Economic Transfers
in the United States

Studies in Income and Wealth
Volume 49

National Bureau of Economic Research
Conference on Research in Income and Wealth

Economic Transfers in the United States

Edited by **Marilyn Moon**

The University of Chicago Press

Chicago and London

Marilyn Moon is a senior research associate at the Urban Institute, Washington, D.C.

The University of Chicago Press, Chicago 60637
The University of Chicago Press, Ltd., London

Library of Congress Cataloging in Publication Data

Main entry under title:

Economic transfers in the United States.

  (Studies in income and wealth; v. 49)
  Papers presented at the Conference on Social Accounting
for Transfers held in Madison, Wis., on 14–15 May, 1982.
  Bibliography: p.
  Includes index.
  1. Transfer payments—United States. 2. Income
distribution—United States. I. Moon, Marilyn. II. Con-
ference on Social Accounting for Transfers (1982: Madison,
Wis.) III. Series.
HC106.3.C714 vol. 49 [HC110.I5] 330s [339.5'22] 84-52

ISBN 0-226-53505-3

Contents

Acknowledgments

This volume of Studies in Income and Wealth contains papers presented at the Conference on Social Accounting for Transfers held in Madison, Wisconsin, on 14–15 May 1982. We are grateful to the National Science Foundation for support and to the Institute for Research on Poverty and its director, Eugene Smolensky, for helping with local arrangements. Marilyn Moon served as chairman of the Program Committee and volume editor. Other members of the Program Committee were Alan Blinder, Sheldon Danziger, Milton Moss, and Michael Taussig. Mark Fitz-Patrick prepared the volume for press.

Volume Editor's Acknowledgments

I would like to express my thanks to a number of persons who helped the conference run smoothly. Maureen Kaye and Janet Wasserstein of the National Bureau of Economic Research made many of the physical arrangements and managed much of the correspondence. My special appreciation goes to Eugene Smolensky, Director of the Institute for Research on Poverty, for his support at critical points in both the planning stage and the operation of the meeting. Beverly Neuport of the

Institute helped solve the inevitable problems that arise in the course of a "long distance" conference. Jill Bury of the Congressional Budget Office—with which I was affiliated while working on the conference—helped with much of the correspondence.

Marilyn Moon

Introduction

Marilyn Moon

The papers in this volume were presented in May 1982 at a National Bureau of Economic Research Conference on Research in Income and Wealth held in Madison, Wisconsin. The particular focus of the conference was the measurement of transfer payments and their impact on the level and distribution of economic well-being. Although prior conferences have traditionally focused on measurement and distributional issues, this was the first meeting to exclusively consider transfer payments.

The issues raised at the conference are certainly not unique; indeed, much has already been written on the definition, size, and distribution of transfers. Rather, the contribution of the conference and this volume is more likely to be found in the collection of diverse issues raised and approaches employed in the various papers.

What Are Transfers?

Robert Eisner's paper, which began the conference, appropriately raises definitional issues. Are our standard measures of transfer payments contained in the National Income and Product Accounts too restrictive? In recent years the definition of a transfer—as a payment to an individual or institution that does not arise out of current productive activity—has been subject to ever broader interpretations. Eisner advocates an expanded set of national accounts that would increase the share of transfers from one-sixth to over one-half of total income. He includes in his figures in-kind benefits and transfers within each sector of the economy.

Perhaps the most controversial issue raised, however, is the appropri-

1

ate time period to be used to define "current." For example, deferred payments such as private pension benefits could be defined as transfers if these payments to individuals are viewed as related to earlier rather than current productive activities. The passage of time before receipt of these benefits technically puts them—and similarly other income flows such as interest and Social Security payments—within the bounds of the definition. The issue of time both in this specific context and in others was a recurring theme discussed during the conference.

Edward Budd, Daniel Radner, and Cameron Whiteman also focus on definitional issues in their paper. They concentrate on the household sector using a 1972 data source that matches information from the March Current Population Survey with Social Security earnings and beneficiary records and with summary information from individual tax returns. Budd and his coauthors use income concepts of (1) earnings only, (2) intermediate, production-related income (PRI), which captures income from earnings and property, (3) household income, which adds transfers to PRI, and (4) household disposable income, which subtracts out personal taxes paid and contributions for social insurance. The last concept they discuss, age-related transfers, addresses the issue of the "time period over which the receipt of income and the furnishing of productive services are to be matched." Although the authors do not attempt to calculate a full lifetime approach to incorporating the effects of such transfers, they calculate alternative distributions including and excluding age-related transfers to illustrate their potential importance. Again, the issue of time plays a central role in this discussion.

The final paper in this section, by Harvey Galper and Eric Toder, focuses on the development of one specific transfer. The implicit transfer that Galper and Toder attempt to measure is the benefit to holders of fully taxable assets that accrues when rates of return rise above their equilibrium level because of differential tax treatment among various types of assets. The movement of capital investment into tax-exempt securities lowers the interest rate in that sector and raises the equilibrium rate on fully taxable securities. To the extent that lower-income investors choose taxable securities, an implicit transfer from higher-income (and higher tax bracket) investors would be made to those with less income. To measure such a transfer requires a new and rather complex approach. The model developed by Galper and Toder to measure the size of this implicit transfer attempts to illustrate the nature of interactions between tax burdens and preferential taxation of various types of assets. The authors simulate their results using 101 households treated as representative of various income and capital income classes. They find that their approach suggests large implicit transfers and taxes that are not considered in standard discussions of tax burdens.

In-Kind Transfers

The second set of papers presented at the conference focuses on the increasingly important area of in-kind transfers. Although these public and private resource flows are commonly accepted as transfers, there is considerable disagreement over how they should be measured. Since these transfers are restricted to the services they provide, economists generally agree that the value to recipients may be less than the cost of providing them. Beyond this point, however, controversy centers on how to develop empirical measures to reflect the recipient value of such transfers. The first two papers in this section focus on public in-kind transfers and are likely to continue the debate on this issue.

Timothy Smeeding's paper takes an empirical approach, comparing a number of alternative measures of benefits and implicitly arguing that it is unrealistic to wait for more perfect estimates. Smeeding's paper builds on an earlier ambitious line of research attempting to calculate the value of all major public in-kind transfers. In addition to the value of these transfers to recipients, Smeeding attempts to measure an indirect benefit often attributed to such programs—the value to the provider (taxpayer). This indirect benefit may reflect altruism or the existence of externalities, for example. Such benefits—and their appropriate distributional impact—are even more controversial than the calculation of recipient values for in-kind transfers. Smeeding concludes that the direct subsidies to recipients equalize the distribution of well-being while the indirect benefits operate in the opposite direction.

Edgar Olsen and Kathy York attempt to provide empirical evidence on the measures of in-kind transfers that result from three different approaches: market value, Hicks cash equivalent, and Marshallian consumer surplus. The authors use public housing as the in-kind transfer under study and draw their data from the 1965 New York City Housing and Vacancy Survey. They find that the distributional results are sensitive to the measure of benefit used and the specification of the underlying prediction equations. Consequently, the authors are skeptical of claims about the effects of in-kind programs on the distribution of economic well-being.

The third paper in this section turns to private in-kind transfers. James Morgan's paper emphasizes that transfers within and across households remain an important—albeit sometimes overlooked—source of economic well-being. Although it has sometimes been argued that public transfers have overshadowed private resource sharing, Morgan attempts to dispel this notion by summarizing some of the findings of the Survey Research Center on intrafamily transfers. Central to this argument is the controversial issue of the dollar value to place on time spent in the home.

This in-kind transfer consequently shares some of the same measurement problems as public in-kind transfers. Morgan uses a rate for the value of time that lies between the average hourly rates of working men and women. Is a "full market" value the appropriate measure for time spent in home production? If so, then intrafamily transfers are very large. A second issue that naturally arises from such a discussion is the role of time in the measurement of economic well-being. Attention to the distributional effect of these in-kind transfers only makes sense in the context of a measure of economic well-being that incorporates the value of time.

The Distributional Effects

Since transfers are a distribution of resources from one individual or group to another, the questions of who gains and who loses are paramount in any discussion of transfer payments. The measurement issues involved in this context must focus on the measurement of other resources as well as transfers. For example, before we can know whether the wealthy are gainers, we must agree on the definition of wealth. In addition, we may be concerned about how transfers are distributed across variables such as age or region.

The paper by Sheldon Danziger, Eugene Smolensky, Jacques van de Gaag, and Michael Taussig compares the effects of transfers on the elderly and nonelderly. The bulk of the empirical work centers on developing the appropriate measure of economic well-being against which the distributional impact of transfers may be assessed. The authors consider consumption as well as income measures, but the most sensitive adjustment turns out to be the choice of the economic unit. If well-being is expressed as equivalent adult income (calculated through the use of constant utility equivalence scales), the elderly are about 90 percent as well-off as the nonelderly. If either consumption or income (with no adjustments for household size) is the measure used, the elderly appear to be only 60 percent as well-off as the nonelderly. Cash transfers to the elderly are particularly important to their level of well-being and the equality of the distribution of that well-being. The degree of "success" attributed to these transfers is sensitive indeed to the measure of economic status employed.

The paper by David Betson and Robert Haveman considers the distribution of public transfers by region. Current policy debate over decentralization of such transfers has made the results from a study of the regional impact of transfers of particular interest. Betson and Haveman examine the inequality of pre- and posttransfer incomes across and within regions both at one point in time and across the period of 1967 to 1979. They find that public cash transfers have decreased inequality substantially—and by a greater degree over time. Through use of a Theil index, the authors are also able to calculate the degree to which these changes affect within- as opposed to across-region changes. For example, Betson and Haveman found a 70 percent decline in inequality within states as a result of income transfers in 1975.

Social Security

By far the largest of the public transfers, Social Security represents both an inter- and intragenerational transfer of resources. Because Social Security is a pay-as-you-go system and has a very complex benefit formula, benefits received by a worker may display little resemblance to the contribution paid through the payroll tax. The relevance of this issue is addressed by both of the Social Security papers in this volume.

Robert Moffitt's paper uses aggregate data to consider the extent to which various cohorts have benefited from the Social Security system relative to their contributions. For these intergenerational comparisons, Moffitt constructs a new historical wealth series ending with persons aged 67 in 1977. This series is quite different in content and purpose from other series, like that developed by Martin Feldstein, since Moffitt's series attempts to measure all taxes paid and benefits received. Moffitt finds that the value of net Social Security wealth has risen for each cohort group reaching retirement age in 1977, although the rate of growth in wealth has slowed over time. The overall growth in benefits—particularly those to male retirees—is largely accountable for the overall increase in Social Security wealth. In the early years of the program such benefit growth was largely attributable to increased recipiency rates. Growth in the actual level of benefits has increased in importance over time, although with considerable variation across cohorts.

Jennifer Warlick and Richard Burkhauser follow quite a different tack in their examination of Social Security. Using an allocation scheme developed in an earlier paper that separates the welfare transfer component of Social Security wealth from that which would be obtained under an actuarially fair system, they focus in this paper on the effects of raising the normal retirement age under Social Security. Theirs is not an empirical paper; results are simulated for several representative cases. Even so, the number of adjustments and complications are substantial. They find that postponing normal retirement is in many ways equivalent to an across-the-board reduction in benefits, lowering the welfare transfer component. Large savings are only possible if workers elect to retire at later ages and if the credits that they receive for postponement are less than actuarially fair.

Other Issues

In addition to the specific topics discussed, the papers as a whole raise some common concerns. For example, the papers in this volume illustrate many of the empirical sources available to researchers interested in transfers—and the important limitations of such data. The creative techniques used in the papers have to some extent been mandated by the shortcomings of existing research materials. In fact, two of the papers— Galper and Toder, and Warlick and Burkhauser—use example observations rather than actual data. Since the likelihood of improvements in data in the 1980s seems increasingly dim, the authors have generally chosen to use existing data even though heroic assumptions are sometimes necessary.

Although several of the papers either explicitly or implicitly raise the issue of the treatment of transfers over time, the discussion at the conference helped to underscore the fact that this remains an important, unresolved issue. Time represents a definitional concern for "transfers" that may actually be linked to past or future productive activity but not in a way that can be measured. If so, where do we draw the line between transfers and payments to factors of production? For example, is aid by family members across generations simply an unmeasured quid pro quo or truly a transfer of resources? Perhaps more important, when does this definitional issue actually matter?

A related issue for the role of time in the measurement of transfers is the increasing emphasis on comparisons of the impact of transfers across generations. Estimating intergenerational equity remains a relatively unexplored area, however. In this conference, the two papers on Social Security and the Danziger et al. paper on the economic status of the elderly only begin to consider these issues. Other researchers may wish to attempt to estimate, for example, to what extent transfers such as Social Security are offset by private intergenerational resource flows, or how intergenerational equity changes for different cohorts across time.

Although these papers were not intended to be policy oriented, they address a number of issues of current interest. Public debate since the beginning of the Reagan Administration has focused on the size of transfer payments relative to the size of the "productive" sectors of the economy. Although some focus has been on shifts from public to private transfers, much of the criticism leveled at the effect of transfers on incentives for work and investment relates to the overall size of transfer payments. Major reductions in public transfers have also made the measurement of the distributional impact of such programs a subject of considerable controversy. As the papers in this volume illustrate, many unresolved measurement and distributional issues are likely to add fuel to the policy debate. For example, adjustments in the value of in-kind transfers to allow comparison with other sources of economic well-being are important for considering adequacy of benefits and the contribution of transfers to poverty reduction. Improved measures of private intrafamily transfers provide a benchmark concerning the current level of resource sharing and the potential for additional transfers within families (as discussed in Morgan's paper). The regional distribution of transfers is of concern for assessing the impact of the decentralization of transfers, particularly those directed at low-income populations. Estimates provided by Betson and Haveman help to illustrate such differences by states and regions.

1   Transfers in a Total Incomes System of Accounts

Robert Eisner

1.1   Introduction

I propose in this initial paper of the conference to project a broad horizon for transfers. I shall move beyond the current National Income and Product Accounts (NIPA) to suggest for consideration all payments or transfers of income in money or in kind that are not in return for current services.

Our essential conceptual notion is that factor incomes for current production—the components of national income—are the direct rewards for current services, without which the current production related to those services would not take place. All other shifts of goods and services or command over them may, for certain purposes at least, be considered transfers. This will set a considerably broader net than the framework in NIPA.

The NIPA definition is simple, deceptively simple: "*Transfer payments to persons* is income payments to persons, generally in monetary form, for which they do not render current services. It consists of business transfer payments . . . and government transfer payments" (NIPA 1981a, p. xi).[1] Examination of this definition, however, may quickly suggest several problems: (1) Why the restriction, "generally in monetary form"? (2) What are "services" and what are "current services"? (3) Why restrict transfer payments to persons to business transfer payments and government transfer payments? Why exclude transfers within the consolidated

Robert Eisner is William R. Kenan Professor of Economics, Northwestern University.

The author is indebted to Steven Bender for invaluable assistance and, again, to ever helpful staff of the National Income Division of the Bureau of Economic Analysis. This work has enjoyed the important financial support of National Science Foundation grant SES-7717555.

personal sector, that is, payments from nonprofit institutions and pension funds to households, transfers between households, and transfers within households?

In a recent major article, Danziger, Haveman, and Plotnick (1981) undertook to survey "how income transfers affect work, savings, and the income distribution." These indeed are the major issues usually associated with transfers. By divorcing remuneration from the supply of services for current production, transfers affect work, savings, and output. They also affect savings by their effects on wealth and because of differences in marginal propensities to consume as between transferors and transferees. And of course, except to the extent that they prove self-canceling, they must affect the income distribution. Considering all of these issues, however, is there anything unique about the limited measures of transfer payments in NIPA? Are the transfer items included in NIPA adequate to inform us how transfers affect work, savings, and the income distribution? Might they even be misleading to the extent that they may substitute, at least in part, for transfers not included in NIPA?

Perhaps the most obvious restriction narrowing the measure of transfer payments in NIPA is that requiring that they be "generally in monetary form." This leads to the substantial exclusion of in-kind transfers in education, housing, medical care, and elsewhere.[2] Indeed, the great bulk of government activity—federal, state, and local—entails the transfer of services to business and to persons. Imputations for the value of these services are likely to be considerably higher than either the value of government purchases of goods and services or the value of product originating in government. For NIPA accounts make no allowance for any value of government product corresponding to government capital consumption or government capital income.

A second important restriction narrowing the measure of transfers in NIPA relates to the broad view of payments for current services. First, current payments to the owners of factors of production are generally presumed to be for current services. Yet in many instances employees are paid wages and salaries more than or less than the value of their current services, sometimes in the expectation of longer run employment commitments. Slowing of economic activity is widely believed to bring on substantial labor hoarding, when firms continue to pay employees at their previous rates even though fewer (if any significant) services are being performed. The excess of such payments over the value of current services might well be viewed as transfer payments, if their definition is to be taken literally.

Of course a degree of arbitrariness exists in the definition of the period of time taken to be "current." Viewing salaries earned while employees are on coffee breaks as transfer payments is not considered useful. At the other extreme, if we look at payments over a lifetime, most of what are conventionally viewed as transfer payments involve deferred compensation for previous services and are not transfers from one individual to another. As the period is extended, the discrepancies between payments and services during the period are progressively reduced. Ultimately, not only cyclical unemployment benefits but old age and retirement pensions might be viewed in large part as payment for services of the extended period.

Taking literally the implicit NIPA definition of the period of current services, we are impelled to open the very large question of whether interest and dividends may usefully be viewed as transfers rather than payments for current services.[3] One of the arguments for including government interest as a transfer is that it relates largely to debt on past wars having nothing directly to do with current production. One may argue similarly for business interest, however, that it relates to past debt, for whatever purpose, and that its payment, except for our bankruptcy laws, has nothing to do with *current* production. This would appear true with even less qualification for dividends. Surely there would be little effect on current production if dividends were not paid. One might then wish to treat business profits, gross of dividends and interest payments, as an income charge against gross national product. The dividends and interest payments would constitute transfers of this profit.

In a longer run or equilibrium sense, the dividend and interest payments may be considered necessary for production, given our institutional arrangements, that is, a set of economic relations defined by private capitalism. But again, they are not literally payments for *current* production. As with the components of personal income characterized as transfers in NIPA, fluctuations in dividend and interest payments conform so little to variations in current production as to be viewed as stabilizers of aggregate demand. And like the transfer payments currently recognized in NIPA, dividend and interest payments tend to reduce the elasticity of supply of current production services with respect to payments for those services. Aside from the age-earnings test in current laws, an elderly person with substantial interest receipts may be just as reluctant to work for a current wage or salary as one receiving Social Security benefits.

Another example of the narrowing of the measure of transfer payments in NIPA occasioned by a broad view of factor payments is the inclusion of dependency allowances to personnel of the armed forces as compensation of employees. Since personnel without dependents presumably perform the same duties as those of similar rank and occupation who have dependents, the additional remuneration in the form of dependency allowances may be viewed as a transfer rather than a payment for services necessary to current production.

The third restriction, relating to sectoral consolidation, serves to exclude a vast array of interpersonal transfers. It has been argued that the very growth of intersectoral transfers in the form of government payments to persons, such as for retirement, medical care, and general welfare, has corresponded to a reduction in similar transfers from children to parents and parents to children and from charitable institutions to those in need.

Ignoring these restrictions, we shall undertake to enumerate a variety of transfers, broadly conceived, that are not currently included in NIPA but may have economic consequences for work, savings, and income distribution as significant as the transfer payments currently included. In some cases we shall indicate estimates of dollar magnitudes, where they are readily available. We shall present, in particular, a set of estimates of transfers in kind, mainly of government services, but also some additional business transfers, developed from our Total Incomes System of Accounts.[4] In none of this do we make so bold as to advocate altering the current accounts. In some cases and for some purposes we may readily concede that the narrower, more precise focus in NIPA is preferable. Our suggestions are rather to be viewed as an attempt to fit the discussion of transfers into a larger context. We may perhaps illuminate a bit further a path for a supplementary set of accounts that would give a fuller, systematic view of the role of transfers in the economy.

1.2 A Broad View of Transfers

We shall undertake implementation of a broad concept of transfers which aims to include all changes in command over goods, services, and resources that are not direct remuneration for current production. It will involve payments in kind as well as in money. It will involve taxes and tax expenditures, government services, and government interventions which have been inserted into or superimposed on the production process. It will also involve net revaluations, or capital gains and losses in excess of changes in the general price level. And it will involve a good deal of what are viewed as intrasectoral transfers and hence not included in NIPA.

A semantic discussion of whether all the items regarded are properly labeled transfers would have only limited value. They all appear to have the characteristics of separation from payment for current production in the sense that, in whole or in part, they are not remuneration for services essential to current output. Yet they do convey or take away current goods and services or the means of payment for them.

A framework for presentation of relevant data, other than tax expenditures and net revaluations, may be found in table 1.1, a considerably extended development of formulations found in Lampman (1975). Following earlier suggestions of Cohen and Gainsbrugh (1958), we break the personal sector into three subsectors: nonprofit institutions, insurance and pension funds, and households. We also separate government enterprises from the business sector. Intersectoral transfers will then involve seven sectors, including the rest of the world. In addition, we take into special account transfers within the household sector.

Turning first to business transfers, we note those business transfer payments currently included in NIPA. As shown in appendix A, they entail corporate gifts to nonprofit institutions and insurance payments for auto liability for personal injury, railroad and miscellaneous liabilities, and medical malpractice liabilities. They also include consumer bad debts, losses due to forgeries, and unrecovered thefts. (This last, if taken correctly, would include shoplifting, which seems to be grossly underestimated at $147 million in 1976 and $225 million in 1979.) The NIPA business transfer payments also include a small item for cash prizes.

Our separation of insurance and pension funds from the personal sector points to the inclusion of most of NIPA's nonlabor income (minus directors' fees). This is the item, "Employer contributions to private pension and welfare funds" in table 1.1, a hefty $74.8 billion in 1976, and growing rapidly since then. It was $117 billion in 1979.

In our Total Incomes System of Accounts (TISA) we have generally treated indirect business taxes as payment for government services or "intermediate product transferred from government." Since it is frequently difficult if not impossible to tie such taxes to particular services, it may be more useful to report all taxes as transfer payments to government. Hence among business transfers to government we will here include indirect business taxes, corporate profits taxes, and contributions for social insurance by employers and self-employed.[5] In addition, we list taxes paid to foreign governments.

Next under business transfers we include an item for the consumption value of media services transferred from the business sector to households. This, of course, relates to most of the entertainment and general information services of commercial television, radio, newspapers, and magazines. These do not turn up in NIPA as income or consumption to the extent that they are viewed as intermediate purchases and sales by business. Similarly, we add as business transfers to households the general provision of health and safety services to employees and business expenditures for protection of the environment. Estimates for the years 1946, 1956, 1966, and 1976 of media and health services and other transfers taken from our Total Income System of Accounts are in table 1.2.

We also include business interest payments and dividends as transfers, as suggested by Rolph (1948) and Hagen and Budd (1958). In our tabulation we count all of *net* business interest as going to the consolidated household sector as well as the portion of gross business interest payments corresponding to consumer interest payments to business. Net

Table 1.1 Transfers in an Expanded Set of Accounts, Exclusive of Tax Expenditures and Net Revaluations, 1976[†] (billions of dollars)

Sector Transfer	Business	Government	Government Enterprises	Nonprofit Institutions	Insurance & Pension Funds	Households	Rest of World
Business[†]	−584.3	+290.3		+1.5	+74.8	+168.3	+49.3
Bus. trans. payments from NIPA	−7.9			+1.5		+6.4	
Employer contrib. to priv. pens. & welfare funds	−74.8				+74.8		
Indirect bus. taxes	−151.7	+151.7					
Corp. profits taxes	−63.8	+63.8					
Employer contrib. for soc. insur.	−74.0	+74.0					
Taxes paid to foreign govt's.	−49.3[a]						+49.3[a]
Media consumption services*	−8.6					+8.6	
Health & safety	−2.9					+2.9	
Environment	n.a.						
Net interest	−87.2					+87.2[b]	
Consumer interest	−26.7					+26.7[b]	
Dividends (net)	−37.4	+0.8				+36.5[b]	
Pay in excess of current serv.	n.a.						

Government[†]	+97.8	−645.0	+15.2	+3.3	+521.0	+7.7
Gov't. transfer pay. from NIPA		−189.6			+186.4	+3.2
Military dependents' allowances		−0.6[c]			+0.6[c]	
Medicaid		−9.2			+9.2	
Gov't. interest (net)		−23.1			+18.6[b]	+4.5
Agricultural expenditures	+5.0	−5.0				
Housing subsidies		−3.1			+3.1	
Other subsidies	+2.0	−2.0				
Loan programs		n.a.				
Licenses		n.a.				
Pay in excess of current services		n.a.				
Consumption services*		−77.4			+77.4	
Education services*		−140.8			+140.8	
Health services*		−17.0			+17.0	
R & D*	+14.5	−14.5				
Fixed capital*		−13.1	+13.1			
Intermediate product*	+76.3	−149.6	+2.1	+3.3	+67.9	
Government Enterprises*	+5.2		−10.0	+0.2	+4.6	
Negative surpluses	+1.6		−3.1		+1.4	
Capital income	+0.1		−0.2		+0.1	
Capital consumption allowances	+3.5		−6.7		+3.1	
Nonprofit Institutions				−31.9	+31.9	
Cost of product minus charges				−18.3[d]	+18.3[d]	
Volunteer services*				−13.6	+13.6	

Table 1.1 (continued)

Sector Transfer	Business	Government	Government Enterprises	Nonprofit Institutions	Insurance & Pension Funds	Households	Rest of World
Insurance & Pension Funds					−68.8	+68.8	
Pension & profit sharing					−33.0	+33.0	
Group health insurance					−22.8	+22.8	
Group life insurance					−4.4	+4.4	
Workmen's compensation					−8.2	+8.2	
Supplemental unemployment					−0.4	+0.4	
Other insurance					n.a.		
Households[†]		+232.6		+30.4	+5.7	−269.7	+1.0
Transfer pay. to foreigners (net)						−1.0	+1.0
Gifts to nonprofit instit.				+16.8[e]		−16.8[e]	
Volunteer services				+13.6		−13.6	
Personal taxes		+180.0				−180.0	
Employee contrib. for soc. insur.		+52.0				−52.0	
Pers. contrib. to pension funds					+5.7[f]	−5.7[f]	
Per. pay. to insur. companies						n.a.	
Coerced services* (draftees & jurors)		+0.6				−0.6	
Services in excess of current pay						n.a.	

						Rest of World	
Rest of World	+8.3	+1.4				+4.8	−14.4
Dividends (net)	+3.4[b]	+0.1[b]				+4.8[b,g]	−8.2
Net interest	+4.9	+1.3					−6.2
Totals excluding taxes							
From sector	245.5	645.0	10.0	31.9	68.8	37.7	14.4
To sector	111.3	2.8	15.2	35.4	80.5	799.4	8.7
All sectors 1,053.3							

n.a. = not available.

†Source: NIPA (1981b), except where otherwise indicated. Totals incomplete.

*From Total Incomes System of Accounts (TISA), derived in part from unrevised NIPA data.

a From Bureau of Economic Analysis, by phone, 1977 figures.

b Figure is for consolidated personal sector; breakout of nonprofit institutions and insurance pension funds is not available.

c Estimated from data provided by Assistant Director of Compensation, Office of Assistant Secretary of Defense for Manpower Reserve Affairs and Logistics.

d Assumed equal to sum of household and business gifts to nonprofit institutions and further assumed all to be transferred, at least eventually, to households.

e From U.S. Department of the Treasury, Statistics of Income, 1976. Includes only contribution deductions listed on tax returns.

f From U.S. Department of Labor (1981), interpolated from 1975 and 1977 figures.

g Allocated in proportion to total dividends received.

Table 1.2   Transfers in TISA: 1946, 1956, 1966, 1976

	Billions of Dollars				Percent P.A. Growth Rates			
	1946	1956	1966	1976	1946–56	1956–66	1966–76	1946–76
From government	71.0	85.6	178.3	374.4	1.9	7.6	7.7	5.7
To households	31.8	51.6	115.5	278.2	5.0	8.4	9.2	7.5
Consumption	5.4	10.2	27.6	77.4	6.6	10.5	10.9	9.3
Public schools	5.5	14.9	40.0	115.9	10.5	10.4	11.2	10.7
Health	1.0	2.5	5.5	17.0	9.5	8.1	12.0	9.9
Intermediate product	19.9	24.0	42.4	67.9	1.9	5.9	4.8	4.2
To business	37.5	32.6	59.6	90.8	−1.4	6.2	4.3	3.0
Research and development	.5	3.9	10.9	14.5	22.3	10.9	2.9	11.7
Intermediate product	37.0	28.7	48.7	76.3	−2.5	5.4	4.6	2.4
To nonprofit (intermediate product)	.7	.8	1.9	3.3	.9	9.5	5.6	5.3
To govt enterprises (intermediate product)	.9	.6	1.2	2.1	−4.1	6.7	5.9	2.7
From government enterprises:								
Interest plus negative surpluses	.7	2.1	2.6	3.2	12.5	1.8	2.3	5.4
From business: Media support	.6	1.9	4.0	8.6	11.4	8.0	8.0	9.1
From nonprofit institutions:								
Imputed value of volunteer services	1.7	3.4	5.8	13.6	7.3	5.3	9.0	7.2
Total transfers	73.9	93.0	190.6	399.8	2.3	7.4	7.7	5.8

Numbers may not sum to totals because of rounding.

dividends other than those to government are also recorded as received in the household sector.

Finally, we include a category called "business pay in excess of current services." This will include items such as paid sick leave. But it also involves any payments that, out of consideration for the desirability of long-term employment commitments, do not match current services. These might in principle include some or all of payments to salaried and other workers who become redundant to current production in periods of cyclical downturn and to old employees who may be retained without salary reduction although their productivity has declined significantly from that of their prime years.

In government transfers we again include the major items from NIPA of government transfer payments to persons and to foreigners. (See appendix A for details.) We also include net government interest payments. In addition, we reclassify as transfers at least two government payments now included in government purchases of business services. These are dependents' allowances for members of the armed forces and Medicaid. The first of these may be viewed, as in NIPA, as a form of remuneration to members of the armed forces. On the assumption, however, that members of the armed forces without dependents perform the same duties as those with dependents, it would seem more appropriate to view these allowances as transfers. As for the case of Medicaid, it seems clearly more appropriate to classify it, with Medicare, as a transfer. The different treatment in NIPA, apparently related to distinctions regarding the discretionary role in choice of services, seems of doubtful relevance in terms of a broader view of transfers.

We also count as transfers agricultural subsidies and other expenditures, including government payments for crop supports, which are treated as government purchases of goods and services in NIPA. We add other subsidies in the form of government services offered below cost, such as some low-rental public housing. Analogously, a large portion of government and government-sponsored loan programs involve substantial elements of transfer to business, home owners, and students.[6]

The award of licenses for television and radio stations, for imports, and for other purposes may also best be viewed as transfers.[7] And as with business employees, we include any payments to government employees in excess of the value of their current services.

Next, from our Total Incomes System of Accounts we include the major items of government services provided to the public without charge. We have separated these into categories of consumption (such as parks and recreation services), public education services, health services (in addition to those included in Medicare and Medicaid), and research and development expenditures. Here we should include at least a portion of government payments to nonprofit institutions for R & D.

Also classified as a government transfer is the fixed capital that the government gives to government enterprises (currently included in NIPA merely as government expenditures for goods and services). And last, we recognize the vast amounts of government services, including those of the military and police, that may be viewed as intermediate in the production of final output but are made available without charge to the user.

The sale of government enterprise product below a correct measure of cost also constitutes a transfer. In NIPA government enterprise product is valued, like business product, at market prices. For this sector, however, market prices are not a measure of cost. Government enterprise product in many instances involves a significant government subsidy. First, the price of government enterprise product does not usually reflect all, if any, of the value of capital consumption or the income of capital generally furnished to government enterprises by government. Second, government enterprises not infrequently operate at a loss. Such negative surpluses of government enterprises are akin to the subsidies with which they are lumped in NIPA. We therefore take the sum of negative surpluses and the consumption and income of capital as a measure of transfers by government enterprises.

Similarly, nonprofit institutions may be viewed as transferring income and services to households to the extent that their charges are less than costs. This should in principle amount to at least the value of gifts received by nonprofit institutions. In addition, nonprofit institutions are transferring, in the value of their product, an amount equal to the value of volunteer services which they utilize without cost.

Some components of insurance payments to households, such as various liability payments, are already included in NIPA business transfer payments, as indicated above. Most pension and insurance payments do not enter NIPA accounts as transfers, however, as they do not qualify as intersectoral flows. If pension and insurance company funds are segregated from the household sector, we can argue in an accounting sense that their payments to households are as much transfer payments to recipients as are corresponding pensions out of government insurance funds for old age and retirement or Medicare.[8] Clearly the economic effect on households of such payments out of private insurance and pension funds is similar to corresponding payments by government classified as transfers. Like government transfers, these payments are not related to current services. Like government transfers, these payments will tend to stabilize household purchasing power and demand. And like government transfers, they may reduce the elasticity of labor supply to wages and salaries.

Among intersectoral transfers by households, we take, from NIPA, payments from persons to foreigners. We list gifts to nonprofit institutions and volunteer services, generally presumed also to go to nonprofit institutions. Personal taxes, but not nontax payments, are listed as transfers. In addition, we include the value of services households transfer to government when individuals are coerced into performing these services at less than market remuneration, or less than what would be necessary to induce the services in a free market. This applies particularly to conscription for military service, in the years when it has been in effect, and to jury duty. Finally, in any particular period some workers are offering services whose value exceeds current remuneration. This excess may be viewed as transfers by households to their various employers.

We complete the tabulation by adding two items from the rest of the world account that, consistent with our earlier discussion, also qualify as transfers. These are net dividends and net interest paid by the rest of the world to the United States.

1.3 Summary Tabulations

While no great precision is claimed for our numbers, particularly those not taken from NIPA, and our allocations are in some cases arbitrary, some of the totals may prove interesting. In particular, excluding taxes, we may note that gross business transfers come to $246 billion, as compared to $8 billion for the business transfer payment item in NIPA. Gross government transfers amount to $645 billion, of which only $190 billion was the NIPA government transfer payment item. Transfers received by households amounted to $799 billion, of which $168 billion came from business, $521 billion came from government, $5 billion came from government enterprises, $32 billion came from nonprofit institutions, $69 billion came from insurance and pension funds, and $5 billion came from the rest of the world. These totals are incomplete, as indicated by the items for which we are unable to locate or prepare estimates. In some cases, particularly with interest payments, we have used only net flows. The various totals may be compared with a 1976 gross national product of $1,718 billion.

Some of the substance and logic of all of this may be better grasped by examining the reclassification of net transfers to households by type and sector of origin presented in table 1.3. We note here first that NIPA transfer payments to households for 1976 amounted to $194.3 billion, of which $7.9 billion were from business and $186.4 billion were from government. Our suggested additions to NIPA transfer payments come to $743.3 billion, almost four times the amount of transfers to households included in NIPA.

We break the additions to NIPA transfer payments into three categories: (1) in-kind; (2) NIPA payments for current goods and services which we reclassify as transfers; and (3) NIPA intrasectoral payments which become intersectoral because of our deconsolidation of the NIPA house-

Table 1.3   **Net Transfers to Households by Type and Sector of Origin, Exclusive of Taxes, Tax Expenditures and Net Revaluations, 1976 (billions of dollars)**

Type	Sector of Origin	Transfer		Amount
NIPA transfer payments				194.3
	Business	Bus. trans. payments	7.9	
	Government	Gov't. trans. payments	186.4	
			194.3	
Additions to NIPA transfer payments				743.3
In-kind	Business	Media consumption services	8.6	
		Health & safety	2.9	
		Environment	n.a.	
			11.5	
	Government	Medicaid	9.2	
		Other health	17.0	
		Education	140.8	
		Housing subsidies	3.1	
		Other subsidies	2.0	
		General consumption	77.4	
		R & D	14.5	
		Fixed capital	13.1	
		Government enterprise subsidies	10.0	
		Intermediate product	149.6	
		Loan programs	n.a.	
		Licenses	n.a.	
			436.7	448.2
NIPA payments for current goods and services	Business	Net interest	87.2	
		Consumer interest	26.7	
		Dividends	37.4	
		Payment in excess of current services	n.a.	
			151.3	
	Government	Military dependents allowances	0.6	
		Interest (net)	23.1	
		Agricultural expenditures	5.0	
		Payment in excess of current services	n.a.	
			28.7	

Table 1.3 (continued)

Type	Sector of Origin	Transfer		Amount
	Rest of World	Net interest	6.2	
		Dividends (net)	8.2	
			14.4	194.4
NIPA intra-sectoral payments	Nonprofit	Cost of product minus charges	18.3	
		Volunteer services	13.6	
			31.9	
	Insurance & pension funds	Pensions & profit sharing	33.0	
		Group health insurance	22.8	
		Workmen's compensation	8.2	
		Group life insurance	4.4	
		Supplemental unemployment	0.4	
		Other insurance	n.a.	
			68.8	100.7
Grand total				$937.6

hold sector by splitting off nonprofit institutions and insurance and pension funds. Of these, the in-kind category is by far the largest, encompassing vast amounts of government services, particularly for education, general consumption, and intermediate product given directly to households, or indirectly as ultimate components of final product. Our estimates of total in-kind transfers for which we were able to develop numbers came to $448.2 billion. These are transfers originating in business and, chiefly, in government. Other in-kind transfers to households by the nonprofit sector are classified separately.

The main items in our reclassification of NIPA payments for current goods and services are interest and dividends. Business interest payments to households may be taken to include both net interest and the consumer interest that has been netted out of gross interest payments. The total amount of NIPA payments for current goods and services reclassified as transfers comes to $194.4 billion.

Finally, the NIPA intrasectoral payments reclassified as transfers include $31.9 billion of nonprofit goods and services and $68.8 billion of transfers from insurance and pension funds to households, bringing the total for this category to $100.7 billion. The grand total in our expanded measure of net transfers to households is thus $937.6 billion, almost five times the corresponding NIPA transfers.

1.4 Other Transfer-like Items

Although the framework for transfers we have just discussed is broad, there is a great deal it does not encompass. First, it does not include the current value of real capital gains and losses, which we shall discuss in the next section. Second, it excludes "tax expenditures," which are in many ways similar in their effects, given the tax system, to direct transfers. We are not prepared to fit them into even our broadened framework at this time. We may at least stress the importance of the issue, however, by indicating the magnitude of tax expenditures as most recently estimated by the U.S. Office of Management and Budget (1982), shown in summary form in table 1.4. For fiscal year 1981, it will be noted, a simple addition (perhaps not quite warranted) of the OMB "outlay equivalent estimates for tax subsidies by function" comes to $272 billion.

Finally, also not included in our tabulations are perhaps the largest transfers of all, those within the household sector. Whether or not we are prepared now fully to account for them, we should recognize that many of the economic effects that we attribute to government transfers in fact may largely substitute for or be offset by private transfers within the household sector.[9] This applies most obviously to gifts and bequests, care of the

Table 1.4   **Outlay Equivalent Estimates for Tax Subsidies by Function (millions of dollars)**[a]

	Fiscal Years		
Function	1981	1982	1983
National defense	2,525	2,500	2,615
International affairs	3,835	4,600	4,930
General science, space, and technology	1,060	1,515	−220
Energy	8,475	8,830	8,800
National resources and environment	2,510	2,705	2,910
Agriculture	1,315	1,250	1,180
Commerce and housing credit	117,470	114,355	120,910
Transportation	65	70	105
Community and regional development	275	435	375
Education, training, employment, and social services	15,370	15,620	15,665
Health	25,110	26,895	28,135
Income security	64,070	70,295	72,850
Veterans benefits and services	1,605	1,685	1,660
General government	85	80	80
General purpose fiscal assistance	27,755	29,860	32,060
Interest	480	620	710
Sum	272,005	281,315	292,765

[a]From U.S. Office of Management and Budget (1982), pp. 28–30.

elderly, and care of the young. In addition, of course, there are hosts of other intrafamily and interhousehold transfers.

1.5   Net Revaluations: Capital Gains and Losses

We have yet to account for a major share of household sources of wealth and purchasing power. I refer to capital gains (and losses).

Capital gains are widely viewed as a reward to capital. The logic of including them as transfer income is in one way akin to that underlying our suggested inclusion of dividend and interest return on capital. Capital gains are clearly excluded from the category of payment for services to current production. In fact, however, they constitute a major component of appropriately defined income—of households, business, and government.

Capital gains and losses represent a substantial anomaly with respect to NIPA. Of course they are not included in NIPA. Yet, taxes on realized capital gains constitute subtractions from corporate and personal income. Hence, the higher realized capital gains are, the lower, for example, is disposable personal income.

Capital gains are not included in NIPA, either on the product or income side, because like transfers they are not viewed as corresponding to current production. I have argued elsewhere (Eisner 1980, inter alia) for application of a Hicks-Haig concept of income as that which can be consumed while keeping one's real wealth intact. On the assumption that one-for-one transformation is possible, we may implement this concept as the sum of consumption and net capital accumulation. We should then want to include net revaluations in net capital accumulation. For surely we are concerned with increases in the net *value* of capital. It should not matter, for the individual, firm, industry, or nation, whether the increases in value are from the acquisition or production of additional assets or to increases in the value of existing assets.[10]

It is important to remember that it is *net* revaluations which are relevant. To preserve real wealth intact, the nominal value of assets must rise by as much as the general price level or some other appropriate measure of prices. Where nominal values rise less than the general level, we in fact have capital losses. We should want to consider as capital gains only increases in the nominal value of assets, or ultimately of net worth, in excess of increases in the general price level.

One possible justification for excluding the value of capital gains from national income is that for the nation as a whole they may to a considerable extent be self-canceling. Those owning land and houses and owing on low-interest mortgage loans have proven to be substantial gainers over most of the last several decades in the United States. But then creditors, as such, and others have lost. In fact, there is good reason to expect that net revaluations will not sum to zero for the nation as a whole. Changes in terms of trade can create substantial gains or losses, as oil producing and exporting countries could easily testify, very happily at least until recently. And changes in interest rates may affect at least the income and wealth of the current year as against future years.

The arguments against including net revaluations in national income point all the more sharply to their role as transfers. Capital gains, in the sense of net revaluations as we have defined them, clearly give their beneficiaries command over goods, services, or resources. If they do not correspond to any current production, then they must be transfers. In terms of the broad concept of transfers we have suggested in this paper, even if they are viewed as properly part of net capital accumulation and hence part of net national income and net national product, we may view them as transfers because they are compensation or rewards not essential to current production.

Whatever their role in the aggregate, net revaluations bulk large in sector accounts and for particular classes of assets and liabilities. They hence bulk large as well for the individuals and groups to whom they relate.

It is immediately apparent in table 1.5, drawn from Eisner (1980),[11] that relevant numbers are substantial, though variable. Business net revaluations on land amounted to $80 billion in 1976 and $21 billion in 1977. Business net revaluations on structures and equipment were $46 billion and $31 billion in those years. Household and nonprofit institution net revaluations on land were $29 billion and $18 billion, while those on owner-occupied dwellings were $45 billion and $69 billion.

Net revaluations on financial assets and liabilities were significant. For business these came to $42 billion in 1976 and $4 billion in 1977. Very large government net revaluations were made on financial liabilities in 1977, amounting to $111 billion. These reflected essentially the depreciating real value of the government debt in the face of higher interest rates and higher prices and the depreciating value of non-interest-bearing Federal Reserve obligations in the form of Federal Reserve notes and member bank deposits as the price level rose.

Thus, households and nonprofit institutions lost heavily in their holdings of financial assets other than equities, suffering negative net revaluations of -60 billion, in 1976. However, they gained $219 billion in that year on corporate and noncorporate equities. In 1977, they lost $56 billion on equity holdings (gaining $56 billion on noncorporate businesses but losing $112 billion on corporate equity) and $158 billion in financial assets other than equity. But they gained no less than $62 billion in net revaluations on their mortgage debt, as well as $21 billion on their other liabilities.

It is difficult to fit net revaluations into a set of accounts dealing with intersectoral transfers. In many cases the implicit transfers are intrasectoral. Increased value of business land may thus entail a higher cost in rents for business lessees. However, the increased value of business land and structures and equipment may also be viewed as a transfer to business

Table 1.5   Net Revaluations: Capital Gains and Losses Net of General Price Level Changes (billions of dollars)

	1946	1956	1966	1976	1977
Business, nonfinancial	−10.4	20.7	25.0	92.2	106.8
Land	−9.9	11.4	16.8	80.2	20.7
Structures & equipment	−5.4	4.9	−3.4	47.3	31.1
Inventories	4.7	.5	−4.2	−1.9	−3.1
Financial assets & liabilities	.2	3.9	15.9	−33.3	58.1
Business, financial	−7.0	−12.5	−9.0	74.0	−54.3
Land	−.0	.1	.3	.0	.2
Structures & equipment	.2	.1	.1	−1.0	−.2
Financial assets & liabilities	−7.0	−12.7	−9.3	75.0	−54.3
Business, total	−17.4	8.2	16.0	166.2	52.5
Land	−9.9	11.5	17.1	80.2	20.9
Structures & equipment	−5.4	5.0	−3.4	46.2	31.0
Inventories	4.7	.5	−4.2	−1.9	−3.1
Financial assets & liabilities	−6.8	−8.8	6.6	41.7	3.8
Government[a]	30.4	22.2	10.3	2.1	58.5
Land	−1.9	4.1	5.9	18.3	10.0
Structures & equipment	−4.1	1.9	−1.8	−22.0	−10.7
Inventories	−6.7	−1.3	−1.3	−.9	−1.8
Financial assets & liabilities	43.1	17.6	7.6	6.7	61.1
Financial assets	−16.9	−7.3	−8.0	−10.4	−50.4
Minus liabilities	−59.9	−24.8	−15.6	−17.1	−111.5
Households, Personal Trusts & Nonprofit Institutions	−85.3	.1	−106.7	219.4	−62.5
Land	−1.2	5.9	.5	29.2	18.2
Owner-occupied dwellings	−1.2	−5.1	−11.2	44.7	69.2
Durables	−8.4	−3.9	−7.6	−9.9	−18.4
Nonprofit fixed capital	.2	.3	.3	−1.9	−.8
Financial assets & liabilities	−74.7	2.9	−88.6	157.3	−130.7
Equities	−34.7	13.3	−69.4	218.8	−55.9
Plus other financial assets	−46.2	−21.9	−36.5	−60.4	−157.8
Minus mortgage debt	−3.6	−9.3	−12.6	17.2	−62.0
Minus other liabilities	−2.5	−2.2	−4.7	−16.1	−21.0

[a]Including government enterprises, federally sponsored credit agencies, monetary authority, and mortgage pools.

Numbers may not sum to totals because of rounding.

of claims to future product, at the expense of households who will have to pay more for the product. To those households with equity claims on business, there will be a corresponding positive net revaluation in the current year and shares of increased earnings in future years.

1.6 Conclusion

Even the rough estimates with which we have sketched in an expanded set of accounts for transfers have some interesting implications. We may, for example, think of transfers as reducing work incentives. To the extent that income is received in transfers rather than as remuneration for labor, the incentive to work may well be reduced. This reduction will of course be aggravated by the incidence of higher marginal taxes on labor to pay for the transfers. But to the extent that this may be a problem, government transfer payments in NIPA are only a small part of the problem. For there is much more in the way of transfers not in NIPA which would have a similar effect. Free education services transferred by government and households, as well as the taxes to pay for them, may discourage current labor. The opportunity for earnings in the form of interest, dividends, and capital gains may seriously depress the supply of labor for current output.

One may also trace significant effects of various other items which we would consider in a broader set of accounts for transfers. Interest and dividends may go disproportionately to saving. Net revaluations will generally constitute saving in a broader set of accounts. If saving is seen not as an increase in net worth but more narrowly as income minus taxes minus consumption, as in NIPA, positive net revaluations of households, by contributing to greater current consumption, will reduce the saving measured in NIPA.

As for effects on income distribution, no doubt the impacts of many of the items included in these broadened accounts would be very large. Private pensions, interest and dividends, and in-kind benefits from business, government, and nonprofit institutions may do as much for the welfare of the elderly as Social Security. Public education and health services, or their lack, may affect the welfare of the poor as much as unemployment benefits, aid to families with dependent children, and food stamps. Just how all of our expanded set of transfers affects appropriate measures of the distribution of income and of welfare is a matter which should be high on the agenda for future research.

Appendix A   *Transfer Payments in NIPA and Subsidies Less Current Surplus of Government Enterprises, 1976–79*

Table 1.A.1   Government Transfer Payments to Persons
(millions of dollars)

	Line	1976	1977	1978	1979
Government transfer payments to persons	1	186,353	199,315	214,607	239,949
Federal	2	158,761	169,570	181,806	204,923
Benefits from social insurance funds	3	121,539	132,187	142,133	160,299
Old-age, survivors, and disability insurance	4	74,501	83,239	91,380	102,581
Hospital and supplementary medical insurance	5	18,366	21,704	24,851	29,238
Unemployment insurance	6	14,809	11,981	8,978	9,406
State	7	14,280	11,533	8,612	9,100
Federal employees	8	310	274	175	163
Railroad	9	219	174	191	143
Railroad retirement	10	3,550	3,783	3,985	4,313
Federal civilian employees retirement	11	8,860	9,929	11,271	12,952
Civil service	12	8,723	9,768	11,094	12,741
Other[a]	13	137	161	177	211
Veterans life insurance	14	936	980	1,031	1,062
Workmen's compensation	15	517	571	637	747
Military retirement	16	7,696	8,503	9,428	10,647
Veterans benefits	17	13,399	12,802	12,812	13,336
Pension and disability	18	8,452	9,189	9,713	10,643
Readjustment	19	4,345	3,145	2,823	2,408
Unemployment	20	602	468	276	285
Other[b]	21	....	....	....	....
Food stamp benefits	22	4,598	4,394	4,585	6,311
Black lung benefits	23	981	972	1,038	1,726
Special unemployment benefits	24	975	680	163	....
Supplemental security income	25	4,631	4,743	4,920	5,321
Direct relief	26	....	....	....	....
Earned income credit	27	908	902	880	829
Other[c]	28	4,034	4,387	5,847	6,454
State and local	29	27,592	29,745	32,801	35,026
Benefits from social insurance funds	30	11,292	12,489	14,144	15,879
Government pensions	31	9,581	10,544	11,960	13,380
Temporary disability insurance	32	511	570	622	699
Workmen's compensation	33	1,200	1,375	1,562	1,800
Direct relief	34	12,840	13,439	13,606	14,058
General assistance	35	1,229	1,237	1,205	1,228

Table 1.A.1 (continued)

	Line	1976	1977	1978	1979
Other direct relief	36	11,611	12,202	12,401	12,830
Aid to families with dependent children	37	10,053	10,574	10,699	10,999
Other categorical public assistance[d]	38	1,558	1,628	1,702	1,831
Other[e]	39	3,460	3,817	5,051	5,089

[a]Consists largely of foreign service and Tennessee Valley Authority.

[b]Consists of mustering out pay, terminal leave pay, and adjusted compensation benefits.

[c]Consists largely of payments to nonprofit institutions and aid to students.

[d]Prior to 1974, consists of old-age assistance, aid to the blind, and aid to the permanently and totally disabled. In 1974, these programs were replaced by the Federal Supplementary Security Income (SSI) program. Beginning with 1974 consists of state benefits under the SSI program. Federal SSI benefits are shown in line 25.

[e]Consists largely of educational assistance, medical insurance premiums paid on behalf of indigents, veterans bonuses, other types of veterans aid, and foster care payments.

Table 1.A.2   **Subsidies Less Current Surplus of Government Enterprises (millions of dollars)**

	Line	1976	1977	1978	1979
Subsidies less current surplus of government enterprises	1	973	3,082	3,606	3,053
Federal	2	5,812	8,222	9,343	9,400
Subsidies	3	5,602	7,525	9,267	9,288
Agricultural	4	711	1,764	2,868	1,179
Housing	5	3,083	3,515	4,145	5,253
Maritime	6	501	526	533	580
Air carriers	7	73	83	72	77
Other[a]	8	1,234	1,637	1,649	2,199
Less: Current surplus of government enterprises	9	−210	−697	−76	−112
Postal service	10	−1,647	−2,062	−1,402	−1,266
Commodity Credit Corporation	11	−185	−311	−762	−1,199
Federal Housing Administration	12	190	184	198	218
Tennessee Valley Authority	13	465	591	649	878
Other[b]	14	967	901	1,241	1,257
State and local	15	−4,839	−5,140	−5,737	−6,347
Subsidies	16	189	210	239	327
Less: Current surplus of government enterprises	17	5,028	5,350	5,976	6,674
Water and sewerage	18	1,533	1,480	1,718	1,976
Gas and electricity	19	1,896	2,077	2,391	2,717
Toll facilities	20	814	848	882	908
Liquor stores	21	408	421	448	444
Air and water terminals	22	591	696	794	874
Housing and urban renewal	23	639	670	677	673
Public transit	24	−1,192	−1,304	−1,561	−1,654
Other[c]	25	339	462	627	736

[a]Consists largely of subsidies to exporters of farm products and to railroads.
[b]Consists largely of Federal Deposit Insurance Corporation, Federal Savings and Loan Insurance Corporation, and Bonneville Power Administration.
[c]Consists of state lotteries, offtrack betting, local parking, and miscellaneous activities.

Table 1.A.3   **Business Transfer Payments (from unpublished BEA worksheets) and Transfer Payments to Foreigners (from NIPA table 4.1) (millions of dollars)**

	1976	1977	1978	1979
Business transfer payments	7,920	8,157	8,665	9,443
Corporate gifts to nonprofit associations	1,477	1,507	1,540	1,570
Consumer bad debts	2,452	2,584	2,801	3,085
Auto liability for personal injury	2,797	3,119	3,438	3,760
Railroad & miscellaneous liability payments	15	13	18	17
Medical malpractice liability	845	564	642	720
Unrecovered thefts	147	158	188	225
Cash prizes	55	63	74	84
Losses due to forgeries	132	149	164	182
FOA's	—	—	−200	−200
Transfer payments to foreigners	4,133	4,105	4,555	5,166
From persons (net)	917	859	798	955
From government (net)	3,216	3,246	3,757	4,211

Appendix B *Transfers in the Total Incomes System of Accounts*

A complete description of sources and methods for imputing product of government viewed in this paper as transfers is in Eisner and Nebhut (1981). Expanded measures of government output estimated there included imputed values of the services of government capital, uncompensated factor services of military draftees and jurors, and net revaluations, as well as the usual compensation of employees. Government output was allocated to consumption, capital formation, and product intermediate to other sectors on the basis of classification in ten broad functions: defense, space research, education, health, sanitation, transportation, parks and recreation, natural resources, welfare, and general administration.

Government output of consumption services, viewed as transfers to households, include half of the final product of the space function related to manned space flights, half of health and sanitation services functions, a portion of transportation, all of the product of local parks and recreation services, and all the output of "welfare." All of the final product of education and half of the final product of health are viewed as capital accumulation transferred to households. Government-funded, private research and development expenditures are viewed as capital accumulation transferred to business. The bulk of defense services (except R & D), half of sanitation services, a portion of transportation services, and all of general administration are viewed as intermediate product, transferred to households and to business.

An imputation for the consumption value of media services is viewed as a business transfer to households. This is calculated, following work of Cremeans (1980), on the basis of the proportions of media expenses not devoted to advertising or promotion. Business transfer payments also include the value of business health and safety programs, based on an extension of data and methods in Kendrick (1976). The value of volunteer services is estimated by applying the average time spent in volunteer activities by those aged fifteen and over, obtained from Szalai (1972), to the average hourly earnings rate of nonsupervisory workers in service industries.

Notes

1. Also included in NIPA are government and personal transfer payments to foreigners. Breakdowns of all transfer payments in NIPA for the years 1976–79 are in appendix A.
2. See the papers by Smeeding and by Olsen and York in this volume for discussion of measures of the value of in-kind transfers.
3. Rolph (1948); and Hagen and Budd (1958), for example, have raised this question. But cf. Jaszi (1958), especially pp. 115–19.
4. As presented in Eisner and Nebhut (1981); and Eisner, Simons, Pieper, and Bender (1982).
5. We have no estimate of the unincorporated business portion of personal income taxes and have hence left them with personal taxes.
6. Weidenbaum (1978) estimates total interest subsidies in federal credit programs at $6,443 million in fiscal year 1975.
7. Cf. Boulding (1973), pp. 54–57.
8. Private pension funds, exclusive of Keogh funds and IRA's, received contributions of $47.1 billion in 1977, of which $41.7 billion were employer contributions. They paid benefits of $20.1 billion directly to retirees and $2.8 billion to insurance carriers (U.S. Department of Labor 1981).
9. See paper by Morgan in this volume and a number of the papers cited there for discussion of wide-ranging aspects of private transfers.
10. Cf. Ruggles and Ruggles (1980), especially pp. 24–26, 60, 66.
11. See also Eisner, Simons, Pieper, and Bender (1982); and Eisner and Pieper (1984). The latter paper focuses on net revaluations in a context of measurement of government net worth, net debt, net deficit, and net real interest payments.

References

Boulding, Kenneth. 1973. *The economy of love and fear: A preface to grants economics.* Belmont, Calif.: Wadsworth.

Cohen, Morris, and M. R. Gainsbrugh. 1958. The income side: A business user's viewpoint. In *A critique of the United States income and product accounts*, 187–209. Studies in Income and Wealth, vol. 22. Princeton: Princeton University Press.

Cremeans, John E. 1980. Consumer services provided by business through advertising-supported media in the United States. *Review of Income and Wealth* 26, no. 2: 151–74.

Danziger, Sheldon, R. Haveman, and R. Plotnick. 1981. How income transfers affect work, savings and the income distribution. *Journal of Economic Literature* 19, no. 3: 975–1028.

Eisner, Robert. 1980. Capital gains and income: Real changes in the value of capital in the United States, 1946–1977. In *The measurement of capital*, ed. Dan Usher, 175–346. Conference on Research in Income and Wealth: Studies in Income and Wealth. vol. 45. Chicago: University of Chicago Press for the National Bureau of Economic Research.

Eisner, Robert, and D. Nebhut. 1981. An extended measure of government product: Preliminary results for the United States, 1946–76. *Review of Income and Wealth* 27, no. 1: 33–64.

Eisner, Robert, and P. J. Pieper. 1984. A New View of the Federal Debt and Budget Deficits," *American Economic Review* 74, no. 1:11–29.

Eisner, Robert, E. R. Simons, P. J. Pieper, and S. Bender. 1982. Total incomes in the United States, 1946 to 1976: A summary report. *Review of Income and Wealth* 28, no. 2: 133–74.

Hagen, Everett E., and E. C. Budd. 1958. The product side: Some theoretical aspects. In *A critique of the United States income and product accounts*, 231–74. Studies in Income and Wealth, vol. 22. Princeton: Princeton University Press.

Jaszi, George. 1958. The conceptual basis of the accounts: A reexamination. In *A critique of the United States income and product accounts*, 13–127. Studies in Income and Wealth, vol. 22. Princeton: Princeton University Press.

Kendrick, John W. 1976. *The formation and stocks of total capital*. New York: National Bureau of Economic Research.

Lampman, Robert J. 1975. Social accounting for transfers. In *The personal distribution of income and wealth*, ed. James D. Smith, 31–44. Studies in Income and Wealth, vol. 39. New York: Columbia University Press.

Rolph, Earl. 1948. The concept of transfers in national income estimates. *Quarterly Journal of Economics* 62, no. 3: 327–61.

Ruggles, Richard, and Nancy D. Ruggles. 1980. Integrated economic accounts for the United States, 1947–1978. Yale University, ISPS Working Paper no. 841. (Revised and abbreviated form: 1982. *Survey of Current Business* 62 (May): 1–53.)

Szalai, Alexander, ed. 1972. *The use of time*. The Hague: Mouton.

United States. Department of Commerce. 1976. *The National Income and Product Accounts of the United States, 1929–74, statistical tables (NIPA)*. Washington, D.C.: GPO.

———. 1981a. *The National Income and Product Accounts of the United States, 1929–76, statistical tables (NIPA)*. Washington, D.C.: GPO.

————. July 1981b. *National Income and Product Accounts, 1976–79 (NIPA). Survey of current business.* Special Supplement. Washington, D.C.: GPO.

United States. Department of Labor. Labor-Management Services Administration. 1981. Preliminary estimates of participant and financial characteristics of private pension plans, 1977. Washington, D.C.: GPO.

United States. Department of the Treasury, Internal Revenue Service. 1979. *Statistics of income, 1976, individual income tax returns.* Washington, D.C.: GPO.

United States. Executive Office of the President, Office of Management and Budget. 1982. *The budget of the United States government, 1983, special analysis G, tax expenditures.* Washington, D.C.: GPO.

Weidenbaum, Murray L. 1978. The use of the government's credit power. In *Redistribution through the financial system*, ed. Kenneth Boulding and T. F. Wilson, 211–26. New York: Praeger.

2 An Accounting Framework for Transfer Payments and Its Implications for the Size Distribution of Income

Edward C. Budd, Daniel B. Radner,
and T. Cameron Whiteman

2.1 Introduction

The purpose of this paper is to develop a framework for accounting for transfer payments for the household sector and for estimating the effect of transfers on the distribution of income by size and by selected socioeconomic characteristics, primarily for the year 1972, for which relatively complete and consistently estimated data exist. Section 2.2 discusses the accounting framework and some of the problems in distinguishing between income arising from production and that arising from income redistribution, or payments (and receipts) of transfers. The notion is that in an accounting system for the economy as a whole, although not necessarily for any individual sector of it, transfer payments simply

Edward C. Budd is professor of economics, Pennsylvania State University; Daniel B. Radner is an economist with the Office of Research and Statistics, Social Security Administration; and T. Cameron Whiteman is an economist with the Statistics of Income Division, Internal Revenue Service.

The authors had originally planned to use the microdata files underlying the 1979 Income Survey Development Research Panel for most of the empirical estimates in this paper. Because the processing of these files was terminated while this paper was being prepared, it was necessary to place primary reliance at the last minute on the fully estimated Exact Match-Statistical Match file for 1972, produced by the Bureau of Economic Analysis in cooperation with the Office of Research and Statistics of the Social Security Administration and used with their permission. We are particularly indebted to Jean Karen Salter, Robert Yuskavage, and Daniel McCarron of BEA, Michael Vita, formerly of BEA, and Sharon Johnson of ORS for the major roles they payed in creating the file, and to Sharon Johnson for preparing the tabulations used in this paper.

In addition to the preliminary results presented here for our specially defined income concepts and those for total money income presented in Budd and Salter (1981), BEA plans to publish more complete distributions for family personal income, together with comparisons with the Current Population Survey for 1972, in addition to a more complete description of the file than is presented in our appendix A. BEA also plans to release a public use file tape of the fully estimated Exact Match-Statistical Match file.

redistribute claims to income produced, without raising the total. Perhaps this is little more than a definition—although the indirect effect of transfers and taxes on production may well affect the level of production, a topic beyond the scope of this paper.[1]

Section 2.3 gives a brief description of the microdata file—the fully estimated Exact Match-Statistical Match (EM-SM) file for 1972—from which the redistributive effects of transfers have been estimated and explains some of the further adjustments to the file that make possible the estimates presented in section 2.4. The basic microdata file used is fully corrected for under- and nonreporting of income, and the aggregates for particular income types are consistent with the aggregates for the corresponding income types included in total money and family personal income as estimated in the National Income and Product Accounts (NIPA). A more complete account of the file is provided in appendix A. Estimates of pre- and after-tax and transfer distributions are presented in section 2.4, although we should note that the estimates for taxes are not of the same quality as the other income and transfer components in the file.

While redistributive transfers are made by business, nonprofit, and household sectors of the economy, in addition to the government, the government is by far and away the most important. Two comments should be made at this point. First, our paper discusses government redistribution through the tax and transfer system, not all of its redistributive activities taken as a matter of deliberate policy, such as agricultural price supports, which raise the (pretax and transfer) incomes of farmers. Second, size and other distributions of pretax and transfer income concepts (such as our earnings and production-related income) should not be viewed as those that would have been generated in the absence of government activities and policies. The latter affect the demand for and supply of products and productive services in a variety of ways and, as a result, the wage and rental rates underlying our estimates of pretransfer incomes.[2]

2.2   An Accounting Framework for Transfers

In this section we develop a framework for the alternative income concepts used in this paper and their relation to an accounting framework for transfer payments for households. Our discussion will be restricted to the household sector; the development of an accounting framework for the economy as a whole and its various sectors is the subject of the Eisner paper in this volume. Our household sector is more narrowly defined than the traditional personal sector in the NIPA: for one thing, it excludes nonprofit institutions, such as philanthropic organizations; for another, its coverage is limited to units eligible for interview in census field surveys. Thus, the institutionalized population, military personnel on post and overseas, civilians overseas, and decedents (persons who died before the survey week but whose incomes in the previous year were included in the income aggregates for that year) are excluded from the estimates.

Private insurance companies and uninsured pension funds, it should be noted, are included in the NIPA business sector, not its personal sector. Also, following the NIPA treatment, we include estates and trusts as part of the household sector and impute property income received by estates and trusts from the business and government sectors directly to beneficiary households, whether the income received by estates and trusts is paid out to beneficiaries or retained by the estate or trust for the latters' benefit.

2.2.1   Definitions of Transfer Income and Income from Production

There appears to be general agreement that transfer payments are defined as payments made for which there is no quid pro quo, that is, nothing of value is provided in exchange. Ingvar Ohlsson (1953, p. 13) refers to such transactions as "independent" or one-way, as contrasted with "combined" or two-way transactions in which there is an exchange of equal values. In the context of national income accounting, a transfer is "any income, either in money or in value in kind, accruing to persons or groups which is not in return for current services or products provided by them."[3] Since by definition no current goods or services are being provided in return, transfers enter only the income side of the accounts and do not affect the product side. For a particular receipt or payment to be considered an income transfer, "two tests must be satisfied: (1) it must be income from the point of view of the recipient; and (2) it must be a payment for which no service or product is provided in return" (Rolph 1948, p. 329). A failure to meet the first test would be exemplified by a capital transfer, such as a gift of land by one person to another, or an insurance reimbursement for storm damage to a residence or an automobile.

The second test requires a definition of production or productive activity. The one adopted by Rolph, and implicit, if not explicit, in much of the literature, is the use of real resources, both physical assets and human beings, to produce goods and services over a specified time period. It lies behind the economist's model of a production function, which posits a relation between the flow of services of real resources, measured in physical units or units of time (e.g., man-hours), and the resulting flow of output.

2.2.2   Money Income vs. Income in Kind

Such a definition does not, of course, set rigid bounds on what is considered productive activity. For one thing, it is generally agreed that the goods and services do not necessarily have to be bought and sold in markets to be eligible for inclusion in the output measure. We believe that the concept of income and product should be extended beyond that embodied in market transactions, although we do not attempt in this paper to determine the appropriate boundaries for inclusion of in-kind income. Although the boundary must be justified by the purpose of the particular study, we would probably draw it before reaching such frontiers of imputation as home production and leisure time.

Imputed income types for which we do have estimates, in particular those imputations that are part of NIPA and included in personal income, are also included in our empirical distributions, specifically, wages in kind, imputed food and fuel consumed on farms, imputed rent on owner-occupied dwellings, and imputed interest. From a distributional standpoint, the inclusion of imputed rent is necessary to give equal treatment to the owners of rented structures and owners who live in their own dwellings without any payment of cash rent. An argument similar to that for imputed rent can be made for the inclusion of imputed interest. Investors have the option either of investing in physical and financial assets directly or of acquiring claims to such assets indirectly through holding the deposits or claims of financial intermediaries. If investors select the latter option, they give up part of the interest return they would otherwise have received as an implicit payment for the services of such intermediaries. Imputing a value for these services and adding it to the return of those holding claims on financial intermediaries is one way of providing equivalent distributional treatment for the two groups of investors. Alternatively, one could deduct the (imputed) value of the equivalent services that those who invest directly provide for themselves, if such estimates existed.

Perhaps imputed wages are defined too narrowly in the NIPA. We see no objection, if estimates of their distribution were available, to broadening the concept to include other kinds of employee perquisites, particularly those enjoyed by many executives. Employer contributions to social insurance and private pensions and welfare funds (including group health and life insurance) are already included in employee compensation in the NIPA, although under the heading of supplements to wages and salaries rather than imputed wages. We confine our empirical work to wages and salaries, not on principle, but because we lack estimates of the distribution of supplements by income size.

2.2.3   Capital Gains and Losses

Capital gains and losses present another problem in defining production, since they do not appear to fit nicely with the notion of creation of values through the use of real resources. Insofar as these gains arise from changes in expectations of the future earning power of existing assets and not just from changes in the rates at which those earnings are discounted, there is a good case for their inclusion. Such inclusion is particularly appropriate for income distribution measurement, since such gains are important in determining the relative well-offness or position of different households and groups in the distribution. We exclude them, not as a matter of principle, but simply because we have no comprehensive estimates of their distribution in our microdata file.[4]

2.2.4 Interest Payments

One of the more controversial issues in national income accounting is the treatment of interest: Are such payments to be viewed as transfers or as payments for productive services?[5] Under current accounting methods employed in the NIPA, interest payments do not affect the size of net national product (NNP); interest is not treated as the purchase of a separate service which produces a value in addition to that already included on the product side. A residence, for example, does not render any more housing services to its occupant simply because there is a mortgage held against it on which interest must be paid. Viewed from the income side, interest is simply a transfer or redistribution of business income or income arising from the rental of physical assets (e.g., dwellings). Similarly, government output is measured independently of government interest paid. While it has often been argued that government output is understated by the omission of the value of the services of government-owned capital, it is usually not proposed to measure such services by interest paid on government debt.[6]

This does not mean, of course, that (net) interest paid, whether by business or government, should be excluded from a measure of income receipts simply because it does not give rise to independent values on the product side. The important issue is whether the totals for the various income types have been measured correctly, for example, whether business or rental incomes are shown net of interest paid if interest is shown as a separate income share (an application of Rolph's "deduct-add" rule), rather than whether the resulting interest (or dividend) share is to be called a productive payment of some sort or other, or simply what it is, a transfer payment.

2.2.5 Consumer Interest

One further problem is presented by consumer interest paid. In the NIPA such interest ("personal interest paid to business") is no longer included in NNP in consumer expenditure, but is treated as a separate allocation of personal income, along with personal taxes, consumption expenditure, net foreign remittances, and personal savings.[7] Personal interest income is thus gross of such interest paid by consumers, rather than net. Given the fact that interest does not represent the value of some additional services purchased by consumers (otherwise it would be included on the product side), it should be deducted from interest paid for purposes of showing the correct relative distribution of income among households. This can be seen most easily in connection with one form of consumer interest: installment credit to finance purchases of consumer durables. Suppose that Jones is sufficiently well-off to purchase an auto and finances it by reducing his holdings of other financial assets (e.g., savings deposits; shares in money market funds), thus foregoing the interest he would otherwise have received on those financial claims. Smith, on the other hand, finances the purchase of an identical auto through a loan either because (a) his net worth or wealth is insufficient, or (b) he chooses not to liquidate any of his financial assets and borrows instead. Unless we deduct the interest paid by Smith from the interest he receives,[8] we will show Smith, on the basis of this consideration alone, just as well-off as Jones in case (a) and better-off than Jones in case (b). An identical argument can be made for borrowing against future earning power, or for loans used to purchase financial assets, for example, stocks purchased on margin accounts where the margin buyer is simply paying over to the broker part of his dividend income from the stock purchased.[9]

Of course, if the product side were to include imputed rental income from ownership of consumer durables such as autos, there would be no need to deduct the corresponding consumer interest paid; the latter would simply be a transfer to the creditor of part of the imputed rent (calculated gross of interest paid) from the durable, just as mortgage interest represents a transfer to the mortgage holder of income arising from the imputed rental value of owner-occupied dwellings. To return to our example of Jones and Smith, accounting for the imputed rental income of both persons and deducting the interest paid by Smith from Smith's rental income would show their correct relative income positions: Jones would have more net imputed rental income from the auto than would Smith. This is exactly the procedure followed in calculating net rental income from owner-occupied housing.

It might be noted that our accounting rules for interest are consistent with generally agreed on accounting rules for calculating net worth, as the difference between the value of a person's assets minus the value of his or her liabilities (debts and loans). Thus, if we draw up balance sheets for Jones and Smith, we should include Smith's installment loan among his liabilities, regardless of how we choose to account for consumer durables. Thus, Smith's net worth would always be shown correctly as less than Jones's, whether or not we choose to include the automobiles each of them owns among their assets. Obtaining a measure of net property income consistent with the measurement of net worth requires deducting consumer interest paid from total interest received even in the case where both the income and net worth concepts omit consumer durables and the income they generate.

2.2.5   Transfers in Kind and Collective Consumption

Just as with income from production, transfers may take the form of in-kind benefits—goods or services furnished free of charge by government to households, or whose cost is reimbursed in whole or in part by government when purchased by households in the market place. Again, there is a good case in principle for including such transfers in recipients' incomes and in practice for drawing the line among types to be included or excluded in ways similar to those for earnings in kind. For example, employing sweeping definitions of in-kind transfers, but unduly limiting types of in-kind income included in earnings, particularly those received by upper-income earners, will bias the resulting size distribution toward equality, or distributions by socioeconomic characteristics toward those groups more heavily reliant on transfer income than on earnings.

There is, however, a major difference between the two types of in-kind income: many in-kind earnings types are not now included in NNP, primarily because they are treated as intermediate products when paid for by employers (e.g., business lunches); in-kind transfers, on the other hand, are already counted on the product side as government purchases of goods and services or collective consumption (e.g., school lunches). The problem for government purchases then becomes one of determining which ones to classify as in-kind transfers and allocable to individual beneficiaries, and which ones as collective consumption and in principle not allocable, or, if allocated anyway, distributed in an essentially arbitrary way, as was done in many of the earlier studies of the redistributive effects of government budgets (e.g., Gillespie 1965; Reynolds and Smolensky 1977). The closer the goods are to pure public goods (e.g., national defense; creation of new knowledge), the weaker is the case for treating them as in-kind transfers. External effects generated by government expenditures on such potentially excludable and appropriable goods as education also complicate the problem. We include as in-kind transfers food stamps and Medicare, since they are part of NIPA's personal income and we have estimates of their distributions in our file; we would also include such things as Medicaid, public housing benefits, and rent subsidies if estimates in our file were available. A borderline case is furnished by education: it is farther along the continuum toward the conceptually unallocable pure public goods case, but there are specific beneficiaries who gain more than the public at large from such expenditures. For empirical work, part of the issue of inclusion must turn on whether there is enough information in the microdata file used to permit an estimate of their distribution on the basis of other than arbitrary, ad hoc assumptions.

Since the papers in this volume by Smeeding, and Olsen and York are concerned with the valuation of in-kind transfers, we do not deal with that issue here. Our aggregate income controls for food stamps and Medicare are based on their cost to the government.

2.2.7 Tax Expenditures

Treating tax expenditures as in-kind transfers presents further problems. If the concern is only with the complete post-tax and transfer income distribution, it is unnecessary to take separate account of tax expenditures, since the final size distribution will already reflect the lower taxes paid by the beneficiaries of such expenditures.

If, on the other hand, the purpose is to show a pretax, post-transfer distribution (including tax expenditures as in-kind transfers), or to isolate the separate distributional effects of particular tax expenditures, estimates are needed. If, however, one then wants to arrive at the final post-tax and transfer distribution of income, some hypothetical, reference, or "counterfactual" tax function must be estimated and imposed that would, in the light of the tax expenditures assigned to recipients, achieve the final distribution. Of course, to derive the counterfactual tax function one could fall back on the expedient of simply adding tax expenditures assigned to recipients to the actual taxes they pay. This expedient might make more sense and result in fewer difficulties if income tax rates were proportional rather than, as in our economy, progressive.

2.2.8 Private Insurance

Most private insurance is designed to provide financial protection against catastrophic events, whether to property or persons. Insurance compensation for property damage, for example, a house lost in fire or an auto demolished in an accident, is simply a capital transfer, designed to make good a capital loss suffered by the claimant, and not part of his or her current income.

Households also purchase insurance to provide protection against loss of income, for example, life and disability insurance. In this case, we would add continuing benefits paid, such as private annuities and monthly disability payments (although not lump-sum settlements, which should be treated as capital transfers), and deduct premiums paid (net of insurance company operating expenses) from the post-transfer income concept (e.g., our household disposable income). This treatment corresponds with the way social insurance is handled in NIPA's definition of personal disposable income: social insurance benefits (e.g., Social Security, unemployment compensation) are included; personal and employer contributions to social insurance funds are excluded.

Another form of private insurance covers extraordinary expenses, such as medical and hospital outlays in connection with an accident or serious illness. Benefits from this kind of insurance we would exclude from pre- and post-transfer income (and include premiums paid). Of course, having incurred a $10,000 medical bill for a serious illness, Jones is better-off if he has insurance that will reimburse him for the bill than if he does not. However, in size distributions we are comparing, not Jones's position with and without insurance coverage for extraordinary expense, but Jones's position with that of others like Smith, who has remained healthy during the same period and hence received no settlement. It would be difficult to maintain, other things equal, that Jones is better-off than Smith to the extent of the $10,000 reimbursement. Indeed, this is one of the reasons we assign Medicare benefits as an imputed premium to all those eligible and not as benefits to those actually receiving health care. (The other is that we have no way of distinguishing between the ill and the healthy aged in our file.)

2.2.9   Pre- and Post-Transfer Income Concepts

Our various income concepts are defined more precisely in table 2.1, and the aggregates for selected income and transfer types (for somewhat broader categories than in table 2.1) contained in our microdata file (the fully estimated EM-SM file) are shown in table 2.2. A description and rationale for each, together with a comparison with alternative concepts, is presented below.

It should perhaps be reemphasized that the accounting framework represented in these tables is restricted to the household sector. In an accounting system for the economy as a whole, by definition transfers paid must be equal to transfers received; since the algebraic sum of transfers paid and received equals zero, the economy's pretransfer income aggregate must equal its post-transfer income aggregate. On the other hand, since a sector's receipts from transfers may exceed or fall short of its payments of transfers to other sectors, there is no necessary relation between its pretransfer and post-transfer income aggregates. Thus, no particular significance should be attached to the virtual equality of our pre- and post-transfer concepts (earnings and household disposable income), quite apart from two intermediate concepts (production-related income and household income).

Primary Income or Earnings (EARN)

Our first concept includes income arising directly from participation by household members in the productive process, either as suppliers of labor services or as proprietors of enterprises (farm and nonfarm) furnishing their own labor services or the services of assets under their immediate control. It includes wages and salaries plus proprietors' income, and omits employer contributions to social insurance and to private health,

Table 2.1   Definitions of Pre- and Post-Transfer Income Aggregate

1. Primary income or earnings (EARN) =	Wages and salaries + Nonfarm proprietors' (self-employment) income + Farm proprietors' (self-employment) income + Money rental income + Imputed rent on owner-occupied dwellings (farm and nonfarm) + Imputed wages and salaries + Imputed food and fuel consumed on farms
2. Production-related income (PRI) =	EARN + Dividends + Money interest received + Imputed interest − Consumer interest paid (exclusive of mortgage interest) + Estate and trust income
3. Household income (HI) =	PRI + Public assistance + Unemployment compensation + Workers' compensation + Veterans' benefits + OASDI benefits* + Railroad retirement benefits* + Government pensions received* + Private pensions and annuities* + Food stamp bonuses + Medicare benefits*

welfare, and pension funds only because our file does not include estimates of the distribution by size of NIPA's supplements to wages and salaries.

Net rental income of persons is also included in EARN, since it is more nearly akin to income of unincorporated enterprises, the distinction between the two, so far as rental property is concerned, depending on whether rental receipts are the major, or merely an incidental, source of income to the recipient (Budd 1958, pp. 355–56). (In the former case, such "net rental income" is classified as proprietors' income originating in the real estate industry.) As previously noted, our household sector includes the results of business operations for proprietors, renters of property, and owner-occupants, not their entire business activities. While there is something to be said for including all the business activities of home ownership in the household sector, as Ruggles and Ruggles (1982) have suggested, and perhaps extending it to self-employed pro-

Table 2.1 (continued)

4. Household disposable income (HDI) =	HI − Personal contributions for social insurance* − Federal personal income tax − State and local income tax − Personal property tax + State income tax refund
5. Household disposable income exclusive of net age-related transfers (HDI − ART) =	HDI − OASDI benefits − Railroad retirement benefits* − Government pensions received* − Private pensions and annuities* − Medicare benefits + Personal contributions for social insurance
6. Production-related income inclusive of net age-related transfers (PRI + ART) =	PRI + OASDI benefits* + Railroad retirement benefits* + Government pensions received* + Private pensions and annuities* + Medicare benefits* − Personal contributions for social insurance*

*Age-related items.

prietors and landlords as well, it is not necessary for the purposes of this paper. In any case, such an extension should not be interpreted as undermining the case for the rental imputation, nor as precluding the handling of interest payments as transfers to other sectors or within the household sector itself.

With due allowance for possible transfer elements included in EARN that we cannot extract (e.g., deferred compensation of employees extending beyond the current year; income arising from long-term rental contracts), EARN is the closest we can get to a concept of income arising from current production and accruing directly to participants without the interposition of transfers or transfer-type payments. While there is nothing analogous to EARN in the NIPA, it is similar to the concept of primary income proposed by the United Nations (UN) for the collection and preparation of income distribution statistics, differing from the latter in its inclusion in primary income of rental income, which is classified by the UN as property income (1977, pp. 1, 11). The United Nations' proposal to define proprietors' or "entrepreneurial" income as well as rental income gross of capital consumption (whereas ours is net) seems to be more a matter of expediency in measurement than one of principle.

Table 2.2   Pre- and Post-Transfer Income Concepts for the Household Sector, 1972 (millions of dollars)

	Total	Money	In Kind
1. Wages and salaries	624,133	621,690	2,443
2. Proprietors' (self-employment) income	78,699	78,358	341
a. Farm	18,348	18,007	341
b. Nonfarm	60,351	60,351	—
3. Net rental and royalty income	19,928	7,535	12,393
4. *Primary income or earnings (EARN)* [1 + 2 + 3]	722,760	707,583	15,177
5. Dividend income	21,728	21,728	
6. Net interest income	40,777	27,779	12,998
a. Interest income received	60,363	47,365	12,998
b. Less consumer interest paid	− 19,586	− 19,586	—
7. Estate and trust income	4,418	4,298	120
8. *Production-related income (PRI)* (earnings plus property income) [4 + 5 + 6 + 7]	789,683	761,388	28,295
9. Government transfer payments	88,444	78,202	10,242
a. Non-age-related transfers	28,385	26,428	1,957
1) Unemployment and workers' compensation	7,814	7,814	—
2) Public assistance and food stamp bonuses	12,642	10,685	1,957
3) Veterans' benefits	7,929	7,929	—
b. Age-related transfers	60,059	51,774	8,285
1) Social Security, railroad retirement, and Medicare benefits	48,050	39,765	8,285
2) Government employee pensions (federal, state, and local)	12,009	12,009	—
10. Private pensions and annuities (age-related)	9,297	9,297	—
11. *Household income* (HI) [8 + 9 + 10]	887,424	848,887	38,537
12. Personal contributions for social insurance (age-related)	− 33,265	− 33,265	—
13. Taxes paid	− 127,630	− 127,630	—
a. Federal personal income	− 90,956	− 90,956	—
b. State and local	− 18,337	− 18,337	—
1) Personal income	− 17,467	− 17,467	—
2) Personal property	− 870	− 870	—
14. *Household disposable income* (HDI) [11 − 12 − 13]	726,529	687,992	38,537

Addenda
Income Concepts for Age-Related Transfer Comparisons

	Total	Money	In Kind
15. Household disposable income exclusive of net age-related transfers (HI − ART) [14 − 9b − 10 + 12]	690,438	660,186	30,252

Table 2.2 (continued)

	Total	Money	In Kind
16. Production-related income inclusive of net age-related transfers (PRI + ART) [8 + 9b + 10 − 12]	825,774	789,194	36,580

SOURCE: Computed from the fully adjusted EM-SM file described in section 2.3.

Production-Related Income (PRI)

Our second income concept takes account of transfers arising out of the nature and distribution of ownership rights in the economy. Since production originates in and income accrues directly to business firms outside the household sector, the transfer of a part of this income to households through interest and dividend payments (directly, or indirectly through estates and trusts), based on the particular kinds of ownership rights or claims that households have in or on business, must be accounted for. Production-related income (PRI) is thus the sum of earnings and property income. We use the term, production-*related* income, partly out of recognition of the transfer character of some privately distributed income, partly because of the necessity of including interest paid by governments to households. Government obligations are bought and sold in private markets; owners of debt instruments do not view their holdings, or the interest income received from them, differently simply because some of the obligations they own are claims against the government, as distinguished from claims on business firms or owners of rental properties. If one feels it necessary to find a production base for payment of government interest similar to that in the private sector, he or she may suppose that it is a distribution of (part of) the income arising from the (not-now-imputed) services of government-owned physical assets.

In accordance with our earlier discussion of consumer interest as a transfer payment, in calculating PRI we have deducted for each household or consumer unit in our file its payment of interest from interest it receives, to derive "net interest received," which may, of course, be negative for individual units.

While in our view EARN is the preferable pretransfer income concept and PRI a concept intermediate between pre- and post-transfer income, others, who are uncomfortable with the treatment of property income as transfer income, may wish to consider PRI as the appropriate pretransfer concept with which our later concepts are to be compared. Our tabulations permit such an alternative treatment. We should also note in passing that in the United Nations' conceptual framework for income distribution statistics there is no concept similar to our PRI. Property income is simply added, along with other private and government transfers, to primary income to obtain the United Nations' total household income.

Production-related income is the concept by which consumer units are ranked for that set of distributions in section 2.4 in which the ranking of units is the same for all distributions, in contrast to the other set in which units are ranked by size of own income concept, that is, the income concept on which the distribution is based.

Household Income (HI)

Adding other government and private transfer payments to production-related income yields our household income. We restrict private transfers to private pension payments, although, as noted earlier in our discussion of private insurance, we would include estimates of benefits paid from private sickness and disability insurance (to replace losses in earnings) if we had them, as well as the imputed value of medical insurance premiums paid by employers. A similar remark applies to receipts of interfamily transfers.

With the exception of the treatment of capital consumption (noted above), consumer interest paid, and the coverage of the institutionalized population, which the United Nations recommends, HI is virtually identical with the United Nations concept of total household income (United Nations 1977, pp. 5, 9–11, 48). It is also similar to the Census Bureau's total money income (TMI), insofar as the latter concept can be said to have a precise definition; important differences are our inclusion of income in kind (excluded from TMI) and our netting of consumer interest paid against interest received. The Bureau of Economic Analysis's (BEA) concept of family personal income (FPI) differs from HI in our netting out interest paid by consumers and our inclusion of personal contributions for social insurance. So far as personal income (PI) is concerned, in addition to the differences already noted between HI and FPI, there are matters of population and sector coverage and the inclusion of employer contributions to private health, welfare, and pension funds ("other labor income") in, and exclusion of private pension payments from, PI. Further, a number of specific transfers in PI are excluded from both FPI and HI, partly for conceptual reasons, partly because of difficulties in estimating their distribution by income size. Examples are lump-sum settlements of various sorts (equivalent to capital transfers), consumer bad debts, and auto insurance liability for personal injuries.

It can be argued that HI and concepts similar to it, such as the United Nations' total household income and the Census Bureau's TMI, involve a form of double-counting, since they include both personal and employer contributions to private and social insurance, in addition to benefits

resulting from the latter. While this is true in part for HI, in our accounting system—as well as the United Nations'—household income is simply
an intermediate concept between a pretransfer, purely production-
oriented income concept (EARN) and a complete post-transfer income
concept (HDI); its purpose is simply to show the effect of transfers
received by the household sector before taking account of transfers
household pay (including taxes).

Household Disposable Income (HDI)

Household disposable income is simply household income less personal contributions for social insurance and personal (income and property)
taxes paid. It is virtually the same as the United Nations' total available
household income, with the exceptions noted above for differences between HI and the United Nations' total household income. For a comparison with BEA's personal disposable income, all the previous differences noted between HI and PI are relevant as well. In addition, BEA
deducts estate and gift taxes (essentially capital transfers) and nontax
payments (on whose distribution we have no information). We have not
made a further deduction for sales and gasoline taxes in figuring HDI,
partly because they are components of indirect business taxes, which
have already been deducted in going from NNP to national income and
personal income and hence implicitly to FPI and our HI, and partly
because of the quality (or lack thereof) of the data available to us from the
itemized deductions on individual tax returns.[10]

Income Concepts Associated with Age-Related Transfers (ART)

One problem in defining transfers is the time period over which the
receipt of income and the furnishing of productive services are to be
matched. At one extreme, most of the wages paid on the last day of a
month for a entire month's labor services ought to be considered a
transfer, if for some reason we were interested in measuring income only
for that one day. At the other extreme, it might be argued that pensions
are simply deferred compensation for services rendered over one's working life and ought to be counted as payments for productive services if the
relevant time period were viewed as the entire life of the wage earner.
One approach might be to measure either the present discounted value of
future wages (net of employer and employee contributions to pension
funds) plus pensions paid, or alternatively, the present value of wages
inclusive of such contributions, but excluding pensions, although, for a
given rate of discount, there is no assurance that these two different
lifetime concepts would come to the same thing. Yet there are serious
difficulties in such a lifetime approach, not the least of which are selecting
the appropriate discount rate and making sense of the recipient unit
concept in a lifetime context, unless the unit is taken to be the individual

earner. Even apart from these considerations, interpreting a size distribution of lifetime incomes for consumer units whose heads are in different stages of their life cycles is no easy matter either.[11]

In any case, it is impossible for us to resolve these problems with the data at hand. We have therefore experimented with a more limited approach, showing the distributional effects of using two different methods of accounting for pensions and retirement contributions and retirement income.[12] One way is to include in current income employer and employee contributions to age-related social insurance and pension plans as employee compensation and to exclude pension payments and retirement benefits, both public and private, from transfer payments. An alternative accounting treatment is to deduct such contributions from employee compensation and add the retirement benefits and pensions paid to the current retirees. A comparison of these two different accounting schemes shows only the net effects of age-related transfers (ART) on the distribution of current year income, given the age distribution of (the heads of) households in the file; it does not show a distribution with a consistent treatment of units independent of or standardized for their age structure. Indeed, for reasons cited earlier, although our discussion of this issue is by no means complete, we doubt that this can be done.

Income concepts used in distributional work are more closely related to the second accounting scheme than the first. Family personal income is perhaps the best example, with the Census Bureau's TMI perhaps a close second, although the latter fails to deduct employee and self-employed contributions to social insurance from earnings. In addition, neither concept deducts—primarily for estimating reasons—employee contributions to private pension plans, although such contributions are of minor importance. On the other hand, the NIPA's concept of personal income does not give consistent treatment to government and private retirement plans—indeed, to social and private insurance schemes in general. Contributions to social insurance (including government employee contributions to federal, state, and local pension plans) are excluded from personal income and the corresponding benefit payments added, whereas employer (and any employee) contributions to provide pension plans are included in employee compensation and private pension payments are excluded. While there is a long-standing rationale in the NIPA for this treatment, it is of limited use in distributional analysis; indeed, personal income is not a concept that can be used without some modification in income size distribution work.

There are two ways to compare our distributions, inclusive and exclusive of age-related transfers. The first is by comparing the distribution of PRI with the distribution that results from deducting from PRI personal contributions for social insurance and adding age-related benefits (Social Security benefits, Medicare, and private pension and annuity payments), denoted as PRI + ART in our tables. The other is to take HDI as the base for the comparison, then deduct age-related benefits and add personal contributions (our HDI − ART). Whichever comparison is used, it will not be complicated by the net effect of *other* transfers—government transfers which are not age-related and personal taxes. In effect, the first method asks: How would the distribution of PRI look if we modified it *only* by including age-related transfers? In the second method, on the other hand, we ask: How would HDI be affected if we were to exclude only age-related transfers from it? Judging by the results in section 2.4, there is little actual difference between the two methods in the extent of change in inequality, pre- and post-transfer, whether measured by changes in selected quantile shares or by the change in the Gini concentration ratio. The implied Lorenz curves for the concepts, as distinguished from their shifts, are, of course, quite different.

Given the data available to us, the comparisons are not based on ideal concepts. For one thing, we lack size distribution estimates of employer and employee contributions to private pension plans; for another, while it would be possible to impute to wage and salary workers employer contributions for social insurance, we have had neither the time nor resources to do so. Thus, the PRI distribution is unfortunately *already* net of employer contributions to social insurance and pension plans, and we cannot show their distributional impact. Neither can we add these contributions back in going from HDI to HDI − ART. For another, our division between age- and non-age-related transfers is only an approximation, although a relatively close one. While nearly all personal contributions are for age-related programs, a few transfers, such as Social Security benefits and veterans' benefits, could not be separated into the two components, given the data in our file. Social Security was classified as age-related, veterans' benefits as non-age-related.

2.3 How the Estimates Were Made

This section provides a brief description of the data base underlying the tabulations in section 2.4. It is based on the fully estimated Exact Match-Statistical Match (EM-SM) file constructed by a joint effort of the Bureau of Economic Analysis (BEA) and the Office of Research and Statistics (ORS) of the Social Security Administration (SSA).

The starting point was the 1972 Exact Match (EM) file, which was an exact match of persons surveyed in the March 1973 Current Population Survey (CPS) with (extracts from) their SSA earnings and beneficiary records and information from their individual tax returns contained in the Internal Revenue Service (IRS) Individual Master File (IMF). Since the amount of tax return information in the IMF was quite limited, ORS carried out a statistical match between the EM file and a subsample of the

Statistics of Income file (which has relatively complete tax return information), itself exact-matched to SSA earnings records to incorporate certain demographic information (age, race, and sex) needed to improve the quality of the statistical match. The income types in each return in the file were then corrected for the effects of audit by using the results of the IRS Taxpayer Compliance Measurement Program for 1972. In our tabulations, wages and salaries, interest, and dividends were taken from the EM portion of the file; proprietor's income, rent, royalties, and estate and trust income, from the SM portion. Since state and local bond interest does not have to be reported on federal tax returns, its distribution had to be estimated separately by using the limited information available from other field surveys. The earnings and property income of nonfilers were taken from the CPS portion of the EM file. All the above earnings and property income types were then adjusted so that their aggregates would reflect their corresponding NIPA control totals. The latter were derived by adjusting the amount of each income type in the NIPA personal income to make it consistent with the CPS population universe and income concepts.

Since most cash transfer payments are not subject to federal income tax, they could not be estimated from the tax return part of the EM-SM file. The starting point was therefore the CPS portion of the file, the major exception being Social Security benefits. With some minor adjustments, the latter were taken from the benefit portion of the Social Security administrative record.

In-kind income, including imputed wages and imputed farm income, was distributed by a variety of methods, using information already in the EM-SM file, as well as information from the 1972 portion of the Consumer Expenditure Survey (CEX), the latter incorporated into the EM-SM file by means of a statistical match between the CEX and CPS portion of the EM-SM file. Imputed interest on checking and savings accounts was distributed on the basis of the value of asset holdings reported by consumer units in the CEX. Imputed net rental income for each owner-occupant was estimated from gross rental value and individual expense components (repair and maintenance, mortgage interest, insurance, and depreciation), from information from the CEX and control totals for gross rent and types of housing expenditures from the NIPA. Medicare benefits were treated as imputed insurance premiums for hospital and medical care and a mean amount assigned to each eligible aged person. Food stamp bonus values were assigned to eligible units based on family size and the number of weeks worked by the head.

Personal contributions for social insurance were based largely on the amount of wages and salaries reported on the tax return and occupational and employment information reported in the CPS, with numerous refinements introduced for specific kinds of contributions, such as contributions by state and local workers to retirement funds. Federal income taxes were taken off tax returns added to the file in the statistical match. State and local income and property tax liabilities were estimated from itemized deductions for those who itemized, with income tax amounts imputed to those who did not itemize, based on amounts reported by itemizers.

A more complete description of the EM-SM file is given in appendix A.

2.4   Pre- and Post-Transfer Income Distributions for 1972

In this section we present estimates of pre- and post-transfer income distributions for consumer units (families plus unrelated individuals) and for selected socioeconomic groups. Relative size distributions and relative mean incomes for all units are shown in tables 2.3 through 2.5, and relative means and shares for socioeconomic groups are given in tables 2.9 and 2.10. Estimates for families may be found in appendix B; since they are similar to those for consumer units, they are not discussed separately.

Table 2.3 gives the income share for each vigesile and the top 1 percent in each of the six distributions; table 2.4 shows the corresponding relative means. Looking at the first two distributions, shifting the definition of income from earnings to production-related income raises the share, and hence the relative mean income, of the bottom two quintiles of the distribution by 20 percent, reduces the share of those in the 41st to 95th percentile range by 4 percent, increases the share of the top 1 percent by over 16 percent, and the share of the 4 percentiles immediately below it by 2 percent. The Lorenz curves for the two distributions intersect just above the 75th percentile. Because of this fact, not too much stress should be placed on the change in a single-valued measure of inequality such as the Gini concentration ratio, although the latter does fall slightly, from .49 to .48. The addition of property income to aged units with little or no earnings or rental income is a factor in the increase at the bottom, with the number of consumer units with zero income falling from 6.5 percent to 2.2 percent of all units. Substantial amounts of property income accrue to those units at the top of the distribution, producing the rather large increase in the share of the top 1 percent.

When the definition is changed from production-related income (PRI) to household income (HI), the income share of the bottom half of the distribution is increased by over 31 percent and by even greater proportions for the lower parts of the distribution, with the income share of the lowest 30 percent of consumer units being more than doubled. The share of the upper half of the distribution, on the other hand, is reduced by about 6 percent, with that of the top 5 percent falling by over 8 percent.

Table 2.3   Income Shares, Families and Unrelated Individuals Ranked by Size
of the Income Definition, 1972
(percent)

Percentile Groups	EARN	PRI	HI	HDI	HDI− ART	PRI+ ART
Total	100.00	100.00	100.00	100.00	100.00	100.00
1–5	− .52	− .41	.05	− .22	− .63	− .25
6–10	.01	.09	.90	1.01	.39	.58
11–15	.20	.37	1.25	1.40	.78	1.00
16–20	.46	.76	1.60	1.77	1.21	1.39
21–25	.91	1.26	1.95	2.14	1.70	1.79
26–30	1.50	1.78	2.32	2.50	2.17	2.19
31–35	2.14	2.29	2.69	2.87	2.63	2.59
36–40	2.76	2.81	3.07	3.23	3.09	2.99
41–45	3.35	3.31	3.47	3.61	3.54	3.40
46–50	3.90	3.82	3.87	4.00	4.00	3.81
51–55	4.46	4.29	4.27	4.39	4.46	4.24
56–60	5.02	4.81	4.69	4.79	4.93	4.69
61–65	5.60	5.35	5.15	5.22	5.42	5.16
66–70	6.21	5.90	5.63	5.68	5.94	5.66
71–75	6.87	6.51	6.17	6.20	6.50	6.21
76–80	7.59	7.23	6.83	6.82	7.16	6.91
81–85	8.52	8.14	7.64	7.61	7.98	7.76
86–90	9.73	9.35	8.73	8.66	9.12	8.89
91–95	11.67	11.35	10.55	10.43	10.94	10.82
96–100	19.60	21.00	19.20	17.90	18.66	20.17
100	6.70	7.81	7.06	6.14	6.37	7.54
Gini concen- tration ratio	.49	.48	.42	.40	.44	.44

The Lorenz curve for HI thus lies everywhere above the curve for PRI,
implying an overall decrease in inequality; the Gini ratio is reduced from
.48 to .42. This change in definition adds various government transfers,
which tend to be concentrated in the bottom half of the distribution. The
number of units with zero income is reduced from 2.2 percent to less than
0.2 percent of all units.

When the definition is shifted from household income to household
disposable income (HDI), the share of the lower three quarters of the
distribution rises, although by only a little over 3 percent. Even when the
share of the bottom vigesile (whose share goes from positive to negative)
is excluded from the calculation, the increase is still only 4 percent. For
the top 1 percent the reduction is 13 percent. The Gini ratio falls slightly
from .42 to .40. These results suggest that the combined effect of personal
contributions for social insurance and personal taxes is only mildly progressive, at least for consumer units below the top 1 percent of the

Table 2.4   **Relative Mean Incomes, Families and Unrelated Individuals Ranked by Size of the Income Definition, 1972**

Percentile Groups	EARN	PRI	HI	HDI	HDI − ART	PRI + ART
Total	1.00	1.00	1.00	1.00	1.00	1.00
1–5	−.10	−.08	.01	−.04	−.13	−.05
6–10	.00	.02	.18	.20	.08	.12
11–15	.04	.07	.25	.28	.16	.20
16–20	.09	.15	.32	.35	.24	.28
21–25	.18	.25	.39	.43	.34	.36
26–30	.30	.36	.46	.50	.43	.44
31–35	.43	.46	.54	.57	.53	.52
36–40	.55	.56	.61	.65	.62	.60
41–45	.67	.66	.69	.72	.71	.68
46–50	.78	.76	.77	.80	.80	.76
51–55	.89	.86	.85	.88	.89	.85
56–60	1.00	.96	.94	.96	.99	.94
61–65	1.12	1.07	1.03	1.04	1.08	1.03
66–70	1.24	1.18	1.13	1.14	1.19	1.13
71–75	1.37	1.30	1.23	1.24	1.30	1.24
76–80	1.52	1.45	1.37	1.36	1.43	1.38
81–85	1.70	1.63	1.53	1.52	1.60	1.55
86–90	1.95	1.87	1.74	1.73	1.82	1.78
91–95	2.33	2.27	2.11	2.08	2.19	2.16
96–100	3.92	4.20	3.84	3.58	3.73	4.03
100	6.67	7.79	7.06	6.14	6.36	7.51

distribution. These comparisons are, of course, complicated by our inability to deduct personal income taxes on capital gains from the distribution, which may explain the perverse behavior of the share of the bottom vigesile.

The effect of age-related transfers on the distributions can be shown in two ways—by deducting such transfers from HDI, or by adding the transfers to PRI. When the definition is changed from HDI to HDI − ART, the share of the bottom 45 percent of the distribution falls, while the share of the top half rises. The Lorenz curve for HDI − ART lies below the curve for HDI, showing an increase in inequality; the Gini ratio rises from .40 to .44. In this definitional change, various retirement benefits, as well as personal contributions, are excluded, thus affecting the bottom of the distribution substantially.

When the definition is changed from PRI to PRI + ART, the share of the bottom 45 percent of the distribution rises, while the share of the top half falls, with the Lorenz curve for PRI + ART lying above the curve for PRI. The two sets of comparisons produce quite similar results, although, of course, opposite in sign; the (absolute value of the) percentage point change in the Gini ratio for the two comparisons, for example, is identical.

The above comparisons are based on ranking individual consumer units by the size of income for the particular definition employed. Part of the difference in inequality between any two income concepts may be the result of the reranking of units when moving from one income concept to another. To measure this effect, relative distributions for all six definitions were recalculated, using the ranking of consumer units in just one concept (PRI) for each distribution. The results are shown in table 2.5. Each vigesile in this table is composed of exactly the same consumer units, for example, if Jones and Smith are both in the 5th vigesile based on their ranking in PRI, they will also be in the 5th vigesile for purposes of calculating shares in the other five income concepts, irrespective of what happens to the size of their incomes when the other definitions are applied.

As might be expected, for each of the five income types (other than PRI, of course) the degree of inequality is reduced as compared with its corresponding distribution in table 2.3. The largest differences between

Table 2.5   Income Shares, Families and Unrelated Individuals Ranked by Size of Production-Related Income, 1972 (percent)

Percentile Groups	EARN	PRI	HI	HDI	HDI− ART	PRI+ ART
Total	100.00	100.00	100.00	100.00	100.00	100.00
1–5	−.42	−.41	.72	.78	.10	.22
6–10	.07	.09	1.17	1.37	.53	.87
11–15	.32	.37	1.38	1.60	.71	1.19
16–20	.66	.76	1.66	1.91	1.09	1.51
21–25	1.17	1.26	1.96	2.21	1.63	1.79
26–30	1.72	1.78	2.26	2.49	2.11	2.14
31–35	2.25	2.29	2.61	2.84	2.60	2.53
36–40	2.80	2.81	2.99	3.19	3.07	2.93
41–45	3.37	3.31	3.42	3.58	3.53	3.37
46–50	3.97	3.82	3.81	3.93	4.00	3.76
51–55	4.48	4.29	4.21	4.32	4.45	4.18
56–60	5.04	4.81	4.64	4.72	4.92	4.63
61–65	5.63	5.35	5.10	5.16	5.42	5.12
66–70	6.20	5.90	5.56	5.60	5.93	5.60
71–75	6.86	6.51	6.08	6.08	6.48	6.14
76–80	7.55	7.23	6.73	6.69	7.14	6.82
81–85	8.49	8.14	7.52	7.43	7.96	7.65
86–90	9.67	9.35	8.66	8.53	9.12	8.81
91–95	11.53	11.35	10.43	10.18	10.88	10.70
96–100	18.62	21.00	19.08	17.40	18.33	20.04
100	5.99	7.81	7.06	5.87	6.11	7.52

tables 2.3 and 2.5 may be found in the lowest part of the distribution. Ranking by size of PRI produces substantially larger shares for the bottom of the HI and HDI distributions, as well as HDI − ART and PRI + ART. Differences at the top of the distribution, on the other hand, are relatively small. Despite the changes for individual vigesiles, it should be noted that a given vigesile never ends up with a larger share than the one immediately above it in the distribution. The implied Lorenz curves for the five income concepts all preserve their normal shape, that is, their slopes are everywhere increasing.

On the other hand, as table 2.6 shows, substituting the PRI-ranked distributions for those ranked by own income concept does not result in uniformly *increasing* the degree of equality as one moves from EARN to HI to HDI. While the extent of equalization is greater in the HDI distribution as compared with HI when the two distributions are ranked by PRI rather than own income, the opposite is true when comparing EARN with either HI or HDI. (Comparisons of the distributions resulting from other concepts with that from PRI are not, of course, affected, since by definition the PRI distribution is not altered by reranking.)

Another way of looking at the effect of reranking units when shifting from one income concept to another is through a cross-tabulation between the two concepts. Table 2.7 contains such a cross-tabulation between PRI and HDI by deciles of consumer units. For all PRI deciles, at least three-fourths of the units remain in the same decile or move no more than one decile in the HDI distribution. Very few units are shifted downward more than one decile; more units are shifted upward more than one decile. Units in the middle of the PRI distribution are shifted downward much more often than upward.

Table 2.6   Ratios of Selected Quantile Shares in Earnings, Household Income, and Household Disposable Income, Families and Unrelated Individuals Ranked Alternatively by Size of Own Income Definition and by Production-related Income, 1972

	(1) HI/EARN		(2) HDI/HI		(3) = (1) × (2) HDI/EARN	
Percentiles	Own	PRI	Own	PRI	Own	PRI
1–20	25.33	7.83	1.04	1.15	26.40	8.98
21–40	1.37	1.24	1.07	1.09	1.47	1.35
41–60	.97	.95	1.03	1.03	1.00	.98
61–80	.91	.89	1.01	1.00	.91	.90
81–95	.90	.90	.99	.98	.89	.88
96–99	.94	.95	.97	.96	.91	.91
100	1.05	1.18	.87	.83	.92	.98

SOURCE: Calculated from tables 2.3 and 2.5.

Table 2.7 Joint Distribution of Production-Related Income and Household Disposable Income, Families and Unrelated Individuals, 1972 (percent)

PRI Percentile Groups	HDI Percentile Groups										
	1–10	11–20	21–30	31–40	41–50	51–60	61–70	71–80	81–90	91–100	Total
1–10	54	27	11	5	2	1	0	0	0	0	100
11–20	36	29	17	10	4	2	1	0	0	0	100
21–30	9	39	23	14	7	5	2	1	0	0	100
31–40	0	5	47	24	11	6	4	2	1	0	100
41–50	0	0	3	45	30	11	5	3	2	0	100
51–60	0	0	0	2	43	36	10	6	2	1	100
61–70	0	0	0	0	2	37	43	12	5	1	100
71–80	0	0	0	0	0	1	34	52	11	2	100
81–90	0	0	0	0	0	0	1	24	64	10	100
91–100	0	0	0	0	0	0	0	0	14	85	100
Total	100	100	100	100	100	100	100	100	100	100	100

Numbers may not sum to totals because of rounding.

It is interesting to ask, what kind of tax (and/or transfer) rate is implied by the difference between any set of pre- and post-transfer distributions. The difference, for example, between HI and HDI for any given quantile of the HI distribution can be expressed as a tax (actually, a combined tax and social insurance contribution) rate for that quantile. The implied tax rate for a quantile in HI is equal to one minus the ratio of its dollar mean HDI to its dollar mean HI. Table 2.8 shows, in addition to the pertinent relative mean incomes (RMI), two sets of rates: one, the (percentage) tax rate implied by the proportional difference between HI and HDI; the other, the combined (percentage) tax and transfer rate implied by the proportional difference between PRI and HDI. For each set, rates have

Table 2.8   **Relative Mean Incomes and Implied Tax and Transfer Rates, Household Income and Production-related Income, Families and Unrelated Individuals Ranked Alternatively by Size of Own Income Definition and by Production-related Income, 1972**

	(1)	(2)	(3)	(4)	(5)	(6)	(7)
		Tax Rates, Units Ranked by Size of:			Tax Minus Transfer Rates, Units Ranked by Size of:		
	Income Definition		PRI		Income Definition		PRI
Per-centiles	RMI	Rate	RMI	Rate	RMI	Rate	Rate
1–20	.19	12.8%	.25	4.0%	.04	−361.1%	−559.1
21–40	.50	10.4	.49	8.6	.41	−24.4	−24.3
41–60	.82	13.8	.80	13.9	.82	2.4	3.7
61–80	1.19	15.9	1.17	16.2	1.25	9.7	11.2
81–95	1.79	17.0	1.77	17.8	1.92	12.7	14.5
96–99	3.04	19.0	3.01	19.8	3.30	15.9	17.5
100	7.06	27.3	7.06	30.5	7.81	25.8	29.1
All units	1.00	16.4	1.00	16.4	1.00	5.7	5.7
Addendum:							
5–20	.25	6.8	.28	3.1	.08	−223.2	−277.3

SOURCE: Calculated from tables 2.3, 2.5, and 2.9.
KEY TO COLUMNS:
(1) Relative mean income, HI, units ranked by HI.
(2) Tax rate implied by the proportional difference between HI, units ranked by HI, and HDI, units ranked by HDI.
(3) Relative mean income, HI, units ranked by PRI.
(4) Tax rate implied by the proportional difference between HI and HDI, units ranked by PRI in both distributions.
(5) Relative mean income, PRI, units ranked by PRI.
(6) Tax minus transfer rate implied by the proportional difference between PRI, units ranked by PRI and HDI, units ranked by HDI.
(7) Tax minus transfer rate implied by the proportional difference between PRI and HDI, units ranked by PRI in both distributions.

Fig. 2.1   Tax and transfer rates implied by relative size distributions of household income and household disposable income, 1972

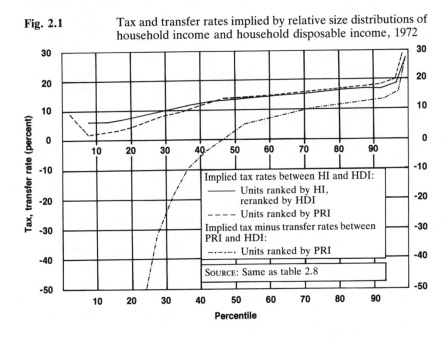

been calculated for recipient units ranked by pretransfer income (HI or PRI) and reranked by post-transfer income (HDI), and for units ranked consistently by PRI. Three of the four tax, transfer rates are plotted in figure 2.1, using the data for vigesiles and the top 1 percent.

For the consistent PRI ranking, the implied tax rates increase uniformly with HI (except for the bottom vigesile in figure 2.1), although, as previously noted, the effect is only mildly progressive, except for the top 1 percent. The rates based on reranked units show the same behavior, except for the bottom quintile, whose rate (12.8 percent) exceeds that for the second quintile (10.4 percent). This difference is the result of the negative share in HDI of the bottom vigesile, precluding the calculation of a tax rate in figure 2.1; the rate for the next three vigesiles comprising the remainder of the bottom quintile is 6.8 percent.

The net tax (tax minus transfer) rates implied by the difference between PRI and HDI rise more steeply than the implied tax rates for HI, although remaining below the latter, even for the top 1 percent; for the bottom two quintiles transfers exceed the sum of taxes and personal contributions, and the implied tax rates shown in table 2.8 are negative. Little significance should be attached to very large negative rates at the bottom; consumer units in this part of the PRI distribution are so heavily dependent on transfers, and those transfers sufficiently unrelated to the small amounts of earnings and property income they receive, that the concept of an average negative tax rate has little interpretive value.

Table 2.9 shows relative mean incomes by socioeconomic groups for each of the six income concepts. The largest changes in relative means for six groups classified by age of head are for the age 65 and over group, with the relative mean for the latter group rising sharply from .35 for EARN to .85 for HDI. Of course, the inclusion or exclusion of age-related transfers can be expected to have a large impact on the relative mean for those 65 and over. The four youngest age groups, on the other hand, show declines as the definition is changed from EARN to HDI.

Female unrelated individuals, many of whom are aged, show the largest change among family type and sex of head groups—a large increase. Other female heads also show a substantial rise. The black group shows a decline from EARN to PRI, followed by a rise to HDI, with no significant change between EARN and HDI.

Income shares for the selected socioeconomic groups are shown in table 2.10. The impact of the shift from EARN to PRI differs greatly by age of head. The youngest age group shows little change in shares. The next three age groups all show a small increase in inequality, whereas for the age 65 and over group just the opposite is the case. Only in the 55–64 group is there evidence of a Lorenz curve intersection, which, as was noted earlier, characterizes the two distributions as a whole. For the younger age groups, the effect of including property income in the

Table 2.9   **Relative Mean Incomes of Socioeconomic Groups, Families and Unrelated Individuals, 1972**

Socioeconomic Group	EARN	PRI	HI	HDI	HDI − ART	PRI + ART
Age of head						
Less than 25	.56	.50	.48	.49	.54	.46
25–34	1.04	.95	.89	.88	.97	.87
35–44	1.35	1.26	1.18	1.17	1.26	1.18
45–54	1.45	1.39	1.31	1.28	1.36	1.32
55–64	1.11	1.14	1.12	1.11	1.12	1.13
65 and over	.35	.56	.80	.85	.57	.81
Family type & sex						
Families						
Headed by couples	1.31	1.28	1.24	1.23	1.26	1.25
Other male head	1.05	1.07	1.13	1.15	1.09	1.12
Other female head	.54	.56	.69	.73	.68	.61
Unrelated individuals						
Male	.57	.58	.60	.59	.58	.59
Female	.29	.39	.46	.48	.41	.46
Race of head						
Black	.67	.60	.65	.68	.69	.59
White & other	1.04	1.05	1.05	1.04	1.04	1.05
Total mean ($)	9,955	10,876	12,221	10,258	9,762	11,372

Table 2.10   Income Shares for Selected Socioeconomic Groups, Families and Unrelated Individuals, 1972

Group	Percentiles	EARN	PRI	HI	HDI	HDI−ART	PRI+ART
Age of head							
Under 25	1–40	9.8	9.7	13.1	14.2	13.8	10.0
	41–80	44.4	44.4	43.2	43.4	43.7	44.0
	81–95	30.0	30.0	28.7	27.8	27.8	29.9
	96–100	15.7	15.9	15.0	14.6	14.6	16.1
25–34	1–40	16.5	16.3	18.7	19.6	19.4	16.4
	41–80	44.3	43.9	42.8	42.9	43.2	43.5
	81–95	25.3	25.4	24.6	24.1	24.1	25.4
	96–100	13.9	14.5	13.9	13.5	13.2	14.7
35–44	1–40	15.8	15.4	17.6	18.3	18.0	15.7
	41–80	42.5	41.7	41.0	41.5	41.9	41.3
	81–95	25.4	25.3	24.6	24.5	24.6	25.2
	96–100	16.3	17.6	16.8	15.7	15.5	17.8
45–54	1–40	14.6	14.5	16.4	17.1	16.5	15.2
	41–80	42.4	41.4	41.0	41.6	42.1	40.9
	81–95	26.4	26.2	25.5	25.4	25.5	25.9
	96–100	16.6	17.9	17.1	15.9	15.9	18.0
55–64	1–40	9.2	10.1	13.6	14.2	11.8	12.4
	41–80	41.3	40.3	39.9	40.7	41.3	39.7
	81–95	29.3	28.6	27.1	27.1	28.2	27.6
	96–100	20.3	21.0	19.4	18.0	18.7	20.3

65 or over	1–40	−1.1	1.8	12.1	12.8	3.6	10.8
	41–80	20.6	26.6	33.7	35.7	29.9	33.6
	81–95	39.9	33.5	28.0	28.1	33.4	28.4
	96–100	40.5	38.1	26.2	23.4	33.1	27.2
Families							
Married couples	1–40	14.6	15.1	18.3	19.1	16.8	17.3
	41–80	42.3	40.6	39.6	40.2	41.4	39.5
	81–95	26.2	25.7	24.6	24.5	25.3	25.0
	96–100	17.0	18.6	17.5	16.2	16.5	18.2
Other male head	1–40	11.2	11.8	16.6	17.5	14.8	14.7
	41–80	42.8	40.7	39.8	40.2	40.7	40.1
	81–95	28.5	27.8	25.6	25.2	26.5	26.5
	96–100	17.5	19.7	17.9	17.1	18.0	18.7
Other fem. head	1–40	3.0	3.9	14.9	15.9	13.5	7.1
	41–80	41.1	40.0	39.4	40.0	39.9	41.0
	81–95	34.4	33.2	27.9	27.1	28.3	31.3
	96–100	21.5	22.9	17.8	17.0	18.3	20.7
Unrelated individuals							
Male	1–40	4.3	5.8	12.2	13.3	8.6	10.3
	41–80	40.9	39.4	38.6	39.6	40.8	38.5
	81–95	32.0	30.4	27.5	27.0	29.0	28.3
	96–100	22.8	24.5	21.7	20.2	21.6	22.9
Female	1–40	.3	2.7	12.5	13.5	5.6	10.3
	41–80	33.5	34.8	36.1	37.0	36.8	36.3
	81–95	40.0	33.3	27.8	27.1	31.4	28.6
	96–100	26.1	29.2	23.6	22.4	26.2	24.8

Table 2.10 (continued)

Group	Percentiles	EARN	PRI	HI	HDI	HDI − ART	PRI + ART
Race of head							
Black							
	1–40	5.4	5.4	13.9	15.1	11.6	9.3
	41–80	42.9	42.7	41.1	41.6	42.4	42.0
	81–95	33.3	33.3	28.9	28.1	29.9	31.1
	96–100	18.4	18.6	16.1	15.2	16.1	17.6
White and other							
	1–40	8.0	9.6	14.2	15.0	11.6	13.0
	41–80	43.0	41.1	40.0	40.6	42.0	39.9
	81–95	29.5	28.4	26.6	26.5	27.8	27.1
	96–100	19.5	20.9	19.2	17.9	18.6	20.0
All units							
	1–40	7.5	9.0	13.8	14.7	11.3	12.3
	41–80	43.0	41.2	40.1	40.7	42.0	40.1
	81–95	29.9	28.8	26.9	26.7	28.0	27.5
	96–100	19.6	21.0	19.2	17.9	18.7	20.2

income concept is relatively small, since these groups are primarily dependent on earnings, particularly wages and salaries; further, perhaps not surprisingly, the property income that is received by these groups tends to be positively correlated with their earnings. For older groups the opposite is true: property income is more important as an income source, and the correlation is reversed—retired persons and those with limited earnings receive relatively more property income than those with larger earnings.

The shift from PRI to HI, on the other hand, produces a uniform movement to less inequality for all age groups, with a substantial increase in the share of the bottom two quintiles. The change is particularly large for the 65 and over group, although the degree of inequality within the aged group for HI is still greater than it is within any other age group. Going from HI to HDI produces a further reduction in inequality for every age group, with the share of the bottom 80 percent gaining at the expense of the top 5 percent.

Removing age-related transfers from HDI (i.e., comparing HDI − ART with HDI) results in very little change in shares for the three younger age groups, although what change there is suggests a Lorenz curve intersection phenomenon, resulting from the greater incidence of personal contributions for social insurance on middle income groups, which rely more heavily on wages and salaries, on which such contributions primarily impinge. As would be expected, for the two older age groups there is a movement toward more inequality, especially pronounced for the 65 and older group. The results in going from PRI to PRI + ART (i.e., adding only age-related—not all—transfers to production-related income) are virtually the same as those discussed above in comparing HDI and HDI − ART, whether one looks at percentage or at percentage point changes in shares, although the relevant changes are, of course, opposite in sign.

In contrast to the effects for age groups, those for family type and sex of head groups in general are similar to those for all units. The shift from EARN to PRI increases the shares of the bottom and top 5 percent and decreases the share in the 41–95 percentile range; that from PRI to HI increases the share of the bottom 40 percent and decreases the shares of the groups above it; that from HI to HDI increase the share of the bottom 80 percent and reduces that of the top 20. The only exception to the direction and extent of change is for female unrelated individuals. For that group the extent of change is generally greater in moving from one concept to another; in addition, the change for the 41–80 percentile group sometimes differs in sign, as compared with the other groups.

The effects for blacks are similar to those for the white and other group, except for the shift from EARN to PRI. The shift produces little change in the shares for blacks because of the relatively small amount of property income received by blacks.

2.5 Conclusion

The major purposes of this paper have been to develop a consistent framework for the accounting of transfers, as receipts of, and payments by, the household sector from, and to, other sectors and to compare the effect of alternative definitions of pre- and post-transfer income on the distribution of income among households by size and by socioeconomic characteristics. We started from a concept of earnings (wages, proprietors' income, and net rental and royalty income), then added net transfers of property income from the business and government sectors (dividends received from corporate business, interest received from business and government net of interest paid to business, and estate and trust income) to obtain a concept reflecting primarily, although not entirely, the results of productive activities, including the resultant distribution of property income arising from the underlying ownership of property rights by the household sector. Our resulting concept of production-related income showed less inequality at the bottom, and more inequality at the top, of the distribution than earnings (i.e., a Lorenz curve intersection). Household income, another intermediate stopping point between our pure pretransfer income concept (earnings) and our complete post-transfer concept, added transfers received (government transfers from both entitlement and means-tested programs and private transfers), but did not deduct transfers paid. As compared with the two preceding concepts, it resulted in a substantial reduction in inequality at the bottom of the distribution and raised substantially the mean incomes of those socioeconomic groups heavily reliant on transfer income. The complete, post-transfer income concept, household disposable income, was net of transfers—personal contributions to social insurance programs and income property taxes—paid by households. Compared with the effect of adding transfers received, deducting transfers paid had only a relatively mild equalizing effect. Although their effects on our concepts are clear enough, we were not able to provide estimates of the redistributive effects of interhousehold receipts and payments of transfers.

Appendix A *Construction of the Estimates*

The estimates shown in this paper were tabulated from the fully estimated 1972 Exact Match-Statistical Match (EM-SM) file, which was constructed in a cooperative effort by the Bureau of Economic Analysis

(BEA), U.S. Department of Commerce, and the Office of Research and Statistics, Social Security Administration (SSA). That file contains estimates of income produced by adjusting estimates from several data sources to be consistent with independent control totals derived primarily from the National Income and Product Accounts (NIPA). The file also includes estimates of several types of tax liability. The construction of that file is described in this appendix.[13]

The 1972 Exact Match File

The starting point for the construction of the file was the 1972 Exact Match (EM) file, which is an exact match of the March 1973 Current Population Survey (CPS), the Internal Revenue Service's 1972 Individual Master File (IMF), an extract of the SSA Summary Earnings Record (SER), which contains earnings covered by the Social Security system, and SSA benefit data. Records from the IMF, SER, and benefit files were matched to CPS records by identifiier linkage variables (Social Security number, name, address, sex, race, and date of birth). About 87 percent of the CPS file was finally matched, and the matched portion was re-weighted to population control totals (Kilss and Scheuren 1978 and discussion by Budd). Not all records included in the three-way link contain all three types of records. For example, some CPS units did not file tax returns. The completed CPS-IMF-SER linked file includes approximately 38,600 matched families and unrelated individuals.

The Statistical Match of Statistics of Income Tax Return Data with the 1973 EM

While there is no doubt that the 1972 EM is superior to any individual microdata file hitherto available, the absence of complete tax return information is a serious limitation; in particular, tax liabilities and income amounts other than adjusted gross income (AGI), wages, interest, and dividends in AGI are missing from the file. To rectify this deficiency and bring in missing information on tax return income types and federal income tax liabilities, a statistical match (SM) was carried out between the EM and the 1972 Augmentation File (AF)[14] The AF was a subsample of Statistics of Income tax returns, which was itself exact matched to SER records to obtain age, race, sex, and Social Security taxable earnings, primarily for the purpose of improving the quality of the statistical matching by adding more good matching variables. The SM was carried out in three steps: the initial match, the rematch, and the high-income match. The initial match and the rematch were similar matches whose purposes were to add tax liabilities and more accurate and complete income data to the EM; the rematch respecified and improved the initial matching for about 15 percent of the records in the file. The high-income match, on the other hand, was performed to add more high-income returns to the statistically matched file to reduce the sampling variance for high-income records.

Twenty-two variables were employed in the match, either for defining "cells" within which matching of records was to occur, or for choosing AF records within the cells. These variables included (amounts) of AGI, interest, dividends in AGI, and Social Security taxable earnings; sex, race, age, number of tax return exemptions, and presence of various tax return schedules. In general, the AF record whose information most closely resembled the EM record's information was chosen as the match for that EM record.[15]

Correction of Tax Return Income Types for the Effects of Audit

The statistical match of the EM and the AF produced complete tax return income type information for each EM record, resulting in what we have previously referred to as the EM-SM file. The next step was the correction of each IRS income type in this file for the effects of audit, as evidenced in the 1973 Taxpayer Compliance Measurement Program (TCMP) file. The methodology proceeded along two related lines: (1) a ratio correction technique for returns in which income, by type of income, went from one amount to another amount, and (2) a net change procedure for returns in which the income type was changed from a loss to a positive amount, or from "none" to a nonzero amount, the latter being of primary importance for self-employment incomes, rent, and interest. Each of these two procedures was implemented separately, for each income type, for eight correction cells based on the type of tax return filed: joint, and all other; one or more exemptions for age 65 and over, and no such exemptions; and short and long tax form.[16]

Final Adjustment of Taxable Income Types to Aggregate NIPA Income Control Totals

Once the size distribution of each IRS income type had been estimated, the final step was to bring the level of each type implicit in the EM-SM file up to its corresponding NIPA control total. The control totals were derived by adjusting the amount of each taxable income type in the NIPA personal income account to make it consistent with the CPS population universe and income concepts. Income received by decedents (persons who died between 1 January 1972 and 15 March 1973), military personnel on post and overseas, and recipients other than persons, such as nonprofit institutions, were excluded. For some income types adjustments were carried out to make the control more nearly consistent with the ways in which the type is reported on the tax return. For example, interest, dividends, rent, and proprietors' income paid to estates and trusts were transferred to a separate control for estate and trust income, since the latter, although not a separate income type in the NIPA, is reported separately on Schedule E of the tax return.

The blow-up procedure for income types with positive income only (no losses) was designed to leave the relative size distribution for each income type unaffected. A correction factor, defined as the ratio of the NIPA control total to the aggregate implicit in the IRS data base (after audit correction), was applied to each nonzero observation. For income types involving loss as well as gain incomes (self-employment incomes, rents, and royalties), losses were reduced in roughly the same proportion as gains were increased. In addition, for particular tax return types a small constant term was added to each record to make the proportion of losses more nearly consistent with evidence from other sources on the proportion of loss incomes.

Estimation of Nontaxable Money Income Types

Since most types of transfer income are not subject to federal income tax, the only estimates for such types are those in the CPS portion of the EM-SM records, with the important exception of Social Security benefits. For the latter, the amount contained in the benefit portion of the Social Security administrative record was substituted for the CPS reported amount. This substitution, together with a limited amount of file editing and inflation of individual amounts by less than 1 percent, brought the aggregate up to the independently derived BEA control.

The CPS was the starting point for the estimation of the remaining transfer payments, including railroad retirement, public assistance, other government transfer programs (unemployment compensation, workers' compensation, government pensions, and veterans' benefit payments), and private transfers (which were limited to private pensions and annuities). For these types of transfer income, the underestimates of aggregate income in the CPS appeared to be primarily the result of underestimates of the number of recipients. The basic strategy was therefore to select additional recipients among the potentially "false zeroes" (those who responded "none" even though they received an amount), rather than raising individual reported amounts.

Although there were some variations in the estimating procedures among individual program types, the following general steps were employed: (1) An income control total was derived from the NIPA estimates and adjusted for consistency with the CPS population coverage, and a recipient unit control was estimated for each program from program data. (2) CPS nonresidents were reallocated amounts and, where the CPS contained only combined amounts, amounts for specific transfer types were estimated. (3) Within cells defined by selected CPS demographic characteristics, additional recipients in each cell were drawn at random from among nonrecipients to meet the recipient unit controls and were assigned amounts reported by or allocated to recipients. Each person drawn had a greater probability of being assigned a smaller amount reported by a recipient than a larger amount to take account of the fact that in field surveys smaller amounts of a transfer type more often go unreported than larger amounts. (4) For some types, assigned amounts were then inflated or deflated (by relatively small ratios) to meet the corresponding income control for the transfer type.[17]

For state and local bond interest, there were essentially no data in the EM-SM records. That income type was estimated using several other data sources—the 1972–73 Consumer Expenditure Survey (CEX), which had been statistically matched to the EM-SM file; the 1962 Survey of Financial Characteristics of Consumers; and the 1977 Michigan Survey of Consumer Attitudes.

Estimation of In-Kind Income

Free food and lodging (included in wages and salaries) were assigned to a small number of employees in a few selected industries. Food and fuel consumed on farms (included in farm income) were imputed to consumer units reporting farm residence in the CPS. The amounts assigned, averaging $100, were a function of family size.

Both imputed rent and imputed interest were distributed on the basis of information collected in the CEX. A statistical match between the CEX and EM-SM files referred to earlier was used to incorporate the CEX estimates into the latter file. Size of consumer unit, race and sex of the head, home ownership, size of total money income, and the size of interest income were among the variables controlled for or used in the statistical match of these two separate files.

Imputed interest on checking and savings accounts was distributed in proportion to the value of these asset holdings reported by consumer units in the CEX. The distribution of imputed interest on equity in life insurance policies was not estimated in this file, and the corresponding amount of imputed interest (approximately $7.1 billion) is not included in the aggregates in table 2.2.

The imputation for net rent on owner-occupied nonfarm dwellings was based on drawing up an income and expense, or production, statement and estimating its components separately for each home owner. Gross rental values and home owners' expenditures on repair and maintenance, mortgage interest, and property insurance were estimated from the CEX. Imputed rent on owner-occupied and tenant-occupied farm operator dwellings was estimated by a somewhat different technique to allow for differences in the method used by USDA to estimate aggregate rent, as compared with BEA methodology, and was incorporated in net rental income rather than in farm income.

Medicare benefits were treated as imputed insurance premiums for hospital and medical care whose full cost was paid by the federal government. The value of the full-year imputed premium assigned to aged persons was $425.

Food stamp bonus values were assigned to eligible recipient units based on the size of the unit and the number of weeks worked by the head. Average bonus values as a function of these two characteristics were based on reported values computed from the CEX, as corrected for underreporting. Participating units were selected from among eligible units, with probabilities of selection a function of the size of the unit and whether it received public assistance.

Estimation of Personal Contributions for Social Insurance, Taxes, and Interest Paid

Assignments of OASDI tax to wage and salary workers were made at the statutory rate, up to the OASDI taxable limit, based on wages reported on the tax return and occupational information drawn from the CPS. The self-employment tax was assigned to persons filing a Schedule SE, based on the amount of self-employment income on the return before correction by audit. The assignment procedure took account of any OASDI tax which the self-employed person may have paid on his or her wage earnings. Contributions to railroad retirement were assigned at the statutory rate for this program.

Employee contributions to state and local retirement plans were distributed on the basis of the tax return amount of wages to those reporting such employment in the CPS. Account was taken of the joint coverage by both state and local plans and by Social Security of some workers, who were assumed to pay a somewhat lower contribution rate than employees covered only by a state or local plan. Retirement contributions of federal employees were based on the statutory contribution rate. The method used for allocating supplementary medical insurance premiums paid by the aged was virtually identical to that used in estimating Medicare benefits, as described above.

Federal personal income tax liabilities were taken without change from the tax returns added to the file in the statistical match. The definition used was total income tax (i.e., income tax after credits plus minimum tax).

For federal tax returns with itemized deductions, state and local income tax liability was estimated as the itemized deduction for state and local income tax less the state income tax refund. Personal property tax liability was estimated as the itemized deduction for the personal property tax.

For federal tax returns which had nonitemized deductions, itemized deductions for state and local income taxes and state income tax refunds were assigned using a hot deck imputation procedure. The assignment was performed within sixteen cells based on type of return (joint, non-joint), number of dependent exemptions (0, 1, 2, 3 +), and number of age or blind exemptions (0, 1 +). Within each of these cells a return was chosen (with replacement) for each nonitemizer. The assignment of the items was based on percent of AGI—that is, if the item was X percent of AGI in the itemized return, X percent of the nonitemized return's AGI was assigned. All assigned amounts were decreased by about 5 percent to bring the aggregate down to the control.

Because of our resource constraints, units with no federal income tax returns were assumed to have no federal, state, and local, or personal property tax liability. In addition, it was not possible to estimate and deduct that portion of the federal personal income tax which was from tax liability on realized capital gains. Deduction of such tax liability would have been desirable since realized capital gains are not included in PRI or HI. This fact should be kept in mind in interpreting the results for the bottom vigesile for the HDI distributions shown in section 2.4.

For federal tax returns with itemized deductions, interest paid was estimated as the itemized deduction for interest (excluding mortgage interest). For federal tax returns with nonitemized deductions, the hot deck imputation procedure mentioned above in connection with taxes was used to impute interest paid. All assigned amounts were reduced by about 20 percent to bring the aggregate down to the control.

Appendix B *Tables for Families*

Table 2.A.1   **Income Shares, Families Ranked by Size of the Income Definition, 1972 (percent)**

Percentile Groups	EARN	PRI	HI	HDI	HDI−ART	PRI+ART
Total	100.00	100.00	100.00	100.00	100.00	100.00
1–5	− .47	− .37	.34	.10	− .44	− .16
6–10	.19	.33	1.30	1.45	.84	.94
11–15	.61	.88	1.70	1.89	1.40	1.47
16–20	1.23	1.45	2.06	2.25	1.89	1.90
21–25	1.85	1.96	2.40	2.59	2.33	2.29
26–30	2.43	2.44	2.74	2.91	2.74	2.65
31–35	2.92	2.88	3.09	3.24	3.13	3.01
36–40	3.37	3.30	3.41	3.55	3.51	3.35
41–45	3.81	3.68	3.73	3.86	3.87	3.68
46–50	4.23	4.07	4.04	4.15	4.22	4.03
51–55	4.65	4.47	4.37	4.46	4.57	4.37
56–60	5.07	4.86	4.72	4.79	4.95	4.73
61–65	5.51	5.28	5.08	5.14	5.33	5.10
66–70	5.98	5.72	5.49	5.53	5.74	5.52
71–75	6.49	6.24	5.97	5.99	6.21	6.04
76–80	7.11	6.86	6.53	6.53	6.76	6.62
81–85	7.87	7.63	7.21	7.18	7.47	7.34
86–90	8.90	8.68	8.20	8.16	8.46	8.37
91–95	10.57	10.45	9.83	9.70	10.05	10.09
96–100	17.68	19.21	17.78	16.51	16.97	18.69
100	6.01	7.07	6.48	5.60	5.73	6.91
Gini concentration ratio	.42	.42	.37	.35	.39	.40

Table 2.A.2   Relative Mean Incomes, Families Ranked by Size of the Income Definition, 1972

Percentile Groups	EARN	PRI	HI	HDI	HDI−ART	PRI+ART
Total	1.00	1.00	1.00	1.00	1.00	1.00
1–5	−.09	−.07	.07	.02	−.09	−.03
6–10	.04	.07	.26	.29	.17	.19
11–15	.12	.18	.34	.38	.28	.29
16–20	.25	.29	.41	.45	.38	.38
21–25	.37	.39	.48	.52	.47	.46
26–30	.48	.49	.55	.58	.55	.53
31–35	.58	.57	.62	.65	.63	.60
36–40	.67	.66	.68	.71	.70	.67
41–45	.76	.73	.75	.77	.77	.74
46–50	.85	.81	.81	.83	.84	.81
51–55	.93	.89	.87	.89	.92	.87
56–60	1.01	.97	.94	.96	.99	.95
61–65	1.10	1.06	1.02	1.03	1.07	1.02
66–70	1.20	1.14	1.10	1.11	1.15	1.10
71–75	1.30	1.25	1.19	1.20	1.24	1.21
76–80	1.42	1.37	1.31	1.31	1.35	1.32
81–85	1.57	1.53	1.44	1.44	1.49	1.47
86–90	1.78	1.74	1.64	1.63	1.69	1.67
91–95	2.11	2.09	1.97	1.94	2.01	2.02
96–100	3.54	3.84	3.55	3.30	3.39	3.74
100	6.01	7.07	6.48	5.60	5.72	6.90

Table 2.A.3   **Income Shares, Families Ranked by Size of Production-Related Income, 1972**

Percentile Groups	EARN	PRI	HI	HDI	HDI– ART	PRI+ ART
Total	100.00	100.00	100.00	100.00	100.00	100.00
1–5	−.37	−.37	.90	1.00	.27	.30
6–10	.30	.33	1.58	1.83	.80	1.28
11–15	.82	.88	1.86	2.13	1.32	1.62
16–20	1.41	1.45	2.05	2.29	1.83	1.89
21–25	1.93	1.96	2.37	2.60	2.29	2.25
26–30	2.46	2.44	2.70	2.91	2.72	2.62
31–35	2.97	2.88	3.05	3.23	3.13	2.97
36–40	3.42	3.30	3.39	3.54	3.51	3.32
41–45	3.84	3.68	3.68	3.81	3.87	3.63
46–50	4.27	4.07	4.01	4.11	4.21	3.99
51–55	4.68	4.47	4.33	4.42	4.57	4.33
56–60	5.10	4.86	4.69	4.77	4.95	4.69
61–65	5.55	5.28	5.01	5.06	5.33	5.04
66–70	5.97	5.72	5.43	5.45	5.72	5.47
71–75	6.46	6.24	5.89	5.87	6.18	5.96
76–80	7.15	6.86	6.42	6.37	6.74	6.52
81–85	7.85	7.63	7.14	7.05	7.46	7.25
86–90	8.80	8.68	8.13	8.03	8.45	8.30
91–95	10.49	10.45	9.70	9.46	9.99	9.96
96–100	16.92	19.21	17.69	16.07	16.66	18.61
100	5.41	7.07	6.47	5.32	5.46	6.89

Table 2.A.4   Joint Distribution of Production-Related Income and Household Disposable Income, Families, 1972 (percent)

PRI Percentile Groups	HDI Percentile Groups										
	1–10	11–20	21–30	31–40	41–50	51–60	61–70	71–80	81–90	91–100	
1–10	57	25	10	5	2	1	1	0	0	0	100
11–20	39	26	16	8	6	3	1	1	0	0	100
21–30	3	46	25	9	7	4	2	1	1	0	100
31–40	0	3	45	29	11	6	4	2	1	0	100
41–50	0	0	3	47	31	9	5	3	2	0	100
51–60	0	0	0	2	43	36	10	6	3	1	100
61–70	0	0	0	0	2	40	42	10	5	1	100
71–80	0	0	0	0	0	1	33	52	11	2	100
81–90	0	0	0	0	0	0	1	25	63	11	100
91–100	0	0	0	0	0	0	0	0	14	85	100
Total	100	100	100	100	100	100	100	100	100	100	100

Numbers may not sum to totals because of rounding.

Table 2.A.5   **Relative Mean Incomes of Socioeconomic Groups, Families, 1972**

Socioeconomic Group	EARN	PRI	HI	HDI	HDI−ART	PRI+ART
Age of head						
Less than 25	.60	.55	.54	.55	.59	.51
25–34	.92	.86	.81	.82	.88	.80
35–44	1.18	1.12	1.06	1.06	1.13	1.06
45–54	1.33	1.29	1.24	1.21	1.27	1.24
55–64	1.11	1.14	1.13	1.11	1.11	1.14
65 and over	.45	.66	.91	.96	.66	.93
Family type & sex						
Families						
Headed by couples	1.09	1.09	1.07	1.06	1.07	1.08
Other male head	.87	.91	.97	.99	.93	.97
Other female head	.45	.47	.59	.63	.58	.53
Race of head						
Black	.67	.61	.66	.69	.70	.61
White & other	1.04	1.05	1.04	1.04	1.04	1.05
Total mean ($)	11,937	12,812	14,203	11,879	11,471	13,220

Notes

1. For a review of the literature on the effects of transfers on labor supply and savings, as well as their purely redistributive effects, such as are examined in this paper, see Danziger, Haveman, and Plotnick (1981).

2. For an excellent discussion of the appropriate pretransfer income concept from which to measure the redistributive effect of government fiscal policy, see Behrens and Smolensky (1973).

3. Rolph (1948), p. 331. Our discussion of transfers draws heavily on Rolph's article. A criticism of Rolph's treatment, which we do not find convincing, may be found in Jaszi (1958), pp. 115–119.

4. The tax return data in our file do contain data on realized capital gains (Schedule D). However, they have not been corrected for audit, as have the other tax return types. Since real capital gains (money gains adjusted for changes in the price level) are the more meaningful concept, it would also be necessary to develop a method for deflating them, no easy task since the underlying asset values giving rise to such gains, on which such a correction would have to be based, are not included in microdata files of tax returns. Further, estimates of accrued capital gains are not available from this source. Realized capital gains are not likely to be a very good proxie for total gains (realized plus accrued) in any case.

5. For a fuller treatment of this issue than is necessary here, see Ohlsson (1953), pp. 160–62; and Rolph (1948), pp. 332–43. Ruggles and Ruggles (1982, pp. 14–16) present an opposite argument. Strangely enough, this controversy has not involved dividend payments, which constitute distributions of corporate earnings (net of interest and taxes) to shareholders. The latter receive such (transfer) income payments because, as legal owners of the corporation, they are entitled to participate in its earnings, not because in some sense or other they are furnishing productive services to the corporation. Such transfers are voluntary rather than legally required, in contrast to interest payments which Rolph defines as contractual transfers (Rolph 1948, pp. 332, 336–37).

6. E.g., Ohlsson (1953), pp. 82–83; Hagen and Budd (1958), pp. 269–70. In the same volume (*A Critique of the U.S. Income and Product Accounts*), Jaszi comments that "the decision [to exclude government interest payments] is a matter of common sense: since in practice there is no determinate relation between government interest payments and the use of government property, there is no realistic ground for including these payments as an approximation to the services rendered by government property" (Jaszi 1958, p. 50).

For an alternative view, see Ruggles and Ruggles (1982), p. 14. Perhaps they would be sympathetic with a further argument Jaszi makes, although not with the final conclusion he draws: "It is true, of course, that with only moderate ingenuity one could define a factor of production, such as lending or abstinence, as standing behind government interest. The concept of factor of production is vague in economic theory, and anyone is free to define it as it suits him best. But all these interpretations of government interest as a factor payment are highly artificial; such interest would be excluded regardless of them in any realistic analysis of resource use" (Jaszi 1958, pp. 50–51).

7. Interest paid by one consumer to another is presumably netted out as a transfer within the personal sector in the NIPA. Even though intrapersonal interest receipts and payments are netted out of this aggregate, their distributive effects should be accounted for in the post-transfer distribution.

8. Of course, net interest received (interest received minus interest paid) could well be negative for individual consumer units such as Smith.

9. Perhaps, as Ruggles and Ruggles (1982, p. 15) argue, part of the interest payment may be hidden in the purchase price of the car, so that Smith pays a higher price than Jones for the identical car. The theoretically correct procedure would be to count the two identical

cars that Jones and Smith purchased at the same price (i.e., with the same weight) in NNP and assign the difference Smith pays to consumer interest paid, although empirically this would be difficult to do. For this and other reasons, actually observed market prices are not always the most appropriate weights for counting individual products in NNP.

10. The argument that indirect business taxes have already been deducted is compelling only if we confine ourselves to the distribution of money income. Excise and sales taxes can affect relative wages and prices, and hence relative real incomes, depending on the composition of consumption expenditure of different households and groups of households (e.g., the aged vs. the non-aged). If one cannot deflate the money incomes of the relevant groups by price indexes which incorporate the effects of indirect taxes, the next best thing may be to deduct the taxes from each household's income.

11. For an excellent discussion of the issues associated with lifetime income accounting and, among other things, its relation to Social Security and age-related transfers, see Taussig (1976), pp. 34–42.

12. Social Security benefits are included along with pensions in retirement benefits. It is true that OASDI was originally conceived as a social insurance program which would insure covered workers against the loss of earnings because of age as well as other factors causing partial or total disability. However, it is well known that the problem of "moral hazard" is even greater for an age-related program such as Social Security than for other forms of insurance. Thus, workers may voluntarily retire, from age sixty-two on, and receive Social Security benefits, even though many could keep on working with possibly little loss of earning power. Mandatory retirement schemes and other institutional restrictions also complicate the interpretation of moral hazard in connection with Social Security. Here we simply assess the effects of Social Security when interpreted as a retirement system and leave aside its other elements.

13. This appendix draws heavily on a description by Budd and Salter (1981) of the EM-SM file and the methods used in its creation.

14. In a statistical match, observations in different files are matched on the basis of similar characteristics, rather than personal identifying information. Only in rare cases do the observations matched represent the same person.

15. A more complete discussion of the statistical match may be found in Radner (1981) and Salter (1980), chap. 6.

16. For a more complete discussion of the audit correction, see Salter (1980), chaps. 7 and 8.

17. While the work on public assistance was hampered by the absence of information on which particular program the respondent participated in, the results of a detailed study of (categorical and financial) eligibility for program participation (by state) for the March 1973 CPS file and exact matched to the EM file were used (Projector and Murray 1980).

References

Behrens, Jean, and Eugene Smolensky. 1973. Alternative definitions of income redistribution. *Public Finance/Finances Publiques* 28:315–32.

Budd, Edward C. 1958. Treatment of distributive shares. *A critique of the U.S. income and product accounts.* Studies in Income and Wealth, vol. 22. New York: National Bureau of Economic Research.

Budd, Edward C., and Jean Karen Salter. 1981. Supplementing household survey estimates of income distribution with data from other sources: The U.S. distribution of total money income for 1972. Paper presented at the 17th General Conference of the International Association for Research in Income and Wealth, 18 August 1981, Gouvieux, France. Mimeo.

Danziger, Sheldon, Robert Haveman, and Robert Plotnick. 1981. How income transfers affect work, savings and the income distribution. *Journal of Economic Literature* 19:975–1028.

Gillespie, W. Irwin. 1965. Effect of public expenditures on the distribution of income. In *Essays in fiscal federalism*, ed. Richard A. Musgrave. Washington, D.C.: The Brookings Institution.

Hagen, Everett E., and Edward C Budd. 1958. The product side: Some theoretical aspects. In *A critique of the U.S. income and product accounts*. Studies in Income and Wealth, vol. 22. New York: National Bureau of Economic Research.

Jaszi, George. 1958. The conceptual basis of the accounts: A reexamination. In *A critique of the U.S. income and product accounts*. Studies in Income and Wealth, vol. 22. New York: National Bureau of Economic Research.

Kilss, Beth, and Fritz Scheuren, 1978. The 1973 CPS-IRS-SSA exact match study: Past, present, and future (and discussion by Edward C. Budd). In *Policy analysis with Social Security files*. Office of Research and Statistics, Social Security Administration, Research Report no. 52, HEW Publication no. (SSA) 79-11808.

Lampman, Robert J. 1972. Public and private transfers as a social process. In *Redistribution to the rich and the poor*, ed. Kenneth E. Boulding and Martin Pfaff. Belmont, Calif.: Wadsworth.

———. 1975. Social accounting for transfers. In *The personal distribution of income and wealth*, ed. James D. Smith. Studies in Income and Wealth, vol. 39. New York: National Bureau of Economic Research.

Ohlsson, Ingvar. 1953. *On national accounting*. Stockholm: Kojunkturinstitutet.

Projector, Dorothy S., and Ellen G. Murray. 1980. Eligibility for welfare and participation rates, 1970. *Studies in Income Distribution*, no. 7. Office of Research and Statistics, Social Security Administration.

Radner, Daniel B. 1981. An example of the use of statistical matching in the estimation and analysis of the size distribution of income. *Review of Income and Wealth* 27: 211–43.

Reynolds, Morgan, and Eugene Smolensky, 1977. *Public expenditure, taxes, and the distribution of income: The United States, 1950, 1961, and 1970*. New York: Academic Press.

Rolph, Earl. 1948. The concept of transfers in national income estimates. *Quarterly Journal of Economics* 62: 327–61.

Ruggles, Richard, and Nancy D. Ruggles, 1982. Integrated economic accounts for the United States, 1947–80. *Survey of Current Business* 62 (May): 1–53.

Salter, Jean Karen. 1980. *Improving the quality of income data reported in field surveys and on individual tax returns.* Ph.D. diss., The Pennsylvania State University.

Taussig, Michael K. 1976. Trends in inequality of well-offness in the United States since World War II. Conference on the Trend in Income Inequality in the U.S. Institute for Research on Poverty, Special Report, University of Wisconsin.

United Nations. Department of Economic and Social Affairs. Statistical Office. 1977. *Provisional guidelines on statistics on the distribution of income, consumption, and accumulation of households.* Studies in Method, Series M, no 61. New York.

Comment   Robert Lampman

This is a summary and discussion of the paper by Budd, Radner, and Whiteman (B-R-W). I will begin with their findings as presented in section 2.4 of the paper. If we take their production-related income (PRI) concept as close to what most people would call pretransfer income, we see that they find what sounds familiar to readers of other studies. That is, first, transfers reduce inequality—they double the share of the lowest 30% and reduce the share of the upper half by 6%. Second, personal taxes paid (which exceed transfers received) further reduce inequality but only slightly. Thus household disposable income (HDI) is less unequal in distribution than is household income (HI) than is PRI. Further, leaving out retirement benefits, which are over two-thirds of all transfers, hurts the share of low-income households.

The authors also state (and here we are in less familiar territory) that the Lorenz curves for PRI and primary income or earnings (EARN) intersect and reflect close to the same overall inequality. The difference between the two concepts is that PRI includes dividends, interest net of consumer interest paid, and estate and trust income. The authors suggest that the latter three items may be thought of as transfer income. Transfers received by the personal sector, including the three property income items, just about equal the negative transfer payments made by the personal sector. Compare lines 4 and 14 in table 2.2. The authors do comment on this near identity, but they do not supply any balancing items to equate transfers received and transfers paid. They do instruct us that ". . . for the economy as a whole, although not necessarily for any individual sector of it, transfer payments simply redistribute claims to income produced, without raising the total" (section 2.1). And ". . . transfers enter only the income side of the accounts and do not affect the product side" (section 2.2.1).

Robert Lampman is professor of economics at the University of Wisconsin, Madison.

Section 2.3 of the paper describes the process of producing the microdata base underlying the findings summarized in section 2.4. The amount of work involved in preparing this data base is truly awesome. It started with a matched set of records for a sample of households from CPS, IRS, and SSA records. Further information was grafted on to this sample from tax audits, the Consumer Expenditure Survey, the Survey of Financial Characteristics of Consumers, and other sources. All items were brought into conformity with the totals in the NIPA after the latter were adjusted for the smaller population covered by CPS. (This explains why the totals in table 2.2 do not reconcile with those for similar concepts in NIPA.)

One wonders whether we should or will ever again have such a data file for another year. One also wonders whether a single sample survey directed at pre- and post-transfer income could produce a data base that is as useful as this one. It should be noted that numerous items of interest for such a study are not yet estimated in the file.

Section 2.2 is a presentation of the B-R-W accounting framework for transfer payments. In designing such a framework, we must decide what sectoring is important, what income items (positive and negative) will be included, and what income period is appropriate. B-R-W accept the personal sector as it exists in NIPA except that they throw out nonprofit (philanthropic) organizations. This leaves families and unrelated individuals, unincorporated business, estates and trusts, insurance and pension funds in their "personal sector." I suggest an alternative sectoring that would show separate sectors for families, an imaginary interfamily transfer fund, philanthropic organizations, and insurance and pensions. This would create a way to show transfers within the present personal sector as well as between that sector and the corporate business and government sectors.

Transfer income (positive and negative) must be distinguished from income arising out of production or exchange and also from changes on capital account. Decisions must be made about what in-kind items are to be included as income and how far to go in imputing income where there is no transaction. In considering these matters, B-R-W point us to controversies among experts and to differences in accounting practice in BEA, the Census Bureau, and the UN. They also refer to the different income concepts now employed in income size distribution work (section 2.2.9).

Where do we get an income measure for family pretransfer income? National income (production at factor cost) would seem to be a logical beginning, but certain transfer items are taken out in the move from net national product to national income. Further, B-R-W reminds us that some components of national income, such as interest, are identified by some as "transfers arising out of the nature and distribution of ownership rights." This classical view relies on a definition of production (nontransfer) income as payment for the use of real as opposed to financial resources. For most real business assets, which are located in the corporate sector, the primary income payment goes to that sector. The payment from the corporation to the stockholder and bondholder in the personal sector (who have only provided money) is a secondary or transfer income item. With respect to corporate paid interest, productive income flows to the asset and is no greater simply because the asset may be encumbered by a bond issue. This concept guides the UN system of accounts. Somewhat related to this is the notion that income items that have no counterpart on the product side—government interest and consumer interest paid—should be identified as transfers.

Our search for a starting point of pretransfer income is not helped by going to personal income since that includes certain transfer payments and transfer contributions. We can get around this tangle by defining pretransfer family income as income arising out of market or two-way transactions, including certain financial transactions, where the income recipient provides something of value. This covers the case of the bondholder.

I have no great quarrel with the B-R-W concept of PRI as pretransfer income. That includes wages and salaries, proprietor's income, net rental and royalty income, dividends and net interest received, and estate and trust income. They also say they would include capital gains and losses and employer contributions to social insurance and private insurance.

Positive and negative transfer items are listed in lines 9, 10, 12, and 13 in table 2.2. The positive transfers include some but not all public and private transfers. Some of these shown are in kind. The negative transfers shown are personal taxes only. The positive transfers amounted to $97.7 billion, which is equal to 8% of GNP. By contrast, the total of social welfare expenditures under public and private programs was equal to over 20% of GNP in that same year. This latter series, which was developed by the Social Security Administration, includes education, health care, and other services not included in table 2.2. B-R-W indicate that they would include some of these items if they had more data in their file. I agree with them that an arbitrary decision must be made about what in-kind items should be counted as personal income. I would also like to include contributions to and from both philanthropic organizations and an imaginary interfamily fund. I would like to see a double-entry account of where the funds come from to pay for the transfers to families. In this connection, I assume that B-R-W would, if they had the data, subtract employer contributions to social and private insurance in going from HI to HDI.

B-R-W rightly point out that the income period is an important issue in accounting for transfers. This is true not only with respect to old-age-related benefits, which they emphasize, but also for certain other episodic benefits, including education. Virtually the whole set of transfers under consideration here can be considered as insurance or as a method of averaging payments over a long period for expenses that occur infrequently. But when is the benefit actually experienced? Consider schooling—does the benefit flow when one is a child in school or later in life? This raises questions about the equalizing effects of transfers suggested by use of a one-year accounting period. Surely, a longer income period would show less equalization.

The development of an accounting framework for transfers will require a consensus answer to the question: "Transfers for what?" If we can center attention on the redistribution that leads to a meaningful and limited concept of "consumer-power income," then I think we can reach agreement on sectoring, distinguishing primary from secondary income, and selecting an income period. B-R-W have moved us a step closer to such a consensus.

3 Transfer Elements in the Taxation of Income from Capital

Harvey Galper and Eric Toder

3.1 Introduction

In an earlier paper (Galper and Toder 1981), we developed a model of firm investment behavior and household portfolio behavior to examine the effects of changing the relative supplies of tax-preferred and fully taxed assets on resource allocation and on government revenues. This present paper is an extension of that earlier work. Here, however, our concern is less with allocation than with distributional effects. In particular, we examine the implications of the availability to households of a number of differentially taxed assets for the measurement of tax burdens and transfer benefits. We develop a framework of analysis and an operational model to demonstrate how the tax system affects the before-tax returns earned by savers on different types of financial and real assets. We then show how traditional measures of tax incidence are altered when account is taken of the effects of the tax system on the portfolio decisions of households.

The traditional calculation of tax burdens, or effective tax rates, relates taxes paid to measured income. In contrast, we define what might be called *full* tax burdens or *full* effective tax rates. The full effective tax rate calculation differs from the traditional effective tax rate calculation by explicitly accounting for the effect of the tax structure on the before-tax return on an asset.

Harvey Galper is senior fellow at the Brookings Institution in Washington, D.C.; and Eric Toder is deputy director, Office of Tax Analysis, Department of the Treasury, Washington, D.C.

The authors would like to acknowledge the extraordinary computer work of Gordon Wilson and the typing of Donna Harrell. They also benefited from helpful conversations with Roger Gordon, Charles Hulten, John Shoven, and Joel Slemrod. The views expressed in this paper do not necessarily represent those of the Brookings Institution or the Treasury Department.

87

For example, in the case of tax-exempt bonds, the traditional calculation assumes that the before-tax return equals the after-tax return and that, consequently, no tax is paid on the income from the asset—the literal meaning of a tax-exempt security. The full effective tax rate calculation, on the other hand, compares the before-tax return on a tax-exempt asset with the return that would be available to the saver if there were no taxes on any asset. In doing so, this method recognizes that savers bid up the price (bid down the yield) of tax-exempt assets to avoid taxes and that this decline in the before-tax yield constitutes an implicit tax on the holder of the tax-exempt bond.

By similar logic, tax preferences, in causing some households to shift from heavily taxed to lightly taxed assets, not only reduce before-tax returns on the latter but also increase before-tax returns on heavily taxed assets. These increases in before-tax returns can be viewed as implicit transfers to wealth holders in relatively low marginal tax brackets. The total redistributive effects of the tax system must incorporate all taxes and transfers inherent in the combination of a progressive rate structure and preferentially taxed assets. It is entirely appropriate that these transfers, even though of an implicit nature, be recognized in a complete accounting of transfers provided through the public sector.

In this paper, we have developed an analytical model to demonstrate these points. This model is a stylized approximation to the real world designed to illustrate the general nature of the interactions between tax burdens and preferential taxation of various classes of assets rather than to provide definitive quantitative estimates of these tax burdens. In our illustrative model, households choose their portfolio mix to maximize their after-tax returns. On the other side of the market, firms, governments, and households supply tax differentiated assets to finance the acquisition and maintenance of productive physical capital. When household demands for each kind of asset are equilibrated with firm, government, and household supplies, the sectoral allocation of the capital stock, the distribution of asset holdings among households, and before-tax yields on different assets held by households are all simultaneously determined. The rates of return and the distribution of asset holdings determine the relative tax burdens and, as we shall see, transfer benefits by income class resulting from differential taxation by kind of asset. This latter relationship is the main area of investigation in this paper—the translation of tax preferences as applied to specific *categories of assets* to the distribution of tax burdens and transfer benefits by *income class*.

The road map for the remainder of this paper is as follows. Section 3.2 presents algebraically the concept of full effective tax rates incorporating implicit taxes and transfers and contrasts this approach to traditional measures of tax incidence. Section 3.3 discusses the formal model for asset demands and supplies used to estimate implicit taxes and transfers. Section 3.4 then presents model simulations that compare conventional tax burden measures under 1979 law with measures of full effective tax rates. These simulations illustrate how taking account of implicit taxes and transfers increases the measured progressivity of the tax structure. Section 3.5 summarizes the results.

3.2   Tax Burdens and Changes in Before-Tax Returns

It is well known that a full analysis of the incidence of the tax system must take into account not only the taxes actually paid by each income class but also the changes in before-tax income induced by the tax system itself. The problems inherent in accurately specifying before-tax income under alternative tax structures have caused earlier critics of statistical studies of the distributional effects of taxation almost to despair of our ability to produce any meaningful results.[1] This same point has been emphasized more recently by Martin Bailey (1974), who has shown that pre-tax returns on particular real and financial assets are affected by the special tax treatment that may be accorded to those assets. In other words, before-tax returns on those assets cannot be assumed to be invariant with respect to the tax structure itself. Changes in before-tax returns can be regarded as implicit taxes and transfers.

The concept of full effective tax rates incorporating implicit taxes and transfers may be formalized in the following way. We may define the effective tax rate, t_e, on the yield from an asset in terms of its before-tax return, r_b, and its after-tax return, r_a. Thus,

$$(1) \qquad t_e = \frac{r_b - r_a}{r_b}.$$

The after-tax return on an asset that is only partially subject to tax may be represented as follows:

$$(2) \qquad r_a' = r_b' \, (1 - \alpha t),$$

where r_a' is the after-tax return, α is the portion of the return subject to tax, r_b' is the before-tax return, and t is the taxpayer's tax rate. The conventional measure of the effective tax rate substitutes r_a' and r_b' into equation (1) and derives $t_e = \alpha t$. Thus, if the asset's return were only 40 percent taxed, the effective tax rate by the conventional measure would be 40 percent of the tax rate of the household holding the asset.

In fact, the before-tax return on a preferentially taxed asset will tend to fall below the return that would prevail in the absence of taxes on capital income. This may be represented as

$$(3) \qquad r_b' = (1 - \beta) \, \bar{r}_b,$$

where $\bar{r}_b$ is the before-tax return in the absence of all taxes on capital income, and $\beta \leq 1$ is a measure of the decline in the before-tax return on the preferentially taxed asset relative to the return in the absence of taxation of capital income. Substituting equations (2) and (3) into (1), one derives

(4) $$t^f_e = \alpha t (1 - \beta) + \beta,$$

Where t^f_e is the full effective tax rate when the before-tax return is taken to be $\bar{r}_b$. The first term on the right side of equation (4) is the explicit tax. Its value is exactly the same as the explicit tax, αt, under the conventional measure which is based on r'_b rather than $\bar{r}_b$. The β term by itself is a measure of the implicit tax or the reduction in the before-tax return from holding the tax-preferred asset. The full effective tax rate is composed of both explicit and implicit taxes.

For some assets, of course, the before-tax return as a result of the tax structure may be greater than $\bar{r}_b$ since, as households move to tax-preferred assets, returns on fully taxed assets will be driven up. In terms of equation (3), this implies a value of β of less than 0. Equation (4) would continue to hold, but in this case, the full effective tax rate would be less than the traditional measure. A negative value of β would constitute an implicit *transfer* provided by the tax system, and if β, in absolute terms, is great enough, the effective tax rate may even be negative.

3.2.1   The Traditional Approach to Tax Incidence

The best example of the traditional approach to tax incidence is the now classic Pechman-Okner study of tax burdens for the year 1966.[2] It is the most meticulously done and most thoroughly documented study of its kind. Since our concern is with federal taxes on capital income, we will concentrate on only two of the taxes examined by Pechman-Okner (henceforth P-O)—the personal income tax and the corporation tax.

In the case of the corporate tax, P-O explicitly adjust the before-tax incomes of households to account for the assumed incidence of the tax. Thus, if the corporate tax is assumed to be borne by corporate shareholders, then both the before-tax income of shareholders and the taxes paid by them reflect this. As P-O note, this is the assumption implicit in the treatment of corporate taxes in the national income accounts. If, as an alternative assumption, the corporate tax is taken to fall on all capital income, then taxes and the before-tax income of all recipients of capital income are correspondingly increased. For the corporation income tax, then, before-tax income flows are not invariant but change with the assumed incidence of the tax.[3]

One fairly minor point in their methodology of allocating the corporate tax to all capital income should be noted here. This allocation is based on measured household income before the personal income tax but after the corporate income tax. As they correctly note, "Ideally the allocation should have been based on income shares as they would have been before any taxes were imposed" (Pechman and Okner 1974, p. 96). Thus, to the extent that measured before- (personal) tax capital income for a particular income class differs significantly from what the before-tax income of that class would have been in the absence of all taxes, the allocation of the corporate tax burden in the P-O study is not fully consistent with the assumption that the corporate tax burden falls equally on all capital. However, since in our model the corporate income tax turns out to be quite small, this source of difference between us and P-O is of only minor importance.[4]

In contrast, the treatment of personal income taxes on capital income is of much greater importance. Despite their use of a range of incidence assumptions for other taxes, P-O assume no shifting of the individual income tax (Pechman and Okner 1974, p. 37). This implies that the before-tax capital income of a household is not changed by the tax system itself.[5]

3.2.2   Allocational and Distributional Effects of the Structure of Taxation of Capital Income

The major elements of the structure of capital income taxation at the personal level are a rising schedule of marginal tax rates combined with an array of preferences for particular assets held by households. These preferences include the exemption of interest on state and local bonds; exclusion of the return to owner-occupied housing and other consumer durables combined with the deductibility of interest to finance such assets; accelerated depreciation and the investment tax credit on eligible property held in the form of partnerships and sole proprietorships and thus taxed directly to individuals; capital gains treatment for corporate equities on that portion of the return resulting in appreciation in the value of the stock; and effective tax exemption of income on assets held in pension funds on behalf of individuals. Other more specialized provisions relating to the taxation of capital income for specific industries also exist, but the ones listed above are the most important preferences in the individual income tax.[6]

As pointed out by Bailey (1974), the response of households to this structure of tax provisions gives rise to major allocational and distributional effects. As a result of competition among taxpayers, all of whom are trying to maximize after-tax rates of return, "tax favored activities come to equilibrium at lower pre-tax rates of return than normally taxed activities" (Bailey 1974, p. 1159). Thus, taxpayers in higher marginal tax brackets are willing to sacrifice before-tax returns to hold preferentially taxed assets that provide greater after-tax returns. This sacrifice of before-tax income constitutes the *implicit tax* mentioned above. In addition, the taxable yield itself is increased as a result of the same portfolio shifts by high-bracket savers. The increase in the taxable yield generates implicit transfers, or higher before-tax incomes for those continuing to hold fully taxed assets.

These implicit taxes and transfers give rise to both allocational and distributional effects. The allocational effects result because tax preferences lower the cost of capital in particular sectors of the economy, such as housing and state and local government. The distributional effects result from the equilibrium changes in after-tax incomes once households have adjusted their financial portfolios in response to the tax structure.

The distributional implications of implicit taxes and transfers were discussed in the Treasury Department's 1977 study of broad-based tax reform options and were taken into account in defining before-tax incomes. However, the measurement of implicit taxes and transfers in the Treasury study was not based on an analytical model of household portfolio choice (U.S. Treasury Department 1977).

3.2.3 Related Research

While the effects of implicit taxes and transfers on the distribution of tax burdens by income class have not been specifically modeled, the implications of the structure of taxation of capital income for household portfolio choice and for the allocation of physical capital have been pointed out in a number of studies. Martin Feldstein (1976), using data from a 1962 survey of income and assets undertaken by the Federal Reserve Board, found that households with higher incomes (and consequently in higher marginal tax brackets) tend to hold larger shares of preferentially taxed assets in their portfolios than do lower income households. Similarly, Galper and Zimmerman (1977), using 1972 data generated by the Internal Revenue Service, found that a disproportionately large share of the income flows from industries that are the most preferentially taxed accrue to households in the highest marginal tax brackets.

Allocational effects of the structure of taxing capital income, including the effects of the corporate income tax, have also been the subject of considerable research. This research includes studies of specific assets such as owner-occupied housing (De Leeuw and Ozanne 1981; Aaron 1972) and tax-exempt bonds, (Ott and Meltzer 1963; Galper and Toder 1981; Hendershott 1981), analyses of the effects of taxation on corporate financial policies (Cordes and Sheffrin 1981), and general equilibrium models emphasizing the effects of differential taxation of capital income on the allocation of capital among industrial sectors.[7] More recently, Joel Slemrod (1983) and Hendershott and Shilling (1982) have developed general equilibrium models that not only explicitly incorporate tax considerations into household portfolio choices, but introduce risk aversion into these choices as well.[8]

Since the Slemrod and Hendershott-Shilling models focus explicitly on household holdings of differentially taxed assets, they could be used to measure distributional effects if expanded to include a sufficiently large number of households. However, Hendershott and Shilling, using a model that takes each household's marginal tax rate as given, deal with four representative households. Slemrod's approach specifically treats the marginal tax rates of individual households as endogenous when each faces an exogenous schedule of rates, but has only nine representative households.

Nonetheless, these as well as earlier cited works suggest the possibility of significant implicit tax and transfer effects resulting from our current tax structure or from changes in it. For example, Hendershott (1981) and Galper and Toder (1981) both find that substantial increases in the supply of tax-exempt bonds will not only tend to increase tax-exempt rates, thereby reducing implicit taxes for holders of tax-exempt bonds, but will also cause taxable rates to rise, generating increases in implicit transfers at the same time. In a similar vein, Hendershott and Shilling (1982, p. 269) find that changes in tax law enacted in 1981 could give rise to an equilibrium response of an almost two percentage point rise in the real before-tax rate of return on fully taxable securities.

Thus, the structure of taxing capital income has the potential of creating substantial implicit taxes and transfers. To address the source of these effects more formally, we develop in the next section an illustrative model of the demand and supply of differentially taxed assets.

3.3   Model of Capital Allocation and Portfolio Choice

This section outlines the basic structural features of the model developed to examine the long-run allocational and distributional effects of changes in the taxation of income from capital. A formal presentation of this model is provided in appendix A. The model can be used to solve simultaneously for the value of physical capital in each productive sector, aggregate supplies of each type of financial claim, rates of return on financial claims and physical assets, after-tax income of each representative household, and total federal revenue, given assumptions about the tax rules, the level of federal debt, the parameters of the demand schedules for the services of physical assets, and total factor supplies of each household.

The model takes account of major features of the tax system—the two-level tax on corporate income, the tax preferences made available for investments in business machinery and equipment, the favorable taxation of capital gains relative to dividend and interest income, the exemption from tax of interest on state and local bonds, the deductibility of interest paid to finance housing and other consumer durables, and the graduated tax rate structure. On the other hand, differences in the effective rate of taxation among industries are not modeled, although the impacts of these interindustry tax differences can readily be incorporated into an expanded model based on the same general framework used in this paper. In addition, the model at this stage of development fails to account for differential perceived risks from holding different assets.

In the model, households finance the entire capital stock either directly or indirectly through the purchase of financial claims issued by other sectors. The capital stock so financed consists of capital used in private business, capital used by state and local governments, and capital used within the household sector (owner-occupied homes and other consumer durables). In addition, households finance a predetermined level of federal debt. The model assumes that total factor endowments (labor and wealth) of each household are fixed. Therefore, the total capital stock is equal to household wealth minus the federal debt.

Corporations, state and local governments, and the federal government issue claims to households to finance capital investments in the business and state and local sectors and to finance the federal debt. In addition, some households issue debt to other households to finance investments in business sector capital by unincorporated enterprises and to finance capital used within households. Each capital-using sector finances its stock of capital with assumed fixed proportions of taxable bonds, tax-exempt bonds, and equity claims unique to that sector. Each saver allocates its wealth among these competing assets to maximize after-tax income, given the before-tax returns available on alternative assets, the tax treatment of each asset, and the schedule of marginal tax rates.

The net cost of capital to each capital-using sector, and thus the desired holdings of physical capital, depend on the rates of return (gross of personal taxes) on the claims issued to finance its capital stock and the taxes imposed at the enterprise level (the corporate tax). The entire economy is in equilibrium at the set of yields at which the demand for each type of claim by households is equal to the supply of each type of claim issued by corporations, governments, and other households to finance the acquisition and maintenance of the capital stock.

3.3.1   Household Demand for Assets

The five types of assets available to households, ordered by degree of taxability, are: (1) fully taxed claims (corporate bonds, loans for home mortgages and other purchases of consumer durables, loans to unincorporated enterprises, and federal government bonds); (2) partially taxed claims (corporate equity); (3) noncorporate equity capital (the noncorporate capital stock net of debt incurred to finance shares in partnerships and proprietorships); (4) tax-exempt bonds (state and local public purpose bonds and industrial development bonds); and (5) equity in consumer durables (capital employed directly within the household sector, net of home mortgages and other debt incurred to finance holdings of housing and other consumer durables).

The first four assets provide market-determined returns in the form of interest, dividends, capital gains, and net earnings of unincorporated enterprises; the fifth asset provides in-kind returns in the form of a flow of services (net of interest, depreciation, and operating costs). In the remainder of the paper, the two general categories of assets are denoted as "market assets" and "consumer durables."

The before-tax return received by a household from any market asset is independent of the quantity of the asset it holds. However, the after-tax return to a household on market assets depends on the household's entire portfolio allocation because the higher the net taxable income from the portfolio, the higher is the household's tax bracket. In contrast, for consumer durables, the amount of the asset purchased by any single household affects both its before-tax and after-tax return. As its stock of consumer durables increases, the household realizes diminishing marginal utility, and thus a lower before-tax return, from durables.

Households are assumed to issue a fixed amount of debt per dollar of equity in unincorporated enterprises and a separate fixed amount of debt per dollar of equity in consumer durables. The resulting interest deductions reduce, but do not eliminate, the tax on net income from unincorporated business. For equity in consumer durable holdings, the net tax is negative because interest deductions reduce taxable income, while the service value from durables is not taxed. The model at this stage does not permit borrowing for purchases of corporate equity and, following current law, also does not permit borrowing for tax-exempt bonds.

Since the four market assets available to households differ only in tax characteristics, households can compute the after-tax return on each market asset given the before-tax rate of return, the tax law treatment, and the household's marginal tax rate. Figure 3.1 illustrates how these after-tax returns vary with the marginal tax rate. In figure 3.1, the most heavily taxed asset is fully taxed claims (F), followed in successive order by partially taxed claims (P), equity in noncorporate capital (B), and tax-exempt claims (E). The before-tax rates of return on each asset—i_f, i_p, i_b and i_e—are illustrated on the vertical axis passing through the origin; the after-tax returns in the 70 percent bracket—y_e (.70), y_b (.70), y_p (.70), and y_f (.70)—are illustrated along the vertical line on the right side of the graph. The slope of each line represents the decline in after-tax return per unit increase in the marginal tax rate. For the fully taxed asset, the slope of the line F, dy_f/dt_j, is equal to $-i_f$; for the less heavily taxed assets, the

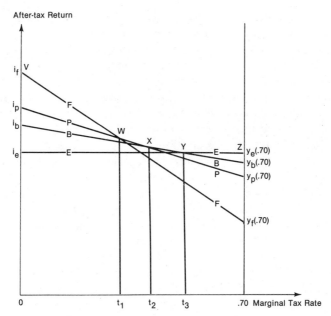

Fig. 3.1   After-tax returns on financial assets

slopes of lines *P, B,* and *E* become successively flatter. Line *E* has a zero slope, reflecting the fact that the after-tax return is equal to the before-tax return on tax-exempt bonds for any marginal tax rate.

The before-tax yield on each asset must be sufficiently high to make the after-tax yield dominate for at least *some* marginal tax rate brackets. Figure 3.1 shows that the steeper lines—that is, the most heavily taxed assets, dominate in the lowest tax brackets, while less heavily taxed assets provide the highest after-tax returns in the highest tax brackets. In figure 3.1, asset *F* dominates for marginal tax rates less than t_1; asset *P*, for marginal tax rates between t_1 and t_2; asset *B*, for marginal tax rates between t_2 and t_3; and asset *E*, for marginal tax rates greater than t_3.

Under current law, taxpayers are faced with a marginal tax rate schedule that increases in discrete steps. Except for the unusual case where after-tax returns on two assets are *exactly the same* at one statutory marginal tax rate, one asset will generally dominate all others at any point on the marginal tax rate schedule. That is, given a marginal tax rate, there will be one market asset that any household should hold to maximize after-tax income. The series of linear segments—*VWXYZ*—trace out the maximum after-tax marginal yields available for every marginal tax rate bracket.

However, the marginal tax rate facing any household is itself determined in part by its portfolio allocation. As a household replaces less heavily taxed with more heavily taxed assets in its portfolio, its marginal tax rate will rise. Thus, solving for the optimal portfolio allocation involves solving for both the marginal tax rate and the optimal allocation of assets at that marginal tax rate.

Figure 3.2 gives some indication of how the household should allocate its wealth to maximize after-tax income in a two-asset world, where taxpayers are not allowed deductions for interest costs incurred to finance tax-exempt assets. In figure 3.2, the two assets are taxable bonds and tax-exempt bonds. For purpose of illustration, the tax-exempt rate is taken to be 7 percent and the before-tax taxable rate to be 10 percent. The line segments WXY trace out the efficient portfolios at any marginal tax rate. Below a 30 percent marginal tax rate, taxable bonds dominate; above a 30 percent rate, tax-exempt bonds dominate.

In this situation, there are three general types of households:

(1) Household 1 has a marginal tax rate of less than 30 percent when all of its assets are in taxable bonds. That is, when total taxable income is equal to wage income (net of the zero bracket amount and excess item-ized deductions) plus 10 percent of wealth, the household has insufficient taxable income to reach the 30 percent marginal tax rate. It can be seen from figure 3.2 that household 1 should hold its entire portfolio in taxable bonds.

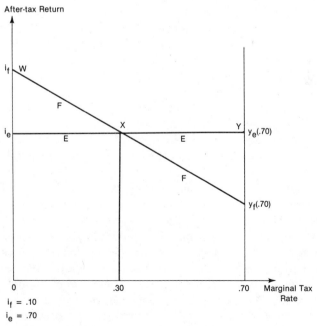

Fig. 3.2   After-tax returns in a two-asset world

(2) Household 2 is faced with a marginal tax rate above 30 percent from wage income (net of deductions and the zero bracket amount) alone. Figure 3.2 shows that household 2 should hold its entire portfolio in tax-exempt bonds.

(3) Household 3 has a marginal tax rate of less than 30 percent based on wage income alone. If all its wealth were in tax-exempt bonds, its marginal tax rate would remain unchanged from that based on net wage income, and taxable bonds would have a higher after-tax yield than tax-exempt bonds. Household 3 will therefore substitute taxable for tax-exempt bonds in its portfolio. As taxable bonds are substituted for tax-exempt bonds, the marginal tax rate of the household rises, moving it in the direction of point X. At point X, when the marginal tax rate reaches 30 percent, further substitution of taxable for tax-exempt bonds will reduce the after-tax yield on the portfolio because it will move the household into the tax bracket where tax-exempt bonds dominate. Therefore, household 3 will be in equilibrium *at the portfolio mix* which makes its marginal tax rate exactly equal to the marginal tax rate at which the after-tax yields of the two assets are equalized.

If the household faces a discrete tax rate schedule, with the marginal tax bracket jumping from 28 percent to 32 percent, it will hold the mix of assets such that one more dollar of taxable income will place it in the 32 percent bracket. The household will be right on a cliff—it will pay a 28 percent top rate (therefore, after-tax income will decline if tax-exempt bonds are substituted for taxable bonds), but would pay a 32 percent rate if it increased its taxable income by one dollar (therefore, after-tax income will also decline if another dollar of taxable bonds is substituted for tax-exempt bonds).

Thus, we can see that there are solutions where one asset dominates and solutions where the household holds both assets. The key feature of the two-asset solution is that it occurs at a critical point in the tax rate schedule. The household holds just enough of the taxed asset to make its taxable income exactly at the break point where one dollar more of taxable income would be taxed at the higher rate, and one dollar less at the lower rate.

This discussion of the optimal allocation of wealth among financial claims in a two-asset world can be generalized to a world of multiple assets with differential tax characteristics. Each market asset will be dominant in a particular tax bracket. Solutions are of two types—single-asset solutions and mixed-asset solutions. In single-asset solutions, the household holds one asset; the taxable income from that asset combined with the taxable income from wages, net of personal exemptions and deductions other than for interest payments incurred to finance business assets, places the household in a marginal tax rate bracket where the after-tax return from that asset is higher than the after-tax return on all other market assets. In mixed-asset solutions, the household is holding two assets adjacent to each other in tax rate characteristics (either fully taxable and partially taxed, partially taxed and noncorporate business, or noncorporate business and tax-exempt bonds). The taxable income from the more heavily taxed of the two assets is just enough, when combined with net taxable income from other sources, to place the household on the border between two marginal tax brackets. In the lower tax bracket, the more heavily taxed of the two market assets being held is preferred; in the higher tax bracket, the less heavily taxed of the two assets is preferred.

A computer algorithm has been developed to allocate household wealth among market assets and consumer durables, based on these general characteristics of a solution to the problem of maximizing the after-tax return on a portfolio of tax-differentiated assets. The algorithm first solves for the allocation of wealth among market assets, given an initial value of consumer durables. Then, optimal holdings of consumer durables are recomputed, given the holdings of market assets. A solution is reached by successive iterations in which the after-tax return from the entire portfolio is maximized.

In this final equilibrium, the after-tax return on holding consumer durables must equal the opportunity cost of holding them. The opportunity cost is the incremental after-tax return received by the household on the optimally invested portfolio when one additional dollar of wealth is available for investment in market assets. The after-tax return from a dollar of equity in consumer durables (which must be equated to this opportunity cost) is a function of the marginal service value per unit of durables and the after-tax cost to the household of borrowing to finance durables (itself a function of the interest rate on fully taxed securities and the household's marginal tax rate). In equilibrium, therefore, the household is maximizing its after-tax return from its portfolio of financial assets and holding an amount of consumer durables that makes the after-tax return on consumer durables equal to the after-tax return that could be earned if the household optimally invested a one dollar larger financial portfolio.

The entire tax-filing population is represented by 101 households. Appendix B describes the characteristics, method of selection, and allocation of wealth to these households. Each household has a fixed labor income, a fixed amount of wealth to allocate among the five assets, and a fixed amount of wealth assumed to be in pension funds. Pension wealth is invested on behalf of the household in fully taxed claims. Since capital income accumulated within pension funds is not subject to tax, after-tax income is maximized when this component of wealth is invested in fully taxed claims, the asset class with the highest before-tax return. For other income, each household faces the 1979 tax rate schedule for joint returns and is assigned a zero bracket amount, which includes the value of itemized deductions other than interest deductions or the standard deduction, whichever is greater. It is assumed that the first dollar of interest cost is deductible.

3.3.2 Supply of Assets by Business and Government

As noted above, business firms and governments supply market assets to households to finance their holdings of productive capital. Each type of enterprise is assumed to issue a fixed ratio of financial claims per dollar of capital stock used by the enterprise. Thus, reallocations of the capital stock among types of enterprises cause changes in the relative amounts of the four tax-differentiated market assets available to households.

Corporations and noncorporate enterprises are assumed to produce the same goods and services which sell for the same price. Corporations supply a fixed ratio of corporate equity (P), taxable bonds (F), and tax-exempt bonds (E) to households. The net cost of capital to corporations is a function of the rates of return (before individual taxes) on the three claims $(i_p, i_f,$ and $i_e)$, the corporate tax rate, and the rules for measuring taxable corporate income (including any available tax credits). Corporate tax rules are assumed parameters of the model. Noncorporate enterprises receive the same gross-of-tax return as corporations.

The total supply of all claims issued by business enterprises is determined by the demand for productive capital in the business sector. This demand for capital, derived implicitly from the demand for private goods and services in the economy and from a business sector production function, is a downward sloping function of the net cost of capital to corporations. Thus, the total supply of all claims issued by business enterprises is also a function of the corporate cost of capital.

In equilibrium, corporations and noncorporate enterprises must earn the same before-tax return on physical capital, since they are assumed to supply the same goods and services, despite the tax advantage to noncorporate enterprises from not having to pay the corporate income tax. To replicate current aggregate household holdings of corporate and noncorporate market assets, given this noncorporate tax advantage, we assume the rate of return to households on noncorporate equity claims is lower than the net cost of capital to corporations. Specifically, we assume that the supply price or before-tax rate of return to households on noncorporate equity, i_b, is a constant fraction of the corporate cost of capital, reflecting a presumed inefficiency of noncorporate compared to corporate enterprises. In the absence of this presumed inefficiency, the tax advantages to the noncorporate sector from not being subject to the tax on corporate income would virtually eliminate the corporation as a form of business organization. (This relative ''inefficiency'' of noncorporate business could result from limited liability, economies of large-scale capital accumulation, or any other advantages of the corporate form. For a further discussion of this assumption and of alternative ways of modeling an economy with both corporate and noncorporate enterprises, see appendix A.)

State and local governments supply tax-exempt bonds to finance the public sector capital stock. (Industrial development bonds, tax-exempt bonds used to finance private business investments, are modeled as claims issued by private corporations.) The supply of tax-exempt bonds issued by state and local governments is a function of the net cost of capital in the state and local sector—the tax-exempt interest rate (i_e).

The supply of taxable bonds issued by the federal government is taken as predetermined in the model.

3.3.3 Equilibration of Supply and Demand

Given the implied household demand functions for market assets and consumer durables, the enterprise supply functions for market assets, and the fixed financing coefficients, the model solves for a set of yields on financial claims, i_f, i_p, and i_e, at which household demands for and enterprise supplies of market assets are equilibrated.

The aggregate demand for the four market assets and consumer durables held by households can be computed once one knows the before-tax returns on the three financial assets, i_f, i_p, and i_e. The return on equity in noncorporate enterprises, i_b, is, as noted above, a fraction of the net cost of capital to corporations. In turn, the net cost of capital to corporations can be computed directly from the interest rates on the three financial assets and the fixed financing coefficients for the corporate capital stock. The return on consumer durables for each household is expressed as a function of the household's stock of consumer durables. Given the four market rates of return and its demand schedule for the services of consumer durables, the model allocates each household's wealth among the five assets to maximize after-tax income. Aggregate demands for the five assets are then computed by summing the resulting individual household demands. Thus, household demands for the five assets can be represented implicitly as a function of the three rates of return on financial claims $(i_f$, i_p, and $i_e)$.

The net household demand for fully taxed claims supplied by business enterprises and governments is equal to gross household demand for fully taxed claims minus household borrowing for consumer durables and noncorporate business. Since all other market assets are only supplied by business and government, net and gross household demands for these assets are equal.

On the other side of the market, the demand for the services of physical capital by governments and business enterprises can be represented, as discussed above, as a function of the rates of return on financial assets.

For any given allocation of the capital stock between governments and business enterprises, the supply of each market asset can be computed from the fixed financing coefficients once one knows the allocation of the business capital stock between corporate and noncorporate enterprises. The additional supply relationship which permits this latter allocation of the business capital stock to be calculated is the relationship between the before-tax rate of return on noncorporate capital and the net cost of capital to the corporate sector.

Thus, the net supplies of the four market assets to households can be calculated in two steps. First, the three relationships for the three capital stocks, in conjunction with the supply price relationship—the rate of return on noncorporate equity—determine the stocks of corporate and noncorporate capital, state and local capital, and federal debt. Second, the capital stocks used in each sector can be multiplied by the fixed financing coefficients to compute the supplies of the four market assets.

In summary, the model represents the two sides of the market in different ways. The supply of market assets by enterprises (and the demand for the services of consumer durables by households) is based on cost of capital considerations and fixed financing coefficients for each real sector of the economy; this analysis is similar to the sectoral analysis usually found in models concerned primarily with allocation effects. In contrast, the household demand for assets is based on the techniques of microsimulation rather than a series of equations in which the demand for each asset is represented as an explicit function of the relevant interest rates. To determine aggregate household demand, each representative household allocates a fixed total wealth among the five alternative assets, given before-tax yields and its tax circumstances, to maximize its total after-tax income. Then, the aggregate demand for each asset is calculated as a weighted sum of representative household demands.

An equilibrium solution is arrived at iteratively by varying the yields on the three financial claims until all asset demands match all asset supplies. The solution values for the yields on the three financial claims and the capital used in each sector can then be used to calculate the cost of capital to different capital-using sectors, the before-tax and after-tax incomes of each household, and total tax revenue.

3.3.4   Qualifications

A number of simplifying assumptions were made in developing the model sketched in this section. Since the major focus of this paper is distributional, we have tried to keep these simplifications in a form that does not limit the analysis of distributional effects, even though important allocational effects are not explored. For example, the business sector is represented as producing one uniform good even though current tax law is characterized by a range of effective tax rates across industries that have important effects on the allocation of the capital stock.[9] In our model, the various preferences for capital investment are summarized in a single parameter estimate of the percentage of business sector income included in the tax base. This parameter is then used to compute effective tax rates on the return to corporate and noncorporate capital.

The suppression of sectoral allocational effects should not greatly affect the findings in this paper because the major distributional effects at the household level depend on the relative supplies of differently taxed financial claims available to households and not on the types of physical capital financed by these claims. For example, the effects of aggregate changes in relative supplies of debt and equity can be examined directly in the model (by changing the assumed debt/equity ratios) without specifying separate industrial sectors.[10] However, the assumption of only one partially taxed financial asset and a uniform treatment of income from noncorporate capital does have direct effects on the measured income distribution. Representation in the model of a wider choice of noncorporate activities (e.g., tax-sheltered industries) and financial claims (e.g., stocks with different dividend payout ratios) would raise after-tax returns for taxpayers in the middle tax brackets.

Some of the simplifying empirical and behavioral assumptions in the model are worth special mention. First, households are assumed to finance all physical capital directly, thereby eliminating financial intermediaries from consideration, with the important exception of pension funds. Pension funds are included in the model because they are a means of changing the tax characteristics of asset earnings, allowing households to pay no tax on earnings from fully taxed securities. However, other tax benefits from purchasing securities through financial intermediaries—such as the tax exemption afforded to the accumulation of life insurance reserves—are not included in the model.

The general lack of financial intermediaries does give rise to one specific problem—the need to take account of the fact that, in 1979, about 75 percent of tax-exempt state and local bonds were held by commercial banks and other financial institutions and only 25 percent were held directly by households. It would be inappropriate for the model to place the entire stock of tax-exempt bonds in households' portfolios since such portfolio behavior would be inconsistent with maximization of after-tax income at the observed structure of interest rates. At the same time, state and local governments must be represented as benefiting from lower financing costs on the entire stock of bonds, not just the share absorbed directly by households.

To resolve this problem, we have assumed an intermediation role for the federal government. The federal government is assumed to pay an explicit subsidy to state and local governments equal to the difference between the tax-exempt and the taxable interest rate, inducing these governments to issue taxable securities. In our model, this subsidy is represented as a negative tax, the counterpart of the subsidy actually provided by the tax system under current law. The subsidy under current law results from the fact that financial institutions can deduct borrowing costs incurred for the purpose of holding tax-exempt securities and can, as a result, earn arbitrage profits by reducing their tax liabilities attributable to other sources of income.

A second simplification in the model is that, as a consequence of the assumption of direct household financing, liquidity considerations do not enter into household portfolio decisions. Each security of a given type is in effect assumed to be of a single maturity, bearing a before-tax yield appropriate to that maturity.

Third, in allowing households to adjust their portfolios immediately in response to tax factors, we assume that such adjustments are costless. In that sense, the analysis of alternative tax regimes in the model is a comparative statics exercise, comparing alternative long-run equilibrium solutions, although the long run in this case involves no changes in aggregate factor supplies.

Fourth, the model only analyzes the main elements of the tax structure. Relatively exotic tax shelters and complex financial transactions are ignored.

Finally, and most important, the model fails to account for the existence of risk as influencing individual and corporate portfolio decisions. In abstracting from risk considerations, the model differs from the work of Slemrod (1981), Hendershott and Shilling (1981), and Gravelle and Zimmerman (1984), each of whom specifically examines interactions between the tax system and risk taking. In contrast, our model in its current stage of development can examine the distributional and allocational effects of the major structural elements of the tax system only for a hypothetical risk-free world. Even in this form, the model can illustrate the general way in which structural tax provisions can give rise to implicit transfer benefits as well as implicit tax burdens compared to a world with no taxes on capital income. Moreover, if significant implicit transfer benefits can be generated under risk-free conditions, it is unlikely that adding risk to the model would change this general result. Recall that the implicit transfer payments arise because the before-tax returns on fully taxed assets increase as households shift their portfolios into tax-preferred assets. Even though the tax-preferred assets—in particular, equity in corporate and noncorporate business—are the riskier assets, a similar portfolio switch into tax-preferred assets and a similar increase in fully taxed yields would still occur in a world with risk, although the shifts may be moderated as household portfolios become increasingly risky.

The assumption of a risk-free world does, however, have two important implications that should be noted here. First, households do not need to diversify their portfolios to reduce risk, since all assets are risk free. Thus, household utility is maximized when after-tax income is maximized. Given its tax situation, each household, as shown above, will tend to choose the one asset (or in some cases two assets) that will maximize after-tax income. Some diversification will occur because of holdings of consumer durables and through the intermediation of pension funds, but in general households will tend to be plungers in the particular assets that maximize their after-tax incomes.

Second, the yield from the corporate income tax is vastly reduced—to a simulated level of $11.5 billion annually in 1979—in our model of a risk-free world. One main reason for this result is that the return to corporate equity, as noted, is much lower when both debt and equity have zero riskiness. Therefore the simulated pre–corporate tax return to equity and the corporate tax are both much lower than actual returns and taxes. In fact, under the parameters assumed in the model, any increase in pre–corporate tax returns to equity to compensate for risk is likely to be taxed at virtually full 46 percent rates, thereby generating substantial additional corporate tax revenues.[11]

3.4   Calibration of Model and Simulation Results

3.4.1   Base Case Conditions

The model developed in the previous section was calibrated to replicate the 1979 values of the holdings of each market asset by all households in the aggregate, each individual household's holdings of consumer durables, and the physical capital stocks used by each sector given a before-tax yield on fully taxed assets equal to 12 percent. This calibration was done by assuming unitary elasticities in the sectoral demand for physical capital functions and in each household's demand for consumer durables and then choosing values for the scale parameters in these functions. The model then generated rates of return for the market assets other than fully taxed securities.

The year 1979 was selected for the base period because it is the last year for which tax return information is available from the Treasury's individual income tax model. This tax return information was used in conjunction with data from the Board of Governors of the Federal Reserve System (1981) on national balance sheets for 1979 to estimate the physical capital stocks used by each sector, the financial claims issued to finance these stocks, and the holdings of market assets and consumer durables by each household. The data base was assembled in two stages. In stage one, a consistent set of aggregates for financial and physical capital stocks were developed; in stage two, the relevant assets were distributed to house-holds according to information on individual tax returns. These estimation procedures are discussed in more detail in appendix B.

The results of the calibration for the 1979 base case are shown in tables 3.1 through 3.4. Table 3.1 shows the financing of the capital stock by sector and the aggregate volume of claims—over $7 trillion—thereby generated. For example, based on the national balance sheets, adjusted as discussed in appendix B, the corporate capital stock is one-quarter debt financed, including a small proportion of tax-exempt debt financing, and about three-quarters equity financed. Unincorporated business is over 85 percent equity financed, and household durable capital is financed one-half by debt and one-half by equity.

Table 3.1   **Financing of Capital Stock and Aggregate Household Claims: Base Case (1979 law) ($ billions)**

Financing of Capital Stock	
Corporate capital	2,017.1
Equity	1,508.6
Taxable bonds	487.3
Tax-exempt bonds[a]	21.2
Capital in unincorporated enterprises	1,709.7
Equity	1,463.5
Taxable bonds	246.2
Household sector capital	2,473.4
Equity	1,236.7
Taxable bonds (mortgages and other consumer loans)	1,236.7
State and local capital	276.4
Tax-exempt bonds[a]	276.4
Federal debt	600.0
Total	7,076.6
Household Claims	
Taxable bonds[b]	2,792.5
Corporate equity	1,508.6
Equity in unincorporated enterprises	1,463.5
Equity in consumer durables	1,236.7
Tax-exempt bonds	75.3
Total	7,076.6

[a]Households hold directly $75.3 billion of total tax-exempt issues of $297.6 billion. The other $222.3 billion are held by financial intermediaries that finance their purchases by issuing fully taxable claims to households.

[b]Of this amount, households hold $598.6 billion in pension funds and the other $2,193.9 billion directly. Households pay no tax on the income from assets held in pension funds.

Table 3.2   Capital Allocation and Rates of Return: Base Case (1979 law)

Capital Stock ($ billions)

Business sector capital	3,726.8
Corporate capital	2,017.1
Capital—unincorporated enterprises	1,709.7
Household sector capital[a]	2,473.4
State and local capital	276.4
Total capital stock	6,476.6
Federal debt	600.0
Total household wealth	7,076.6

Rates of Return (percent)

$i_f = 12.000$
$i_p = 9.357$
$i_e = 7.100$
$r_c = 10.544$
$hr_c = 9.109$

Numbers may not sum to totals because of rounding.
i_f = yield on fully taxed claims, i_p = yield on partially taxed claims, i_e = yield on tax-exempt claims, r_c = before-tax yield on corporate capital, hr_c = before-tax yield on noncorporate capital.
[a]Owner-occupied housing and consumer durables.

Table 3.2 shows more directly the sectoral allocation of the physical capital stock (including federal government debt) and the before-tax rate of return on fully taxed bonds (i_f), partially taxed corporate equities (i_p), and tax-exempt bonds (i_e). Table 3.2 also shows the net of depreciation cost of capital for the corporate sector (r_c) and the before-tax return available to holders of noncorporate capital (hr_c).

The rate of return on equities (i_p) is a risk-adjusted return. The spread between taxable and tax-exempt yields—about 40 percent—is almost identical to that used by Slemrod (1981) and reflects a combination of the 45–50 percent spreads betwen tax-exempt and taxable bonds in shorter maturities and the 30–35 percent differential between long-term taxable and tax-exempt bonds in the late 1970s.

Tables 3.3 and 3.4 show total wealth and simulated asset holdings by wealth class and income class in the 1979 base case. Other than pensions and consumer durables, the tendency toward asset specialization is clear. As an extreme case, table 3.3 shows that only those with wealth greater than $5 million hold tax-exempt bonds. The concentration of wealth is also evident. The wealthiest 8.3 percent of tax returns—those with wealth of $200,000 or more—hold 58.4 percent of total wealth. Similar results may be seen in table 3.4, where wealth holdings are arrayed by income class. For example, households with income of $100,000 or more account for 1.5 percent of total returns and hold 27.5 percent of total wealth.

Table 3.3   Simulated Holdings of Wealth by Wealth Class; Base Case (1979 law) ($ billions)

Wealth Class ($ thousands)	Number of Returns (thousands)	Fully Taxed	Partially Taxed	Equity in Noncorp. Business	Tax-Exempt	All Market Assets[a]	Pensions	Equity in Consumer Durables	Total Wealth
0–10	30,198	0	0	0	0	0	41.0	201.0	242.0
10–50	34,761	224.4	0	0	0	224.4	194.0	461.3	879.8
50–100	13,197	407.7	58.0	1.5	0	467.2	158.0	249.1	874.3
100–200	6,821	634.7	102.7	17.5	0	754.9	76.7	112.7	944.3
200–500	5,395	589.1	720.5	79.6	0	1,389.2	70.0	112.2	1,571.4
500–1,000	1,695	337.9	359.5	304.0	0	1,001.4	33.7	51.5	1,086.6
1,000–5,000	530	0	268.0	569.8	0	837.8	19.4	33.5	890.7
5,000+	92	0	0	491.2	75.3	566.5	5.7	15.3	587.5
Total	92,690	2,193.9	1,508.6	1,463.5	75.3	5,241.3	598.6	1,236.7	7,076.6

Numbers may not sum to totals because of rounding.

[a] Excluding pensions.

Table 3.4   Simulated Holdings of Wealth by Income Class: Base Case (1979 law) ($ billions)

Income Class ($ thousands)	Number of Returns (thousands)	Type of Claim							Total Wealth
		Fully Taxed	Partially Taxed	Equity in Noncorp. Business	Tax-Exempt	All Market Assets[a]	Pensions	Equity in Consumer Durables	
0–5	17,354	13.7	0.0	0.0	0.0	13.7	5.7	104.9	124.3
5–10	17,966	152.5	0.0	0.0	0.0	152.5	32.9	133.8	319.2
10–15	12,740	287.0	0.0	0.0	0.0	287.0	46.5	98.3	431.9
15–20	8,882	165.5	0.0	0.0	0.0	165.5	51.2	93.4	310.2
20–30	15,895	642.8	0.0	0.0	0.0	642.8	130.7	230.7	1,004.2
30–50	14,997	665.6	561.6	0.0	0.0	1,227.2	191.2	356.7	1,775.1
50–100	3,433	266.8	640.8	60.0	0.0	967.6	78.1	121.7	1,167.4
100–200	1,096	0.0	306.2	504.5	0.0	810.8	40.3	56.7	907.7
200+	327	0.0	0.0	899.0	75.3	974.2	22.1	40.3	1,036.7
Total	92,690	2,193.9	1,508.6	1,463.5	75.3	5,241.3	598.6	1,236.7	7,076.6

Numbers may not sum to total because of rounding.

[a]Excluding pensions.

3.4.2 Simulation Results: Elimination of Taxation of Income from Capital

Starting from the base case, we have simulated the long-run effects of eliminating all taxes on capital income on the portfolio choices of households, rates of return, and the allocation of physical capital. This simulation was performed by solving the model for the case where there is only one market asset, with no taxes imposed on its return, the corporate income tax is eliminated, and households are no longer allowed tax deductions for interest on consumer, mortgage, or business loans. Since the portfolio choices facing households are differentiated only by tax and not by risk characteristics, only one type of market asset emerges in the model when taxes on the return to savings are eliminated. The household's portfolio then reduces to a choice between holding consumer durables, which provide a return in terms of service value, and holding the one undifferentiated market asset. Holdings of pension funds are assumed to remain unchanged.

On the capital-using side of the model, corporations and state and local governments continue to demand capital services and supply the one market asset according to the previously calibrated functions specifying their demand for physical capital.

In equilibrium, the household demand for this one market asset equals the total supply issued by all capital-using sectors. The equilibrium interest rate is the rate at which the household demand matches the supply by corporations, governments, and those households that borrow to finance their holdings of consumer durables.

When taxation of capital income is eliminated, there is effectively only one business sector, and the distinction between corporate and noncorporate enterprise disappears. In terms of the model, this is accomplished by having all activity performed in the corporate sector inasmuch as less efficient noncorporate enterprises can no longer compete with corporations once their relative tax advantages have been removed. Furthermore, since there are no longer tax-differentiated assets in the absence of capital income taxes, the distinction between corporate and noncorporate enterprise has no significance for the distribution of tax burdens.

We assume that the revenue loss from eliminating capital income taxation is balanced either by an increase in taxation of wage income or a reduction in public services. Neither of those changes would affect the allocation of the stock of capital in our model once the returns on capital income were not subject to tax. However, an increase in federal debt to offset the tax reduction would affect capital allocation because federal debt absorbs some private wealth holdings and therefore "crowds out" investments in physical capital by private firms, households, and state and local governments.

Because we do not specify how the revenue effect of eliminating capital income taxation is compensated for, our results do not show the differential incidence from alternative tax structures. Rather, we provide estimates of the specific incidence of taxation among income groups without identifying who would otherwise pay tax or who benefits from public services.

Tables 3.5 through 3.10 summarize the results of our simulation. Table 3.5 shows the allocation of the capital stock among uses and the interest rate on all assets in the case where capital income taxation—$42 billion of revenue in our estimates—is eliminated. The equilibrium interest rate of 9.282 percent is between the tax-exempt rate in the base case (7.1 percent) and the fully taxable rate in the base case (12 percent). This change in interest rates means that the cost of capital financed by tax-exempt claims (mostly state and local capital) rises while the cost of capital financed by fully taxed claims falls. The net (of depreciation) rental cost of corporate sector capital declines from 10.544 percent to 9.282 percent.

As a result of these changes in the cost of capital compared to the base case, capital in the private business sector (all business enterprises) increases by 6.5 percent, capital in the household sector (consumer durables) declines by 7.2 percent, and capital in the state and local sector declines by 23.5 percent. Since the state and local sector is relatively small in the base case, this large proportionate decline does not free up substantial resources for other capital-using sectors. The federal debt remains constant by assumption.

The effect on consumer durables from eliminating taxation of capital income is a more complicated story. The decline in overall holdings of consumer durables masks important differences in the effects on consumer durable investment for different households. The 9.282 percent cost of capital in the no-capital-income-tax world is lower than the cost of holding consumer durable capital under 1979 law for some households

Table 3.5   Capital Allocation and Rates of Return: No Capital Income Taxes

Capital Stock	Amount ($ billions)	Change from Base Case	
		($ billions)	(%)
Business sector capital	3,969.0	242.3	+6.5
Household sector capital	2,296.1	−177.3	−7.2
State and local capital	211.4	−65.0	−23.5
Federal debt	600.0	0.0	—
Total household wealth	7,076.6	0.0	—

Rate of return on all assets = 9.282%.

Numbers may not sum to totals because of rounding.

and higher than this cost of capital for others. For households in the zero tax bracket, the cost of holding household capital declines and the equilibrium stock of consumer durables *rises* when capital income taxes are eliminated because they previously had to pay 12 percent after-tax for borrowed funds and could earn 12 percent on financial assets by buying fully taxed securities. In contrast, for households in higher brackets, the cost of holding consumer durables increases significantly because they lose the benefits of deducting interest payments and because the returns they could formerly earn on market assets were relatively low. On average, the cost of holding household capital rises, and the equilibrium stock of consumer durables declines.

Table 3.6 shows how removal of capital income taxation alters the simulated holdings of wealth by wealth class. Households in the lowest wealth class ($0–$10,000) hold wealth only in the form of pensions and consumer durables in the 1979 base case and, therefore, have no opportunity to increase consumer durable holdings in the simulated no-capital-income-tax world. However, the second lowest wealth class contains some households for whom the cost of holding consumer durables declines and the opportunity exists to increase such holdings, and other households for whom the cost of durables rises. On balance, this wealth class shifts $0.2 billion in wealth out of market assets into consumer durables. All other wealth classes increase their net holdings of market assets and reduce holdings of consumer durables; the largest proportionate drop in consumer durable holdings occurs in the highest wealth classes.

Table 3.6   Simulated Holdings of Wealth by Wealth Class: No Capital Income Taxes ($ billions)

Wealth Class ($ thousands)	Type of Claim			Change in Market Assets[b]	Total Wealth
	Market Assets[a]	Pensions	Consumer Durables		
0–10	0	41.0	201.0	0.0	242.0
10–50	224.2	194.0	461.5	−0.2	879.8
50–100	491.3	158.0	225.0	24.1	874.3
100–200	768.7	76.7	98.9	13.9	944.3
200–500	1,409.7	70.0	91.7	20.5	1,571.4
500–1,000	1,014.9	33.7	38.0	13.5	1,086.6
1,000–5,000	848.8	19.4	22.5	11.0	890.7
5,000+	572.3	5.7	9.4	5.9	587.5
Total	5,330.0	598.6	1,148.0	88.7	7,076.6

Numbers may not sum to totals because of rounding.
[a]Excluding pensions.
[b]Compared to base case (equal and opposite to change in consumer durables).

The differences between base case yields on market assets and consumer durables and the uniform return to wealth in a world with no capital income taxes constitute the implicit taxes and transfers that are the basic subject of this paper. These implicit taxes and transfers for groups of households can be measured by comparing capital income in the 1979 law base case with income from capital when there are no capital income taxes. These comparisons are presented in tables 3.7 and 3.8. Table 3.7 shows the distribution of capital income and total income by income class under both the 1979 law base case and a tax system with no capital income taxes. Table 3.8 shows the distribution of explicit and implicit taxes by income class.

The concepts used to measure capital income and taxes in tables 3.7 and 3.8 merit further discussion. In table 3.7, the column labeled "Capital Income, 1979 Law" is the measure of capital income that most closely conforms to the income concept used by P-O. Capital income under 1979 law is measured as the sum of the before-tax yield on all financial assets, the before-tax yield on equity in unincorporated business (net of interest payments), the imputed rental income from consumer durables (again, net of interest costs), and the imputed corporation income tax. Following the procedure recommended, though not strictly applied, by P-O for the case where all capital bears the corporate income tax, we allocate the imputed corporate tax to households in proportion to wealth.

The column "Capital Income: No Capital Income Taxes" shows the distribution of income computed by our simulation of capital allocation and returns from investment in a world without capital income taxes.

Table 3.7   **Distribution of Income by Income Class ($ billions)**

Income Class ($ thousands)	Number of Returns (thousands)	Capital Income		Implicit Tax[a]	Labor Income	Total Income
		1979 Law	No Capital Income Taxes			
0–5	17,354	15.1	15.9	0.7	41.8	57.7
5–10	17,966	33.5	31.3	−2.2	114.5	145.9
10–15	12,740	46.9	40.5	−6.4	126.6	167.2
15–20	8,882	32.1	28.9	−3.2	129.2	158.1
20–30	15,895	105.9	93.3	−12.6	293.7	387.1
30–50	14,997	170.4	164.8	−5.6	407.5	572.2
50–100	3,433	110.0	108.4	−1.6	132.8	241.2
100–200	1,096	78.9	84.3	5.3	62.3	146.5
200+	327	87.0	96.2	9.2	30.8	127.0
Total	92,690	679.9	663.6	−16.3	1,339.3	2,002.9

Numbers may not sum to totals because of rounding.

[a]Capital income when no capital income taxes minus capital income under 1979 law.

Since in this world there is only one rate of return that is common to all capital, including consumer durables, the capital income of each household is simply equal to its wealth multiplied by the rate of return. Implicit taxes and transfers arise because this rate of return differs from the rate of return *before-tax* that households receive under current law.

The calculation of 1979 law capital income shown in table 3.7 raises two important conceptual points. The first concerns the method of measuring imputed rental income from housing and other consumer durables, and the second, the method of accounting for the subsidy that the tax system provides to commercial banks for their holdings of tax-exempt securities.

Our measure of imputed rental income differs from the conventional measure used in the national income accounts. The problem we confront is what before-tax return to impute to a household from an asset that provides its return in the form of services rather than dollars. It is tempting to use the market rental value of those services as the measure of the return—the method used to estimate the imputed income from owner-occupied housing in the national income accounts. This measure would be correct in a world with no taxes. However, because the tax advantages to consumer durable investment are contingent on the fact that the capital services are *not* rented, there is no reason to expect the household to equate the marginal productivity of its capital in consumer durables to the market return on durables. Rather, when the household, behaving as a business firm would, equates the marginal productivity of the capital with the cost of obtaining it, marginal productivity is in general not equal to the market rent because tax provisions differentially affect the cost of capital in household and market activities.

To be consistent with the measurement of the before-tax return to financial claims and corporate assets, we must impute to the household a return on equity in consumer durables equal to the opportunity cost, in terms of foregone returns on market assets, of holding an extra dollar of equity in consumer durables.[12] This opportunity cost in most, but not all, cases is *lower* than the market rental value of the services of durables because the cost of capital to *most* households for investment in durables is *lower* than the cost of capital to the corporate sector. For households in the zero tax bracket, however, the cost of capital for consumer durables is higher than the cost of capital to corporations because in our simulated base case the before-tax return on fully taxed securities, i_f, is greater than the cost of capital to the corporate sector, r_c.

Using this measure of imputed rental income from consumer durables, the net imputed before-tax capital income from *equity* in consumer durables is equal to:

$$[1/(1 - f_4)] \, (y_d - f_4 i_f),$$

where y_d is the opportunity cost of equity in consumer durables, f_4 the fraction of consumer durable capital financed by debt, and i_f the fully taxed interest rate.

It is important to stress that this procedure for measuring the before-tax income from consumer durables is conceptually distinct from the measurement of implicit taxes and transfers. The issue discussed here concerns the correct measurement of before-tax returns from capital realized under existing tax rules. In contrast, implicit taxes and transfers arise because current before-tax returns to capital are themselves different from what they would be in the absence of taxation.

The income measures reported in table 3.7 must also reflect the assumed subsidy to tax-exempt financing. As discussed above, banks and other financial institutions receive benefits in the form of lower taxes for holding state and local debt. In this way, these institutions serve as a vehicle for conveying a federal subsidy that lowers the cost of capital to state and local governments, relative to the return received by households, without directly altering tax liability at the household level. This subsidy or negative tax is treated as part of the tax system and, accordingly, is reflected in net taxes and before-tax income of households in the 1979 base case. The subsidy (negative tax) is allocated among households in proportion to their simulated holdings of fully taxed securities.

Table 3.8 provides a breakdown of explicit and implicit taxes by household income class. Explicit taxes include individual income taxes—allocated between capital income and labor income—the corporate income tax, and the negative tax (i.e., the subsidy) for tax-exempt bonds. Implicit taxes are broken down into two categories—changes in before-tax interest received from holdings of federal debt and all other changes in before-tax capital income resulting from the entire system of capital income taxation. Individual income taxes are allocated between taxes on labor income and taxes on capital income by stacking labor income first. This means that the first dollar marginal tax rate on income from capital is the marginal tax rate on the last dollar of taxable wages, net of all deductions other than interest.

In table 3.8, explicit taxes on individual capital income are zero for the lowest income class because those households are all in a zero tax bracket. Total explicit taxes on individual capital income are negative for households with income between $5,000 and $10,000 because of the deductibility against labor income of interest costs incurred to finance holdings of housing and other consumer durables. Explicit taxes are positive for all classes with income greater than $10,000 and increase relative to labor taxes, reflecting the composition of income, as income increases.

The corporate income tax is allocated in proportion to total household wealth. The tax-exempt subsidy is allocated according to holdings of taxable securities. The total simulated corporate income tax for all house-

Table 3.8   Distribution of Taxes by Income Class ($ billions)

Income Class ($ thousands)	Explicit Taxes				Implicit Taxes				
	Individual Income Taxes			Corporate Income Tax	Tax-Exempt Subsidy[a]	Change in Federal Bond Interest	Other	Total Capital Taxes	Total Taxes
	Labor	Capital	Total						
0–5	0	0	0	0.3	0.1	−0.1	0.9	0.9	0.9
5–10	6.4	−1.3	5.0	0.5	0.7	−1.1	−1.1	−3.7	2.7
10–15	10.6	2.9	13.5	0.7	1.3	−1.9	−4.4	−4.1	6.5
15–20	13.4	1.5	15.0	0.5	0.8	−1.3	−1.9	−2.0	11.5
20–30	37.1	9.8	46.9	1.6	3.0	−4.5	−8.1	−4.2	33.0
30–50	68.9	11.9	80.8	2.9	3.3	−5.0	−0.6	5.8	74.7
50–100	30.6	4.7	35.3	1.9	1.3	−2.0	0.4	3.6	34.2
100–200	18.1	5.0	23.1	1.5	0.2	−0.2	5.6	11.7	29.8
200+	10.0	6.8	16.8	1.7	0.1	−0.1	9.3	17.6	27.6
Total	195.1	41.4	236.5	11.5	10.9	−16.3	0.0	25.7	220.9

Numbers may not sum to totals because of rounding.

[a]Treated here as a negative tax.

holds is almost exactly offset by the tax-exempt subsidy, leaving total explicit taxes on capital income only slightly above simulated taxes paid directly at the household level.

Table 3.8 also shows implicit taxes by income class. Since it is assumed in the model that the elasticity of demand for capital services is unit elastic with respect to the net (of depreciation) cost of capital, total before-tax income from all physical capital assets—capital used in corporate and noncorporate business, in state and local governments, and in households—does not vary with changes in the cost of capital. However, since the quantity of Federal debt is assumed to be fixed, total interest earnings on federal debt vary directly with changes in the rate of interest.

As shown in Table 3.5, the equilibrium interest rate simulated when there are no capital income taxes is 9.282 percent. The difference between this return and the yield on fully taxed securities in the 1979 base case represents an implicit subsidy to holders of fully taxed bonds. Since the federal government issues a fixed quantity of fully taxed bonds, federal borrowing costs and total income to holders of federal debt are higher in the 1979 base case than in the no-capital-income-tax equilibrium. In other words, the simulation results imply that the 1979 system of capital income taxation increased the cost of federal borrowing by $16.3 billion. This net implicit subsidy to holders of taxable securities offsets part of the revenue gain from taxing capital income, although the offset takes the form of an increased outlay rather than a reduction in federal revenue.

Implicit taxes for each income class measure the difference between capital income in the absence of capital income taxes and before-tax capital income under 1979 law. Since total before-tax income from capital is fixed, the total implicit tax, net of the increased interest on the federal debt, is zero. However, as table 3.8 shows, the tax system does affect the distribution of before-tax capital income by income class because it alters the pattern of before-tax yields among tax-differentiated assets. In general, before-tax capital income is increased (implicit taxes are negative) for taxpayers in lower and middle income groups, and reduced (implicit taxes are positive) for taxpayers in the highest income groups.

The last two columns of table 3.8 show total capital taxes and total taxes by income class. Total capital taxes are computed by adding explicit and implicit taxes. Thus, while total explicit taxes on capital income (net of the tax-exempt subsidy) add up to $42.0 billion, the total tax on capital income is only $25.7 billion. The difference of $16.3 billion represents the increased interest paid on the federal debt. Total taxes are the sum of taxes on capital income and taxes on labor income. The top income class with 14.5 percent of capital income and 6.3 percent of all income pays 68.5 percent of total capital income taxes and 12.5 percent of all taxes.

Table 3.9 shows the computation of effective tax rates by income class

Table 3.9   Effective Tax Rates (ETR) by Income Class

Income Class ($ thousands)	Effective Tax Rate on Capital Income		Effective Tax Rate on All Income	
	Traditional Method[a] (percent)	Full ETR Method[b] (percent)	Traditional Method[c] (percent)	Full ETR Method[d] (percent)
0–5	1.3	5.9	0.4	1.6
5–10	−4.4	−11.7	3.3	1.8
10–15	4.8	−10.1	7.4	3.9
15–20	3.7	−6.9	9.1	7.2
20–30	8.0	−4.4	11.4	8.5
30–50	6.7	3.5	13.9	13.1
50–100	4.8	3.4	14.8	14.2
100–200	8.0	13.9	17.3	20.3
200+	9.7	18.3	15.6	21.7
Total	6.2	3.9	11.7	11.0

Numbers may not sum to totals because of rounding.
Income is as reported in table 3.7; taxes as shown in table 3.8
[a](individual capital income tax + corporate tax − tax-exempt subsidy)/(capital income, 1979 law).
[b](total capital taxes)/(capital income, no capital income taxes).
[c](total explicit taxes)/(labor income + capital income, 1979 law).
[d](total taxes)/(total income).

on capital income and on all income under the traditional and full effective tax rate (ETR) methods. Under the traditional method, the tax rate, as discussed in section 3.2, is defined as the ratio of explicit taxes paid to before-tax income. The tax rate on capital income rises to 8.0 percent for households with income between $20,000 and $30,000, then declines to 4.8 percent for households with incomes between $50,000 and $100,000, and rises again to 9.7 percent for households with income greater than $200,000. In contrast, the full effective tax rate on capital income—with the exception of the bottom class, the peculiarity of which is discussed below—rises throughout the income scale except for a minor dip at the $50,000–$100,000 class. The full effective tax rate is negative for households with income between $5,000 and $30,000, remains less than 4 percent for households with income between $30,000 and $100,000, and then jumps to 13.9 percent for households with income between $100,000 and $200,000 and to 18.3 percent for households with income greater than 200,000.

The tax rate on all income, measured by the traditional method, increases as income rises up to a peak of 17.3 percent for the $100,000–$200,000 income class, but then declines to 15.6 percent for households with income greater than $200,000. The full effective tax rate rises throughout the income scale as income rises. Thus modifying the measure of tax burdens, to take account of implicit taxes and subsidies, reverses the finding that tax rates begin to decline at the highest income levels.

Two further points should be made about the data shown in table 3.9. First, the measure of full effective tax rates is independent of the assumptions used to allocate corporate taxes and the tax-exempt subsidy among income classes. The full effective tax rate calculation depends only on a comparison between after-tax income in the 1979 base case and before-tax income in a world with no capital income taxes. Since corporate taxes and the tax-exempt subsidy alter the measures of explicit taxes paid and before-tax capital income by the same amount, they do not affect the measure of after-tax income in the base case.

The second point is an explanation of the high effective tax rate in the lowest income class. The general result that implicit taxes are greater for high-income taxpayers than for low-income taxpayers—a consequence of the fact that high-income taxpayers hold tax-preferred financial assets with lower before-tax returns—does not apply to the measure of implicit taxes on holdings of consumer durables by some households. The reason for this anomaly is that households' total holdings of consumer durables are constrained in the model (by an assumption that consumer durables are 50 percent debt financed) to be no more than twice total household wealth. For some households, consumer durable holdings represent their entire asset portfolio in the 1979 base case. If these households are in very low tax brackets, they would prefer to hold more consumer durables in the zero tax world because their after-tax interest costs are lower. However, these households are constrained by total available wealth because the model does not permit additional borrowing for the purchase of consumer durables.

Since holdings of consumer durables for these households are the same in both the base case and the no-tax case, the total service value must be the same; however, interest costs are higher in the 1979 base case. Thus, for selected households—those with low marginal tax rates who are constrained from increasing their holdings of durables—the net before-tax income from consumer durables (i.e., the difference between the service flow and the interest costs) is lower in the 1979 base case than in the no-tax world. These selected households pay a positive implicit tax in the form of higher financing costs on holdings of consumer durables. This accounts for the 5.9 percent effective tax rate for the lowest income class in table 3.9. (Relaxing the borrowing constraint in subsequent development of this model would eliminate this effect. Low wealth taxpayers would be permitted to increase consumer durable holdings in the no-capital-tax case, driving down their before-tax returns, and to decrease their holdings as the cost of borrowing rises, thereby maintaining the same net before-tax income from durables.)

Table 3.10   Rates of Return in Different Marginal Tax Brackets

Marginal Tax Rate (percent)	Dominant Market Asset[a]	Rate of Return (percent)			Effective Tax Rate (percent)	
		Before Individual Tax	After Tax	No Capital Income Taxes	Traditional Method[b]	Full ETR Method
0	F	12.000	12.000	9.282	−1.93	−29.28
14	F	12.000	10.320	9.282	12.34	−11.18
16	F	12.000	10.080	9.282	14.38	−8.60
18	F	12.000	9.840	9.282	16.42	−6.01
21	F	12.000	9.480	9.282	19.48	−2.13
24	F	12.000	9.120	9.282	22.53	1.75
28	F	12.000	8.640	9.282	26.61	6.92
32	F	12.000	8.160	9.282	30.69	12.09
37	P	9.357	7.972	9.282	16.26	14.11
43	P	9.357	7.748	9.282	18.61	16.53
49	B	8.622	7.526	9.282	14.33	18.92
54	B	8.622	7.414	9.282	15.61	20.12
59	B	8.622	7.302	9.282	16.88	21.33
64	B	8.622	7.190	9.282	18.16	22.54
68	B	8.622	7.101	9.282	19.17	23.50
70	E	7.100	7.100	9.282	2.25	23.51

[a]F = fully taxed claims
P = partially taxed claims
B = net equity in noncorporate business.
E = tax-exempt claims.
[b]Includes imputed corporate tax equal to .1631 cents per dollar of wealth and tax-exempt subsidy equal to .3901 cents per dollar of wealth in fully taxed claims.

Table 3.10 gives some further indication of what lies behind the results in table 3.9 by showing how taxation affects the returns earned by households in different marginal tax brackets. The column labeled "Dominant Market Asset" in table 3.10 shows the asset with the highest after-tax return (other than consumer durables) in each marginal tax bracket. As marginal tax rates increase, after-tax returns available to savers decline; however, the rate of decline is slowed by the existence of tax-preferred assets. The before-tax rate of return declines in three discrete steps at those marginal tax rates where it just pays to switch to a less heavily taxed asset.

The effective tax rate as measured by the traditional method increases in each tax bracket up to the point where the investor switches to a less heavily taxed asset. Where the investor is holding fully taxed assets, the effective tax rate is slightly less than the statutory marginal tax rate because the tax-exempt subsidy is greater than the imputed corporate tax for holders of fully taxed securities. Above the 32 percent bracket, the measured effective tax rate drops sharply with the shift from fully taxed to partially taxed assets because the measured before-tax income declines.

At each other switch point, the marginal tax rate again declines, falling to 2.25 percent (all attributable to the corporate tax) in the 70 percent bracket.

In contrast, the full effective tax rate measure shows a negative tax rate in the lowest tax brackets because the tax system, by raising the yield on fully taxed assets, enables low-bracket taxpayers to earn higher after-tax yields than they would earn in a world with no capital income taxes. The full effective tax rate increases monotonically with marginal tax rates because after-tax yields decline. However, as taxpayers switch to more tax-preferred assets, the inclusion percentage also declines; therefore, increases in marginal tax rates beyond a certain point are associated with smaller reductions in after-tax yields. At the extreme, where the preferred asset is the tax-exempt claim, further increases in statutory marginal tax rates have no effect on full effective tax rates. Thus, while the full effective tax rate calculation, in contrast to the traditional method of estimating effective tax rates, shows that the effective tax rate increases continuously with increases in the statutory tax rate, the progressivity of the tax system is much milder than it would be in the absence of preferences. In comparison with the top statutory rate under 1979 law of 70 percent (plus an imputed corporate tax), the results of the simulations show a maximum marginal tax rate on capital income, using the full ETR method, of only 23.51 percent.

3.5   Conclusions

The complex structure of capital income taxation in the United States causes significant changes in the relative returns to wealth ownership realized by different groups of taxpayers. By altering the relative before-tax yields on assets with different tax treatments, the tax system provides transfers to some capital income recipients in the form of higher before-tax and, in some cases, higher after-tax yields than would have been available absent any taxation of capital income; at the same time, the tax system imposes implicit taxes, in the form of reduced before-tax yields, on other capital income recipients. These implicit transfers and taxes are not captured in traditional approaches to measuring the burden of taxes on capital income.

The simulations shown in this paper indicate that these implicit transfers and implicit taxes might be quite large and that taking their existence into account could alter qualitative conclusions about the distribution of tax burdens. In particular, the preliminary results suggest that the pre-1981 system of capital income taxation provided net transfers to lower- and middle-income households (with income less than $30,000) and imposed much larger taxes on upper-income households than would be shown by traditional methods of measuring tax burdens.

The results presented in this paper were generated using a model of portfolio choice and capital allocation in which households allocate available wealth to maximize after-tax returns and in which the demand for physical capital by capital-using sectors is a function of the net cost of capital services. The model specifically accounts for the interaction between after-tax returns and the tax rate structure for a diverse and representative sample of U.S. households. However, further modifications of the model will be necessary to verify and to expand the tentative conclusions reached in this paper.

The major changes required are to expand the model to take account of risk as well as after-tax return as a determinant of portfolio choice, to increase the number of capital-using sectors, to allow households a greater choice among financial claims, and to specify more explicitly the production relationships and the demand for final goods. While these revisions in the model would enable us to refine our results and to increase the range of issues that could be considered, they are unlikely to alter the basic conclusion that the taxation of capital income gives rise to significant transfer effects by changing the relative before-tax yields of different assets.

Appendix A Formal Presentation of Model of Capital Allocation and Portfolio Choice

This appendix presents formally the equations of the model outlined in section 3.3 and provides further explanation of the assumptions embodied in the model.

Assets Available to Households

Households allocate their wealth among five types of assets—fully taxed claims, partially taxed claims (corporate equity), noncorporate equity capital, tax-exempt bonds, and equity in consumer durables. For the purposes of the model, households regard all assets within each asset type as equivalent.

The five assets available to households are characterized as follows:

Fully Taxed Claims

Fully taxed claims include corporate bonds, loans for home mortgages and other purchases of consumer durables, loans to unincorporated enterprises, and federal government bonds. All of these assets have the same before-tax yield and are therefore indistinguishable to the households who own them, although they are issued by different borrowers to finance different types of investments.

The after-tax return on fully taxed claims available to household j is:

(A1) $$y_{fj} = i_f(1 - t_j),$$

where i_f is the before-tax return and t_j is the marginal tax rate of household j. The total stock of fully taxed claims is equal to F.

Partially Taxed Claims

Partially taxed claims consist of corporate equity. All equity shares are assumed to have the same dividend payout rate and the same expected holding period before realization of capital gains becomes a taxable event. The income from corporate shares is treated as partially taxed at the shareholder level because taxation of the portion of that income that accrues in the form of appreciation in the value of shares is deferred until realization and at that time partially excluded from the tax base.

The after-tax return on corporate equity available to household j is:

(A2) $$y_{pj} = i_p (1 - at_j),$$

where i_p is the return available to shareholders before individual income taxes (but net of any corporate level tax) from corporate equity and a is the fraction of i_p that is effectively included in the tax base. The value of a is taken to be equal to 0.4 in the simulations shown in section 3.4. Note that tax preferences at the corporate level increase the before-tax yield available to all households by the same amount, while the tax savings from preferences at the shareholder level vary with the household's marginal tax rate.

The total stock of partially taxed claims is equal to P.

Noncorporate Equity Capital

Noncorporate capital includes all capital used in partnerships and proprietorships. In the model, one business sector produces all private goods and services, although some enterprises are organized as corporations and others as partnerships and proprietorships. We assume that corporations and noncorporate enterprises hold the same mix of capital and are subject to the same rules for defining taxable business income. However, for corporations taxes are imposed on taxable income of the entity and on dividends and capital gains received by shareholders. In contrast, for noncorporate enterprises taxable business income (net of interest deductions) is attributed directly to households.

Households are assumed to borrow from other households to finance a fixed fraction of equity in unincorporated enterprises. The ratio of debt to total wealth invested is f_3. The after-tax return, per dollar of *equity*, in unincorporated enterprises available to household j is:

(A3) $y_{bj} = [1/(1 - f_3)]$
$$[(1 - zt_j)i_b - f_3 i_f (1 - t_j)].$$

In equation (A3), f_3 is the share of *all* assets in unincorporated enterprises financed by debt, z is the percentage of business income subject to tax, and i_b is the before-tax rate of return, per dollar of capital invested in unincorporated enterprises. The expression $(1 - zt_j)i_b$ represents the gross after-tax income per dollar invested in unincorporated enterprises; net of tax interest costs equal to $f_3 i_f (1 - t_j)$ are subtracted to obtain after-tax income net of interest costs. The term $1/(1 - f_3)$ converts yield per dollar of total capital to yield per dollar of equity.

The term z summarizes the effects of all business sector tax preferences, including tax depreciation at rates faster than economic depreciation and the investment tax credit. Conceptually, z should vary with both the discount rate (which determines how an acceleration of deductions translates into the equivalent of a permanent change in taxable income) and the marginal tax rate (which determines the value of tax credits in terms of tax deductions). Thus, z should vary among individual taxpayers and should also vary with other changes in tax policy that affect equilibrium market interest rates. However, for simulating the model we collapsed all of these provisions into one parameter representing the average percentage of business income included in the tax base. The value of z used in the model is equal to 0.4. In contrast, if there were no investment credit and if tax depreciation matched economic depreciation in a world with no inflation, the value of z would be equal to 1.0.

In this model, z serves two important functions. It both approximates the degree of tax preference directly available to households from ownership of assets in unincorporated enterprises and also measures the effective tax rate at the corporate level.

As noted, the model has only one business sector. Since corporations and unincorporated enterprises compete with each other in the same markets, the rental price of capital services must be the same for both types of enterprises.

If activities in corporate and noncorporate forms were equally efficient, unincorporated businesses would displace most corporate activity because their tax advantages would enable them to provide a higher after-tax return to most households who supply equity financing. The tax advantages to noncorporate enterprises relative to corporations result because the former are not subject to a separate tax at the enterprise level.[13]

To account for the existence of a large corporate sector in the model, despite the tax advantages of partnerships and proprietorships, we assume noncorporate activity is, in some sense, inherently less efficient than corporate activity.[14] In other words, if r_c is the total return to corporate capital (on both debt and equity), then hr_c ($h < 1$) is the return to noncorporate enterprises. Recall that this return is represented in equation (A3) as i_b. Although less efficient, unincorporated enterprises can compete successfully with corporations because of preferential tax treatment.

The total amount of equity in noncorporate enterprises is denoted as B. The total stock of capital employed in noncorporate enterprises is B^*, where $B^* = B/(1 - f_3)$.

Tax-Exempt Bonds

Tax-exempt bonds are issued directly by state and local governments to finance all capital stocks held by those governments and also on behalf of corporations to finance a portion of the private capital stock. Tax-exempt bonds used to finance corporate sector investments, generally referred to as industrial development bonds, are indistinguishable to households from traditional tax-exempt bonds.

The after-tax yield available to all households on tax-exempt bonds is:

(A4) $y_e = i_e$,

where i_e is the before-tax return on tax-exempt bonds.

Equity in Consumer Durables

Consumer durable capital consists of housing, automobiles, furniture, and other durable goods employed directly within the household sector. Households issue to other households a fixed amount of debt per dollar of equity in consumer durables. The after-tax return, per dollar of leveraged equity in consumer durables, is:

(A5) $y_{dj} = [1/(1 - f_4)] [i_{dj}(D_j^*) - f_4 i_f(1 - t_j)]$.

In equation (A5), f_4 is the fraction of *all* consumer durable capital financed by debt, and D_j^* is the total amount of consumer durable capital owned and used by household j. The value of household j's equity in consumer durables is $D_j = (1 - f_4)D_j^*$.

Equation (A5) expresses the fact that households pay no tax on the income from consumer durable capital (i_{dj}) but are allowed to deduct the costs of debt incurred to hold consumer durables. This deduction reduces the cost of borrowing from $f_4 i_f$ to $f_4 i_f(1 - t_j)$.

As discussed in the text, households receive a before-tax return from holding consumer durables in the form of a flow of services rather than monetary income. The marginal value of these services, i_{dj}, is computed from the equation:

(A6) $D_j^* = D_{0j}/i_{dj}$.

Equation (A6) represents the demand for consumer durable services of household j as a downward-sloping function of the net rental cost of household capital (i_{dj}) with a demand elasticity of -1.0. The value D_{0j} is a constant assigned to household j; this value is set in calibrating the model so that each sample household will hold its estimated stock of consumer durables under 1979 law.

Summing over all households, the total value of household equity in consumer durable capital is denoted as D. The total value of consumer durable capital is $D^* = D/(1 - f_4)$.

Household Demand for Assets

Households choose among the five available assets to maximize after-tax income, where income includes the dollar value of services from consumer durables and is net of after-tax interest costs.

The computer algorithm that allocates each household's wealth among the five assets is discussed in the text. Summing over all households, the results of this maximization procedure can be summarized in the equation:

$$(A7) \qquad (F, P, B, E, D) = f(i_f, i_p, i_b, i_e).$$

The before-tax return on consumer durables, i_d, can be solved for any household from the function $i_{dj}(D_j^*)$ described in equation (A6).

As noted, households issue fully taxed securities to finance holdings of equity in noncorporate enterprises and consumer durables. Therefore, the net household demand for fully taxed securities issued by corporations and governments is equal to:

$$(A8) \qquad S = F - f_3 B/(1 - f_3) - f_4 D/(1 - f_4),$$

where S is net demand of the household sector for fully taxed securities.

Supply of Financial Assets by Business Firms and Governments

Private corporations, unincorporated enterprises, state and local governments, and the federal government all supply financial claims to households to finance the private and public physical capital stock and federal government debt.

Private Corporations

Corporate sector capital is financed by taxable debt, tax-exempt debt, and partially taxed claims (corporate equity). The share of each type of claim in the corporate financial structure is taken to be fixed. The net (of depreciation) rental cost of capital, r_c, is equal to:

$$(A9) \qquad r_c = [1/(1 - zu)]$$
$$[f_2 i_f(1 - u) + e_2 i_e(1 - u) + p_2 i_p].$$

In equation (A9), f_2 is the share of corporate capital financed by fully taxable bonds, e_2 is the share of corporate capital financed by tax-exempt bonds, p_2 is the share of corporate capital financed by equity, u is the corporate tax rate (.46), and z is the proportion of corporate income subject to tax. This formulation implies that, while interest is deducted at the statutory corporate rate of 46 percent, the market return need only be enough to cover the "effective" corporate tax rate of zu.[15]

The total demand for capital services in the business sector (corporate and noncorporate) is taken to be a downward function of the net cost of capital services, with a demand elasticity of -1.0. This can be expressed as:

(A10) $\qquad K = K_0/r_c,$

where K is the demand for capital in private business activity.

The total amount of physical capital in the business sector can, in turn, be expressed as the sum of the capital employed within corporations, C, and the capital employed in noncorporate enterprises, hB^*. Thus, for any amount of household holdings of noncorporate equity, the supply of each financial asset by corporations can be computed by multiplying the fixed financial ratios for corporate capital by $(K - hB^*)$, the total capital employed in the corporate sector. Equations (A11a)–(A11c) summarize these relationships:

(A11a) $\qquad E^c = e_2 \left[K(i_f, i_p, i_e) - hB^*(i_b) \right],$

(A11b) $\qquad P^c = p_2 \left[K(i_f, i_p, i_e) - hB^*(i_b) \right],$

(A11c) $\qquad F^c = f_2 \left[K(i_f, i_p, i_e) - hB^*(i_b) \right].$

In equations (A11a)–(A11c), E^c, P^c, and F^c represent the volume of tax-exempt, partially taxed, and fully taxed assets supplied by corporations to households.

Noncorporate Enterprises

From equations (A11a)–(A11c) it can be seen that the supply of claims by corporations depends on the demand for physical capital in the corporate sector and the rate of return available to households on noncorporate equity capital, i_b. This supply price relationship can be expressed as:

(A12) $\qquad i_b = hr_c,$

where h, as noted above, represents the ratio of the productivity of capital in the noncorporate and corporate sectors, and r_c is the net of depreciation cost of capital services supplied by corporations.

State and Local Governments

For state and local governments, no taxation occurs at the enterprise level. All capital is assumed to be financed by tax-exempt bonds. The net rental cost of capital is equal to i_e. The demand for capital services by state and local governments can be expressed as:

(A13) $L = L_0/i_e$,

where L_0 is a constant. Equation (A13) expresses the demand for the services of state and local capital as a downward-sloping, unit elastic function of the net cost of capital to state and local governments.

Finally, the supply of tax-exempt bonds by state and local governments can be expressed as:

(A14) $E^L = L(i_e)$.

Federal Government

The federal government issues fully taxable claims to finance a government debt set equal to G. Therefore, we can express the supply of claims by the federal government as:

(A15) $F^G = G$,

where G is taken to be exogenous.

The equations for the demand for capital services by households (D^*), business firms (K), and state and local governments (L) are all expressed as unit elastic functions of the net cost of capital. These demand functions may be viewed as a convenient way of summarizing production function relationships for each use of capital (the elasticity of substitution of labor for capital), relative factor shares in output, and the price elasticity of demand for final output (see Allen 1964, pp. 369–74). We do not deal with these production and demand-for-final-output relationships explicitly in this stage of the model's development.

Equilibration of Supply and Demand

The entire model can be solved for a set of yields on financial assets, i_f, i_p, and i_e at which household demands for and firm and government supplies of all assets are equilibrated.

The model can be summarized by a system of eight equations in eight unknowns: i_f, i_p, i_e, i_b, S, P, E, and B. From equations (A7) and (A8), we can characterize net household demands for the four assets as a system of four equations implicitly solved by the computer algorithm developed for maximizing after-tax income of households:

(A16) $S^d = S^d (i_f, i_p, i_b, i_e)$,

(A17) $P^d = P^d (i_f, i_p, i_b, i_e)$,

(A18) $B^d = B^d (i_f, i_p, i_b, i_e)$,

(A19) $E^d = E^d (i_f, i_p, i_b, i_e)$.

On the other side of the market, the supply of each asset can be expressed as the sum of the amount of the asset issued by each capital-using sector. As described above, the total supply of each asset depends on the shares of business sector capital accounted for by corporate and noncorporate enterprises. This division of the business capital stock is solved for by an equation which expresses the supply price of equity in unincorporated enterprises as a function of the rates of return on financial claims.

The four supply equations can thus be expressed as:

(A20) $S^s = F^C + F^G = f_2 [K(i_f, i_p, i_e) - hB^* (i_b)] + G,$

(A21) $P^s = P^C = p_2 [K(i_f, i_p, i_e) - hB^* (i_b)],$

(A22) $E^s = E^C + E^L$

$\quad\quad = e_2 [K(i_f, i_p, i_e) - hB^* (i_b)] + L(i_e),$

(A23) $i_b = hr_c(i_f, i_p, i_e).$

Equations (A16)–(A23) are solved by a process of iteration in which initial trial values of i_f, i_p, and i_e are altered to equilibrate all demands and supplies.

The equilibrium solutions can then be used to compute equilibrium values of total household holdings of each asset, the capital stocks financed by those assets, and the cost of capital to different sectors, given the fixed financing coefficients ($e_2, f_2, p_2, f_3,$ and f_4) for corporate sector capital, capital in unincorporated enterprises, and consumer durables, and the formula for computing the cost of capital to the corporate sector (eq. [A9]).

Appendix B *Estimation of Household Wealth*

The estimation of household wealth distributions for use with the simulation model presented in appendix A entailed three separate operations: (1) the selection of a sample of households to represent the entire tax-filing population;[16] (2) the calculation of the total amount of wealth to be allocated to these households; and (3) the development of allocation procedures to distribute these wealth totals to the selected households. This appendix discusses each of these steps in turn.

The tax-filing population is represented by 101 tax returns categorized as a matrix of ten labor income classes and ten capital income classes, and one extra return from the highest labor and capital income classes. The income classes were selected from the 1979 Treasury individual tax model. Each labor income class represents approximately 10 percent of wage income; each capital income class represents approximately 10 percent of capital income, other than income from consumer durables and pension funds. The lowest capital income class, however, has no capital income (other than imputed rent from consumer durables and the return on pension funds) and accounts for about 40 percent of all households. To compensate for this, the other nine capital income classes account for about 11 percent of capital income each, again excluding the return to durables and pension funds. In addition, the two lowest labor income classes together account for 10 percent of wage income, and the other eight classes each account for slightly more than 10 percent of wages. The 100th cell of the ten-by-ten matrix, in the highest labor and capital income classes, has been subdivided into two cells of equal size to capture a part of the extreme variation in wages and wealth among the highest income households.

Each sample tax return is assigned the mean labor income and capital income for all tax returns represented by its labor and capital income cell. The sample returns are then weighted by the number of returns in each cell to represent the total tax-filing population.

The second operation, the calculation of wealth totals, begins with national balance sheet data developed by the Board of Governors of the Federal Reserve System (1981). These national balance sheets have then been adjusted to make the data internally consistent and to implement our basic framework of having the household sector finance all physical capital and the debt issues of the federal government.

To assure internal consistency, it was necessary to resolve the discrepancy in the Federal Reserve Board data between two measures of net worth of the corporate sector: (1) corporate net worth as measured by the difference between corporate physical assets valued at replacement cost and financial liabilities net of financial assets, and (2) corporate net worth as measured by the market value of equities. The difference between these two measures of net worth is substantial—over $1 trillion in 1979 values. A resolution is needed to assure that households, through their holdings of corporate debt and equity, exactly finance the physical capital stock used by corporations. Following the wisdom of Solomon, we split the difference—that is, we increased the market value of equities by about one-half trillion dollars and reduced the value of the physical capital stock used by corporations by the other half trillion dollars.

The percentage decrease in the value of reproducible physical assets held by corporations was then applied to the value of the corresponding physical assets used by other sectors, again as taken from the national balance sheets, in order not to change the relative size of the capital stock in each sector. To match the financing with the physical capital, nondebt financing was correspondingly adjusted in each case. In this way, physical capital stocks for each sector, along with the claims issued to finance this capital, were derived.

Also, in developing the data, we explicitly account for special tax provisions that encourage certain financial intermediaries—commercial banks and fire and casualty insurance companies—to hold tax-exempt bonds in their portfolios. As a result, the volume of tax-exempt bonds issued by state and local governments and corporations in 1979 (about $300 billion) does not match the volume held by households (about $75 billion). To preserve this difference between tax-exempt bonds held by households and those issued by state and local governments and corporations, we have assumed, as noted in the text, that about $225 billion of bonds considered to be tax-exempt to their issuers are considered to be taxable in the hands of households.

Furthermore, since the household sector in the Federal Reserve Board data includes balance sheet information for nonprofit institutions as well, physical capital held by nonprofits, and a corresponding volume of debt, was subtracted from the balance sheet totals to derive financial statements appropriate to the household sector alone. The results are presented in table 3.1.

The third step in developing the wealth distributions is the allocation of these wealth totals among the 101 sample tax returns. For this purpose we used information on each sample tax return to allocate each type of asset individually. Corporate equities were allocated in proportion to dividends reported on tax returns; taxable bonds, in proportion to interest income; equity in noncorporate enterprise, by business income (adjusted for losses); consumer durables, in proportion to mortgage and other nonbusiness interest expense (imputed to the file by the Treasury Department for tax returns not itemizing deductions); and pension wealth, according to a rough estimate of each household's total wage earnings over its previous work history. Because no tax return information exists on earnings from tax-exempt assets, such assets were assigned only to tax returns in the highest wealth classes.

Wealth has been allocated on an asset-by-asset basis primarily to derive as accurate a distribution of total wealth as possible. With the exception of consumer durables and pension wealth, use of the simulation model (see appendix A) requires a figure for only the size of each household's portfolio and not its composition. Given its total portfolio (other than pensions and consumer durables), each household chooses an asset mix that maximizes its after-tax return. A separate estimate is required for pension wealth since its return is tax-exempt, and households, accordingly, always invest pensions in the highest yielding asset before taxes. Consumer durables are also a special case in that the return to durables is not a market yield but an in-kind flow of services. The value of these services for any level of consumer durable holdings is determined by a demand schedule, unique to each household, for the services of consumer durables. Values are selected for the scale parameters in these demand schedules to replicate each household's assigned consumer durable holdings. In our simulations, households then reevaluate their optimal consumer durable holdings in response to changes in the tax structure.

While the distributions of wage income and wealth are as accurate as we could make them short of embarking on a major data gathering effort, these distributions, nonetheless, remain only approximations, in part because data on tax returns are not perfect allocators of total taxpayer wealth. Pension wealth and equity in noncorporate business, in particular, could be subject to substantial misestimation. However, for the purpose of this current paper, which is largely expository, we believe that our allocation methods provide usable approximations of wealth ownership. Tables 3.3 and 3.4 show these distributions.

Notes

1. See, for example, Prest (1955).
2. Pechman and Okner (1974). This study was updated by Okner (1980). In this later study, Okner used the same methodology and found essentially the same results for 1970 as for 1966.
3. Alternative assumptions regarding the incidence of the corporate tax are also examined by P-O, such as forward shifting to consumers and backward shifting to labor. In each case, the before-tax incomes of those ultimately bearing the tax are adjusted accordingly.
4. In fact, in the simulations shown in section 3.4, we assume that the traditional method correctly allocates the corporate tax burden in proportion to household wealth rather than realized capital income.
5. This before-tax income is not necessarily the same as income reported for tax purposes since items not subject to tax, such as state and local bond interest and net rent on owner-occupied homes, are imputed by P-O to individual households.
6. Some of these other provisions are discussed in Galper and Zimmerman (1977).
7. The most comprehensive general equilibrium model of the tax system, itself an elaboration of the pathbreaking work of Harberger (1962), has been developed by John Shoven and his colleagues. See, for example, Fullerton, Shoven, and Whalley (1983) and Goulder, Shoven, and Whalley (1983). Also see Hendershott and Hu (1980; 1981). For a more general discussion of the economic effects of the structure of capital income taxation, see Steuerle (1982) and Bradford (1980). Bradford emphasizes that our current structure, as a "halfway" house between an income tax and a consumption tax, affords numerous opportunities for manipulation by taxpayers, yielding gains to them but little, or even negative, social product.
8. The model developed by Hendershott and Shilling draws heavily on Slemrod's work. Furthermore, just as the general equilibrium model of Shoven et al. can be considered an extension of Harberger, Slemrod's work is an extension of an earlier paper written jointly with Feldstein (Feldstein and Slemrod 1980) that modified the basic Harberger approach. The Feldstein-Slemrod paper suggests that an understanding of the effects of the corporate income tax also requires an analysis of household portfolio behavior since, for some higher bracket taxpayers, the corporate tax may not be an additional tax but rather a way of avoiding even higher individual taxes. This can occur because, for corporations that retain earnings rather than distribute dividends, the combination of the corporate tax plus capital gains taxes ultimately paid by households on income retained by the corporation may be less

than individual taxes paid on dividends received. Gravelle and Zimmerman (1984) also have developed a model in which both tax and risk considerations affect household portfolio decisions.

9. See, for example, *Economic Report of the President* (1982), p. 124, and Jorgenson and Sullivan (1981).

10. Of course, there may be some systematic causal relationships between the degree of preferential taxation by industry and the use of debt and equity financing. Such relationships are lost by our simplification.

11. The simulated finding of a greatly reduced corporate tax in a risk-free world is consistent with the recent work of Roger Gordon and Burton Malkiel, who analyze the corporate tax as essentially a tax on risk taking (Gordon 1981; Gordon and Malkiel 1981). In particular, Gordon is critical of models of capital allocation that ignore risk and uncertainty while at the same time assuming that corporate returns to capital (and tax collections) would be unchanged in a risk-free world. One implication of Gordon's position is that corporate taxes in a risk-free world would indeed be quite small.

12. For a similar analysis applied to household holdings of automobiles and other conventional consumer durables, see Katz and Peskin (1980).

13. However, the combination of the corporation tax and capital gains treatment of retained earnings could impose lower total taxes on high-bracket households (under 1979 law) than would direct allocation of all business taxable income to the household with no corporation income tax. See Feldstein and Slemrod (1980).

14. This assumption represents a compromise between (1) the view that pre-tax returns must be the same for both corporate and noncorporate activity because they both exist in the same market, and (2) the alternative view that corporate and noncorporate enterprises are essentially supplying different goods and services, and therefore before-tax returns need not be equalized. This latter view is consistent with the approach of Harberger (1962) to corporate income taxation. The need to modify the strict Harberger view has been suggested by Feldstein and Slemrod (1980) and Gravelle and Zimmerman (1984). Our approach equilibrates returns on corporate and noncorporate capital in a world with only one private sector output. The "efficiency differential" allows the marginal product of capital to be higher for corporate investments than for noncorporate investments, while at the same time after-tax returns at the margin for owners of equity claims in corporations and noncorporate enterprises are equalized. The differential could arise from limited liability, economics of large-scale capital accumulation, or other advantages of the corporate form. Further work will expand the model to allow for more than one business sector with corporations specializing in some activities, unincorporated business firms in others, and still more sectors containing both types of enterprises.

15. Our characterization of the net cost of capital is a simplified version of the approach developed by Hall and Jorgenson (1967).

16. Nonfilers were thus not considered explicitly, thereby introducing some degree of error into the estimates but probably of small magnitude, since total household wealth was not affected by this procedure but only its distribution.

References

Aaron, Henry J. 1972. *Shelter and subsidies.* Washington, D.C.: Brookings Institution.

Allen, R. G. D. 1964. *Mathematical analysis for economics.* New York: St. Martin's Press.

Bailey, Martin J. 1974. Progressivity and investment yields under U.S. income taxation. *Journal of Political Economy* 82:1157–75.

Board of Governors of the Federal Reserve System. 1981. *Balance Sheets for the U.S. Economy 1945–80.* Washington, D.C.

Bradford, David. 1980. The economics of tax policy toward savings. In *The government and capital formation*, ed. George M. Von Furstenberg. Cambridge, Mass.: Ballinger.

Cordes, Joseph J., and Steven M. Sheffrin. 1981. Taxation and the Sectoral Allocation of Capital in the United States. *National Tax Journal* 34:419–32.

De Leeuw, Frank, and Larry Ozanne. 1981. Housing. In *How taxes affect economic behavior*, ed. Henry J. Aaron and Joseph A. Pechman. Washington, D.C.: Brookings Institution.

Economic Report of the President. 1982. Washington, D.C.: GPO.

Feldstein, Martin. 1976. Personal taxation and portfolio composition: An econometric analysis. *Econometrica* 44:631–50.

Feldstein, Martin S., and Joel Slemrod. 1980. Personal taxation, portfolio choice, and the effect of the corporation income tax. *Journal of Political Economy* 88:854–66.

Fullerton, Don, John B. Shoven, and John Whalley. 1983. Replacing the U.S. income tax with a progressive consumption tax: A sequenced general equilibrium approach. Journal of Public Economics. 20:3–23.

Galper, Harvey, and Eric Toder. 1981. Modelling revenue and allocation effects of the use of tax-exempt bonds for private purposes. In *Efficiency in the municipal bond market: The use of tax-exempt financing for "private" purposes*, ed. George G. Kaufman. Greenwich, Conn.: JAI Press.

Galper, Harvey, and Dennis Zimmerman. 1977. Preferential taxation and portfolio choice: Some empirical evidence. *National Tax Journal* 30:387–97.

Gordon, Roger H. 1981. Uncertainty and the analysis of corporate tax distortions. Proceedings of the 1981 Annual Conference of the National Tax Association, Chicago, Illinois.

Gordon, Roger H., and Burton G. Malkiel. 1981. Corporation finance. In *How taxes affect economic behavior*, ed. Henry J. Aaron and Joseph A. Pechman. Washington, D.C.: Brookings Institution.

Goulder, Lawrence, John B. Shoven, and John Whalley. 1983. Domestic tax policy and the foreign sector: The importance of alternative foreign sector formulations to results from a general equilibrium tax analysis model. In *Behavioral Simulation Methods for Tax Policy Analysis*, ed. Martin Feldstein. Chicago: University of Chicago Press.

Gravelle, Jane G., and Dennis Zimmerman. 1984. Tax progressivity and the design of tax incentives for investment. *Public Finance Quarterly* (forthcoming).

Hall, Robert E., and Dale W. Jorgenson. 1967. Tax policy and investment behavior. *American Economic Review* 57:391–414.

Harberger, Arnold C. 1962. The incidence of the corporation income tax. *Journal of Political Economy* 70:215–40.

Hendershott, Patric H. 1981. Mortgage revenue bonds: Tax-exemption with a vengeance. In Kaufman, George G., ed., *Efficiency in the municipal bond market: The use of tax-exempt financing for "private" purposes*, ed. George G. Kaufman. Greenwich, Conn.: JAI Press.

Hendershott, Patric H., and Sheng-Cheng Hu. 1980. Government induced biases in the allocation of the stock of fixed capital in the United States. In *Capital, efficiency, and growth*, ed. George M. Von Furstenberg. Cambridge, Mass.: Ballinger.

———. 1981. Inflation and extraordinary returns on owner-occupied housing. Some implications for capital allocation and productivity growth. *Journal of Macroeconomics* 3:177–203.

Hendershott, Patric H., and James D. Shilling. 1982. Capital allocation and the economic recovery tax act of 1981. *Public Finance Quarterly* 10:242–73.

Jorgenson, Dale W., and Martin A. Sullivan. 1981. Inflation and corporate capital recovery. In *Depreciation, inflation, and the taxation of income from capital*, ed. Charles E. Hulten. Washington, D.C.: Urban Institute.

Katz, Arnold J., and Janice Peskin. 1980. The value of services provided by the stock of consumer durables, 1947–77: An opportunity cost measure. *Survey of Current Business* 60, no. 7: 22–31.

Okner, Benjamin. 1980. Total U.S. taxes and their effect on the distribution of family income in 1966 and 1970. In *The economics of taxation*, ed. Henry J. Aaron and Michael J. Boskin. Washington, D.C.: Brookings Institution.

Ott, David, and Allan H. Meltzer. 1963. *Federal tax treatment of state and local securities*. Washington, D.C.: Brookings Institution.

Pechman, Joseph A., and Benjamin Okner. 1974. *Who bears the tax burden?* Washington, D.C.: Brookings Institution.

Prest, A. P. 1955. Statistical calculations of tax burden. *Economica* 22:234–45.

Slemrod, Joel. 1983. A general equilibrium model of taxation with endogenous financial behavior. In *Behavioral Simulation Methods for Tax Policy Analysis*, ed. Martin Feldstein. Chicago: University of Chicago Press.

Steuerle, Eugene. 1982. Is income from capital subject to individual income taxation? *Public Finance Quarterly* 10:283–303.

United States Treasury Department. 1977. *Blueprints for basic tax reform*. Washington, D.C.: GPO.

Comment   Benjamin A. Okner

The Galper-Toder (G-T) paper is obviously an extremely ambitious undertaking. However, much work is still needed to improve and refine it. To their credit, the authors note several deficiencies and improvements that they feel are needed at several places within the paper.

In the model, the lack of any existence of risk is especially serious. Other changes they did not emphasize but that I believe would be fruitful include: splitting noncorporate business into a farm and nonfarm sector; separating proprietorships and partnerships; and developing a somewhat different approach to the demand for durable goods. I find it extremely unreal to think of grouping the things that influence the demand for automobiles or owner-occupied houses with the factors influencing the demand for toasters, vacuum cleaners, and hair dryers.

When they started to implement their model, the researchers obviously discovered that the data they needed do not exist. Lacking real data, G-T obviously did what other researchers have been doing for many years: they allocated aggregates among their population in accord with some proxy. This may have introduced two errors into their data base. The Federal Reserve Board aggregates for the household sector, in addition to being a not-too-reliable residual, also include data for schools, hospitals, and nonprofit institutions. Some adjustment should have been made to derive a number suitable for the universe of "people households." The other potential problem has to do with whether all of the aggregate asset values were distributed among the tax-filing population represented in the individual income tax file. For 1979, the CPS reports a total of 84.0 million families and unrelated individuals. The statistics in the paper indicate that there were 92.7 tax-filing units. While they may have adjusted for an alignment problem between the two data sets, the authors do not comment on this in the paper.

The exclusion of nonfilers may have had a deleterious effect on the G-T results. A large proportion of nonfilers are in the 65-and-over age groups and hold substantial amounts of assets. While I do not think that the omission of nontaxable nonfilers would influence any changes in the distribution of implicit and explicit transfers and taxes, they should have an effect on the initial yields of various types of assets. This again is an area worth looking into.

The lack of production functions and especially labor-supply functions is an extremely serious omission from the model. Without these, it is impossible to say anything serious about the incidence of any tax or

Benjamin A. Okner is an economist with the Office of the Secretary, Department of the Treasury, Washington, D.C.
The views expressed in this comment are those of the author only.

transfer changes. Since they did not have labor supply functions, the authors were forced into some very weak statements about "specific incidence" when, I believe, they should have been discussing "differential incidence."

In a differential incidence analysis, the 1979 distribution of income would probably appear much more progressive than the one that would be inferred from the paper. This occurs because the government would have to lower the tax on income from labor to "get rid of" the $45 billion raised by the explicit tax on income from capital (see table 3.7). And while wealth is concentrated among the rich, labor income accrues mainly to those at lower income levels. Of course, this need not occur if the government instead uses the money to increase spending on items that benefit only the rich. The "increased progression" results from the combination of a specific incidence analysis and a no-capital-income-tax economy used as the comparison case in the paper. In the future, I would strongly urge the authors to alter their model to include labor supply functions and to employ differential incidence and a comparison base that is either current tax law or some other tax structure that is more realistic than a no-tax world.

The counterfactual adopted (the no-tax-on-capital-income world) for the analysis not only contributes greatly to some extremely confusing wording, but is *unknown* and *unknowable*. Not only would the amount and allocation of capital be totally different if such a world existed, but it seems very likely that the same would be true of the amount and allocation of labor. It also seems likely that we would have different institutional arrangements (including forms of enterprise), laws, regulations (or lack thereof), and so forth. I do not know what my preferred comparison situation would be for this analysis (perhaps a graduated, two-step, equal-yield tax), but I feel confident that it would not be a *no-tax* world.

Careful reading leads me to question whether I would label the empirical work that was undertaken a "microsimulation." While the full tax file was used to derive average amounts and types of income for each of the 101 cells in the household sector, the calculations involved working with average or representative tax returns. For some analyses, the concept of an "average tax return" makes sense. For this one, I have grave doubts about the procedure. If there is such an entity as the "typical millionaire," I've never come across it. The people we are most interested in for wealth analysis are characterized by diversity and variation, yet that was all lost in creating 101 *average households*. A stratified sample of 10,000–20,000 returns in the household sector would have been far preferable and would not have used an enormous amount of computer space or time.

Finally, I think that it is appropriate to ask what was learned from the analysis. The major findings of the paper are that lower-wealth households received significant implicit transfers from the very rich and that when implicit taxes were added to their explicit tax burdens the richest of the rich were actually taxed more heavily than was generally thought. (Both conclusions, of course, depend on the model and the assumptions on which the model was formulated.)

This, of course, fails to convey the full richness of the results that can be derived from the G-T model. Yet a little thought makes it obvious that any progressive tax is going to yield a less-unequal after-tax distribution of income from wealth than will be the case in a no-tax world. And given a fixed total supply of wealth, a less-unequal wealth distribution must imply that there must be transfers occurring from the very rich to the less rich. It is not as obvious that one could deduce the magnitude of the additional implicit taxes imposed on the really, really rich. In an equal yield, differential analysis, such a tax increase would obviously be required, but that is not the case here. One would have to study the relationship between yields on tax-exempt and taxable bonds and recognize why tax-exempt bonds are attractive investments only for those in very high tax brackets to deduce this latter conclusion.

At this time, I find it impossible to give an overall evaluation of the Galper-Toder paper. Because so many important segments either need to be amplified or added to the model, any judgment at this point would be akin to asking an art critic to give his opinion of a canvas where the artist had run out of several colors of paint and where he also planned to enlarge the size of the total picture before he exhibited it.

The analysis represents a good start on what could turn out to be a very important tax policy tool in future years. The trick to success in building models of this kind seems to involve simultaneously formulating segments that are realistic (in the sense of having a recognizable counterpart in how people behave in the real world) and keeping the model simple enough to be comprehensible to other researchers (and policymakers).

Galper and Toder seem to have made a good start. I look forward to seeing their future work in this area.

4   Approaches to Measuring and Valuing In-Kind Subsidies and the Distribution of Their Benefits

Timothy M. Smeeding

4.1 Introduction

In recent years much attention has been focused on public in-kind subsidies for food, education, medical care, and housing. While the majority of past efforts have dealt with in-kind transfers, recent attention has been drawn to other types of public subsidies for similar commodities (e.g., tax expenditures for employer-provided medical care and for home mortgage interest deductions). Often the value of these non-means-tested in-kind subsidies dwarf the more readily available and noticeable value of means-tested in-kind transfers. For instance, the market value of means-tested in-kind transfers for rented public housing in 1980 was $5.0 billion as compared to $20.8 billion in tax deductions for mortgage interest and property taxes, and foregone revenues from tax-exempt bonds to finance mortgages (Smeeding 1982, table A-1).

In response to criticisms of the increasingly limited value of money income statistics, the U.S. Bureau of the Census began in 1980 to collect data on recipiency of several types of in-kind subsidies: major in-kind transfer benefits and employer-provided, tax-subsidized health and pen-

Timothy M. Smeeding is professor of economics and director of the Division of Social Science Research, Center for Public Affairs, University of Utah at Salt Lake City.

This research was supported in part by the American Statistical Association Research Fellowship Program at the U.S. Bureau of the Census, where the author was a research fellow when the paper was written. However, this paper should in no way be interpreted as the position of the Census Bureau. The technical assistance of Daniel Burkhead and John Coder of the Census Bureau, Joseph Minarik of the Congressional Budget Office, and Susan Abu-Zahra is gratefully appreciated. The author has benefited from conversations with Irwin Garfinkel, Paul Ginsburg, Robert Lampman, Marilyn Moon, and Eugene Smolensky, and from seminars given at the Congressional Budget Office and the 43d Session of the International Statistical Institute. The author retains full responsibility for all errors and omissions.

sion benefits (U.S. Bureau of the Census 1981). Further, the 1978 and 1979 Income Survey Development Program (ISDP) research panels for the planned Survey of Income and Program Participation (SIPP) extended these efforts to cover government-subsidized mortgages, tax-free employer-provided subsidies, and income tax information (see Manser 1981; 1982). However, while surveys can fairly easily assess noncash benefit recipiency, subject to sampling and nonsampling error, the measurement and valuation of these benefits are much more problematic. Researchers in this area should be quick to discover that no one measure of the value of in-kind benefits is adequate for all uses of such data. Rather, depending on the purposes to which the data will be put, different approaches to measuring and valuing in-kind subsidies will be appropriate.

This paper proposes a set of conceptual approaches for measuring and valuing in-kind subsidies for budgetary purposes and for distributing their benefits to recipients and nonrecipients. Section 4.2 presents a set of alternative measures of the value of public in-kind subsidies which, for purposes of this paper, are defined below. Although this analysis could be extended to include nonpublic in-kind subsidies (e.g., employer-provided meals, housing, and free transportation; or private charitable provision of food and shelter), we will concentrate only on public sector in-kind subsidies. Section 4.3 illustrates the use of these various approaches by providing alternative estimates of the efficiency of government-provided subsidies and estimates of the size distribution of in-kind benefits for a selected set of medical care and housing subsidies in 1979. Section 4.4 summarizes the results of the paper and the implications of these measures for social accounting for public in-kind subsidies.

This paper will consider both direct and indirect public in-kind subsidies. Direct public in-kind subsidies, or in-kind transfers, are defined as publicly provided benefits in the form of goods and services of a private good nature which are received without fully reciprocal quid pro quo provision of goods or services by the recipient. These direct subsidies include traditional types of means-tested in-kind transfers, such as Medicaid or public housing, and also direct subsidies such as FHA, FHMA, and VA mortgage interest subsidies for home ownership. Indirect in-kind subsidies take the form of tax expenditures that reduce the market price of specific private goods or services by exclusion from tax, by deduction from the tax base, or by tax credit. While these subsidies do not directly enter government budgetary accounts as expenditures, they can generally be thought of as alternatives to direct subsidy programs of equal dollar cost, despite practical differences that may lead Congress to choose indirect subsidies over direct subsidies, or vice versa (Congressional Budget Office 1981). For purposes of this paper, the important point is the realization that a certain amount of foregone tax revenue has the same effect on government budgets as an equal-cost direct expenditure. In accounting for the budgetary cost and distributional effects of public in-kind subsidies both direct and indirect subsidies need to be explicitly recognized.

4.2 Conceptual Approaches to Measuring and Valuing In-Kind Subsidies

Researchers and policymakers need to realize that no single measure of the value of in-kind subsidies is adequate for all uses. Strategies for valuing in-kind benefits depend on how the data will be used. Unfortunately many research studies have not established the conceptual basis for their approach to measuring and valuing in-kind benefits, despite the fact that use of inappropriate measures of value may lead to incorrect conclusions concerning their efficiency cost or distributional effect, and thus to incorrect policy decisions.

Before examining each valuation technique in detail, it is useful to understand the major conceptual differences between them and their general relationship to one another. Market value is the private market cost of the goods and services transferred to the recipient net of any required recipient payment. Government cost is the total delivery cost of these goods, which may be provided by government at, below, or above their private market value. If government cost falls below market value, efficiency benefits accrue from government production of the good or service being transferred. On the other hand, if government cost exceeds market value the efficiency costs are borne by the taxpayer. These differences are important in determining whether the government should actually produce a given good, or whether they should merely provide the good by means of subsidizing private market consumption. The social benefit value to recipients and taxpayers must be at least as large as the government cost if the provision of a given benefit is to be efficient in an economic sense.[1]

While market value, government cost, and social benefit value are essentially valuation concepts related to economic efficiency, other measures of value are preferred for assessing the distributional impact of in-kind subsidies. For instance, recipient or cash equivalent value is the cash amount for which recipients would be willing to trade their right to the in-kind subsidy given their current incomes (including cash and other in-kind subsidies). In general, the cash equivalent value is no more than the market value of the in-kind benefit and is the proper concept for measuring the distributional impact of in-kind subsidies on beneficiaries incomes and well-being.

For distributional purposes, the aggregate difference between the social benefit value of an in-kind subsidy and the cost of a cash transfer program, with total recipient benefits equal to the cash equivalent value of the in-kind subsidy, serves as an upper-bound measure of nonrecipient benefits. Because we cannot estimate social benefit value, these nonrecipient benefits are approximated by the extra government cost involved in providing in-kind transfers instead of lesser amounts of cash transfer which would have the same welfare value to recipients. Several potential types of nonrecipient benefits will be mentioned, and their aggregate value will be distributed among taxpayers. A framework similar in part to this one has been previously suggested for public housing programs (DeSalvo 1971), though no actual estimates of value were presented and nonhousing programs were not considered. The remainder of this section discusses these different concepts of value with reference to housing and medical care subsidies.

4.2.1 Market Value

The market value of an in-kind transfer is equal to the private market cost or the purchasing power of benefits received by the individual. In-kind transfers present beneficiaries with control over some amount of economic resources that usually can be bought and thus have been explicitly valued in the private market. Because market value is intuitively appealing to economists and relatively easy to estimate in many cases, it is the measure most often used in studies of the value and distribution of in-kind transfer benefits. In some cases (e.g., food stamps) the market value is directly measurable as the dollar value of food coupons in the market.

In other cases, however, market value must be estimated. For instance, the market value of medical care transfers (e.g., Medicare) as medical insurance can be estimated as the sum of vendor payments net of beneficiary charges (e.g., the Medicare supplemental medical insurance premium), plus private sector claims-processing cost, plus selling costs. In the case of public housing transfers the conceptual measure of market value is easily defined as the difference between the private market rental value of the unit and the rent actually paid by public housing tenants. Estimating market value for public housing becomes problematic because the private market rental value is not known.

The market value of indirect subsidies from exclusion of employer-provided benefits is the income and payroll tax savings (i.e., the dollar value of untaxed income times the appropriate marginal federal income and payroll tax rate). In the area of health care two types of indirect subsidies may be noted: the tax exclusion of employer-paid health insurance premiums, and the tax deductibility of the first $150 of direct health insurance expenses, plus out-of-pocket expenses in excess of 3 percent of adjusted gross income. Indirect tax subsidies for housing primarily benefit home owners in the form of mortgage interest and property tax deductions, deferral of capital gains on home sales, and the exclusion of the first $125,000 of capital gain for qualifying elderly home owners.

When measuring the market value of indirect tax subsidies it may be important to realize that estimates are based on current lost tax revenues and do not account for the behavioral response of taxpayers to changes in the amount or form of the subsidy. For instance, Ginsburg (1981a, p. 8) has predicted that full taxation of employer-provided health insurance might decrease the proportion of medical expenses covered by insurance (and thus we assume health insurance purchases) by 25 percent. As long as the 25 percent decline in health insurance purchases are not deferred to other nontaxable forms of compensation (e.g., pension plan contributions), the estimated market value of the tax subsidy and its budgetary effects will not differ considerably. However in the case of housing subsidies, removal or limitation of mortgage interest tax deductibility may lead to windfall capital losses for home owners and thus may substantially affect capital gains tax revenues. In estimating both the market value and government cost of indirect housing and medical subsidies we do not account for the effects of behavioral response.

The market value concept is sometimes used for program budgeting by administering agencies and, in some cases, by the Congressional Budget Office. In situations where overhead costs can be assumed not to vary with the proposed program adjustment, changes in market value can be an accurate predictor of the net change in government or budgetary cost. However, in cases where government cost and market value vary significantly the government cost measure should be used to estimate the budgetary impacts of program changes. Market value has also been used, though, as we will argue below, incorrectly, in studies of the distributional impact of in-kind programs and their effect on poverty status (Congressional Budget Office 1977; Hoagland 1980; Paglin 1980; Browning 1976).

4.2.2 Government Cost

To measure the net budgetary impact of a proposed change in an in-kind subsidy program, or to compare the economic efficiency of public sector provision vs. public sector production of an in-kind subsidy, a measure of the total government cost of producing (or providing) the given benefit is required. Government cost includes the dollar cost of benefits provided plus all of the associated economic costs of production (or provision) and program management.[2] Government cost is net of recipient contributions to the program, should there be any. Because, as generally calculated, it includes all direct costs of providing a given benefit, government cost is normally the proper measure to determine net changes in budget outlays resulting from a given change in program rules and regulations. For instance, in the case of indirect tax subsidization, the government cost is simply the market value of the subsidy—the foregone tax revenue plus the administrative-processing and enforcement costs associated with the additional tax preference provisions.

Government cost may also be compared to the market value of in-kind subsidies to determine the net efficiency cost or efficiency benefits from the form in which the transfer is provided. For instance, consider the Medicare program wherein government is the producer as well as the provider of health insurance coverage. The government cost is the cost of vendor payments plus claims-processing and enforcement costs. Suppose that, as has been recently suggested, the delivery mechanism for Medicare was changed to an equal outlay voucher system whereby the government provided beneficiaries with a voucher which could be used to purchase private health insurance (Ginsburg 1981b). Unfortunately such a change would not be cost efficient. Private insurance carriers typically have high selling and marketing costs, or load factors, which would be reflected in premiums charged Medicare voucher holders. Because Medicare avoids these selling and marketing costs, and because of comparable claims-processing costs for government and private insurers, fewer benefits in terms of covered medical services could be purchased through the private sector with equal cost vouchers for all beneficiaries, as compared to the current Medicare program. Based on this discussion, the government cost of the Medicare program appears to be below the private market value of the medical care benefits provided by the program. If this is so, efficiency benefits are being realized from the current method of Medicare health insurance provision. Changing to an alternative form of benefit provision, such as a voucher plan, would probably increase government cost to the private market value of benefits being provided.[3]

On the other hand, current public housing programs have been criticized because of their high cost in excess of the market value of housing benefits provided (Rydell, Mulford, and Helbers 1980; Weinberg 1982). Recent analysis of the Experimental Housing Allowance Program (EHAP) whereby tenant beneficiaries received vouchers for a specified portion of their rent indicates far lower cost for equivalent market value housing benefits (Rydell, Mulford, and Helbers 1980). These findings suggest that changing the form of public housing subsidies could substantially reduce the government cost of providing housing benefits by reducing the attendant efficiency costs associated with current program designs.

4.2.3 Social Benefit Value

The social benefit value of a public transfer program must be at least as great as the government cost to justify the program. The social benefit value should include spillover effects (consumption and production externalities) and other efficiency and equity benefits accruing to taxpayers who finance the program, as well as benefits to the program recipient net of recipient charges. Social benefit values will not be presented in this paper because of difficulties in estimating their dollar value. However most social benefit values from in-kind transfers take the form of nonrecipient benefits, which are discussed below.

The market value, government cost, and social benefit value concepts are useful in determining the efficiency of government-provided in-kind subsidies and their budgetary impact. They are less well suited for assessing the distributional effects of in-kind subsidies, where measures of recipient (cash equivalent) value and nonrecipient value are preferable.

4.2.4   Recipient or Cash Equivalent Value

If in-kind subsidies distort consumption patterns, they add less to a recipient's economic well-being than an equal-dollar-cost cash subsidy. If so, they should be discounted to their recipient value to reflect this fact. If consumption patterns are not distorted by the in-kind transfer, the recipient value and market value of the subsidy will be equal.[4] Only in this case is market value an acceptable substitute for recipient value when measuring the distributive effect of recipient benefits from in-kind subsidies. Recipient value reflects the program beneficiary's own valuation of the benefit and can be measured by the amount of cash transfer that would make the recipient just as well-off as the in-kind transfer. The recipient value is also known as the cash equivalent value and is formally termed the "Hicksian equivalent variation" after Sir John Hicks (1943). Most economists agree that cash equivalent value is the proper measure for valuing in-kind transfers to evaluate their impact on economic well-being and the income size distribution because it translates the market value of goods into cash values conceptually equivalent to the money incomes to which they are added (Smeeding and Moon 1980; Smeeding 1982).

In theory, the recipient or cash equivalent value can be estimated by assigning a utility function to subsidy recipients. The cash equivalent value measure is the amount of cash subsidy that would leave the recipient at the same level of well-being or utility as the market value of the in-kind transfer. However, because utility functions cannot be observed and measured with any degree of accuracy, and because of difficulties with current consumption data, a simplified measure of recipient value, which is explained in section 4.3.2, has been developed as a substitute.

While the recipient value of indirect in-kind subsidies are conceptually no different than those for direct subsidies, cash equivalent values for indirect in-kind subsidies have not yet been estimated. A major problem with estimating cash equivalent value for both direct and indirect subsidies is the absence of a relevant counterfactual. For instance, in estimating the cash equivalent value of the tax exclusion for employer-provided health insurance it is necessary to observe individual purchases of health insurance by similar persons in the absence of tax advantages. While it may be possible to infer such values from estimates of the price elasticity of demand for medical insurance, we are not able to observe the health insurance purchases of a group of unsubsidized individuals similar to those who now benefit from the tax advantages of employer-provided health benefits. Thus, while cash equivalent value is conceptually preferable to other measures of in-kind transfer value in assessing the distributional impact of in-kind subsidies, it is not easily or accurately estimated in many cases.

4.2.5 Nonrecipient Benefits

In most cases of in-kind transfer, particularly in the case of medical care benefits, the cash equivalent value of in-kind subsidies is less than both the market value and government cost of the in-kind benefit (Smolensky et al. 1977; Cooper and Katz 1978; Smeeding 1982). Because transfer recipients could therefore be made just as well-off with a lower-cost cash subsidy, nonrecipient taxpayers and policymakers must also receive some of the benefits from in-kind subsidies. In allocating this portion of the benefits from in-kind transfers we would ideally want to distribute the difference between the social benefit value of the in-kind subsidy and the cost of a cash transfer program, with benefits equal to the recipient value of the in-kind program, to nonrecipient beneficiaries. However, because social benefit value is not easily estimated, we assume that total benefits are at least as great as the government cost of in-kind subsidies. We can then derive a lower-bound estimate of nonrecipient benefits by taking the difference between government cost and the lower-cost cash transfer which leaves beneficiaries just as well-off as the in-kind program.[5]

Recent research suggests a number of efficiency and equity benefits that one might want to count in measuring the value of nonrecipient benefits. For instance, in addition to production and consumption externalities, and the paternalism of "donor benefits" (Hochman and Rodgers 1969; Thurow 1974), in-kind subsidies may have additional efficiency advantages over an equal-cost cash transfer program. For instance, Krashinsky (1980) and Nichols and Zeckhauser (1981) argue that the "target efficiency" (Weisbrod 1969) of subsidy programs is greatly improved by imposing restrictions on the choices made by the intended beneficiaries. Murray (1981) has shown that means-tested in-kind transfers lead to a smaller labor supply reduction than an equal-cost cash transfer. In fact, certain types of in-kind transfers, such as work training subsidies or subsidized day care, may actually increase labor supply relative to an equal-cost cash transfer program. In addition, worker training subsidies and child health and nutrition programs, such as the Maternal and Child Health Care Program and the Women, Infants, and

Children Nutrition Program, may have long-term health-related invest-ment benefits to both the individuals and society that would not be realized by an equal-cost cash transfer (Garfinkel and Smeeding 1981).

In addition to these efficiency benefits, in-kind subsidies may have equity benefits (even more difficult to value). For instance, in-kind benefits in the form of subsidized education or health care may enhance equality of opportunity to a greater extent than an equal-cost cash trans-fer. Equity arguments for guaranteed minimum availability of certain merit goods (such as health care) can also be made (Tobin 1970; Mus-grave 1959), as can arguments for social risk sharing (tax subsidies for those experiencing catastrophic medical expenses, or Medicare coverage of renal dialysis).

Having argued for the existence of nonrecipient benefits, we need to decide who the nonrecipient beneficiaries are. In general, we will argue that all taxpayers receive nonrecipient benefits in proportion to federal income tax payments. In this sense nonrecipient benefits can be treated as a public good.[6]

However, a case can be made that specific types of in-kind transfers benefit particular individuals who in the absence of the in-kind transfer would have provided a similar benefit to the in-kind subsidy recipient. For instance, take the case of Medicaid-financed nursing home expendi-tures. Because of attendant program rules and regulations, Medicaid nursing home beneficiaries receive little if any net welfare gain from qualifying for these benefits (Smeeding 1982, pp. 53–56). If it can be argued that most such direct beneficiaries are no better-off in an eco-nomic sense with the transfer than without it, who benefits from these expenses? It can be argued that Medicaid nursing home benefits protect taxpayers against the direct monetary costs and indirect opportunity costs of looking after aged or disabled relatives who need constant care and attention. On the one hand, all taxpayers are protected against this eventuality should it ever arise. Thus an argument for the public good approach can be made. On the other hand, in any given period specific taxpayers (sons, daughters, other relatives) who would have otherwise paid for these services become "secondary beneficiaries" (Lampman and Smeeding 1982). But because of lack of information on specific secondary beneficiaries, we will not be able to allocate relevant types of nonrecip-ient benefits to such individuals.

4.3 Applications and Examples

We are not able to provide estimates of either the efficiency measures or the distributional measures of the value of all types of in-kind sub-sidies. However, we can provide some rough estimates of the effect of the proposed measures of value on both program efficiency comparisons and

Table 4.1   The Current Government Cost and Alternative Government Cost of Medicare and Public Rental Housing in 1980 ($ billions)

Program/ Choice of Delivery Mechanism	Current Government Cost				Alternative Government Cost				Government Cost vs. Alternative Cost	
			Overhead and Administration:				Overhead and Administration:		Difference in Overhead and Administration:	
	Total	Value of Benefits[a]	Dollar Cost	(as % of benefits)	Total	Value of Benefits[a]	Dollar Cost	(as % of benefits)	Dollar Cost	(as % of benefits)
A. Medicare										
1. Current program	$29.356	$28.391	$ .965	(3.4)						
2. Voucher program:					$37.382[b]	$28.391	$ 8.991	(31.7)	$ −8.026	(−28.3)
High estimate					46.306	28.391	17.915	(63.1)	−16.950	(−59.7)
Medium estimate					34.041	28.391	5.650	(19.9)	−4.685	(−16.5)
Low estimate					31.798	28.391	3.407	(12.0)	−2.442	(−8.6)
B. Public housing										
1. Current programs										
Low-rent public housing	3.126	2.039	1.087	(53.3)						
Rent supplement	.382	.258	.124	(48.1)[c]						
Section 236	1.017	.709	.308	(43.5)						
Section 8 (new)	1.297	.860	.437	(50.8)						
Section 8 (existing)	1.767	1.220	.547	(44.8)						
Total	$7.589	$5.086	$2.503	(49.2)						
2. Voucher program:					5.888[b]	5.086	.802	(15.8)	1.701	(33.4)
High estimate					6.064	5.086	.978	(19.2)	1.525	(30.0)
Low estimate					5.712	5.086	.626	(12.3)	1.877	(36.9)

the distribution of program benefits for a selected set of medical care and housing benefits.

4.3.1 Efficiency Measures

In determining the net budgetary impact of a particular in-kind subsidy, and in estimating the efficiency costs of government production vs. government provision of benefits, both the market value and government cost measures are important. In table 4.1 we have calculated the government cost of both Medicare and public housing as currently designed and the alternative cost of a voucher program that provides the same total value of benefits to recipients.[7] The differences between overhead and administration under the current government cost and the alternative government cost options (in the final two columns of table 4.1) measure the net costs (if negative) or benefits (if positive) of changing the existing program delivery mechanism to a voucher program.

In the current Medicare program (table 4.1, part A) overhead and administration charges for claims processing averaged 3.4 percent of benefits (or claims) in 1979 (U.S. Department of Health and Human Services 1980). The costs of a change to a voucher system has been estimated in three ways. First, the high estimate is based on total expenses as a percent of claims for a sample of large and medium private insurance carriers providing a comprehensive major medical insurance policy to an employer with one employee in 1978 (Thexton 1978). While total insurance premiums for the elderly will differ from that of employees, the majority of the expenses of providing the policy, or the "load factor," should be quite similar. Of the total load factor of 63.1 percent,

---

Notes to Table 4.1

SOURCES: Medicare, current program: *Social Security Bulletin* (1982), table M-2; U.S. Department of Health and Human Services (1980).

Medicare, voucher program: Thexton (1978); Schuttinga (1981); Ginsburg (1981b).

Public housing, current programs: benefit values: Doyle et al. 1980; overhead and administration: low-rent public housing: Morrall and Olsen (1980); U.S. Department of Housing and Urban Development (1974); Section 236: Mayo et al. (1980); Murray (1980); Section 8 (new): Mayo et al. (1980); Weinberg (1982); Section 8 (existing): Rydell, Mulford, and Helbers (1980).

Public housing, voucher program: Rydell, Mulford, and Helbers (1980); U.S. Department of Housing and Urban Development (1979).

[a]Value of benefits are net of beneficiary contributions. These include the supplementary medical insurance premium in Medicare and the subsidized rental payment by public housing beneficiaries. Value of benefits in the Medicare program are measured by vendor payments, and in public housing programs by the difference between the private market rental value and the subsidized rent.

[b]Alternative cost is the simple average of the high, low, and medium estimates from the voucher programs in the Medicare case; and then high and low estimates in the public housing case.

[c]Overhead and administration for the rent supplement program is the simple average of all other overhead and administration charges.

3.8 percent covers state insurance premium taxes, 25.5 percent goes to direct sales overhead and commissions, 5.5 percent for claims processing, and 28.3 percent "other," which includes all remaining expenses of marketing and sales promotion, experience rating individuals, and profits.

It should be recognized that significant economies of scale in total overhead expenses exist. For instance, if a local senior citizens group endorses a plan with fifty participants, expense charges fall to 19.9 percent of claims (as shown under the medium estimate). Thus the high estimate assumes that all Medicare voucher holders would enroll with private insurers and that none of the advantages of economies of scale in overhead expenses would be developed through group sales. The medium estimate is based on the assumption that all Medicare voucher holders enroll with private insurers, but that groups of fifty enrollees are formed so that economy of scale advantages would be realized. Larger (smaller) groups would experience lower (higher) overall expenses. For instance, groups of 500 (5) would experience total load factors of 9.8 (46.8) percent of claims (Thexton 1978).

The low estimate is based on Blue Cross/Blue Shield (BC/BS) load factors (Schuttinga 1981) for single policies. They are lower than the private insurance company expenses for several reasons. First of all, BC/BS offers larger numbers of comprehensive health insurance policies than supplemental policies which have a higher ratio of load factor to claims. Secondly, BC/BS is a nonprofit company which in most states avoids the state insurance premium tax. Finally, there is some evidence that BC/BS cross-subsidizes single individuals at the expense of larger groups (Schuttinga 1981).

The overall total cost is the simple average of the alternative cost options, implicitly assuming that some voucher holders will end up in each of the three alternative scenarios. The fact that all three scenarios currently exist despite the large differences in overhead costs apparent in table 4.1 justifies this averaging technique. The result of this comparison indicates that a Medicare voucher plan would likely have cost the U.S. taxpayer an additional $8.0 billion, or 28.3 percent of vendor payments (claims) in 1980. These comparisons indicate that the current Medicare delivery system, which benefits from large economies of scale in claims processing, and which avoids the marketing, selling, and other costs associated with private insurance carriers, confers substantial efficiency benefits to taxpayers when compared to the alternative cost (or market value) of an equal benefit voucher plan.

In the case of public housing (table 4.1, part B) we find the opposite conclusions. The net market value of public housing benefits is equal to market rent minus the tenant contribution (or subsidized rent). This value has been estimated to be $5.086 billion in 1980 by the Congressional

Budget Office (Doyle et al 1980, p. 241) Various authors (see sources to table 4.1) have estimated the overhead or delivery cost per dollar of housing services. These costs have been expressed as a percent of benefit value, which differs from the value of housing services by the amount of the tenant contribution. Depending on the specific housing program in question, these expenses averaged 49.2 percent of benefits and include such items as construction costs and FHA loan subsidies for public housing construction, program-induced increases in rent, and the costs of administering the program (payments processing, eligibility recertification, periodic reinspection of public housing units to ensure code compliance, and other participant services). The difference between the market value of benefits delivered by public housing programs and the total government cost of these programs is quite large, totaling over $2.5 billion in 1980. Administrative costs and overhead for public housing are far above the administrative costs for other in-kind programs.[8]

The alternative costs of the voucher program were derived from EHAP (U.S. Department of Housing and Urban Development 1979). Under EHAP tenants received vouchers for the difference between the estimated standard cost of adequate housing (or the fair market rent) and 25 percent of their adjusted household income. Beneficiaries were then free to use this voucher to rent any dwelling that meets code requirements in the local area. EHAP was actually three different housing experiments, two of which (the Supply Experiment [SE], which was designed to determine the effects of vouchers on local housing markets; and the Administrative Agency Experiments [AAE], which were designed to gather information on the costs of delivering housing allowances) are used to obtain the alternative cost estimate in table 4.1.

The SE indicates that because the housing allowance voucher plan subsidizes housing demand in a local area, these areas experienced a 1.2 percent short-run increase in rental housing prices. This translates into a 1.5 percent increase in program costs relative to the net value of benefits (total rent minus a tenant contribution of roughly 30 percent of total rent). Additional overhead costs derived from both the SE and the AAE programs are added to this amount. The high cost estimate of $256 per unit per year or 17.8 percent of net benefits in table 4.1 is taken from the AAE experiments, while the low cost estimate, $156 or 10.8 percent of net benefits, is taken from the SE experiment (U.S. Department of Housing and Urban Development 1979, table V-1). The SE costs fall below the AAE costs because of economies of scale. Each site participating in the AAE experiments, had no more than 900 households, while each of the SE sites served at least 3500 households. The implication of these estimates is that combining the best features of the AAE experiments with the economies of scale experienced in the SE experiment (which are liable to be even greater in a nationwide program) might lead to administrative costs below those found in the low estimate in table 4.1. However, conservatively assuming that not all such economies would be realized, we have avaraged these estimates to derive the overall government cost of a voucher program with benefit values equal to those paid under current public housing programs. Comparing the voucher estimates with the current system, we find that the net efficiency costs from the current public housing system are estimated to be $1.7 billion or 33.4 percent of the market value of benefits received by public housing tenants.

Some care must be taken in interpreting these figures. Because of existing public housing program commitments, such as contracts promising to maintain subsidies for thirty years in the section 8 program (Congressional Budget Office 1979), and because of government-owned public housing complexes, the costs of changing the current phalanx of housing programs into a voucher system may be prohibitive. However, the estimates in table 4.1 do indicate that future low-income rental housing programs of the EHAP voucher type should be much more cost effective than additional units provided under current housing programs.

4.3.2   Distributional Implications

Measures of the value of in-kind subsidies are crucial in determining their distributional impact. Often public policy focuses only on means-tested direct subsidies or in-kind transfers because of their rapid growth and impact on the poverty status of low-income households (Paglin 1980; Smeeding 1982). For instance, the market value of means-tested benefits in the form of Medicaid and public housing have increased from $7.2 billion in 1970 to $31.6 billion in 1980 (Smeeding 1982, table 1). Indeed Medicaid, with vendor payments of $26.2 billion in 1980, is our largest means-tested transfer benefit, far outweighing *all* means-tested cash transfer benefits combined ($18.9 billion in 1980). In contrast, little attention has been focused on the distributional effects of conceptually similar indirect subsidies for health care or housing. In fact, only once in recent years has the Treasury Department even published estimates of the (market) value of tax expenditures by income class (U.S. Department of the Treasury 1978).

The distributional impact of direct in-kind subsidies is most often presented in terms of their market value with little attention focused on recipient value (e.g., Browning 1976; Congressional Budget Office 1977; Hoagland 1980). However, if one accepts the argument that recipient value is the proper conceptual approach for measuring the distributional impact of in-kind subsidies, and if reasonable measures of recipient value can be estimated, the distributional impact of in-kind subsidies is quite different from that observed when using the conventional market value approach. Moreover, accepting the concept of recipient value, and given the rapidly growing literature on the efficiency advantages of in-kind transfers, one is led to the notion of nonrecipient benefits and their distribution.

In this section of the paper we examine the mean value and size distribution of a subset of both direct and indirect in-kind subsidies for medical care and housing, comparing the results of conventional measures of their value to the conceptual approaches suggested above. A brief explanation of the derivation of these estimates precedes the analysis.

The government cost and market value of direct in-kind subsidies have recently been estimated by Smeeding (1982). Medical care benefits from Medicare and Medicaid are treated as insurance benefits accruing to the entire covered population according to broad beneficiary risk class (aged, disabled, adult, child). The government cost of these benefits as insurance is equal to total vendor payments plus claims-processing costs per state and risk-class specific recipient. In effect this approach measures the price that the government would have to charge beneficiaries for insurance coverage to just break even. In the past, this measure has often been confused with treating the market value of medical benefits as insurance (e.g., Hoagland 1980; Smeeding and Moon 1980; Smeeding 1982).[9] However, as demonstrated in section 4.2, the private market value (or market cost) of insurance with vendor payments equal to those of Medicare (or, we assume, Medicaid) are estimated to be 28.3 percent more than the government cost. Both measures have been calculated from the March 1980 Current Population Survey (CPS) and are presented below.

The market value of public housing was estimated using a hedonic regression model employing the Annual Housing Survey (AHS) to determine the private market rental value of public housing based purely on the characteristics (quantity and quality) and location of the housing unit. Subtracting the reported rents paid by public housing beneficiaries (as reported in the AHS) from these estimates of market rent, we arrive at the market value of the subsidy. Because the government cost of public housing has not been confused with market value, we present no distributional estimates of the government cost of public housing.

Recipient or cash equivalent value is estimated by assuming that the recipient value of an in-kind transfer is equal to the normal expenditure on that item by unsubsidized consumer units. This procedure involved matching subsidized units to unsubsidized units with similar characteristics (income, size, location, and age). If this similar nonrecipient normally spent less than the market value of the in-kind benefit on the subsidized good, the recipient value was measured by the level of normal expenditures. If normal expenditures exceed market value, recipient value equals market value. That is, because the in-kind transfer recipient would normally spend at least as much as the market value of the transfer on the subsidized good, it is not restrictive and therefore has the same income value as a cash transfer with equal dollar benefits (Smeeding 1982). This method of estimating recipient value does not explicitly employ utility functions. However, given the current state of the art in estimating cash equivalent value using empirical utility functions, it has been suggested that the normal expenditure approach is preferable to such methods (Manser 1982).

Nonrecipient value is measured by subtracting the government cost of a cash transfer program, with benefits equal to the aggregate recipient value of the in-kind subsidy, from the government cost of the given medical care or housing transfer. Overhead costs of the cash transfer program are estimated to be 4.5 percent of benefits, roughly the administrative costs in the current Supplemental Security Income (SSI) program and in the Seattle-New Jersey Negative Income Tax Experiment. The market value of nonrecipient benefits is distributed by money income decile in proportion to federal personal income tax payments.

Recipient value for indirect subsidies has not been calculated and cannot be derived from the recipient value estimates for direct in-kind subsidies. Even if we were able to estimate recipient value, the nonrecipient value of tax subsidy benefits would be distributed to all taxpayers in a fashion similar to the distribution of the market value of recipient benefits. And so total recipient plus nonrecipient value for these benefits would be roughly equivalent to the distribution of their market value, which is shown in tables 4.2–4.6.

Nonrecipient value and the market value of indirect subsidies were distributed using information from several sources. Of primary importance is a recent document (U.S. Department of the Treasury 1981) which presents information on federal personal income tax payments by adjusted gross income class. Using CPS estimates of money income transfers by money income decile, and assuming one tax return per CPS household at higher income levels, we estimated the distribution of taxes by CPS money income decile.[10] While the resulting distribution is only a rough estimate of the true distribution of federal income tax liability by money income decile, it is quite similar to that found in other studies (e.g., Okner 1980). These taxes were then subtracted from money income to arrive at the "post-tax" money income distribution in tables 4.3 and 4.5. Data from this source were also used to allocate indirect subsidies for personal health care deductions (in proportion to taxes paid by itemized tax returns claiming these deductions) and for property tax and mortgage interest deductions (also in proportion to taxes paid by itemized returns claiming these deductions).

Tax subsidies for employer-provided health insurance and sickness/accident insurance were calculated directly from a March 1980 CPS data tape estimating the cost of employer-provided health insurance and marginal federal income tax and payroll tax rates (Smeeding 1981). The overall, average, marginal federal personal income and payroll tax subsidy was calculated to be roughly 36 percent of the employer contribution and was directly distributed by CPS money income decile.

Because a prorich pattern of benefits is most likely disequalizing, we will refer to patterns of mean benefits increasing by income decile as regressive. The inverse of this logic indicates that a propoor, mean benefit pattern is progressive. When referring to the size distribution of aggregate benefits, those which have a greater (lesser) share of total program subsidies for the lower income decile than their after-tax money income share of 1.5 percent are termed equalizing (disequalizing). Again the inverse applies to the share of benefits for the highest decile, which receives 24.5 percent of after-tax income.

4.3.3 Medical Care Subsidies

The distributional impact of a subset of medical care subsidies is presented in tables 4.2 and 4.3. Both the mean value of benefits per beneficiary (table 4.2) and the size distribution of subsidies (table 4.3) have been calculated by CPS money income decile for 1979. The size distribution of CPS money income minus personal income taxes is also presented in the first row of table 4.3. Each table presents various measures of both direct (part A) and indirect (part B) subsidies. In part C of table 4.3 we have aggregated direct, indirect, and total subsidies to determine their net impact on the after-tax income size distribution.

Direct subsidies in tables 4.2 and 4.3 include only Medicaid and Medicare. Roughly $14.3 billion in outlays for veteran's medical care, CHAMPUS (military health care), worker's compensation, maternal and child health care, and Indian health programs are omitted (Health Insurance Institute 1980; *Social Security Bulletin* 1982). Roughly 40 percent of these benefits accrue to military living on base and to the institutionalized who are not covered in the CPS. Indirect subsidies exclude $1.3 billion in tax deductible charitable contributions for health (Congressional Budget Office 1981). These omissions should not have a great effect on the net distribution of the $68.9 billion in subsidies which are included in table 4.3.

The first two rows of table 4.2 present estimates of mean government cost and market value of direct medical subsidies. Our government cost estimate has been termed the "market value" in most studies (Hoagland 1980; Smeeding 1982). Our estimate of market value exceeds this estimate by 28.3 percent in each decile (as estimated in table 4.1). Mean benefits to the 22.7 million recipient households are fairly even across the income distribution. On the other hand, recipient value in row 3 rises with income, reflecting increased willingness to pay for medical care at higher income levels. "Benefit weights" (Smolensky et al. 1977), the ratio

Table 4.2   Distributional Impact of Medical Care Subsidies by Household Money Income Decile: Mean Value per Recipient Household in 1979

Benefit Measures Row and Type	Overall Mean Value[a]	Money Income Decile									
		Lowest	Second	Third	Fourth	Fifth	Sixth	Seventh	Eighth	Ninth	Highest
A. Direct subsidies (Medicare and Medicaid)											
1. Government cost	$1760	$1514	$1784	$1915	$1924	$1852	$1797	$1800	$1741	$1763	$1503
2. Market value	2258	1942	2289	2457	2468	2376	2306	2309	2234	2262	1928
3. Recipient value	832	442	648	802	893	1029	1080	1072	1080	1074	1077
4. Nonrecipient value[b]	323	17	51	79	117	168	219	264	351	521	1408
B. Indirect subsidies[c] (tax expenditures)											
5. Employer-provided health insurance	530	63	119	187	260	333	407	501	504	688	912
6. Employer-provided sickness & accident insurance	32	1	3	6	10	15	20	27	34	44	83
7. Tax deductible health care expenses	153	35	95	108	116	121	128	137	145	160	330

SOURCES: Rows 1, 2, 3, 5, 6: Calculated from March 1980 CPS data tapes. See Smeeding (1982) for the basis of rows 1, 2, and 3, and Smeeding (1981) for rows 5 and 6.

Row 4: Estimated from March 1980 CPS data tapes; U.S. Department of the Treasury (1981); Congressional Budget Office (1981).

Row 6: Estimated from Steuerle and Hoffman (1979); U.S. Department of the Treasury (1981).

[a]Mean value per recipient household.

[b]Nonrecipient value equals government cost of Medicaid and Medicare minus (1.045 × recipient value). These benefits were distributed as equal proportions of federal personal income taxes paid by each household with federal income tax liability and divided by the number of taxpaying households in each decile to arrive at mean decile values.

[c]All indirect subsidies are measured at their market value.

of recipient value to market value, rise from 22.8 percent in the lowest decile to 55.9 percent in the highest with an overall mean value of 36.8 percent. This pattern reflects not only low willingness to pay for medical benefits at low-income levels but also almost a complete lack of willingness to pay for the portion of medical insurance that protects against need for institutional care at all income levels. Institutional care benefits were $11.8 billion on a government cost basis in 1979, 27 percent of the government cost of Medicare and Medicaid subsidies.

Nonrecipient benefits (row 4) averaged $323 per taxpaying household with a very regressive benefit pattern reflecting the size distribution of federal income tax payments by money income decile. Mean indirect benefits are also regressively distributed, not only because of rising marginal federal personal income tax rates, but also because mean employer cost per beneficiary for employer-provided health insurance increases from $446 in the lowest decile to $1309 in the highest decile. Employer subsidies for sickness and accident insurance follow a similar pattern. Because only those who itemize deductions can benefit from these deductions, and because itemizers are largely in the highest three deciles, benefits are regressively distributed. The regressivity of tax deductions for health insurance and other tax deductible health care expenses has previously been established by Steuerle and Hoffman (1979). Because mean benefits are calculated per beneficiary household we cannot generally add benefits together. However, because over 90 percent of those covered by either employer health insurance or employer sickness and accident insurance are covered by both programs we can add these benefits together with little loss in accuracy (Smeeding 1981). Combining these items we find that a typical employee in the highest decile receives an indirect subsidy of almost $1000—somewhat more than the average recipient value of direct medical subsidies of $832.

Turning to table 3 we can more readily assess the distributional impacts of medical subsidies. The conventional method of valuing in-kind benefits, at their government cost as in row 2, produces a benefit distribution which is quite equalizing in nature. The $8.6 billion of government cost allocated to the lowest income decile is over 42 percent of their aggregate post-tax money income share of $20.3 billion. Using a true market value measure (row 3) increases this fraction to 54.2 percent of disposable income. Switching to recipient value (row 4), we find that benefits from Medicare and Medicaid are still equalizing in nature, but to a much lower degree. In this case, benefits to the lowest decile are only 15.3 percent of their disposable income share. Adding recipient and nonrecipient value to arrive at our preferred measure of the value of direct subsidies (row 9) further reduces the equalizing impact of medical subsidies. These results can be compared to the conventional method of distributing the value of Medicare and Medicaid in row 2. Large differences can be noted, particu-

Table 4.3   Distributional Impact of Aggregate Medical Care Subsidies by Money Income Decile in 1979 (in $ billions) (percent distribution in parentheses)

Benefit Measure and Type — Row	Aggregate Value	Money Income Decile									
		Lowest	Second	Third	Fourth	Fifth	Sixth	Seventh	Eighth	Ninth	Highest
1. Post-tax money income	$1341.2 (100.0)	$20.3 (1.5)	$39.0 (2.9)	$62.1 (4.6)	$83.5 (6.2)	$105.6 (7.9)	$130.3 (9.7)	$156.2 (11.6)	$186.1 (13.9)	$263.0 (17.1)	$329.1 (24.5)
A. Direct subsidies (Medicare and Medicaid)											
2. Government cost	43.7 (100.0)	8.6 (19.7)	9.7 (22.2)	7.3 (16.7)	5.2 (11.9)	3.6 (8.2)	2.5 (5.7)	2.1 (4.8)	1.7 (3.9)	1.5 (3.4)	1.5 (3.4)
3. Market value	56.1 (100.0)	11.0 (19.7)	12.4 (22.2)	9.4 (16.7)	6.7 (11.9)	4.6 (8.2)	3.2 (5.7)	2.7 (4.8)	2.2 (3.9)	1.9 (3.4)	1.9 (3.4)
4. Recipient value	23.8 (100.0)	3.1 (12.9)	4.4 (18.4)	3.8 (16.0)	3.0 (12.5)	2.5 (10.5)	1.9 (8.0)	1.5 (6.3)	1.3 (5.5)	1.2 (5.0)	1.2 (5.0)
5. Nonrecipient value[a]	22.8 (100.0)	.1 (.4)	.4 (1.8)	.6 (2.6)	.8 (3.5)	1.2 (5.3)	1.6 (7.0)	1.9 (8.3)	2.5 (11.0)	3.7 (16.2)	10.1 (44.3)
B. Indirect subsidies (tax expenditures)											
6. Employer-provided health insurance	17.1 (100.0)	[b] ([b])	.1 (.6)	.3 (1.7)	.6 (3.3)	1.2 (6.7)	1.6 (9.0)	2.2 (12.4)	2.9 (16.3)	3.8 (22.0)	5.0 (28.1)

	Total										
7. Employer-provided sickness & accident insurance	1.4 (100.0)	(b) (b)	(b) (b)	(b) (b)	(b) (b)	.1 (7.1)	.1 (7.1)	.1 (7.1)	.2 (14.3)	.3 (21.4)	.6 (42.9)
8. Tax deductible health care expenses	3.1 (100.0)	(b) (b)	.1 (3.2)	.1 (3.2)	.1 (3.2)	.2 (6.5)	.2 (6.5)	.3 (9.7)	.4 (12.9)	.4 (12.9)	1.3 (41.9)
C. Total subsidies											
9. Value of direct subsidies[c] (4+5)	46.6 (100.0)	3.2 (6.9)	4.8 (10.2)	4.4 (9.4)	3.8 (8.1)	3.7 (7.9)	3.5 (7.5)	3.4 (7.3)	3.8 (8.1)	4.9 (10.5)	11.3 (24.2)
10. Value of indirect subsidies (6+7+8)	22.3 (100.0)	.1 (.4)	.2 (.9)	.4 (1.8)	.7 (3.1)	1.5 (6.7)	1.9 (8.5)	2.6 (11.7)	3.5 (15.7)	4.5 (20.2)	6.9 (30.9)
11. Value of direct plus indirect subsidies (9+10)	$68.9 (100.0)	$3.3 (4.8)	$5.0 (7.3)	$4.8 (7.0)	$4.5 (6.5)	$5.2 (7.5)	$5.4 (7.8)	$6.0 (8.7)	$7.3 (10.6)	$9.4 (13.6)	$18.2 (26.4)

Numbers may not sum to totals because of rounding.

SOURCES: Rows 1, 5: Estimated from March 1980 CPS data tapes; U.S. Department of the Treasury (1981). Rows 2, 3, 4, 6, 7: Estimated from March 1980 CPS data tapes. See Smeeding (1982) for the basis of rows 2, 3, and 4, and Smeeding (1981) for rows 6 and 7. Row 8: Estimated from Steuerle and Hoffman (1979); U.S. Department of the Treasury (1981).

[a] Nonrecipient value equals government cost of Medicaid and Medicare minus (1.045 × recipient value). These benefits are distributed as equal proportions of federal personal income tax paid by each household with federal income tax liability.

[b] Less than $.1 billion or less than .1 percent.

[c] Value of direct subsidies is estimated by combining recipient and nonrecipient values.

larly for the highest and lowest deciles. For instance, the share of direct subsidies accruing to the highest decile is $1.5 billion or 3.4 percent of benefits using the conventional government cost approach, as compared to $11.3 billion or 24.2 percent of benefits when recipient and nonrecipient values are aggregated in row 9.[11]

4.3.4 Housing Subsidies

The distribution of housing subsidies are shown in tables 4.4 and 4.5. Neither mean nor aggregate government cost was distributed across beneficiaries because our definition of market value is akin to the definition used by others who have distributed these benefits. Excluded from the estimates of direct subsidies are estimates of the annual value of FHA, VA, and FHMA mortgages. The available information on recipients of these subsidies indicates that the majority of benefits were received by households with above average incomes in 1978 (Manser 1981, p. 52–53). Thus, if we were able to estimate their value they apparently would be disequalizing. Also excluded were $2.4 billion in tax expenditures for municipal housing bonds, for tax-deferred capital gains for those selling their homes and purchasing another within the specified time limit, and for the capital gains exclusion for qualifying elderly. These would also accrue mainly to upper-income groups (Congressional Budget Office 1978). Thus, if data on omitted types of public subsidies for housing were available we would find their distribution disequalizing.

Mean market value for public housing (table 4.4, row 1) are progressively distributed for two reasons. First, over 99 percent of public housing benefits accrue to households in the lower 50 percent of the income distribution; secondly, the market value of these benefits is equal to the private market rental value of the housing unit net of tenant contributions. Because tenant contributions are roughly 25 percent of net income, the tenant contribution increases and the net subsidy decreases as income increases, all else equal. Recipient values are also propoor because of the first reason mentioned above. However, because recipient willingness to pay for housing rises with income, the pattern of recipient values is much less propoor. Mean benefit weights for public housing increase only from 59 percent in the lowest decile to 79 percent in the highest decile, with a mean value of 65 percent.

Mean nonrecipient benefits are prorich because of their income tax payments distributor. Mean direct subsidies are even more prorich because of the unequal distribution of taxes paid by those with itemized returns claiming interest deductions, and those with itemized returns claiming deductions for state and local taxes paid. Because of the great deal of overlap between these two groups of indirect subsidy beneficiaries we may again add mean values with little loss of accuracy. If so we find overall mean benefits of $635—about the same as mean recipient values

Table 4.4   Distributional Impact of Public Housing Subsidies by Household Money Income Decile: Mean Value Per Recipient Household in 1979

Row	Benefit Measures and Type	Overall Mean Value[a]	Money Income Decile									
			Lowest	Second	Third	Fourth	Fifth	Sixth	Seventh	Eighth	Ninth	Highest
	A. Direct subsidies											
1.	Market value	$980	$1205	$1070	$796	$531	$552	b	b	b	b	b
2.	Recipient value	636	715	739	496	372	436	b	b	b	b	b
3.	Nonrecipient value[c]	54	3	8	13	19	27	37	44	59	86	239
	B. Indirect subsidies[d] (tax expenditures)											
4.	Mortgage interest	383	23	114	133	184	235	271	319	377	428	613
5.	Property tax	252	19	51	75	98	123	135	165	198	274	405

SOURCES: Rows 1, 2: Calculated from March 1980 CPS data tapes; Doyle et al. (1980). Rows 3, 4, 5: Estimated from March 1980 CPS data tapes; U.S. Department of the Treasury (1978, 1981); Congressional Budget Office (1978).

[a]Mean value per recipient household.

[b]Less than 30,000 households in this cell.

[c]Nonrecipient value equals government cost minus (1.045 × recipient value). These benefits are distributed as equal proportions of federal personal income taxes by each household with federal income tax liability and divided by the number of taxpaying households in each decile to arrive at mean decile values.

[d]All indirect subsidies are measured at their market value.

Table 4.5   Distributional Impact of Aggregate Housing Subsidies by Money Income Decile in 1979
(in $ billions) (percent distribution in parentheses)

Benefit Measure Row and Type	Aggregate Value	Money Income Decile									
		Lowest	Second	Third	Fourth	Fifth	Sixth	Seventh	Eighth	Ninth	Highest
1. Post-tax money income	$1341.2 (100.0)	$20.3 (1.5)	$39.0 (2.9)	$62.1 (4.6)	$83.5 (6.2)	$105.6 (7.9)	$130.3 (9.7)	$156.2 (11.6)	$186.1 (13.9)	$229.0 (17.1)	$329.1 (24.5)
A. Direct subsidies											
2. Market value	4.6 (100.0)	2.2 (47.4)	1.4 (29.9)	.6 (12.7)	.2 (4.1)	.1 (2.0)	.1 (2.0)	b (b)	b (b)	b (b)	b (b)
3. Recipient value	3.0 (100.0)	1.3 (46.1)	1.0 (38.5)	.3 (13.0)	.1 (.7)	.1 (.5)	.1 (.5)	b (b)	b (b)	b (b)	b (b)
4. Nonrecipient value[a]	3.7 (100.0)	b (b)	.1 (2.6)	.1 (2.7)	.1 (2.7)	.2 (5.4)	.3 (6.8)	.3 (8.1)	.4 (10.8)	.6 (16.2)	1.7 (44.6)

B. Indirect subsidies (tax expenditures)

	Total										
5. Mortgage interest	9.3 (100.0)	b (b)	.1 (.7)	.1 (.8)	.2 (1.5)	.3 (3.2)	.6 (5.7)	1.0 (9.6)	1.6 (16.6)	2.0 (21.7)	3.4 (39.5)
6. Property tax	6.4 (100.0)	b (b)	b (b)	.1 (1.3)	.1 (1.4)	.2 (3.1)	.3 (5.3)	.5 (7.7)	1.0 (15.5)	1.4 (22.3)	2.8 (43.5)

C. Total subsidies

	Total										
7. Value of direct subsidies[c] (3 + 4)	6.7 (100.0)	1.3 (19.3)	1.1 (16.3)	.4 (5.9)	.2 (3.0)	.3 (4.5)	.4 (5.9)	.3 (4.5)	.5 (7.5)	.6 (8.9)	1.7 (25.2)
8. Total value of indirect subsidies (5 + 6)	15.7 (100.0)	b (b)	.1 (.6)	.2 (1.2)	.3 (1.9)	.5 (3.2)	.9 (5.7)	1.5 (9.6)	2.6 (16.6)	3.4 (21.7)	6.2 (39.5)
9. Value of direct plus indirect subsidies (7 + 8)	22.4 (100.0)	1.3 (5.7)	1.2 (5.4)	.6 (2.7)	.5 (2.2)	.8 (3.6)	1.3 (5.7)	1.8 (8.0)	3.1 (13.8)	4.0 (17.9)	7.9 (35.1)

Numbers may not sum to totals because of rounding.

SOURCES: Rows 1, 2, 3: Calculated from March 1980 CPS data tapes; Doyle et al. (1980); U.S. Department of the Treasury (1981). Rows 4, 5, 6: Estimated from March 1980 CPS data tapes; U.S. Department of the Treasury (1978, 1981); Congressional Budget Office (1978).

[a]Nonrecipient value equals government cost of public housing minus (1.045 × recipient value). These benefits are distributed as equal proportions of federal personal income tax paid by each household with federal income tax liability.

[b]Less than $1 billion or less than .1 percent.

[c]Total value of direct subsidies is estimated by combining recipient and nonrecipient value (rows 3 and 4).

for direct subsidies. In the highest decile total mean indirect subsidies of $1018 are above the overall mean market value of direct housing subsidies.

In table 4.5 benefits as measured by both the conventional market value approach and the recipient value approach (rows 2 and 3) are equalizing, while nonrecipient benefits are disequalizing. Adding recipient and nonrecipient value (row 7) nets out both types of effects, though the lowest decile still receives benefits far in excess of their post-tax money income share in row 1. Indirect subsidies (row 8) are quite disequalizing, with their size distribution benefiting only the top three deciles in excess of their disposable income share. When direct and indirect subsidies are combined in row 9 we find a U-shaped distribution with beneficiaries in the first and second deciles and in the top two deciles benefiting in excess of their post-tax income shares. The net effect seems to be slightly propoor with benefits in the bottom two deciles exceeding their money income shares to a greater extent than those in the top deciles. If we were able to distribute the housing subsidies not measured in this table, the net effect of all housing subsidies would be roughly neutral with respect to both ends of the distribution. Only the middle portion of the distribution would have benefits below their money income share.

4.3.5 Combined Values

Finally, we can add overall medical care subsidies (table 4.3, row 11) and housing subsidies (table 4.5, row 9) to get an idea of their net effect on the money income size distribution. In addition, we can compare the distributional impact of direct in-kind subsidies using the conventional market value (or government cost for medical care) approach as compared to the recipient value–nonrecipient value approach recommended in this paper. Table 4.6 presents these results.

Part A of table 4.6 clearly indicates a large difference between the conventional market value/government cost approach and the suggested recipient plus nonrecipient benefit approach to valuing direct in-kind subsidies. The suggested approach is much less propoor than the conventional approach, particularly as far as the highest money income quintile is concerned. Adding the value of indirect subsidies to our suggested approach, we arrive at an estimate of the total net distributive effect of these subsidies. As expected, the post-tax money income share of the lowest quintile is below their share of total in-kind subsidies, but not as expected, so is the top quintile's share! That is, accepting our framework, the richest 20 percent of households receive a larger share of in-kind housing and medical subsidies than their share of money income.

As one moves down the rows of table 4.6 away from the conventional measure of the size distribution of direct subsidies toward a different

Table 4.6   The Net Effect of Medical Care and Housing Subsidies on the Size
Distribution of Post-Tax Money Income in 1979 (in $ billions)
(percent distribution in parentheses)

Row	Benefit Measure and Type	Value of Benefits (billions)			
		Aggregate Value	Lowest Quintile	Middle Three Quintiles	Highest Quintile
1.	Post-tax money income	$1341.2 (100.0)	$59.5 (4.4)	$723.6 (54.0)	$558.1 (41.6)
A.	Direct subsidies only				
2.	Conventional approach[a]	48.3 (100.0)	21.9 (45.3)	23.4 (48.4)	3.0 (6.2)
3.	Suggested approach[b]	53.3 (100.0)	10.4 (19.5)	24.4 (45.8)	18.5 (34.7)
B.	Total subsidies				
4.	Direct plus indirect subsidies[c]	91.3 (100.0)	11.3 (12.4)	40.5 (44.4)	39.5 (43.3)

Numbers may not sum to totals because of rounding.
SOURCES: Tables 4.3 and 4.5.
[a]Market value for public housing (table 4.5, row 2) plus government cost for medical care (table 4.3, row 2).
[b]Recipient plus nonrecipient value of direct subsidies (table 4.3, row 9, plus table 4.5, row 7). Row 3 exceeds row 2 above as a result of the treatment of the institutionalized and the allocation of government cost in excess of the market value of public housing to nonrecipient beneficiaries.
[c]Recipient plus nonrecipient value of direct subsidies (row 3) plus value of all indirect subsidies (table 4.3, row 10, plus table 4.5, row 8).

approach which includes measuring the effect of all types of public subsidies on the income size distribution, the share of subsidies accruing to the bottom quintile continues to decline while that of the top quintile increases to a much greater degree. Clearly one's choice of the types of in-kind subsidies to include in a distributional analysis, one's approach to valuing those subsidies, and their distributors all have an important role to play in determining their impact on the income size distribution.

4.4   Summary and Implications for Social Accounting

The purpose of this paper was to demonstrate the policy use of several alternative measures of the value of public in-kind subsidies. Applications were made to a subset of medical care and housing subsidies. Rough estimates of the efficiency gains or losses from the program delivery system were made. The efficiency benefits from the current Medicare program and the efficiency costs of current public housing programs were shown. Rough estimates of the effect of various valuation approaches on the money income size distribution were also made. Once all types of medical care and housing subsidies covered in this paper were combined, we find that both the poor and the rich benefit in excess of their post-tax money income shares. Several implications for social accounting can be drawn from these results.

One immediate recommendation is to group all direct and indirect subsidies by subsidy category (health care, housing, food, etc.) to determine their net budgetary impact and distributional effect. The Congressional Budget Office (1981) now groups tax expenditures by subsidy area, but does not include direct subsidies for the same commodity. Few if any analyses of the total impact of public subsidies on income distribution are available even in rough form (Wilensky 1981).

In the area of efficiency considerations two suggestions can be made. First of all, additional analyses of the delivery mechanism for public in-kind subsidies comparing the government cost, market value, and alternative government cost of providing various subsidies is necessary. While we have examined only Medicare and public housing, this analysis can and should be extended to other direct and indirect subsidies. For instance, can we design a direct federal catastrophic health insurance subsidy that achieves the objectives of the current tax deduction subsidy system more effectively and more equitably? Second, the concept of social benefit value demands additional attention. When all equity and efficiency considerations are considered, in-kind subsidies may be more efficient and equitable means for reaching certain public goals than are equal value cash transfers.

In the area of assessing the distributional impact of in-kind subsidies, we must begin to clearly differentiate between recipient and nonrecipient benefits, particularly in the area of health care and education subsidies. The size distribution of the market value or government cost of a particular subsidy may suggest misleading conclusions about their impact on the extent of poverty or on the inequality of income. In particular, we must develop better estimates of the recipient value of public subsidies and realize that these values are the conceptually appropriate concept for estimating the impact of in-kind subsidies on poverty, affluence, and inequality. The value of nonrecipient benefits, which might lead us to prefer in-kind subsidies to cash transfers on efficiency or overall equity grounds, should be distributed to the true beneficiaries not just allocated to recipients by the conventional market value/government cost methodology.

We hope this paper will stimulate discussion of these issues and further refinement of the concepts suggested above. In our judgment, this line of research will prove a cost-effective investment in more efficient and equitable public policy.

Notes

1. We implicitly assume that social cost and government cost are synonymous.

2. Government cost may also be defined to include the deadweight loss or welfare costs associated with the additional taxes or public debt needed to fund a given subsidy. Further, if means-tested subsidies reduce beneficiary labor supply, an additional indirect cost element may arise (see Moffitt 1981; Murray 1981). However, we do not estimate these costs in this paper.

3. This conclusion must be tempered by the possibility that a substantial growth in HMOs and other forms of prepaid health care may reduce health care costs below those currently experienced in the predominant fee-for-service health care system (Ginsburg 1981b).

4. The reader should note that in cases where the government cost of a particular in-kind benefit falls short of the market value of the benefit *and* where the recipient value exceeds the market value of the benefit, recipient value can exceed government cost. For instance, suppose a Medicare beneficiary finds that he would have spent an amount on health insurance exceeding the market value of the Medicare benefit package if presented with an equal cash transfer. In this case the cash equivalent value of the medical care benefit exceeds the government cost of providing that specific set of medical care benefits because of the selling cost advantages of Medicare over private insurance providers.

5. Again we ignore behavioral response to such a change. For instance, transforming an in-kind program into an equal welfare benefit cash program may increase participation in the cash program (because of lower stigma cost or other factors), in which case the cost of the cash program would rise.

6. There are a number of potential distributors for nonrecipient or nonexclusive public good benefits (Reynolds and Smolensky 1977; O'Higgins and Ruggles 1981). We chose the equal proportion of income tax distributor, implicitly assuming an income elasticity of demand in excess of unity for these benefits (because of the progressive personal income tax). It makes sense to argue that higher-income households have a relatively higher demand for in-kind benefits than recipients. Presumably the majority of in-kind benefit recipients, lower-income persons and the elderly, pay lesser portions of federal taxes and would prefer equal-cost cash transfers over in-kind transfers because they put a higher value on the cash benefits. Further support for such a distributor has been indirectly provided by Aaron and McGuire (1970). Alternative distributors could provide a more progressive (e.g., if distributed in proportion to capital income) or less progressive (e.g., if distributed on a per capita or per household basis) nonrecipient benefit distribution than the alternative we have chosen. For these reasons, we feel that our choice of distributors is both plausible and sensible.

7. Entries in the value of benefits column in table 4.1 are exactly equivalent to market value as defined in section 4.2 in the case of public housing. In the case of Medicare, however, the value of benefits equals the cost of vendor payments excluding the overhead and administrative charges which are appropriately part of market value when medical benefits are measured by their insurance value. This differentiation was necessary to bring out the fact that the value of medical benefits in terms of vendor payments, or insurance claims, are held constant when comparing alternative government cost and current government cost in table 4.1.

8. For instance, the Food Stamp program costs roughly 8.5 percent in excess of the market value of the stamps (MacDonald 1977), while the Medicaid program experiences claims processing costs averaging 5.4 percent of vendor payments (Smeeding 1982).

9. In the earlier literature, it was generally assumed that the market value and government cost of Medicare and Medicaid were equal. However, recent evidence (Ginsburg 1981b; table 1) strongly suggests that private market value exceeds government cost.

10. We would like to thank Joseph Minarik for suggesting this strategy.

11. The aggregate value of direct subsidies (row 9) exceeds the government cost of subsidies to CPS beneficiaries (row 2) by $2.9 billion because of taxpayers' nonrecipient benefits on behalf of the institutionalized who are not covered by the CPS, but who do receive Medicaid and Medicare coverage.

References

Aaron, H., and M. McGuire. 1970. Public goods and income distribution. *Econometrica* 38:907–20.

Browning, Edgar K. 1976. The trend toward equality in the distribution of net income. *Southern Economic Journal* 42:912–23.

Congressional Budget Office. 1977. *Poverty status of families under alternative definitions of income.* Background Paper no. 17 (revised). Washington, D.C.: GPO.

———. 1978. *Federal housing policy: Current programs and recurring issues.* Background Paper. Washington, D.C.: GPO.

———. 1979. *The long-term costs of public housing programs.* Background Paper. Washington, D.C.: GPO.

———. 1981. *Tax expenditures: Current issues and five-year budget projections for fiscal years 1982–1986.* Report to Congress. Washington, D.C.: GPO

Cooper, C., and A. Katz. 1978. *The cash equivalent of in-kind income.* Stamford, Conn.: Cooper and Company.

DeSalvo, Joseph S. 1971. A methodology for evaluating housing programs. *Journal of Regional Science* 11:173–85.

Doyle, Mary P., David Edson, Norma Pappas, and William Boulding. 1980. *Creation of 1980 and 1984 data bases from the March 1978 CPS, volume I, final report.* Washington, D.C.: Mathematica Policy Research.

Garfinkel, I., and T. Smeeding. 1981. Cash vs in-kind benefits: A conference proposal. University of Wisconsin-Madison. Mimeo.

Ginsburg, Paul. 1981a. Altering the tax treatment of employment based health plans. *Milbank Memorial Fund Quarterly* (Spring).

———. 1981b. Medicare vouchers and the procompetitive strategy. *Health Affairs* 1:39–52.

Health Insurance Institute. 1980. *Source book of health insurance data 1979–1980.* Washington, D.C.: Health Insurance Institute.

Hicks, John R. 1943. The four consumer surpluses. *Review of Economic Studies* 7.

Hoagland, G. William. 1980. The effectiveness of current transfer programs in reducing poverty. Paper presented to Middlebury College

Conference on Economic Issues, 19 April, Middlebury, Vermont. Mimeo.

Hochman, Harold, and James Rodgers. 1969. Pareto optimal redistribution. *American Economic Review* 59:542–57.

Krashinsky, Michael. 1980. The role of in-kind transfers in income distribution. New Haven, Conn.: Yale University. Mimeo.

Lampman, Robert, and Timothy Smeeding. 1983. Interfamily transfers as alternatives to government transfers to persons. *Review of Income and Wealth*, 29:45–66.

MacDonald, M. 1977. *Food stamps and income maintenance.* New York: Academic Press.

Manser, M. 1981. *Analyzing in-kind income receipt using the SIPP panel data.* Washington, D.C.: Mathematica Policy Research.

———. 1982. *Analyzing in-kind housing and medical benefits using the 1979 ISDP panel data.* Washington, D.C.: Mathematica Policy Research.

Mayo, S. K., S. Mansfield, W. D. Warner, and L. Zwetchkenbaum. 1980. *Housing allowances and other rental assistance programs—A companion based on the housing allowance demand experiment, part 2: Costs and efficiency.* Cambridge, Mass.: Abt Associates Inc.

Moffitt, Robert A. 1981. The negative income tax: Would it discourage work? *Monthly Labor Review* 103, no. 4:23–27.

Morrall, John F., and Edgar O. Olsen. 1980. The cost-effectiveness of leased public housing. *Policy Analysis* 6:151–70.

Murray, Michael. 1980. Tenant benefits in alternative federal housing programmes. *Urban Studies* 17:25–34.

———. 1981. A reinterpretation of the traditional income-leisure model, with application to in-kind subsidy programs. *Journal of Public Economics* 14:69–81.

Musgrave, Richard A. 1959. *The theory of public finance.* New York: McGraw-Hill.

Nichols, Albert L., and Richard J. Zeckhauser. 1981. Targeting transfers through restrictions on recipients. Paper presented to the American Economic Association, 29 December, Washington, D.C.

O'Higgins, M., and P. Ruggles. 1981. The distribution of public expenditures and taxes among households in the United Kingdom. *Review of Income and Wealth* 27:298–326.

Okner, Benjamin. 1980. Distributional aspects of tax reform during the past fifteen years. *National Tax Journal* 32:11–27.

Paglin, M. 1980. *Poverty and transfers in-kind.* Palo Alto, Calif.: Hoover Institution Press.

Reynolds, M., and E. Smolensky. 1977. *Public expenditures, taxes and the distribution of income: The United States, 1950, 1961, 1970.* New York: Academic Press.

Rydell, C., J. Mulford, and L. Helbers. 1980. *Price increases caused by housing programs*. Rand Corporation Report R-2677-HUD. Santa Monica, Calif.: Rand Corporation.

Schuttinga, James. 1981. Telephone conversation, June 9.

Smeeding, Timothy M. 1975. *Measuring the economic welfare of low-income households, and the anti-poverty effectiveness of cash and non-cash transfer programs*. Ph.D. diss., University of Wisconsin-Madison.

————. 1981. The size distribution of wage and nonwage compensation: Employer cost vs recipient value. Paper presented to the National Bureau of Economic Research Conference on Labor Cost, 3 December, Williamsburg, Virginia.

————. 1982. *Alternative methods for valuing in-kind transfer benefits and measuring their impact on poverty*. Technical Report 50, U.S. Bureau of the Census. Washington, D.C.: GPO.

Smeeding, Timothy M., and M. Moon, 1980. Valuing government expenditures: The case of medical care transfers and poverty. *Review of Income and Wealth* 26:305–24.

Smolensky, E., L. Stiefel, M. Schmundt, and R. Plotnick. 1977. Adding in-kind transfers to the personal income and outlay account: Implications for the size distribution of income. In T. Juster (ed.), *The distribution of economic well-being*, ed. F. T. Juster. Studies in Income and Wealth, vol. 41. Cambridge, Mass.: Ballantine for the National Bureau of Economic Research.

Social Security Bulletin. 1982. February. Washington, D.C.: GPO

Steuerle, Eugene, and R. Hoffman. 1979. Tax expenditures for health care. *National Tax Journal* 32:101–15.

Thexton, Peter M. 1978. Letter to Morton B. Hess, Office of the Actuary, Social Security Administration.

Thurow, Lester. 1974. Cash versus in-kind transfers. *American Economic Review* 64, no. 2: 190–95.

Tobin, James. 1970. On limiting the domain of inequality. *Journal of Law and Economics* 13:263–77.

U.S. Bureau of the Census. 1981. Characteristics of households and persons receiving noncash benefits: 1979. *Current population reports*, series P-23, no. 110. Washington, D.C.: GPO.

U.S. Department of Health and Human Services. 1980. *Medicare 1979*. Health Care Financing Administration. Washington, D.C.: GPO.

U.S. Department of Housing and Urban Development. 1974. *Housing in the seventies: A report of the National Housing Policy Review Commission*. Washington, D.C.: GPO.

————. 1979. *Experimental housing allowance program: A report of findings*. Washington, D.C.: GPO.

U.S. Department of the Treasury. 1978. Tax expenditures affecting individuals, fiscal year 1977. *Muskie News* 13 (February), appendix.

————. 1981. Individual income tax returns, 1979; Income, deductions, residential energy credit. *SOI Bulletin* 1:1–22.

Weinberg, Daniel. 1982. Housing benefits from the section 8 housing program. *Evaluation Review* 6:5–24.

Weisbrod, Burton. 1969. Collective action and the distribution of income: A conceptual approach. *The analysis and evaluation of public expenditures: The PPB system.* Report prepared for the U.S. Joint Economic Committee, 93d Congress. Washington, D.C.: GPO.

Wilensky, Gail R. 1981. Government and the financing of health care. Paper presented to the American Economic Association, 30 December, Washington, D.C.

Comment   Janice Peskin

Measurement of in-kind income has received increasing attention from academic economists and government statisticians during the last decade. This heightened interest primarily has reflected the growth of government in-kind subsidies and what is perceived as a resulting bias in measures of poverty based on money income alone. In this tradition, the paper by Timothy Smeeding considers the valuation issue—that is, how to place dollar values on the in-kind income—and presents estimates of the distribution of public in-kind subsidies in the areas of health and housing.

Smeeding defines four alternative valuations: (1) market value defined as the cost of the goods and services on the private market; (2) government cost defined as the cost to the government of providing the goods and services, including costs of program management; (3) recipient or cash equivalent value defined as the value of the goods and services to the recipient, which conceptually is the money income that would be required for the recipient to forego the transfer (Hick's equivalent variation concept); and (4) social benefit value defined as the value of the goods and services to recipients and to nonrecipients; as with cash equivalent value this is a welfare concept.

A number of relationships are posited between the valuations and are explored in the empirical sections of the paper. (1) Government cost differs from market value when the government is more or less efficient than the private sector in providing an identical good or service. (2) The cash equivalent value is generally less than the market value and government cost because the subsidy constrains or induces recipients to spend

Janice Peskin is a senior analyst with the Congressional Budget Office, Washington, D.C. The views presented here are the author's and do not necessarily represent those of the Congressional Budget Office.

more on the good than they would choose to spend if given cash. (3) The social benefit value is at least as great as government cost if the subsidy is efficient in an economic sense. (4) The social benefit value is generally greater than the cash equivalent value, giving rise to nonrecipient benefits.

There are two main purposes of the paper. The first is to point out that the different valuations are appropriate for different uses. Specifically, government cost is appropriate for studies of budgetary impacts, and comparisons of government cost and market value can be used in studies of government efficiency. The cash equivalent value is appropriate for including in-kind income in measures of poverty and income distribution. And the social benefit value is appropriate for studies of efficiency and of income distribution. While these points are not new, it is always useful to stress the importance of relating measures to their intended uses. The second purpose of the paper is to illustrate uses of the alternative values of government housing and medical care subsidies in studies of efficiency and of distribution of income.

To illustrate efficiency studies, the author compares the direct provision by the government of health insurance (Medicare) and of public housing to indirect provision through vouchers enabling recipients to purchase health insurance and housing in the private market. In this illustration, the differences between government costs and private market costs of providing identical recipient benefits are compared. He finds that direct provision of health insurance is more "efficient" than are health insurance vouchers but that public housing is less "efficient" than are housing vouchers. Efficiency, which can be interpreted in many ways, is used in a narrow sense in this illustration. Measured costs do not represent true resource costs, which may differ between direct government provision and indirect provision through vouchers, for example, if one is better in controlling upward pressure on prices, in regulating fraud, or in reducing unnecessary use of medical care. Moreover, comparisons of alternative delivery systems on economic efficiency grounds cannot ignore likely differences in outcomes for beneficiaries. For example, without low-rent public housing, would sufficient low-rent housing in inner cities be available to meet the demand, and would it be available to all races? In other words, recipient values are not usually independent of delivery systems.

The author then presents estimates of the aggregate values and distributional effects of medical care and housing subsidies by alternative valuation techniques. Both direct subsidies (Medicare, Medicaid, and public housing) and indirect subsidies through the tax system (tax deductions for employer-provided health and accident insurance, medical care expenses, mortgage interest, and property taxes) are considered. Direct subsidies include benefits to nonrecipients as well as to recipients.

The distributional effects of the subsidies as estimated by the author are generally consistent with our intuition and other studies. The direct subsidies to recipients in 1979 were equalizing in that a greater share of the subsidies went to the lower-income deciles than their existing share of after-tax money income. Of the direct subsidies considered, most are means-tested so that this result is not surprising. The indirect subsidies to recipients or tax expenditures were disequalizing; that is, a greater share went to the higher-income deciles than their existing share of after-tax money income. The indirect subsidies are regressive because to benefit requires itemization on tax returns, because subsidies increase with tax rates, and because employer-provided health benefits rise with income. The value of the subsidies for nonrecipients (that is, the altruistic benefits enjoyed by nonrecipients) were disequalizing because they were distributed in proportion to tax payments. Aggregating all direct and indirect subsidies, which is the author's preferred approach, shows that the shares received by both the lowest and the highest quintiles exceeded their shares of after-tax money income. The middle classes were the big losers.

However, the assumptions that underlie the distributional estimates are often very strong, and the findings are quite sensitive to the assumptions. The least satisfactory aspect of the paper in my view is its measurement of the values of in-kind subsidies for nonrecipients. To estimate the aggregate value for any in-kind subsidy, the author first assumes that the total social benefit value equals government cost. (The author states that in theory the value *at least* equals government cost but the estimates are based on the equality assumption.) Then the value of benefits to nonrecipients is the difference between government cost and the aggregate recipient value plus costs of program management. This nonrecipient value is distributed across income classes in proportion to tax payments.

Both resulting aggregate values and their distributions across income classes have little justification. As to the aggregate values, there is no reason to believe that the social benefit value equals government cost for every, or indeed any, in-kind subsidy. To assume so precludes inefficient government programs or programs where benefit-cost ratios exceed one. It should also be noted that in at least one other study (Smolensky et al. 1977) nonrecipient values have been taken to equal the *full* government cost of the subsidy, not just the difference between government cost and recipient benefits.

As to the distribution of the nonrecipient values, the paper treats them as pure public goods. Yet nonrecipient benefits accrue to the relatives of recipients who would otherwise have paid for some of the consumption of health care and housing, as the paper discusses, and to the health and construction industries in the cases of Medicare-Medicaid and public housing, respectively. Moreover, even if the nonrecipient benefits are treated as pure public goods, distribution by tax payments is theoretically questionable (Musgrave 1959). The distribution of public goods' benefits are, in the real world, unknown (and, given "free rider" problems, some would say unknowable). The wisest course, if they must be distributed, would seem to be to use a variety of alternative distributors, which has been done frequently in the economic literature. The distributors for public goods' benefits in the literature have included families (or households), income, capital income, disposable income, and the reciprocal of the marginal utility of expenditures (Aaron and McGuire 1970; Brennan 1981; Gillespie 1965). These studies have also found the distributive effects of public goods to vary sharply depending on which distributor is used. Because of this sensitivity, and the lack of a theoretical or practical reason for using tax payments as a distributor, the findings on nonrecipient benefits are questionable. Moreover, given how little we know about recipient benefits from in-kind income, I see little reason to embark on such a speculative endeavor as estimating the distribution of nonrecipient benefits at this time.

The estimates of the distributional effects of indirect subsidies or tax expenditures are also unsatisfactory because such subsidies are valued only at cost and not in cash equivalents. The inducement to overspend on direct subsidies, which results in cash equivalent values below cost, applies equally to indirect subsidies. Moreover, if the improvement of income measures for purposes of assessing relative well-being is the goal, measuring income on an after-tax basis is preferred. After-tax incomes of recipients of indirect subsidies are higher because of their receipt of the subsidies. Hence, one cannot add to the after-tax incomes the values of the indirect subsidies without double-counting their value.

The estimates of direct subsidies to recipients are more satisfactory. They are based on cash equivalent values, which rise with income given positive income elasticities. Hence, valuation in cash equivalents (or recipient valuation) leads to distributions of subsidies that are less equalizing than are distributions based on cost valuations. The author's ratios of cash equivalent values to market values (so-called benefit weights) for Medicare and Medicaid rose from 23 percent in the lowest income decile to 56 percent in the highest decile; their average value was 37 percent. One possible reason for this low value for medical care is that subsidies to the institutionalized are included while expenditures on institutional care are for the most part not included in the estimation of cash equivalent values. The weights for public housing subsidies rose from 59 percent to 79 percent, respectively, with an average value of 65 percent.

The estimates of cash equivalent values in the paper are only rough approximations to the true values. True cash equivalent values are measured by the money income that would leave the recipient on the same indifference curve as does the in-kind subsidy. Consequently, cash equivalent values can be estimated only by utilizing assumed utility functions. The author's estimating technique, as I understand it, compares the consumption of the specific good inherent in the in-kind subsidy with the consumption of the same good by similar households without the subsidy. To make the households similar, certain demographic characteristics are controlled for and the income level of the nonsubsidized household is taken to be the money income *plus* market value of the in-kind subsidy of the subsidized household. The cash equivalent value of the in-kind subsidy is then taken to be the consumption of the nonsubsidized household when that consumption is less than the market value of the subsidy or the market value of the subsidy when the consumption of the nonsubsidized household is more than the subsidy.

As compared to true cash equivalent values, the author's approximation has several biases. First and most importantly, the approach may *over*estimate cash equivalent values because the income level of the nonsubsidized household is too high by the difference between the market value and cash equivalent value of the subsidy. This bias is obviously most important when cash equivalent values fall well below market values (for example, in the case of medical care subsidies) and when multiple in-kind subsidies are received. On the other hand, the approach may *under*estimate cash equivalent values because preferences for the in-kind subsidy of recipients will be systematically greater than preferences of nonrecipients who are also eligible for the subsidy but choose not to participate. For example, households with similar incomes and demographic characteristics who choose not to buy into the supplementary medical insurance (SMI) portion of Medicare presumably prefer less health insurance relative to other goods in their consumption bundle than do SMI recipients. It is not clear which of these biases will dominate.

It is true, as the author points out, that estimation by utility functions is problematic, both because the true utility function is unknown and because necessary data, such as geographic price differences, are lacking. Nonetheless, given the biases in the author's approximation, and the uncertainties about cash equivalent values in general, the results presented here should be viewed with caution.

This paper, and others by Smeeding, contribute to the growing literature on income in-kind. But considerable research and reform of our income statistics remain before income in-kind can be treated adequately and income and poverty measures made meaningful.

Our official statistics continue to be deficient in their treatment of in-kind income. Poverty measures exclude noncash income despite the fact that the Food Stamp program was enacted to provide the cost of nutritional diets to low-income families; such costs form the basis of the poverty threshold. Measures of family income based on Bureau of the Census surveys also exclude noncash income. And measures of personal income in the National Income and Product Accounts are inconsistent in their inclusion of in-kind income—for example, including Medicare but excluding Medicaid—and deficient in their valuation of such income, which is by government cost rather than cash equivalent value.

These deficiencies in our official statistics are large and growing. Government in-kind subsidies to the low-income population grew sharply relative to cash income during the 1965–75 period as many of the noncash programs like Medicare and Medicaid were first implemented and expanded. Since 1975, government cash payments to low-income families have declined significantly in real terms. As a result, whereas government cash benefits accounted for around 40 percent of total benefits (cash plus noncash) to low-income families in 1975, by 1983 they are expected to account for only 30 percent of total benefits. In addition, while data are lacking, it is likely that employer-provided noncash income has risen relative to cash income.

Improvements in the treatment of noncash income have been made in recent years. The Bureau of the Census now routinely collects information on the recipiency of a few types of in-kind income in its March Current Population Survey and has recently published a study by Smeeding on valuing public in-kind transfers. If further progress is to be made, the most pressing needs are collection of better data on recipiency of private in-kind income and research developing and comparing alternative estimates of cash equivalent values. Only with the inclusion of this expanded information on in-kind income can we be assured that measures of income and their distribution portray with any reality the distribution of well-being across families and over time.

References

Aaron, Henry, and M. McGuire. 1970. Public goods and income distribution. *Econometrica* 38:907–20.

Brennan, Goeffrey. 1981. The attribution of public goods benefits. *Finances Publiques* 36:347–73.

Gillespie, W. Irwin. 1965. Effect of public expenditures on the distribution of income. In *Essays in fiscal federalism*, ed. Richard A. Musgrave. Washington, D.C.: The Brookings Institution.

Musgrave, Richard A. 1959. *The theory of public finance*. New York: McGraw-Hill.

Smolensky, Eugene, Leanna Stiefel, Maria Schmundt, and Robert Plotnick. 1977. Adding in-kind transfers to the personal income and outlay account: Implications for the size distribution of income. *The distribution of economic well-being*, ed. F. Thomas Juster. Studies in Income and Wealth, vol. 41. Cambridge, Mass. Ballantine for the National Bureau of Economic Research.

5   The Effect of Different Measures of Benefit on Estimates of the Distributive Consequences of Government Programs

Edgar O. Olsen and Kathy A. York

5.1 Introduction

Many different measures of the benefit of an in-kind transfer have been used in benefit-cost analysis. Perhaps the most common is the difference between the market value of the bundle of goods consumed under the program and the market value of the bundle that would have been consumed in its absence (e.g., Aaron 1970; E. Browning 1976, 1979; Fried et al. 1973). This measure ignores the fact that people are not indifferent between all bundles with the same market value; its advantage is that it requires less information than more sophisticated measures. Another common measure of benefit is Marshallian consumer's surplus (e.g., J. Browning 1979; Mayo et al. 1980, pp. 95–102; Olsen 1972). It is now widely known that this measure has no natural interpretation unless the income elasticity of demand for the subsidized good is zero. It is best viewed as an approximation to a measure such as Hicks's price equivalent variation. This equivalent variation is the unrestricted cash grant that would be as satisfactory to the recipient as its in-kind transfer. In recent years many attempts have been made to estimate this measure using estimated indifference maps with various degrees of generality (e.g., De Salvo 1975; Murray 1975; Olsen and Barton 1983; Rosen 1978).

The primary purpose of this paper is to provide empirical evidence concerning whether the more sophisticated measures provide markedly different conclusions about the distributive consequences of government programs. This is done for two programs known to have very different effects, namely, public housing and rent control. To estimate any of the

Edgar O. Olsen is professor of economics at the University of Virginia, Charlottesville; and Kathy A. York is a graduate student in the Department of Economics, University of Virginia, Charlottesville.

three measures of benefit for either program, it is necessary to predict the market rent of the subsidized unit. Our prediction is, in essence, the mean rent of unsubsidized units with the same observed characteristics. The Marshallian and Hicksian measures also require estimates of the trade-offs individuals are willing to make among goods, so indifference maps are estimated for various types of families using data on families living in unsubsidized private rental housing. These indifference maps are assumed to be applicable to similar subsidized families. The various measures of benefit are then calculated for each household in the public housing and the rent control samples. For these two programs, each measure of benefit is regressed on household characteristics. We conclude that the approximations to a satisfactory measure of benefit, such as Hicks's price equivalent variation, will in some cases give a misleading impression of the distributive consequences of government programs.

5.2 Derivation of Benefit Formulas

Before providing the empirical evidence, we must specify more precisely our three benefit measures. We divide all commodities into two composites called housing services and nonhousing goods and assume that all consumers of the same race who live in the same area and buy all goods in uncontrolled markets face the same set of prices and that this set of prices would be the same in the absence of public housing and rent control.[1] In addition, we assume that no household's future consumption is affected by its participation in one of these programs during the current year.[2]

Consider then a family participating in one of the two housing programs. Its preferences are presumed to be representable by the indifference map in figure 5.1. Suppose that the family has an income Y and faces prices (P_m^h, P_m^x) in the private markets for housing services and nonhousing goods. In the program's absence, the family would choose a combination (Q_m^h, Q_m^x) of the two goods. Under the program, however, the family occupies a dwelling providing Q_g^h units of housing services and commanding a rent $P_g^h Q_g^h$. This implies a consumption of nonhousing goods given by the quantity

$$(1) \qquad Q_g^x = \frac{Y - P_g^h Q_g^h}{P_m^x}.$$

Recall that the difference between the market value of the goods consumed under the program and the market value of the bundle consumed in its absence is usually called the subsidy S. That is,

$$S = P_m^h Q_g^h + P_m^x Q_g^x - Y.$$

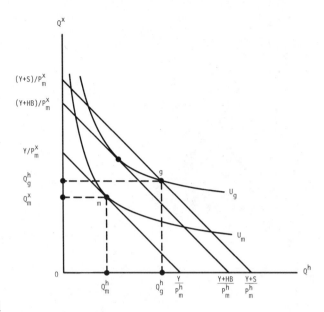

Fig. 5.1

Substituting the expression for Q_g^x from equation (1) then gives

(2) $$S = P_m^h Q_g^h - P_g^h Q_g^h,$$

so the subsidy is just the difference between the market and actual rent of the program unit. Since any combination of goods with the same market value as the bundle consumed under the program involves the same subsidy and since a family is not indifferent among all such combinations, the subsidy is not a satisfactory measure of benefit.

A measure that does not have this defect is Hicks's price equivalent variation. This is the unrestricted cash grant HB which, if given to the family in lieu of the opportunity to occupy the dwelling unit provided through the program, would yield the same level of well-being as the program. In general,

$$HB = V^{-1}(U_g, P_m^h, P_m^x) - Y,$$

where $V^{-1}(U_g, P_m^h, P_m^x)$ is the income that would allow the family to achieve at market prices the same level of well-being as attained under the program.

Another measure that has been used more frequently in empirical research is Marshallian consumer's surplus. This measure is depicted in figure 5.2, where $D(Q^h)$ is the family's Marshallian (money-income-constant) demand curve for housing services. The price-quantity combinations of housing services for the family with and without the program

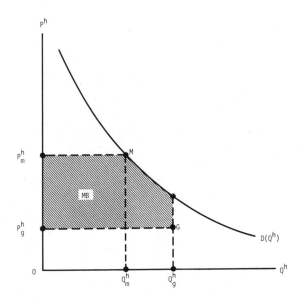

Fig. 5.2

are represented by points G and M in the diagram. The Marshallian benefit of the program MB is equal to the excess of consumer surplus at G over consumer surplus at M. Accordingly,

$$(3) \qquad \text{MB} = P_m^h Q_m^h + \int_{Q_m^h}^{Q_g^h} D(Q^h)dQ^h - P_g^h Q_g^h.$$

This is the shaded area in figure 5.2. If the income elasticity of demand for housing services were zero, then the money-income-constant and real-income-constant demand curves would coincide and the Marshallian and Hicksian measures of benefit would be the same (Blaug 1978, pp. 374–83). Otherwise, the Marshallian measure has no natural interpretation.

Neither the Marshallian nor the Hicksian measure of benefit may exceed the subsidy. A famous proposition in consumer's surplus analysis is that the Hicksian measure exceeds the Marshallian measure if the subsidized good is a normal good (Blaug 1978, pp. 374–83). However, the proof of this proposition assumes that the change in well-being results from a rotation of a linear budget constraint. Since neither public housing nor rent control change budget constraints in this way (Kraft and Olsen 1977, pp. 52–53; Olsen 1972, pp. 1083–84), the Marshallian measure need not be less than the Hicksian measure for these programs. This is easily seen by supposing that point G in figure 5.2 is directly below point M, in which case point g in figure 5.1 would be directly above point m. In this case the Marshallian measure of benefit, MB, is equal to the subsidy, S, but if housing service is a normal good, the Hicksian measure, HB, is less than the subsidy. We estimate that the Marshallian benefit exceeds the Hicksian benefit for about 80 percent of the households in rent controlled units and 6 percent of those in public housing units.

To estimate the Hicksian and Marshallian benefits accruing to a participant family, we posit that each family's preferences are representable by a Stone-Geary or displaced Cobb-Douglas utility function,

(4) $$U = (Q^h - \beta^h)^\gamma (Q^x - \beta^x)^{1-\gamma},$$

where β^h and β^x are usually interpreted as the family's subsistence levels of housing services and nonhousing goods, and γ is the marginal propensity to spend on housing services out of income. All parameters are allowed to vary across families.

Olsen and Barton (1983) show that the Hicksian benefit formula for the Stone-Geary utility function (4) is

(5) $$\begin{aligned} \text{HB} = &[(P_m^h Q_g^h - P_m^h \beta^h)/\gamma]^\gamma \\ &[(P_m^x Q_g^x - P_m^x \beta^x)/(1-\gamma)]^{(1-\gamma)} \\ &+ P_m^h \beta^h + P_m^x \beta^x - Y. \end{aligned}$$

The Marshallian demand function corresponding to the Stone-Geary utility function is

(6) $$P^h = \gamma(Y - P^x \beta^x)/[Q^h - (1-\gamma)\beta^h].$$

Substituting this into equation (3) and evaluating the integral gives the Marshallian benefit formula

(7) $$\begin{aligned} \text{MB} = &P_m^h Q_m^h - P_g^h Q_g^h + \gamma(Y - P_m^x \beta^x)\{\ln[P_m^h Q_g^h \\ &- (1-\gamma)P_m^h \beta^h] \\ &- \ln[P_m^h Q_m^h - (1-\gamma)P_m^h \beta^h]\}. \end{aligned}$$

The subsidy can be calculated from a knowledge of the market rent of the family's subsidized unit and its expenditure on housing under the program. Although the characteristics of the subsidized unit can be observed, its market rent must be estimated since it is not rented in the private, uncontrolled market. The housing expenditure of each subsidized family is directly observed. Estimation of the Hicksian and Marshallian benefit requires, in addition, a knowledge of the family's income and estimates of the parameters of its indifference map. Knowledge of the family's income and housing expenditure under the program and the estimate of the market rent of its subsidized unit determine the location of point g in figure 5.1. This information plus estimates of the parameters of the family's indifference map determine the graph of the indifference curve containing the consumption bundle under the program which together with the family's income determines its Hicksian benefit.[3] The Marshallian benefit depends on the same parameters and variables.

Expenditure on housing in the absence of the program $P_m^h Q_m^h$, which appears in the formula for Marshallian benefit, can be calculated from this information using the demand function (6).

5.3 The Data

The empirical results of this paper are based on data for a stratified random sample of about 35,000 housing units and their occupants from the 1965 New York City Housing and Vacancy Survey.[4] The data are of the sort collected in the Decennial Census of Population and Housing except that information was collected on whether the housing unit was in a public housing project or subject to rent control.

5.4 Predictions of Indifference Map Parameters

5.4.1 Marginal Propensity to Spend on Housing

A family with a Stone-Geary indifference map (4) and paying market prices for all goods will spend a fraction,

$$(8) \qquad P^h Q^h / Y = \gamma + (1 - \gamma)\beta^h (P^h / Y) - \gamma\beta^x (P^x / Y),$$

of its income on housing. Since we do not directly observe the market prices facing households, we cannot estimate the parameters γ, β^h, and β^x in a straightforward way. So we proceed in two steps.

First, we rewrite equation (8) as

$$(9) \qquad P^h Q^h / Y = \gamma + \alpha(1/Y),$$

where $\alpha = (1 - \gamma)P^h\beta^h - \gamma P^x\beta^x$. To allow for the possibility that market prices and the indifference map parameters differ systematically for different types of families, we write γ and α as functions of the variables for location, race, and family size defined in table 5.1. To allow for differences in the observed rent-income ratio among families with the same values of explanatory variables, we add to equation (9) an error term with mean zero. Since the observations are generated by random sampling, the explanatory variables in this regression are stochastic. If the error term is uncorrelated with these stochastic regressors, ordinary least squares (OLS) estimators are consistent. Table 5.1 presents the OLS estimates based on the 4,014 families in the sample living in unfurnished uncontrolled private rental housing for which the values of the required variables are reported.[5]

These results enable us to estimate the mean marginal propensity to spend on housing for different types of families. For example, the estimated mean for two-person black households living in Manhattan is .0356 (= .0978 + .0284 − .0517 − .0389). However, they do not enable us to

Table 5.1   **Estimated Relationship between Rent-Income Ratio and Family Characteristics**

Regressors	Descriptions of Regressors	Coefficients	t-scores
CONS	Constant	.0978	16.9
MANH	1 if unit in Manhattan; 0 otherwise	.0284	5.5
BLACK	1 if black; 0 otherwise	−.0517	−6.6
FS2	1 if family size is 2; 0 otherwise	−.0389	−6.0
FS3	1 if family size is 3; 0 otherwise	−.0382	−4.8
FS4	1 if family size is 4; 0 otherwise	−.0688	−8.5
FS5	1 if family size is at least 5; 0 otherwise	−.0115	−1.1
ININC	Inverse of annual income	832.3	50.0
MANHC	MANH*ININC	393.7	14.5
BLACKC	BLACK*ININC	78.7	2.5
FS2C	FS2*ININC	372.5	14.3
FS3C	FS3*ININC	434.6	10.7
FS4C	FS4*ININC	627.6	17.0
FS5C	FS5*ININC	229.9	4.6

$R^2 = .77$; standard error = .09; number of observations = 4014.

make estimates of the subsistence parameters. The second step in estimating the parameters of the indifference map involves using the estimates of α implicit in table 5.1 and independent estimates of subsistence expenditure on housing $P^h \beta^h$ to estimate $P^x \beta^x$.

5.4.2   Subsistence Parameters

If subsistence housing expenditure $P^h \beta^h$ is the same for all households of a particular type, if the population of households of each type in New York City contains a household at subsistence, and if the rents of all uncontrolled, privately owned apartments are accurately reported and reflect neither public nor private charity, then the sample minimum rent of such units for families of each type is a consistent estimator of $P^h \beta^h$, and its upward bias declines to zero as the sample size approaches the population size. Table 5.2 presents the sample minima for the 5,675 families reported to be living in uncontrolled, private rental housing for whom values of all required variables are available.

The erratic pattern of these minima suggests substantial violations of at least one of the assumptions underlying the use of the sample minimum as an estimate of $P^h \beta^h$. To obtain a more acceptable pattern, we first used the market rent prediction equations discussed in section 5.5 to estimate the difference in the price per unit of housing service in Manhattan and elsewhere in New York City. This is done by using the market rent equations for Manhattan and non-Manhattan to predict rents for all uncontrolled, private rental units in the city and by comparing the means of these predictions. We conclude that rents of units in Manhattan are 46

Table 5.2   Sample Minimum Annual Rents for Private, Uncontrolled Rental
                   Housing

| | Non-Manhattan | | Manhattan | |
FS	White	Black	White	Black
1	480	612	900	720
	(429)	(45)	(564)	(39)
2	240	516	372	660
	(1296)	(95)	(619)	(52)
3	684	648	900	1080
	(883)	(89)	(173)	(20)
4	360	780	864	732
	(692)	(73)	(84)	(23)
5+	300	625	1320	744
	(376)	(88)	(23)	(12)

Number of cases in parentheses.

percent greater than rents of similar units elsewhere. This result is used to express non-Mahattan sample minima in Manhattan prices. We then regress the natural logarithm of these adjusted sample minima on the natural logarithm of family size separately for blacks and whites. The OLS estimates are $6.43 + .086 \ln(FS)$ with $R^2 = .11$ for whites, and $6.66 + .086 \ln(FS)$ with $R^2 = .28$ for blacks. These equations together with our estimate of the difference in the price per unit of housing service between Manhattan and other boroughs are used to calculate the predicted subsistence rents reported in table 5.3. While these estimates clearly leave much to be desired, we believe they are better than the sample minima.

Substituting estimates of γ and α derived from table 5.1 and $P^h \beta^h$ from table 5.3 into the definition of α yields an estimate of $P^x \beta^x$. Specifically

$$(10) \qquad P^x \hat{\beta}^x = [(1 - \hat{\gamma}) P^h \hat{\beta}^h - \hat{\alpha}]/\hat{\gamma}.$$

Table 5.3   Predicted Subsistence Rents

| | Non-Manhattan | | Manhattan | |
FS	White	Black	White	Black
1	425	535	620	781
2	451	568	659	829
3	469	585	685	854
4	479	603	699	880
5+	489	615	713	899

The estimates of this parameter were implausibly large in absolute value for several family types with unusually small estimates of the marginal propensity to spend on housing. Rewriting equation (10) as

$$P^x \hat{\beta}^x = [(P^h \hat{\beta}^h - \hat{\alpha})/\hat{\gamma}] - P^h \hat{\beta}^h$$

makes clear that $P^x \hat{\beta}^x$ will be very sensitive to errors in estimating γ for γ near zero. Since we believe that our estimates of the marginal propensity are implausibly small for several family types, we decided to set it equal to .01 when the results in table 5.1 led to a smaller estimate.

Estimates of $P^x \hat{\beta}^x$ were negative for all family types. This is typical of attempts to estimate the Stone-Geary indifference map with data on individual households (Cronin 1979; Hammond 1982, pp. 102–113; Olsen and Barton 1983, p. 311). In light of the theoretical and statistical reasons for expecting difficulties in estimating subsistence expenditures (Olsen and Barton 1983, p. 313), it is best to think of our estimates as yielding a reasonable approximation of the true indifference map over that part of consumption space containing the consumption bundles in our sample rather than as reliable estimates of subsistence.

The indifference maps estimated in this section are typical of families of each type living in unsubsidized housing. We want to use them to estimate benefits for subsidized families, so we assume that the preferences of families in public housing or rent-controlled units do not differ systematically from those of unsubsidized families. It has been suggested that the typical family in public housing has a stronger than average taste for housing and vice versa for the typical family in a controlled unit. However, a previous study using the same data and the procedures developed by Heckman (1979) concluded that selection bias is not an important objection to using the methods of this paper to estimate the benefits of the public housing program (Olsen and Barton 1983, pp. 314–15).

5.5   Predictions of Market Rent

To estimate benefits using any of the measures requires a prediction of the market rent of the housing unit occupied under the program. To make such predictions we first estimate a linear relationship between annual gross rent per room and the variables listed in table 5.4 together with the product of these variables and a racial dummy variable. The inclusion of the racial interaction terms permits the coefficients of the explanatory variables to be different for blacks and whites. Relationships are estimated separately for Manhattan and other parts of the city. The data are for unfurnished, uncontrolled, private rental housing for which the values of the variables involved are reported.[6]

Table 5.4 presents the results. In the Manhattan regression, the racial interaction for duplex built prior to 1947 does not appear because the two units in this category were occupied by blacks. Other variables were omitted because they had no variance in the sample. In the non-Manhattan regression, the variable for condition of the unit was deleted because it had the wrong sign and was statistically insignificant at conventional levels.

Although we would not, in most cases, reject the hypotheses that the coefficient of the individual racial interaction variables are zero at con-

Table 5.4   **Estimated Relationships between Annual Gross Rent per Room and Housing Characteristics**

Descriptions of Explanatory Variables	Manhattan Coefficients		Non-Manhattan Coefficients	
	Explanatory Variables	Racial Interactions	Explanatory Variables	Racial Interactions
Inverse of the number of rooms	1153.99**	−34.61	920.96**	86.22
1 if duplex built prior to 1947; 0 otherwise	−262.00	—	−174.34**	35.51
1 if duplex built in 1947–59; 0 otherwise	—	—	−91.21**	−13.30
1 if duplex built in 1960–65; 0 otherwise	—	—	−55.15**	−20.81
1 if duplex built prior to 1947 and converted to apartment; 0 otherwise	−196.69**	20.90	−111.87**	−54.14
1 if duplex built after 1947 and converted to apartment; 0 otherwise	−35.54	−345.58	−112.34**	—
1 if apartment built before 1901; 0 otherwise	−324.81**	169.17	−223.06**	91.00
1 if apartment built in 1901–29; 0 otherwise	−160.28**	−84.57	−163.03**	6.74
1 if apartment built in 1930–59; 0 otherwise	−159.90**	71.29	−58.22**	38.36
1 if dwelling in Queens; 0 otherwise	—	—	12.20**	37.03**
1 if dwelling in Richmond; 0 otherwise	—	—	31.38**	−83.13
1 if dwelling in Bronx; 0 otherwise	—	—	−4.30	27.85
Story of unit if less than 7; 0 otherwise	−17.14	17.35	−7.79*	0.76
Story of unit if building has elevator; 0 otherwise	31.10	−18.16	19.15**	−12.53
1 if story of unit is at least 7; 0 otherwise	123.79**	−96.45	89.22**	−94.78**
1 if unit is in sound condition; 0 otherwise	30.73	139.65	—	—
Percentage of rooms that are bedrooms	0.19	−0.04	0.48**	0.30
Constant	421.59**	−341.18	224.59**	−55.37
R^2	.53		.73	
Standard error	235		95	
Number of observations	1526		3827	

Each racial interaction variable is the variable BLACK times an explanatory variable. One asterisk indicates significance at the .05 level; two, significance at the .01 level.

ventional levels of significance, the hypothesis that they are all zero is rejected. The relative magnitudes of the coefficients are as expected in most cases. The main exceptions are for units occupied by blacks which accounted for less than 10 percent of the sample in each location.

To predict the market rent of a subsidized unit, we substitute its characteristics, including the race of its occupants, into the appropriate equation and multiply by the number of rooms. This procedure is satisfactory to the extent that the mean market rent of subsidized units is the same as the mean market rent of unsubsidized units with the same *observed* characteristics.

5.6   Comparisons of Different Benefit Measures

The estimated indifference map parameters, predicted market rents, and information collected in the survey enable us to estimate the alternative measures of benefit given by equations (2), (5), and (7) for each of 1366 families in public housing and 5640 families in rent-controlled units.[7]

5.6.1   Mean Benefits and Correlation Coefficients

The mean values of the subsidy, the Marshallian benefit, and the Hicksian benefit of public housing and rent control, along with the mean values of other key variables, are given in table 5.5; the correlation coefficients between the different benefit measures are given in table 5.6.

For public housing the means of the Hicksian and Marshallian benefit measures differ inappreciably and their correlation coefficient is close to one. This suggests that the more sophisticated Hicksian equivalent variation contributes little above the contribution of the Marshallian consumer

Table 5.5   **Means of Alternative Measures of Benefits and Other Variables**

Description of Variable	Public Housing	Rent Control
Subsidy	$1,242	$ 395
Marshallian benefit	$1,114	$ 204
Hicksian benefit	$1,136	$ 107
Gross income	$4,488	$5,678
Predicted market rent	$2,084	$1,397
Actual rent	$ 842	$ 994
Estimated "subsistence" housing	$ 589	$ 543
Estimated "subsistence" nonhousing	− $27,145	− $17,631
Age of head of household	46	49
Estimated marginal propensity to spend on housing	0.06	0.07
Family size	3.75	2.74
Proportion black headed	0.39	0.15
Proportion female headed	0.24	0.26

All dollar magnitudes are annual.

Table 5.6   Correlations between Different Benefit Measures

	Public Housing	
	MB	HB
S	.952	.961
MB	—	.999

	Rent Control	
	MB	HB
S	.763	.603
MB	—	.956

surplus to our knowledge of the public housing program's distributive consequences. A comparison of the Hicksian benefit and the subsidy leads to somewhat different conclusions. The subsidy overstates the benefit accruing to an average family by approximately 9 percent. Still, the correlation of the Hicksian benefit and the subsidy is quite high.

Rent control is strikingly different from public housing not only with respect to mean benefit but also with respect to the relationships between different measures of benefit. The mean subsidy is more than three times as large as the mean Hicksian benefit, while the mean Marshallian benefit is almost twice as large. Furthermore, the correlations between the subsidy and the other two benefit measures are much lower than for public housing. These findings suggest that the different measures might lead to different conclusions concerning the distributive effects of rent control.

5.6.2   Regressions of Benefit Measures on Family Characteristics

To explore in more detail the effects of different benefit measures on perceptions of the distributive consequences of government programs, we regress each benefit measure on family characteristics. The results for public housing and rent control are reported in tables 5.7 and 5.8.

In the case of public housing, the three measures yield the same qualitative results. Mean benefit is greater for poorer and larger households and for households with a younger white head.[8] Among otherwise similar households, there is little difference in mean benefit between male- and female-headed households. The variation in benefit among households that are the same with respect to the observed characteristics is substantial no matter what measure of benefit is used.

However, substantial differences are present in the quantitative results based on the subsidy and those based on the other two measures. Among otherwise similar families, the estimated difference in the mean subsidy is about twice as large as the estimated difference in either the Marshallian

Table 5.7   Estimated Relationships between Annual Benefit and Family
                   Characteristics for Public Housing

	Benefit Measure		
Family Characteristics	S	MB	HB
Gross annual income	−.050**	−.024**	−.027**
	(−7.013)	(−3.963)	(−4.311)
Family size	102.523**	46.235**	52.137**
	(13.560)	(7.232)	(7.795)
1 if head is black;	−355.742**	−265.979**	−294.169**
0 otherwise	(−13.670)	(−12.088)	(−12.777)
1 if head is female;	70.602*	5.650	14.597
0 otherwise	(2.038)	(.193)	(.476)
Age of head	−2.051*	−3.214**	−3.089**
	(−2.152)	(−3.988)	(−3.663)
Constant	1344.516**	1311.547**	1331.112**
	(18.375)	(21.199)	(20.563)
R^2	.22	.14	.15
Standard error	456	386	403

Numbers in parentheses are t-scores. One asterisk indicates significance at the .05 level;
two, significance at the .01 level.

or Hicksian benefit for a given difference in income or family size. These
discrepancies are easy to explain. Public housing is more stimulative of
housing consumption than a cash grant (in an amount equal to the
subsidy) for almost all participants (Olsen and Barton 1983, p. 322). As a
participating family's income increases, its consumption of nonhousing
goods increases but its housing consumption is unchanged. As a result,
the program distorts its consumption pattern to a lesser extent (i.e., the
Hicksian benefit approaches the subsidy). Larger families in public housing are assigned to larger units but are not required to pay greater rents,
so housing consumption increases with family size but nonhousing consumption is unaffected. Therefore, the program is more distortive for
larger families (i.e., the ratio of Hicksian benefit to subsidy is less). The
implications of the alternative measures for perceived differences in
mean benefit based on the age, race, or sex of the head of the household
are smaller. For example, the estimated difference between the mean
subsidy of a household headed by a person twenty years old and that of a
household headed by a person seventy years old is $103 per year. The
estimated difference in the Hicksian benefit is $155 per year.
    In the case of rent control, the three measures yield similar qualitative
results. Mean benefit is greater for poorer households and for households

Table 5.8   Estimated Relationships between Annual Benefit and Family
                   Characteristics for Rent Control

	Benefit Measure		
Family Characteristics	S	MB	HB
Gross annual income	−.011**	−0.038**	−0.044**
	(−7.235)	(−16.385)	(−12.499)
Family size	−4.817	−2.736	−4.902
	(−1.213)	(−0.443)	(−0.524)
1 if head is black;	−245.995**	−806.917**	−1375.098**
0 otherwise	(−15.377)	(−32.437)	(−36.468)
1 if head is female;	34.504*	60.673**	101.618**
0 otherwise	(2.484)	(2.809)	(3.104)
Age of head	4.112**	2.561**	0.794
	(11.123)	(4.456)	(0.911)
Constant	293.101**	405.470**	510.802**
	(10.662)	(9.485)	(7.883)
R^2	.09	.20	.21
Standard error	416	647	981

Numbers in parentheses are t-scores. One asterisk indicates significance at the .05 level;
two, significance at the .01 level.

with white or female heads.[9] Family size is neither an important nor a
statistically significant determinant of any measure of benefit. The only
qualitative difference is that age of the head of the household is statistically insignificant at conventional levels in the regression explaining
Hicksian benefit but is highly significant in the other two regressions.
Finally, all three regressions suggest that there is nothing approaching
equal treatment of equals under rent control.

For this program both the subsidy and the Marshallian measure give
misleading impressions of the magnitudes of the differences in the mean
Hicksian benefit for various types of households. Among otherwise similar families, the estimated difference in the mean Hicksian benefit is four
times as large as the estimated difference in the subsidy for a given
difference in income. The difference in the Hicksian benefit to otherwise
similar blacks and whites is more than five times as large as the difference
in the subsidy and 70 percent larger than the difference in the Marshallian
benefit. Large differences also exist for family size and the sex and age of
the head of the household.

5.7 Comparisons of Two Hicksian Benefit Measures

Any indifference map that can be specified as a basis for calculating
Hicksian benefit is a special case of some more general indifference map.

Since the more general indifference maps are typically more difficult to estimate and use in predicting benefit, it is desirable to know whether they lead to markedly different conclusions concerning the distributive consequences of government programs. We explore this question by estimating the benefits of public housing and rent control using a Cobb-Douglas indifference map, which is a special case of the Stone-Geary indifference map.

In the two-good case, the Cobb-Douglas indifference map has only one parameter that can be interpreted as the marginal propensity to spend on housing or the rent-income ratio of a household maximizing subject to a linear budget constraint. Since the mean value of this parameter can be different for families of different types, we regress the rent-income ratio of families living in unfurnished, uncontrolled, private rental housing on their characteristics. The results are reported in equation (11), where the numbers in parentheses are t-scores.

(11) $P^h Q^h / Y = .3242 + .0048 \text{ MANH} + .0698 \text{ BLACK}$
              (38.0)   (0.67)   (6.99)

              $- .0724 \text{ FS2} - .0944 \text{ FS3} - .0846 \text{ FS4}$
              $(- 7.92)$ $(- 9.24)$ $(- 7.75)$

              $- .0902 \text{ FS5};$ $R^2 = .04$
              $(- 7.15)$

The huge decline in R^2 when the displacement parameters of the Stone-Geary indifference map are constrained to be equal to zero (compare equation [11] with table 5.1) suggests the possibility that the Cobb-Douglas and Stone-Geary indifference maps will yield markedly different conclusions concerning the distributive consequences of public housing and rent control.

The Cobb-Douglas indifference map has been used in a number of previous studies, for example, Clarkson (1976), De Salvo (1975), and Kraft and Olsen (1977). In an earlier study, Murray (1975, pp. 784–86) noted several differences in the distribution of Hicksian benefits among participants in the public housing program when a Cobb-Douglas rather than a generalized constant elasticity of substitution indifference map was used. Most notably he found that using a Cobb-Douglas indifference map to estimate benefit led to the conclusion that mean benefit varies directly with income among families in a single city. Our results reported in table 5.9 corroborate this finding. They also suggest that using a Cobb-Douglas indifference map to estimate the benefits of public housing will lead to a substantial understatement of the difference in mean benefits among otherwise similar blacks and whites.

In the case of rent control, the results based on a Cobb-Douglas indifference map lead us to be confident that mean benefit is smaller for female-headed households, while the more general displaced Cobb-

Table 5.9   Estimated Relationships between Two Hicksian Benefit Measures and Family Characteristics

Family Characteristics	Public Housing		Rent Control	
	Undisplaced Cobb-Douglas	Displaced Cobb-Douglas	Undisplaced Cobb-Douglas	Displaced Cobb-Douglas
Gross annual income	.064**	−.027**	−.117**	−0.044**
	(9.921)	(−4.311)	(−46.194)	(−12.499)
Family size	52.078**	52.137**	37.680**	−4.902
	(7.581)	(7.795)	(5.591)	(−0.524)
1 if head is black; 0 otherwise	−73.956**	−294.169**	−430.917**	−1375.098**
	(−3.128)	(−12.777)	(−15.870)	(−36.468)
1 if head is female; 0 otherwise	−27.237	14.597	−166.972**	101.618**
	(−.865)	(.476)	(−7.083)	(3.104)
Age of head	−3.615**	−3.089**	−2.884**	0.794
	(−4.175)	(−3.663)	(−4.597)	(0.911)
Constant	677.887**	1331.112**	861.475**	510.802**
	(10.196)	(20.563)	(18.463)	(7.883)
R^2	.24	.15	.29	.21
Standard error	414	403	706	981

Numbers in parentheses are t-scores. One asterisk indicates significance at the .05 level; two, significance at the .01 level.

Douglas leads to the opposite conclusion. The Cobb-Douglas results lead us to be confident that mean benefit varies directly with family size and inversely with the age of the head of the household, while the more general indifference map suggests no such relationships. Finally, the two indifference maps lead to very different impressions of the extent to which mean benefit varies with family income and race.

5.8 Conclusion

The evidence presented in this paper shows that the inferences made about the distributive consequences of a government program can depend importantly on the measure of benefit used and the specification of the underlying prediction equations. Additional studies involving other programs are desirable to judge the extent of the misimpressions created by using approximations to a satisfactory measure of benefit and highly restrictive indifference maps. In the meantime we should avoid these approximations (i.e., the subsidy and Marshallian consumer surplus) and the Cobb-Douglas indifference map whenever time and data permit. More general indifference maps, such as the Stone-Geary and Constant

Elasticity of Substitution, are easy to estimate and to use in estimating a satisfactory measure of benefit, such as Hicks's price equivalent variation. Finally, we should be modest in making claims about the effects of government programs on the distribution of well-being since any satisfactory measure of benefit will depend on individual preferences, and any indifference map that is simple enough to use is likely to provide at best a rough approximation to such preferences.

Notes

1. See Olsen (1972, pp. 1096–99) and Olsen and Barton (1983, pp. 3–5) for a detailed discussion of the assumptions underlying this analysis.

2. Since this is an unsatisfactory model of intertemporal choice, we did estimate intertemporal indifference maps under a number of sets of assumptions. In some cases estimates of the structural parameters could not be recovered from estimates of the reduced form parameters; in other cases the estimates were implausible. Since we have limited confidence in the intertemporal indifference maps estimated and since using them to estimate benefits would be difficult, we did not pursue this matter further. See Olsen and Barton (1983, pp. 14–15 and 38–39) for a discussion of some attempts to estimate intertemporal indifference maps using the data underlying this study, and Hammond (1982) for a policy analysis in which such indifference maps are estimated and used to calculate benefits of several government housing programs.

3. Since market prices are assumed to be the same for similar families and the same with and without the programs, we can define units of output for families of each type such that both prices are 1. Therefore, a knowledge of the differences in prices facing different types of families is not necessary for the purposes of this paper.

4. The stratification was intended to increase the efficiency with which rental vacancy rates could be estimated. Housing units in existence in 1960 and located in census enumeration districts ranking in the top 5 percent in terms of the vacancy rate were placed in one stratum. Other housing units in existence in 1960 were placed in another. Units built more recently were put in strata according to their age. A description of the sample design can be obtained from the authors. The probabilities of selection were used in calculating means but not in estimating stochastic relationships. For a discussion of the latter, see Olsen and Barton, (1983, pp. 328–30).

5. No public housing units and few rent-controlled units are furnished. These controlled units are excluded from our analysis of the distribution of benefits.

6. Units in single-family structures, with eight or more rooms, or in several unusual structure types were deleted from the sample. Few public housing or rent-controlled units have these characteristics, and these deletions reduced the sample used to estimate the market rent equation by only 6 percent.

7. For 3 percent of the rent control sample, the Hicksian and Marshallian measures could not be calculated because predicted market rent is less than our estimate of subsistence housing expenditure. The mean annual difference is $266. In these cases we set $P_m^h Q_g^h = P_m^h \beta^h + 1$. For almost 2 percent of the rent control sample and 1 percent of the public housing sample, the reported subsidized rent exceeds reported income. The annual differences are $157 and $202, respectively. Even though benefit could be calculated in these cases, we set $Y = P_g^h Q_g^h + 1$. Such problems seem inevitable in working with data on individual households.

8. Olsen and Barton (1983, p. 325), using the same data but somewhat different methods for estimating indifference maps and predicting market rents, found essentially no difference between the mean benefits of similar black and white households and households with younger and older heads.

9. The results in table 5.8 also differ from Olsen's (1972, p. 1094) results based on data from the 1968 New York City Housing and Vacancy Survey, a different Marshallian demand curve, and a different equation for predicting market rent. Most notably, Olsen concluded that blacks received somewhat larger benefits than whites. The most likely explanation for this discrepancy is his failure to allow for racial differences in the coefficients of the market rent equation.

References

Aaron, Henry. 1970. Income taxes and housing. *American Economic Review* 60:789–806.

Blaug, Mark. 1978. *Economic theory in retrospect*. 3d ed. Cambridge: Cambridge University Press.

Browning, Edgar K. 1976. The trend toward equality in the distribution of net income. *Southern Economic Journal* 43:912–23.

———. 1979. On the distribution of net income: Reply. *Southern Economic Journal* 45:945–59.

Browning, Jacquelene M. 1979. Estimating the welfare cost of tax preferences. *Public Finance Quarterly* 7:199–219.

Clarkson, Kenneth W. 1976. Welfare benefits of the Food Stamp program. *Southern Economic Journal* 43:864–78.

Cronin, Francis J. 1979. *The housing demand of low-income households*. Report no. 294–25. Washington, D.C.: The Urban Institute.

De Salvo, Joseph S. 1975. Benefits and costs of New York City's middle-income housing program. *Journal of Political Economy* 83:791–806.

Fried, Edward R., Alice M. Rivlin, Charles L. Schultze, and Nancy H. Tetters. 1973. *Setting national priorities: The 1974 budget*. Washington, D.C.: The Brookings Institution.

Hammond, Claire Marie Holton. 1982. The benefits of subsidized housing programs: An intertemporal approach. Ph.D. diss., University of Virginia.

Heckman, James J. 1979. Sample selection bias as a specification error. *Econometrica* 47:153–61.

Kraft, John, and Edgar O. Olsen. 1977. The distribution of benefits from public housing. In *The distribution of economic well-being*, ed. F. T. Juster. Studies in Income and Wealth, vol. 41. New York: National Bureau of Economic Research.

Mayo, Stephen K., Shirley Mansfield, David Warner, and Richard Zwetchkenbaum. *Housing allowances and other rental housing assist-ance programs—A comparison based on the housing allowance demand experiment, part 1: Participation, housing consumption, location, and satisfaction*. Cambridge, Mass.: Abt Associates.

Murray, Michael P. 1975. The distribution of tenant benefits in public housing. *Econometrica* 43:771–88.

Olsen, Edgar O. 1972. An econometric analysis of rent control. *Journal of Political Economy* 80:1081–1100.

Olsen, Edgar O., and David M. Barton. 1983. The benefits and costs of public housing in New York City. *Journal of Public Economics* 20:299–332.

Rosen, Harvey. 1982. The benefits and costs of public housing in New York City. Discussion paper 123, Thomas Jefferson Center for Political Economy, University of Virginia.

———. 1978. The measurement of excess burden with explicit utility functions. *Journal of Political Economy* 86:S121–S135.

Comment   Robert Hutchens

Economists interested in distributional issues have for some time wrestled with the problem of measuring the value of in-kind transfers. In essence the problem is that we do not exactly like what we can measure, and we cannot exactly measure what we like. On the one hand, we can obtain reasonably accurate measures of the market value of in-kind transfers, but for purposes of looking at distributional questions such measures are not entirely satisfactory. On the other hand, we would like to measure the cash equivalent of the transfers, but when we try to do this we have little confidence in the accuracy of our results.

The paper by Edgar Olsen and Kathy York demonstrates the seriousness of this problem. Their work analyzes the distribution of benefits from two government programs—rent control and public housing—in New York City. For each person in their sample they obtain three different measures of the program benefit: market value, Hicks's cash equivalent, and Marshallian consumer surplus. Their purpose is to determine whether the three different measures yield different conclusions about the distributional consequences of the programs. This is a useful approach. If several distributional studies find that Hicksian and Marshallian measures yield about the same conclusions as market value measures, then our problem would be solved. We could rely on the more easily obtained market value measure and safely ignore the more sophisticated measures. Alternatively, if it is found that the three measures yield vastly different conclusions, then we will at least know that our problem is indeed a serious one.

The paper opens with a discussion of the mechanics of computing the different benefit measures. The authors confront three issues here. First,

Robert Hutchens is a professor of economics at Cornell University.

market rents are not observed for the households in subsidized (or controlled) units. Of course, without data on market rents the market value of the subsidy received by the household cannot be determined. Olsen and York resolve this by estimating a hedonic model of rents paid by households in unsubsidized units and then imputing rents to the subsidized units. In this paper then, the market value of the subsidy received by a household is a predicted quantity; it is equal to the predicted market rent minus actual rental payments. The second issue confronted by Olsen and York is lack of data on individual utility functions. Without knowledge of the shape of utility functions, the Hicksian and Marshallian measures cannot be computed. To resolve this the authors assume that the New Yorkers in their sample have a Stone-Geary utility function over two composite goods, housing and nonhousing. The parameters of the utility function may vary by race, family size, and whether or not the family lives in Manhattan. Although there were major difficulties in obtaining plausible empirical results for their utility function, the authors eventually settle on a set of parameters that in their view represents a reasonable approximation of the indifference map over the relevant choice set. The final mechanical issue involves calculating the Hicksian and Marshallian measures. Given information on the market value of the subsidy and the parameters of the utility function, this is a matter of inserting numbers into an appropriately specified mathematical formula.

When Olsen and York compute the three benefit measures for the families in their sample, they find rather striking differences in the resulting distributions. They first analyze means and the correlation coefficients. For public housing the three measures are highly correlated and yield similar mean benefits. For rent control, however, different results emerge. The means are substantially different, and the correlation coefficients are well below one. Next they regress the three different measures on family characteristics and find that each measure yields different regression coefficients. Finally, they analyze a Hicksian benefit measure that is based on a Cobb-Douglas rather than the Stone-Geary utility function. Once again distributional conclusions are sensitive to this change in specification.

We cannot then say that it makes no difference how in-kind benefits are measured. This work suggests that distributional conclusions can be quite sensitive to whether the in-kind benefits are measured at their market value, their Hicksian cash equivalent, or their Marshallian consumer surplus.

I will focus my comments on two aspects of the paper. The first concerns the empirical methods used in obtaining the three measures. The second concerns the distributional consequences of the different measures.

First, it is conceivable that the paper's conclusions are the result of inaccurate information and that in reality the market value measure is closely related to the Hicksian or Marshallian measure of the benefit. The empirical techniques employed in the paper rely on predicted market rents, predicted utility function parameters, and self-reported incomes. Even if one grants the assumption that all utility functions are Stone-Geary and that there are no other in-kind programs, reporting and prediction errors may cause the measured benefits to diverge significantly from the true benefits. Put another way, if the econometrician had all of the information that is available to the consumer, he may come to a different conclusion. This can be illustrated by considering the Hicks cash equivalent benefit. To compute a household's Hicks benefit the authors not only predict the parameters of the household's utility function, but also the size of the household's subsidy. They implicitly assume that errors in predicting the parameters of the utility function are uncorrelated with the subsidy. Suppose this is not true. In particular, suppose that people with tastes for housing that are stronger than the predicted tastes tend on average to obtain lower subsidies. This would seem plausible for rent control. If units with a large subsidy (a large discrepancy between market rents and controlled rents) are less adequately maintained, then people with strong tastes for housing may tend to avoid such units. In this case the estimated Hicks cash equivalent benefit would be biased as would the correlation between the Hicks benefit and the market value of the benefit. A similar story could be told for income reporting. If the people who tend to under report income also tend to live in units with large subsidies, then the Hicks benefit and the correlations computed here will be biased. My point is that it is conceivable that more accurate information on crucial variables or, alternatively, explicit modeling of the covariance structure of prediction errors could overturn the paper's results.

Such an argument can, however, be made for almost any empirical study and is not particularly compelling in this case. If in-kind transfers constrain the behavior of recipients, then a market value measure should diverge from a Hicksian cash equivalent measure. Given differences in income and tastes across a population, it would be surprising to observe a close relationship between the different measures. Although more accurate information on subsidies and utility function parameters could perhaps make the paper more convincing, the conclusion that the different measures have different distributional consequences is in my view quite reasonable.

This leads to the second point. Can anything more be said about the different distributional consequences of the different measures? Does knowledge of the distribution with in-kind benefits measured at their market value tell us anything about the distribution with in-kind benefits measured at their Hicksian cash equivalent? This paper is silent on such questions, and the authors may wish to pursue them in future research. Let me illustrate. Consider an in-kind transfer program that is income conditioned. It provides larger benefits to families with smaller cash incomes, yet does not affect the rank order of families in the income distribution. Suppose we wish to analyze inequality in the distribution of cash plus in-kind income in the population served by this program. For this purpose one might use either a market cost or cash equivalent measure of the in-kind benefits. How would the different measures affect an assessment of inequality in the distribution of cash plus in-kind income? It can be shown that under certain assumptions the market value measure leads to a more equal distribution of cash plus in-kind income than does the cash equivalent measure. That is, a market value measure will indicate the maximum equalizing effect of the in-kind transfer program. This is then a case where knowledge of the distribution based on market value measures gives us some information on the distribution based on cash equivalent measures.

This is, however, a theoretical result. It rests on assumptions like identical utility functions in the population and programs that do not affect the rank order of families in the income distribution. One would like to know whether the result holds in a world where such assumptions are often violated. Is it the case, for example, that a market cost measure of rent control subsidies makes rent control look more redistributive than a cash equivalent measure? Are other generalizations possible? We may find that a distribution based on the more accurate and easily obtained market value measure provides bounding information on the distribution based on cash equivalents. In a world with uncertainty about the shape of utility functions, it is likely that the best we can do is to put bounds on the distribution of cash equivalent benefits.

To conclude, I think Olsen and York have written a very useful paper. It deals nicely with very complicated issues; it points out how sensitive distributional conclusions are to the way in-kind benefits are measured. Finally, it raises fundamental questions about where we go from here.

6   The Role of Time in the Measurement of Transfers and Well-Being

James N. Morgan

6.1   Introduction

The usual analysis of redistribution deals with taxes and the regular money transfer payments made by government and perhaps some institutions. And the usual analysis of income and income distribution makes use of concepts like total family money income measured before taxes but after some transfers. The purpose of this paper is not to provide a comprehensive discussion of an ideal set of national accounts but to touch on a few aspects where we have some data to enliven the theoretical discussion. In the process we need to be conscious of three kinds of models: an institutional model that determines many of the insurance and governmental transfers, a behavioral model that deals with individual decisions about giving and getting help in time or money, and an accounting model that focuses on each individual's net contribution to or benefit from the various transfer mechanisms including voluntary and altruistic (nonreciprocal) ones.

We can think of individuals, in families, where institutional arrangements alter earned incomes into disposable incomes after the regular (involuntary) transfers and taxes. Rules and regulations and insurance principles determine all these, and we pick up the situation after they have done their work. Three types of voluntary transfers take place within the private sector: (a) transfers between individuals and philanthropic institutions; (b) transfers between individuals not living together, between friends or relatives, including alimony and child support; and (c) intrafamily transfers implicit when people live together and some produce or earn more than others.

James N. Morgan is professor of economics and a program director of the Survey Research Center, Institute for Social Research, University of Michigan, Ann Arbor.

6.2 Institutional Voluntary Transfers

A major form of transfer currently attracting attention is private philanthropy, donated in both money and time. We need a behavioral model to deal with these, but we know very little about the sources and motivations for altruism except that we know altruistic attitudes go along with altruism, but that does not explain much (Thiessen 1968); Macaulay and Berkowitz 1970; Smith 1973; Sills 1957). Also giving time and giving money tend to be complementary rather than competitive (Morgan, Dye, and Hybels 1977). Tax provisions make them equal for upper-income people, but giving money is more costly than giving time for those who do not itemize tax deductions. Our study of giving in 1973 is the only one that covered both time and money. Indeed, no full-scale national surveys of details of philanthropy had been conducted prior to that study. The Consumer Expenditure Survey of the Bureau of Labor Statistics generally includes "contributions" as a category (Lamale and Clorety 1959; U.S. Bureau of Labor Statistics 1965). Two rather specialized studies of large givers focused on reactions to tax laws (Commission 1970; Hunter 1968). In the course of studying well-being and its intergenerational aspects, the Survey Research Center in 1960 asked about gifts to friends and relatives, to churches or religious organizations, and to other organizations "like Community Chest, schools, cancer or heart associations, and so forth." A 1965 Survey Research Center Study, *Productive Americans*, asked about time spent doing "volunteer work without pay such as work for church or charity, or helping relatives" (Morgan, Sirageldin and Baerwaldt 1966). The older and more affluent and better educated were giving more money, and the better educated were giving more time.

In the spring of 1973 the Office of Tax Analysis of the United States Treasury asked us to do a small study of the giving of those who itemized and those who did not itemize their deductions (Roistacher and Morgan 1974). With the relatively small sample and no overrepresentation of the upper-income groups, the Treasury study could not distinguish among those with widely differing marginal tax rates; but it could look at those who were itemizing their deductions compared to those who were not. Income, home ownership, and family size largely determined whether it paid to itemize, and income and itemization status largely determined whether the household gave and how much it gave. Indeed, itemization seemed primarily to affect whether the household gave at all. Only at incomes above $10,000 did it affect the amounts givers gave to religious organizations, and only at incomes above $25,000 did it affect the amounts givers gave to nonreligious charities. But as Martin Feldstein pointed out to us, the combination of differences in "whether" and "how much" leads to estimates of substantial "price elasticities" of giving. The Treasury study also showed substantial differences in the age pattern of giving between those giving to religious organizations and those giving to other donees.

Finally, to provide an extensive pretest and some early indications of responses to changed standard deductions, the Filer Commission funded a small national survey in October 1973, repeating the questions of the Treasury study and adding some questions to cover gifts of time and money, itemization and changes in itemization, and the perceived effects of the latter (Roistacher, Morgan, and Juster 1974).

When asked general reasons for recent past changes in giving, almost no one mentioned tax considerations. Among the families who had stopped itemizing, only 7.5 percent said that the change had affected the amount they contributed to charity. On the other hand, just as in the larger study reported here, many (43 percent) felt that people in general would give less without the tax incentive of deductibility, and a substantial minority (26 percent) felt that people like them (in the same financial situation) would give less. At incomes of $25,000 and more, nearly half of the respondents felt that families in financial situations like theirs would give less without deductibility.

The October 1973 data on actual giving also showed substantial effects of tax deductibility (itemization). Once again the effect was greatest on whether the family gave at all; but among the givers, itemizers also gave more. Adjustments for spurious correlation through age and income differences between itemizers and nonitemizers (and nonfilers) reduced the apparent effects but did not erase them. Additional adjustments for differences in education, family size, occupation, race, homeownership, and marital status reduced the differences to the borderline of significance, but such adjustments involve overcorrection. In any case, the remaining differences still indicated that itemization was associated with greater giving.

These data also indicated what we found in the 1974 study—that itemizers also give more time. This would indicate that time and money go together since gifts of time are "tax-exempt" regardless of itemization status. That is, if one had spent the time to earn money and given the money, the result would have been the same as giving time, provided the money gift could have been itemized. Actually, itemizing was mostly associated with whether time was given at all rather than with the amount given.

None of those other studies asked much detail about giving, about information about tax laws, or about the giving of both money and time (in the same interview). Also, none of them provided an adequate sample of upper-income families. Indeed, the 1960 Survey Research Center study oversampled the lower end of the income distribution because of its interest in poverty. In an earlier study made before recent legal changes, we found that even the affluent lacked information about marginal tax rates and made only infrequent gifts of appreciated assets (Barlow, Brazer, and Morgan 1966).

A lot of research has been done on altruism using experiments or studies of organized groups and there is a good deal of historical discussion of the development of philanthropy in the United States (Lenrow 1965; Macaulay and Berkowitz 1970). One of the founders of the Society for the Study of the Grants Economy, Kenneth Boulding, has recently attempted to develop a theoretical structure within economics to handle philanthropy and other transfers, as well as coercive redistributions by war, taxes, robbery, and extortion (Boulding 1973). However, no neat equilibrium or set of maximization rules can handle factors such as gifts, taxes, theft, and war. Nor did this study attempt one. Our purpose was to find out who gives what to whom and to add several kinds of evidence as to why they give.

Studies have been made of voluntarism, but the only national sample surveys of volunteer time in addition to *Productive Americans* were two that were done by the United States Census Bureau, the first in 1965 for the Department of Labor and the second in 1974 for ACTION (U.S. Department of Labor 1969; ACTION 1975; Wolozin 1975) and there have been some recent economic discussions of voluntarism (Becker 1976; Weisbrod 1977; Alchian 1973; Phelps 1975).

Even though sample surveys are more useful for providing data helpful in understanding who gives what to whom and why than for estimating amounts, it is interesting to note that the aggregates derived from the survey covering 1973 totaled $26 billion in philanthropic contributions and nearly six billion hours of volunteer time. Valued at estimated opportunity cost for individuals (by gender and education and age), that volunteer time came to $19 billion for husbands and single household heads, and another $10 billion for wives, totaling more than the money given.[1] In addition, wives who did volunteer work reported an additional $760 million in out-of-pocket costs. Aggregates of skewed distributions from sample surveys are of course crude (and made more so by possible response variance) but it seems clear that private philanthropy is substantial, even relative to public transfers, and that at any reasonable valuation, the time given is as important as the money given.

6.3   Private Interfamily Transfers

Time spent helping friends, neighbors, and relatives on an individual basis was also reported in this study, and a crude estimate of about 83 hours per family for 69 million families comes to more than 7 billion hours. At the same average value per hour calculated above for volunteer time, this time would be valued at $42 billion, though this may be an exaggeration since much of the help was manual labor. These time transfers were reported at all income levels, however.

In our economic surveys we frequently ask about money transfers to individuals to estimate the number of outside dependents affecting income taxes. About 11 percent of families report such out-transfers, but only 4 percent provide more than half of anyone's support, and fewer than 2 percent provide more than half the support for more than one person. If we take the 1980 13th wave of the Panel Study of Income Dynamics reporting on 1979 and the 1974 study of philanthropy in 1973, we can derive the crude estimates, using 1979 prices and 1979 population, in table 6.1. Table 6.1 also uses a 1965 estimate of time spent helping individuals or in volunteer work for organizations and a 1960 estimate of contributions to derive 1979 aggregates, allowing for expansion in population and price levels (Morgan, Sirageldin, and Baerwaldt 1966; Morgan et al. 1962).

Of course, other aggregate sources of information on the main institutional and government transfers are available. Our purpose is neither to estimate aggregates nor to compare survey data with other sources, but rather to put the dollar amounts in perspective with the nonmoney transfers of time or services. The survey data are likely to underreport government transfers received more than they underreport time or money given, and the valuation of the time given is difficult. But the numbers in table 6.1 indicate substantial private transfers ignored in the national accounts. The parenthetical dollar estimates were opportunity cost estimates in 1973 and an arbitrary $6 an hour in 1979.

Returning to our behavioral model, individuals can also make transfers to relatives by doubling up and providing housing and other goods and services directly and probably more efficiently, but at some emotional cost. Clearly people prefer to live in "nuclear families," and, in particular, one person in the kitchen is seen as optimal (Morgan et al. 1962, chap. 14). The nation has seen a long period of undoubling of households since the end of World War II, facilitated, many believe, by the increasing adequacy of the incomes of older people as Social Security benefits improved. At present, fewer than 10 percent of families provide housing for others who are not their young children, and it is most commonly large nuclear families of seven or more who also house other relatives. Between 1970 and 1980 the percentage of those aged 65–74 living as guests in others' households has decreased from 10.4 to 6.9 percent; for those aged 75 or older, the decrease was from 19.5 to 13.9 percent. On the other hand, money contributions to others come largely from families where the taxable income of the head and wife is greater than $25,000, implying that affluent families send money to needy relatives, while less affluent, larger, families invite them to share their home. In our early

Table 6.1   **Annual Giving of Time and Money—Some Crude Aggregates**

	Per Family		Aggregates (billions)		Aggregates (billions)[a]	
	1973 Hours	Dollars	1973 Hours	Dollars	1979 Hours	Dollars
1974 Study of Philanthropy in 1973						
Money philanthropy	—	$459	—	$25.7	—	$63.0
Time to organizations						
Husband or single head	47	—	3.2	(19)	—	—
Wife (48 million wives)	55	—	2.7	(10)	7.2	(43.2)
Per household	85	—	5.9	(20)	—	—
Time helping individuals	83	—.	5.7	(28)	7.0	(42.0)

	1979 Dollars					
1980 13th Wave Panel Study						
Out						
Spent helping relatives	$293.75					$24.9
Interfamily						
Alimony	9.29					0.8
Child support	—					0.8
Help from relatives	46.07					3.9
Contributory—government						
Unemployment comp.	59.51					5.0
Workers comp.	30.73					2.6
Social Security	844.54					71.5
Contributory—nongovernment						
Pensions	530.68					44.9
Other						
Head	80.57					6.8
Wife	83.20					7.0
Total transfers head and wife[b]	1924.72					163.02
Total transfers others	138.80					11.76
1965 Productive Americans						
Time spent helping organizations or individuals	87				7.37	(44.2)

	1959 Dollars					
1960 Income and Welfare in the U.S.						
Contributions to individuals and institutions, including alimony, gifts in kind	$315					66.4

[a]84.7 million families in 1979. Inflation 1959–79 = ×2.48; 1973–79 = ×1.62.
[b]Does not include alimony.

study of income distribution, *Income and Welfare in the United States*, we actually divided families into "adult units" consisting only of those married to each other plus their children (Morgan et al. 1962). For purposes of examining inequality or studying factors affecting doubling up this may still be necessary, but for purposes of estimating transfers, as we shall see, we can deal with families as they live together and estimate the intrafamily transfers.

Some people, about 5 percent of households, live rent-free. Much of the free rent is probably a transfer, but some may reflect a nonmoney income, as when the building engineer lives free in the building.

6.4 Emergency Help—Time and Money

Regular interfamily transfers are not common, nor large, but a natural question arises: Is the insurance value of commitments to provide emergency help in the form of time or money important? While we cannot answer that question in aggregate dollar or hour terms, we do have information from the 1980 13th wave of the Panel Study of Income Dynamics, based on a series of questions about emergency help, actual and potential, in time and money, given and received, to or from friends or relatives, nearby or far away.[2]

Since emergencies may not come every year, respondents were asked about actual help in the last five years. Given the known tendency for people to include some previous year's activity in reports on a single previous year, we should also avoid exaggeration this way, but we also might have some understatement from memory losses, particularly of help received. In fact, whether it is better or not, it is *easier* to remember giving than receiving: 15 percent reported getting help in the form of time, but 28 percent reporting giving it. Twenty-two percent reported getting emergency help in the form of money, but 29 percent reported giving it.

The real bias could be smaller than these figures indicate, of course, since a single family could get help from more than one other family. Since more help goes from parents to children than the reverse, and most parents have more than one child, multiple giving could actually be more common than multiple receiving, resulting in more receivers than givers. On the other hand, couples have two sets of parents from whom to receive help.

At any rate, a substantial minority reported giving or receiving emergency help, and some of the financial help was seen as a gift rather than as a loan. Perceived availability of help was even more common: two-thirds said they could get "several hundred dollars" or more, mostly from parents or siblings, mostly as a loan. Eight in ten said they could call on friends or relatives nearby to "spend a lot of time helping out" in a serious emergency, in two-thirds of the cases with no obligation to repay in some way. If those persons were not available for help, the vast majority said there would be someone else. More than 70 percent said that they could get emergency help from someone who did not live nearby. We have not attempted to estimate probabilities, average amounts, or economic values (net of expected repayments), but there clearly is real sharing in society today. The growth of public transfer systems has not supplanted all of the old private altruism or extended family responsibilities.

The age patterns are interesting and important to note, since we shall find strong age patterns in intrafamily transfers too. The young benefit largely from interfamily emergency help in time and money, and the older-middle-aged but not retired largely provide it (see table 6.2).

6.5   Intrafamily Transfers

We turn now to our third concern, the area where the role of time and other nonmoney transfers becomes most important: transfers inside the family living together. At this point we leave the behavioral model of decisions about who lives with whom and who supports others outside the household, and move to a model where accounting is more important as we attempt to attribute the income and the consumption of the family to individual family members. The difference between them is the net transfer of the individual to or from the family he or she lives with.

We start with the components of a more comprehensive estimate of total family income, then (a) allocate it to the individuals who earned it or account for its presence, and (b) estimate for each individual what fraction of the total is of benefit to that person. The first step requires including nonmoney components of income, and the second step involves estimating the different needs of individuals of different age and gender. We do not have to deal with economies of scale from living together because it is the average, not the marginal, benefit we estimate.[3]

We have a considerable amount of detail on money income in the 1980

Table 6.2	Percent Reporting Giving or Getting Emergency Time or Money Help in the Last Five Years, by Age (6533 family heads reporting in 1980)			
Age	Gave $	Gave Time	Got $	Got Time
18–24	22%	29%	38%	14%
25–34	28	28	35	18
35–44	28	29	19	12
45–54	35	30	17	12
55–64	38	32	7	11
65–74	28	28	5	15
75+	18	19	4	22

Panel Study. We use the net equity in any owned home for estimating imputed rent, and the hours spent on housework and child care for estimating time contributions other than those involved in earning money for the family. In 1979 we asked about other unpaid productive activities—repairing the house or car; growing and preserving food—but did not attempt to divide the hours spent between family members. For those interested in the informal economy, unaccounted for in National Income, people's reports of amounts saved by such work per household in 1978 were $118 for work on the car, $327 for work on the house, and $62 for growing or preserving food. It was mostly the young who worked on cars, the middle-aged on houses, and the older people who grew food (Morgan 1981).

The total real income of the family that must be allocated to individuals can be accounted for and classified as follows:

1. Labor income
2. Other taxable income
   Asset income—rent, interest, dividends, etc.
   Alimony
3. Other earned income (nontaxable)
   Child support received
   Imputed rent (5 percent of net equity, to approximate)
4. Contributory transfers
   Social Security
   Private pensions
   Unemployment compensation
   Worker's compensation
5. Noncontributory transfers
   Aid to Families with Dependent Children
   Supplemental Security Income
   Other welfare
   Value of food stamp subsidy
   Value of heating subsidy
6. Value of time spend on housework and child care

The sequence of questions that elicit this information asks more detail about husband and wife than about other family members. The aggregate income components of "others" (other than head and wife) are coded with assignments of missing information at the family level, but coded for each individual only as taxable or transfer income, with an indication of whether the taxable income was labor, asset income, or both, and the main source of transfers. Appendix B gives the procedures we used for allocating income to individual family members. The most important policy we adopted was to pool and split the asset, contributory transfer, and imputed rental income evenly between husband and wife on the grounds that they contributed equally to it or at least that we do not know the actual contributions of each. Their noncontributory transfer incomes were attributed to family members in the same way that consumption was allocated, neutralizing any "redistribution" of such income.

A variety of estimates of the value of imputed rent are possible. If one believed Irving Fisher, one might argue for 2 or 3 percent as the real return on the net equity, the rest being capital gains eroded by inflation. At the other extreme one might argue for 13 percent, the 10 percent annual increase in the house prices in this period plus a 3 percent net rental income, earned and consumed by the owner. Of course, the real cost and hence net rental income of a house depends on the family's tax bracket and how much mortgage interest it can deduct (Duncan and Morgan 1980). We settled for 5 percent of the net equity, a compromise.

The major problem in estimating intrafamily transfers, however, is how to value the time people contribute. Even the time spent working for money, it might be argued, should be valued somewhat differently from wages, to allow for income taxes and a certain disparity between wages and real contribution arising from "dual labor markets" or other market imperfections (e.g., immobile workers). Housework time is even more difficult, since using "opportunity cost" estimated as hourly earnings of people of similar age, gender, and education involves two possible selection biases arising from people's decisions about working for money and about having children and doing a lot of housework. So before using even a compromise estimate, we look separately at intrafamily transfers of money and of housework time.

This procedure involves some difficult decisions. We can assume that the family money income is consumed roughly in proportion to the food needs of individuals by age and gender (see appendix B for details), but what about time? We have bravely assumed that the benefits of housework time are proportional in the same way, which probably underestimates the benefits to children, who need *more* attention. A not-quite-appropriate bit of evidence is the impact of changing family composition on housework hours, which estimates the *marginal* cost of family members. Table 6.3 shows one set of estimates based on changes from 1975 to 1979, although they are not adjusted for economies of scale, and another set based on 1979 static (long-term?) interfamily differences.

At any rate, if we credit each individual with the housework hours provided and deduct an estimated "consumption" of a fraction of the total housework benefits, we have the net time contributions by age and gender of figure 6.1. It is no surprise, of course, that women are the contributors of such time, and men the beneficiaries. By comparison, if we take the money income (including imputed rent, asset income, and money transfers) and for each individual deduct from his/her contribution his/her estimated consumption of the money's benefits, we have the patterns of figure 6.2. Only in the 35–44 age group, when there are

Table 6.3   **Effects of Family Members on Level and Change in Time Costs (Housework) and Food Costs—Regression Coefficients (for 4730 families with the same head or wife 1975–80)**

		Regression Coefficients			
		1975–79 Change in[a]		1979 Level of[b]	
Gender and Age	Our Scale	House-work	Food Con-sumption	House-work	Food Con-sumption
Children 1–2	.286	341**	96*	356**	91
		(38)	(47)	(45)	(65)
3–5	.571	147**	121**	213**	305**
		(34)	(41)	(39)	(56)
6–13	.857	267**	273**	304**	607**
		(24)	(29)	(20)	(28)
Girls 14–17	1.000	318**	340**	388**	768**
		(35)	(43)	(39)	(56)
Boys 14–17	1.000	296**	456**	310**	819**
		(34)	(41)	(39)	(56)
Females 18–20	1.000	160**	448**	290**	866**
		(50)	(60)	(57)	(81)
Males 18–20	1.000	176**	369**	113*	593**
		(49)	(59)	(54)	(76)
Females 21–29	1.000	140*	678**	170*	677**
		(70)	(85)	(75)	(107)
Males 21–29	1.000	35	579**	270**	672**
		(58)	(70)	(58)	(82)
Adults 30+	1.000	421**	731**	826**	841**
		(38)	(46)	(29)	(41)

[a]Regressing change on change in numbers of family members of each type, controlling also for income component changes.
[b]Regressing level on number of family members of each type, controlling also for overall income/needs.
*Significant at $p < .05$.
**Significant at $p < .01$.

children to benefit too, do women contribute more dollars than their estimated consumption of dollar benefits. We assume, of course, that even dollars saved or used to pay taxes benefit individuals in the family in roughly the same proportions as the dollars spent for living costs.

Another way to compare men and women is to compare their total hours spent in earning money, commuting, or doing housework. Figure 6.3 shows that over most of the life course, things are pretty even in those dimensions. Only when the men retire and the women still do most of the housework does a discrepancy appear. It should be said that we truncated the reports on housework hours at 6000 hours per person per year, which is more than 16 hours, every day.

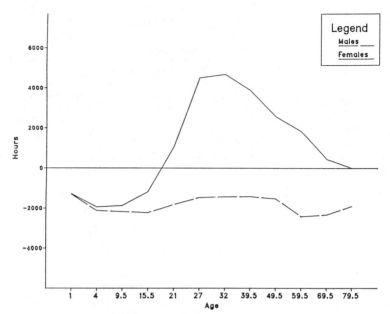

Fig. 6.1   1979 intrafamily transfers of time (housework)—net contributions of males and females, by age.
(truncated at 6000 hours/person, scaled at $6/hour)

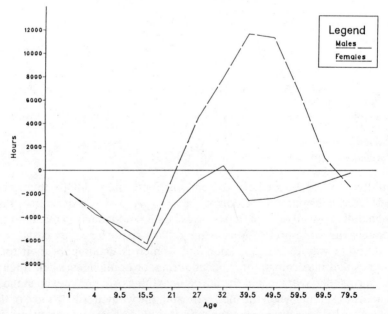

Fig. 6.2   1979 net contribution of $ income to family for males and females, by age, for 18,920 sample and nonsample individuals in 1980
(includes transfers, asset income, imputed rent)

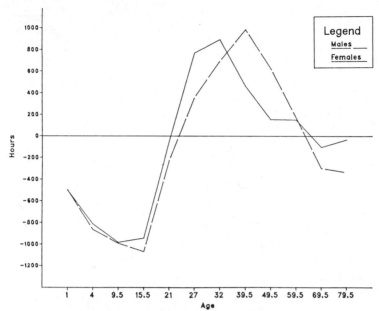

Fig. 6.3   Net contribution of hours to family for males and females, by age, for 18,920 sample and nonsample individuals in 1980 (money work, commuting, housework, consumption of time allocated like consumption of family income)

In estimating the aggregate amount of intrafamily transfers, we cannot of course keep time and money separate. To do so would exaggerate the total amount of transfers—failing to balance money transfers from husband to wife by time transfers the other way. Hence we are driven to estimate the dollar value of housework, however arbitrarily. We settled on $6 an hour, with no distinction between men and women or between education levels, although it is entirely possible to experiment with a variety of assigned values. Figure 6.4 shows the age-gender patterns when we value housework at $6 an hour. We have selected a level at which some net transfer from men to women occurs during the men's peak earning years, and from women to men later on. The average hourly earnings of working wives in 1979 was $5.40, that of all household heads was $8.09, and that of female heads somewhere between. Table 6.4 reports some aggregate estimates from 1970, for 1976 and for 1979 from the Panel Study of Income Dynamics, which are similar to those presented in this study, except that two values of housework time are used in 1976, $5/hour and an opportunity cost wage corrected for selection bias, and in 1970 opportunity cost and a market cost estimate for housework were used (Baerwaldt and Morgan 1973; Morgan 1978).

Table 6.A.1 in appendix B gives the housework data separately at $6/hour, allowing different values for different age and sex groups to be

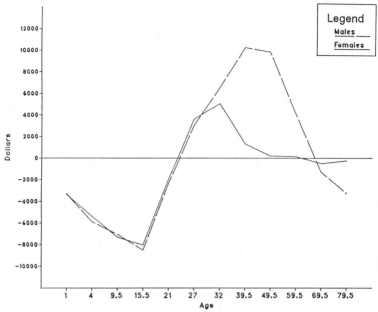

Fig. 6.4   1979 average net contribution to the family living together, by age and sex
(counting housework and child care at $6/hour)

used and the implications spelled out at least for subgroup average net contributions. Given the limitations on available extra work, and on available paid day care, opportunity cost estimates have problems too. On the other hand, it is credible that people do housework and child care believing it is better than what they might pay for.

6.6   Estimating Aggregate Intrafamily Transfers

In the NIPA the flows of money that go to people who did not currently earn it are also called transfer incomes. National income accounting for family transfers should count only the aggregate of the net subsidies received, or the aggregate of the net contributions made, but not both since that would count a dollar transfer twice—once when contributed, once when received. On the other hand, averaging to obtain the net contributions of a group can eliminate offsetting amounts completely. Indeed, except for errors and rounding, the overall average net contribution for the whole population should be zero. If we ignore the sign, add up the contributions and subsidies, and divide by two, we have the amount of transfer flow for either a group or for the whole sample. Table 6.A.1 in appendix B gives such average estimates for the subgroups by age and

Table 6.4   **Intrafamily Transfers—Some Rough Aggregates (assuming 225 million individuals in 1979)**

	1979 Estimates (using 18,930 individuals)	Aggregates (billions)	
	Average Per Person	Hours	Dollars
Absolute average $ transfer	$5396	—	$607
Absolute housework— child care time transfer	440	49.50	297
Absolute total time (hours)	757	85.16	511
Combined average absolute net transfer allowing housework—child care at $6/hr.	6180	—	695

A Comparison of Estimates[a]

Housework Valued At:	1970		1976		1979
	Market Cost[b]	Opportunity Cost[c]	Opportunity Cost[d]	$5	$6
Intrafamily transfers	313	398	528	552	695
Gross national product	982	982	1516	1516	2400
Ratio TR/GNP	327	41	35	36	29

[a]In current dollars and populations. See Baerwaldt and Morgan (1973) and Morgan (1978) for earlier data.
[b]$1.50–2.50 depending on region and city size.
[c]$1.67–4.32 depending on marital status, education, and city size.
[d]Complex estimate allowing for selection bias (see Morgan 1978).

sex, but a more important estimate is the aggregate amount of intrafamily transfer in comparison with the transfers in the national accounts.

Estimating aggregates from a sample is best done by estimating an average per person and then multiplying by an outside, more precise, estimate of the aggregate number of persons. Estimating averages in our sample necessitated using weights to take account of different sampling and response rates, and all the data we have given are so weighted. Some of the individuals were not sample members, yet we had to include them to balance out the families we studied for this purpose. They were given the same weights as the other family members. Actually, weights used in estimating a weighted average of 18,920 cases will make very little difference. Other sources of variation plus conceptual and measurement problems are probably more serious. In fact, omitting nonsample members and using individual weights resulted in 15,317 cases and an average absolute net transfer of $6204 rather than the $6180 of table 6.4.

The results given in table 6.4, assuming 1979 prices and a 1979 population of 225 million, are an aggregate intrafamily transfer of $695 billion. If we look at dollars and time separately, we have $607 billion in dollar transfers, and nearly 50 billion hours of housework transfers, which at $6 is nearly $300 billion.

The implication remains as we stated it some years ago—we have not "socialized" the responsibility for dependent members of society as far as we might think; families remain responsible for most of the burden. The implications of continued sluffing off of responsibility for each other could be a huge increase in the government or institutional transfers to replace the private interfamily and intrafamily transfers. The marketizing or monetarizing of child care will quite likely continue, decreasing intrafamily transfers. In so far as people already pay for child care, the housework hours in our estimates have already been reduced.

Whatever the measurement and conceptual problems, time and its productive use in unpaid ways are clearly important in assessing the amount of transfers taking place. The valuation of that time and the expectations about it underlie much of the discussion of equity between men and women.

6.7   Time in the Assessment of the Results of Transfers

The other side of the coin is that the time-use that produces real income, often for the benefit of others in a family, also affects the well-being of people by reducing their leisure. And even if we despair of estimating the reallocation of resources within the family, we need to know how much time is being devoted to paid and unpaid productive activities by family members if we are to assess their level of well-being and discuss the distribution of "income" in its most meaningful sense.

Perhaps the simplest way to start is to think of family well-being as resulting from two main components: its control over resources relative to its needs, and its time remaining to enjoy those resources after the work it takes to get them. If there is some indifference curve relating leisure and things, or some revealed preference, then there must also be a *ophelimite* function (to use Pareto's term). If we assume this function is similar to a production function with labor and capital, then the question is: What are appropriate exponents to the two terms, income/needs and leisure/adult?

Much discussion of the problem of comparing single-earner and two-earner families implies this issue without coming to grips with it. And the discussions of families with and without children tend to focus on the greater needs, but not on the greater unpaid but productive use of time in housework and childcare.

An initial bit of empirical evidence of the importance of taking account of differences in need and in leisure (or its other face, productive time use) is given in table 6.5. The positive correlation between income and needs implies that using income alone exaggerates the amount of inequality (high-income families tend to be larger and need more income). The high correlation between income and total work hours (paid and unpaid) implies that income alone also exaggerates inequality by ignoring the amount of effort provided by high-income families and the lower amount of time they have left to enjoy their income.

We also looked at the correlations of *change* to see whether changes in well-being were badly measured by changes in income because of correlated changes in needs or in leisure time. Again the correlations are sufficiently large to indicate systematic bias. (Even if the correlations were low, the measurement variance would remain a problem, perhaps made worse because no systematic correction would be possible.)

One more bit of empirical evidence relates to the question of whether the pattern of correlations among the components of well-being is uniform in the population. If the correlations were linear and uniform across population subgroups, then the proper weighting of components would not matter much. But as table 6.6 shows, the relationships vary among subgroups. Among middle-aged couples, accounting for leisure makes very little difference since everyone is working hard, and needs vary less and are only mildly correlated with income. The age extremes are where the disparities among the components of well-being make the use of income alone such a bad measure of well-being and of inequality. This is particularly true for families with no wife present.

Table 6.5   **Some Static and Dynamic Correlations Relevant to Differences among Different Measures of Well-Being (for 5501 individuals who were head or wife in 1976 and in 1980, in families with the same head and wife 1975–80)**

Correlations of 1979 data:	
Total family income and family needs	.239
Total family income and total work hours[a]	.369
Family needs and family work hours	.672
Correlations of change 1975–79	
Change in income and change in needs	.060
Change in income and change in total work hours[a]	.240
Change in needs and change in work hours	.184

[a]Work hours include paid work of head, wife, and others; commuting of head and wife; and housework by head, wife, or others. Needs not adjusted for inflation, so no spurious inflation-trend correlation.

Table 6.6   Intercorrelations and Relative Variances of Components of
                   Well-Being by Life-Cycle Groups

	Correlations			Relative Variability (standard deviation/mean)			
	Needs with Income	Leisure with Income	Leisure with Income/ Needs	Income	Needs	Leisure	Income/ Needs
All	.22	−.24	−.18	.24	.34	.25	.74
Single (no wife present)	.52	−.43	−.35	.37	.46	.31	.94
Under 30	.77	−.31	−.38	.44	.47	.26	.93
30 or older	.43	−.47	−.35	.34	.46	.33	.93
30–59	.10	−.21	−.21	.28	.38	.33	.91
60 or older	.82	−.74	−.57	.50	.66	.33	.98
Married	.15	−.20	−.13	.23	.33	.23	.70
Under 30	.12	−.23	−.25	.16	.18	.21	.52
30 or older	.15	−.19	−.11	.23	.33	.23	.73
30–59	.16	−.19	−.11	.21	.32	.22	.69
60 or older	.13	−.20	−.12	.24	.41	.28	.99

Is there any way to estimate what the exponents of the leisure and income/needs components of a utility function should be? One traditional approach is to infer the shape of an indirect utility function from a labor supply function. In fact, there would have to be two related labor supply functions for husband and wife. So far most such work has assumed a one-worker family and ended up with a utility function based on the main earner's wage rate and all other family income. It is difficult to be enthusiastic about an estimate of family well-being that treats the wife's earnings as exogenous.

Until we can come up with some more convincing empirical, revealed-preference estimate of the family utility function, it might be useful to look briefly at the implications of reasonable if arbitrary well-being functions that take account of income/needs and leisure/adult. Actually these functions have to do more than assign exponents, they also have to deal with economies of scale in the family in the creation of a family "needs" standard to take account of family composition. The needs standard we have been using is the official, federal basis of poverty estimates. It starts with an estimate of food needs for each family member according to age and gender, applies an economy-of-scale correction for total family food costs, multiplies by three to expand to all costs, and applies another economy-of-scale correction. Corrections are also applied for farmers and for single, older people.

The 1981 poverty standard was roughly $2500 plus $1250 per person, so that a family with two children would "need" $7500 if they stayed together, but if each parent took one child, forming two-person families, each would "need" $5000, for a total of $10,000. Hence any income maintenance scheme based on that definition of need would imply substantial attempts to recapture economies of scale and substantial incentives to split.

The importance of the "needs" formula lies in its common use in setting income maintenance standards. Put simply, income maintenance programs attempt to recapture some of the economies of scale of living together, at the cost of providing incentives for families to split up.

Similarly, ignoring work and leisure in a well-being or poverty needs measure also has implications for incentives, both to double or undouble and to work. Particularly if "credit" is given for child care in assessing well-being, taxes and income maintenance payments based on such an expanded measure are more likely to approximate neutrality with respect to individual decisions about work and living together.

One way to see the relevance of an expanded definition of well-being is to define a reasonable one, assume an income maintenance and tax program based on it rather than dollar income, and assess the impact of individual decisions about working and about changing family composition on people's well-being. We provide an example in appendix C.

Not only can a better definition of well-being, justified as a better measurement, be less distorting of people's work, marriage, and child-bearing choices, but, since it provides larger income maintenance for people who are working more, it is also more likely to be politically acceptable. Allowing for child-care time gives more to mothers, but since they get "credit" for either child-care time or market-work time, some neutrality is still preserved with respect to fertility decisions.

One can think, then, of searching for a measure of well-being, and a taxation and income maintenance policy based on it, that would be as undistorting as possible of work and family decisions. No easy definition of "neutrality" exists, but perhaps we can recognize and avoid unduly large, potentially distorting effects.

6.8   Summary and Conclusions

We have examined several ways in which time and its use are important. In the area of private philanthropy, the value of time devoted to helping institutions or other individuals is at least as great as the money given. A whole range of interesting research projects awaits enthusiasts of selection bias to estimate the value of that time.

There is also emergency time and money help, on which we have relative frequency but no real quantitative measurement. Measurement here must deal with the expected value or insurance value of such rights to help, as well as the value of the time component.

Inside the family living together, money flows are unmeasurable, but we can look at the contributions of money and time each individual makes, including housework and child-care time. Once we agree on how to estimate each member's benefit from the family, we can estimate net benefit (plus or minus), particularly by age and sex. At any reasonable assumption about the value of housework time and the division of benefits, the amount of intrafamily transfers is much larger than the $230 billion of transfer payments in the national accounts. The implications for explosion of transfer payments if private responsibility continues to diminish are obvious.

Finally, the level and distribution of well-being and its rate of improvement over time, as well as policy about redistribution, also require dealing with transfers and with time. We suggest the need for a standard definition that takes account of money and nonmoney transfers as both a measure of well-being and a criterion for taxation and income maintenance programs. An illustrative example suggests that better definitions are less likely to have distorting effects on people's decisions about work, having children, and who lives with whom (doubling up).

Appendix A *Questions Asked in the 1980 (13th) Wave of the Panel Study of Income Dynamics on Interfamily Emergency Help Patterns*

K66. Last year did you help support anyone who doesn't live here with you now?

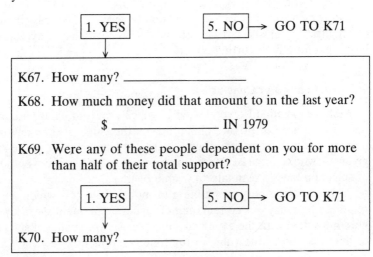

K71. People sometimes have emergencies and need help from others—either time or money. Let's start by talking about time. In the last five years have you (or anyone living with you) spent a lot of time helping either a relative or friend in an emergency?

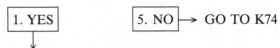

K72. Was the person you helped a relative of (yours/anybody who lives here)?

K73. What kind of help was that? _____

_____

K74. Suppose there were a serious emergency in your household. Is there a friend or relative living nearby whom you could call on to spend *a lot of time* helping out?

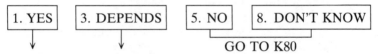

K75. Would that be a relative?

K76. What is that person's relationship to you?

_____

K77. How much would that person mind spending time helping you out—a lot, a little bit, or not at all?

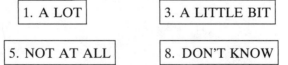

K78. Would you feel you had to repay that person in some way?

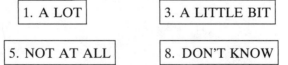

K79. If that person were not available, is there someone else you could call on?

K80. Do you have a relative or friend who *doesn't* live near you who could come to help you in an emergency?

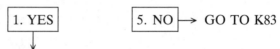

K81. Is that person a relative?

1. YES   5. NO ⟶ GO TO K83

K82. What is that person's relationship to you?

_____

K83. In the last five years has either a friend or a relative spent *a lot of time* helping you in an emergency?

K84. What kind of help did you receive? (Did you receive any other kind(s) of help?)

_____
_____
_____
_____

K85. We've talked about time, now let's talk about money. Do you have any savings such as a checking or savings account, or government bonds?

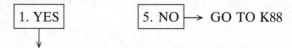

K86. Would they amount to as much as two months' income or more?

1. YES   5. NO ⟶ GO TO K88

K87. Would they amount to as much as a year's income or more?

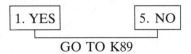

K88. Was there a time in the last five years when you had as much as two months' income saved up?

K89. Suppose in an emergency you needed several hundred dollars more than you had available or could borrow from an institution. Would you ask either a friend or a relative for it?

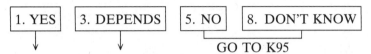

K90. Is the person you would ask a relative?

K91. What is that person's relationship to you?

_____

K92. How much would that person mind helping you out with money— a lot, a little bit, or not at all?

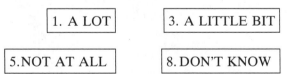

K93. Would this money be a loan or a gift?

K94. Would you expect to pay interest on it?

K95. In the last five years have you received any amount such as several hundred dollars from either a friend or relative?

K96. Was it a loan or a gift?

K97. Did you pay interest on it?

K98. In the last five years have you helped out either a friend or a relative in an emergency by giving or loaning them several hundred dollars or more?

K99. Was the person you helped a relative?

K100. What is that person's relationship to you?

_____

K101. Was that a loan or a gift?

K102. Did (he/she) pay interest on it?

K103. Prices and costs have been rising generally—are there some particular increases that have hit you especially hard?

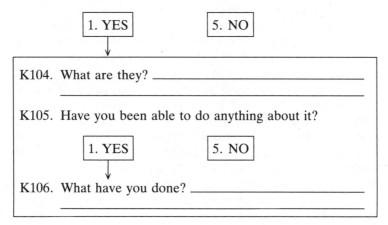

1. YES   5. NO

K104. What are they? _____

_____

K105. Have you been able to do anything about it?

1. YES   5. NO

K106. What have you done? _____

_____

Appendix B *Estimation of Intrafamily Transfers*

Assumptions must be made about the benefit allocation of the family income to its members and about allocation of some income components as to who contributed them. A realistic estimate also requires inclusion of the major nonmoney components of income. We start by defining a more global concept of income consisting of:

Total family money income (before taxes)

Imputed return (at 5 percent) on net equity in the house—free rent

Value of housing received free for those who neither own nor rent

Value of food stamp subsidy

Government subsidy of heating costs

Value of housework hours (at $6 in 1979)

The individual benefits from the family income are assumed with everyone 14 or older counting as one, those 6–13 counting .857, those 3–5 counting .571, and those under 3 counting .286; the sum of these equivalent adult numbers being the base. Thus, an only child aged 4 is assumed to benefit from .571/2.714 of the family income. This implicitly assumes that taxes paid out of income purchase a benefit too.

As for the contribution attributed to individuals, we can identify the earnings of the wife, and the wages, bonus, professional practice, and market gardening labor income of the husband. All taxable income of the head and wife beyond that is divided equally between them, it being mostly asset income from assets that they presumably both helped accumulate. Imputed rent is also allocated 50/50 between husband and wife. The transfer income of head and wife from contributory transfers—Social Security, retirement, unemployment, worker's compensation, child support—is also divided equally between them. Noncontributory transfers of head and wife are divided among the whole family in the same proportions as their estimated share of the consumption of income.

That leaves the income of "others," which appears in each individual's record in two parts: taxable income and transfer income. For the detail in the tables, other individuals' transfer income is considered to be part of their income from "contributory transfers or assets" if it is reported to be from Social Security, retirement pay, unemployment compensation, worker's compensation, or child support, otherwise to be income from noncontributory transfers. Notice that noncontributory transfers are attributed to the individual, even though such transfers to head or wife are allocated as a "contribution" by all family members. Taxable income of these other individuals is allocated between labor income and "asset income or contributory transfers" according to a code that distinguishes those whose taxable income was only labor income, only asset income, or both, with the "both" cases being assigned half-labor and half-asset income.

Our estimates of the family total income come from worksheets that lump the individuals other than the head and wife, but the contributions attributed to those other individuals come from individual records that contain the two figures for taxable and transfer income of that individual. This probably explains why the total net contribution across all family members does not come out to be zero, but the orders of magnitude of the components are reasonable, and it is the age and gender patterns we are concerned with.

To have complete families, we had to retain nonsample individuals, which means that the weighting is not precise. Rather than give nonsample individuals zero weights, we used the family weight for all family members. The effect on the overall average net or absolute contribution is very small.

Table 6.A.1   **Average Gross and Net Contributions to Family, 1979 (for 18,920 sample and nonsample individuals)**

Age	House-work × $6	Total Contribution $ + Hours of Housework at $6		Total Hours Work + Commuting + Housework		Net Contribution	
		Gross	Net	Gross	Net	$	Housework at $6
Men							
0–2	$ 25	$ 158	$ − 3301	4	− 497	$ − 2002	$ − 1291
3–5	147	316	− 5897	25	− 864	− 3771	− 2118
6–13	809	1570	− 7042	170	− 991	− 4854	− 2167
14–17	999	1629	− 8514	334	− 1067	− 6276	− 2222
18–24	1444	4316	− 2357	1696	− 221	− 524	− 1819
25–29	2149	17268	3028	2494	359	4503	− 1471
30–34	2315	21350	6516	2666	695	7942	− 1423
35–44	1989	24158	10235	2693	989	11676	− 1414
45–54	2201	26460	9821	2603	628	11351	− 1519
55–64	2330	20874	4126	2122	170	6536	− 2406
65–74	2956	13230	− 1274	994	− 297	1050	− 2324
75 +	3031	11565	− 3260	700	− 336	− 1372	− 1888
Women							
0–2	9	117	− 3359	1	− 498	− 2056	− 1295
3–5	184	370	− 5383	31	− 812	− 3445	− 1932
6–13	1100	1336	− 7302	185	− 982	− 5408	− 1869
14–17	2351	2886	− 8032	511	− 943	− 6815	− 1189
18–24	4615	9528	− 1972	1829	− 42	− 3032	1068
25–29	7043	14401	1191	2348	357	− 2076	3272
30–34	8026	16454	3601	2496	769	− 880	4505
35–44	8218	17365	5057	2552	896	395	4677
45–54	7998	17312	1301	2417	463	− 2572	3875
55–64	7570	16049	200	2008	154	− 2374	2576
65–74	7264	14901	146	1400	150	− 1681	1832
75 +	5458	11918	− 505	941	− 103	− 952	447
All	3635	11970	− 253	1536	− 33	− 233	− 8

Appendix C *A Test Model*

One way to see the problem of designing a tax and income maintenance system that is reasonably neutral with respect to decisions about working, having children, and sharing housing and child care is to look at the implications of an apparently reasonable system. Let me describe one as an example.

Suppose we have a tax or subsidy system that uses a uniform 50 percent rate; that is, if a unit has an income less than its threshold standard, half the difference is paid them in a "negative income tax," and if they have more, half the excess is taxed away.

We thus focus on the definition of threshold "income," and we propose to define it to set a level of family well-being that takes account not only of the family's money income but also of needs and of the time they have left to enjoy it—that is, how hard they worked to get it. And we shall include in that work a credit for housework and child care.

Threshold income is where well-being is $-1.0 = 100$ percent where

$$\text{Well-Being} = \left(\frac{\$ \text{Money Income}}{\$ \text{Family Needs}} \right)^{1/2} \left(\frac{\text{Free Time per Adult}}{\substack{\text{Free Time if Each} \\ \text{Adult Works Full Time} \\ \text{2,000 Hours per Year}}} \right)^{1/2}$$

By simple algebra, then, the target or threshold income is

$$\text{Target } \$ \text{Income} = (\$ \text{Needs}) \left(\frac{6760}{8760 \text{ work hours per adult}} \right).$$

The tax subsidy rule is that the subsidy should be half of the difference between the target figure and actual money income. If the amount is negative, it is considered a tax.

$$\text{Subsidy} = \tfrac{1}{2}((\$ \text{Needs}) \left(\frac{6760}{\substack{8760 \text{ Work Hours} \\ \text{per Adult}}} \right) - (\$ \text{Actual Income}).$$

We now have only to define needs standards and the work hour allowance for housework and child care.

The well-being function is, of course, analogous to the usual production function—linear, homogenous.

One could argue about the exponents and develop more complex measures (Lazear and Michael 1980). And one can deduct sleep time from the base and make the measure much more sensitive to work hours (too sensitive, I think). But let's proceed to fix the needs standards and work allowances and see the results.

We define needs with no economy of scale adjustments purposely to encourage living together and sharing:

Needs:
Each adult 18 or older	$3,000
Each child 12–17	2,000
Each child 6–11	1,500
Each child under 6	1,000

But we allow for some economies in caring for children:

Work credit for housework and child care:
Household management (each dwelling) 1,000 hours plus 500 hours for each child under 18, plus another 500 if *any* child is under 6. Maximum = 3,500 hours.

One could easily argue with these standards, but it is useful to think of them as a point of departure and see their implications for people's decisions about working, having children, or doubling up. And we can ask whether the results seem equitable, particularly as between families with two, one, or no *earners*.

A set of illustrative cases is given, skipping over the algebra and giving the net subsidy or tax, and the after-tax, after-subsidy disposable income, and the well-being measure. One can see the effects of decisions about market work by moving down the columns, of marrying by looking three columns to the right, of having children (and usually working less in the market) by moving diagonally up to the right.

To keep things as simple as we can, we assume a fixed $3 per hour for market work.

A single adult with one child ends up with $2,000, all subsidy, without doing any market work, $3,840 after earning $3,000 working half-time, or $5,838 working full time. The marginal tax rates on money earnings are 41 percent and 33 percent because of the allowance for work effort and the well-being measure goes from .71 to .90 to 1.01, meaning that the person is better-off working. Some basic guarantee or separate child-care allowance might be necessary—I'll come back to that issue.

A couple with one preschool child ends up with $6,500 if they do only 2,000 hours of market work—both half-time or only one working and the other minding the house and child. Increasing market work by 1,000 hours raises earnings by $3,000, after-tax income by $1,780 ($6,500 to $8,280), implying a marginal tax rate of 41 percent. Another 1,000 hours, meaning both parents work full time, would mean $12,000 in earnings, $10,095 after taxes. In terms of our well-being index, a couple with one child going from one full-time equivalent market worker to one and one-half to two has a well-being measure that goes from .96 to 1.05 and

1.11, a reasonable incentive compared with a straight 50 percent tax or subsidy of differences from the need standard of $7,000, ignoring work effort which would produce well-being measures of .95, 1.01, and 1.05.

More important than work decisions, which have been overstressed anyway, are decisions about who lives with whom and pools resources and decisions about having children. More children always means a lower level of economic well-being even after the subsidies-taxes, even if the parent or parents manage to keep working for money. Presumably we want it that way. Even though we want to be sure children are properly cared for, we don't want it to be economically profitable to parents to have them.

The case where society would most like to encourage combining families is that of two single parents. Suppose they each have one preschool child. Separately they might each work half-time, end up with $3,840 disposable income and a well-being ratio of .90. Together, even without working more than before in the market, the pooled family would have $7,153 in disposable income and a well-being ratio of .93. The total subsidy would fall from twice $840 or $1,680 to $1,153. And if there are economies in living together not incorporated in the needs standard and hence not recaptured by the government, the incentive to double up is still greater. For instance, it might easily be possible, because of shared responsibility for the children, for the parents to do more market work.

A more usual situation is a woman with several children and a man with no children he is taking any direct responsibility for. A woman with three children aged 2, 4, and 6, not working in the market, would get a subsidy of $3,802 and be in difficult shape (well-being = .71). A single man working full time would end up with $4,755 after taxes, well-being = 1.16. Marriage would produce a family with a disposable income of $8,130, $2,130 of it subsidy, and well-being of .89. The government has reduced the cost to the man of acquiring a family. Separately the government collected $1,245 in taxes from the man, gave $3,802 to the mother, net cost $2,557. Together, the government provides a subsidy of $2,130, recapturing almost none of the gains from doubling up. Additional child-support subsidies would help.

In general, as you can see from the tables, marrying is not discouraged, having additional children is discouraged, and you are always better-off, in terms of a sensible measure of well-being, if you work more. Most important of all, there is credit given for work, and the working poor are treated a little better. This may be all it takes to improve public acceptance of adequate income maintenance programs. Put another way, the marginal tax rate on income from work is lower than that on other income, and the needs standard on which subsidies or taxes are based is set higher the more work people do.

These figures and this set of definitions and subsidies and taxes are merely illustrative. The important issue is how to design a system that does not distort in antisocial directions decisions about having children, sharing households and child raising, or working. And the crucial point is that if the standard of well-being the program uses as a goal takes account of work/leisure as well as money income and family needs, it is more likely to be balanced in these three dimensions. The result should be a greater sense of equity between the working and nonworking (for money) poor, and between parents who devote more or less time to children, and between men and women.

As we have said, there is also a concern for the proper care of children, and there is the problem that income maintenance floors sufficient to assure that care might put a money premium on having children, while inadequate support might punish children for the indiscretion of their parents. I have suggested elsewhere the possibility of separate child-care subsidies, paid for by long-term surtaxes on all parents for each child they produced. Instead of trying to squeeze the full current cost out of parents, including divorced ones, we proposed a surtax for forty years on each parent for each child. For normal families, this amounts to an installment plan method of paying for child-raising costs. But it puts "women's work" in the market place, gives her free choice whether to work in the market or raise children, allows the setting of national standards for child care separately from the taxes, which imply a population policy or national fertility policy. Child care is expensive in both time and money, and it would take something like a 5 percent surtax per child to make the system generally self-financed. Remember that the subsidies come during the first eighteen years, the payments spread over forty, and even at 3 percent (real rate) the present value of forty annual surtax payments is only 23 times the annual payment while the eighteen-year cost has a present value of over 14 times the annual cost.

Such schemes are easy to invent, but their popular understanding and acceptance, and their actual effects on behavior, require some advanced research, and I mean more than speculating about the possible effects. A variety of research eliciting responses from representative samples of the population should be done. Are the needs standards and the housework–child-care allowances realistic and fair between different family sizes so they will not distort people's choices about living arrangements?

Our present Panel Study data could be used to be used to make estimates of the impact of any proposed scheme, though only before any effects it might have on behavior. Such impact studies are most useful if a scheme is not expected to alter behavior very much. But a change to a system that was more nearly neutral with respect to individual choices would produce changes by getting rid of past distortions of behavior.

Table 6.A.2   **Amount of Subsidy (or Tax), Disposable Income, and Well-Being Index for Families of Different Composition, Work, and Earned Income under a Program to Maintain Well-Being (not just income)**

		One Adult		
		No Children	One Child Under 6	Children 2,4,&6
Dollar income needs		$3,000	$4,000	$6,500
Hours credit for housework & child care		1,000	2,000	3,000

Market Work

Hours	Earnings	Subsidy or −Tax		
None	None	1,305	2,000	3,802
1,000	3,000	0	840	3,112
2,000	6,000	−1,245	−162	2,850
3,000	9,000	−2,370	−904*	3,459*
4,000	12,000	−3,303*	−1,102*	6,433*
		Net Disposable Income		
None	None	1,305	2,000	3,802
1,000	3,000	3,000	3,840	6,112
2,000	6,000	4,755	5,838	8,850
3,000	9,000	6,630	8,096	12,459*
4,000	12,000	8,697*	10,898*	18,433*
		Well-Being Measure		
None	None	.71	.71	.71
1,000	3,000	1.00	.90	.81
2,000	6,000	1.16	1.01	.87
3,000	9,000	1.25	1.06*	.88*
4,000	12,000	1.27*	1.05*	.86*

		Two Adults			
		No Children	One Child Under 6	Two Children Under 6	Children 2,4, & 6
Dollar Income Needs		$6,000	$7,000	$8,000	$9,500
Hours credit for housework & child care		1,000	2,000	2,500	3,500

Market Work

Hours	Earnings	Subsidy or −Tax			
None	None	2,454	3,048	3,636	4,418
1,000	3,000	1,113	1,755	1,846	3,250
2,000	6,000	−210	500	1,153	2,130
3,000	9,000	−1,500	−720	0	1,058*
4,000	12,000	−2,760	−1,905	−1,092*	−104*
		Net Disposable Income			
None	None	2,454	3,048	3,636	4,418
1,000	3,000	4,113	4,755	4,846	6,250
2,000	6,000	5,790	6,500	7,153	8,130
3,000	9,000	7,500	8,280	9,000	10,095
4,000	12,000	9,240	10,095	10,908*	11,896*
		Well-Being Measure			
None	None	.71	.70	.71	.71
1,000	3,000	.88	.85	.79	.81
2,000	6,000	1.02	.96	.93	.89
3,000	9,000	1.12	1.05	1.00	.95*
4,000	12,000	1.19	1.11*	1.05*	.99*

*Would probably require paying for housework and child care, so net income after that, and well-being, would be smaller.

Notes

1. We did not attempt to deal with the two possible selection biases which would occur if people who work for money earn more than those who do not work for money would have earned, and if people who do volunteer work would be more productive at the work than those who do not volunteer.
2. See the chapter giving details in *Five Thousand American Families*, vol. 10, Ann Arbor, Mich.: Institute for Social Research (forthcoming). See appendix A for the actual questions asked.
3. Measures of family well-being do have to deal with economies of scale in estimating family needs and relating income to needs, and the official poverty standards incorporate such estimates.

References

ACTION. 1975. *Americans volunteer*. Washington, D.C.: GPO.

Alchian, Armen A., et al. 1973. The economics of charity. In *Essays on the comparative economies of giving and selling, with applications to blood*, ed. M. H. Cooper and A. J. Cuyler. London: The Institute of Economic Affairs.

Baerwaldt, Nancy, and James N. Morgan. 1973. Trends in intra-family transfers. In *Surveys of consumers 1971–72*, ed. Lewis Mandell, et al. Ann Arbor, Mich.: Institute for Social Research.

Barlow, Robin, Harvey E. Brazer, and James N. Morgan. 1966. *The economic behavior of the affluent*. Washington, D.C.: The Brookings Institution.

Becker, Gary S. 1976. Altruism, egoism, and genetic fitness: Economics and sociobiology. *Journal of Economic Literature* 14:817–26.

Boulding, Kenneth. 1973. *The economy of love and fear*. Belmont, Calif.: Wadsworth Press.

Bremmer, Robert H. 1960. *American philanthropy*. Chicago: University of Chicago Press.

Commission on Foundations and Private Philanthropy. 1970. *Foundations, private giving, and public policy*. Chicago: University of Chicago Press.

Curti, Merle. 1958. American philanthropy and the national character. *American Quarterly* 10:420–37.

Duncan, Greg, and James N. Morgan. 1980. The effects of inflation and taxes on the costs of home ownership. *Journal of Consumer Affairs* 14:383–93.

Gerson, Janet. 1981. *The allocation of time in the household—A theory of marriage and divorce*. Ph.D. diss., University of Michigan.

Gronau, Reuben. 1977. Leisure, home production, and work—The theory of the allocation of time revisited. *Journal of Political Economy* 85:1099–1123.

Hauskneet, Murray. 1962. *The joiners*. New York: Bedminster Press.

Hunter, Willard. 1968. *The tax climate for philanthropy*. Washington, D.C.: American College Public Relations Association.

Hyman, Herbert, and Charles Wright. 1971. Trends in voluntary membership of American adults: Evidence from national sample surveys. *American Sociological Review* 30:191–206.

Lamale, Helen H., and Joseph A. Clorety. 1959. City families as givers. *Monthly Labor Review* 1303–11.

Lazear, Edward P., and Robert T. Michael. 1980. Real income equivalence among one-earner and two-earner families. *American Economic Review* 70:203–08.

Lenrow, Peter B. 1965. Studies of sympathy. In *Affect cognition and personality, empirical studies*, ed. S. S. Tomkins and C. E. Izard. New York: Springer.

Macaulay, J., and M. Berkowitz, eds. 1970. *Altruism and helping behavior*. New York: Academic Press.

Marts, Arnaud C. 1966. *The generosity of Americans*. Englewood Cliffs, N.J.: Prentice Hall.

Mauss, Marcel. 1967. *The gift*, trans. Ian Cunnison. New York: Norton.

Morgan, James N. 1978. Inter-family transfers revisited: The support of dependents inside the family. In *Five thousand American families— Patterns of economic progress*, vol. 6, ed. Greg J. Duncan and James N. Morgan. Ann Arbor, Mich.: Institute for Social Research.

———. 1981. Trends in non-money income through do-it-yourself activities, 1971 to 1976. In *Five thousand American families—Patterns of economic progress*, ed. Martha S. Hill, Daniel Hill, and James N. Morgan. Ann Arbor, Mich.: Institute for Social Research.

Morgan, James N., Martin H. David, Wilbur J. Cohen, and Harvey E. Brazer. 1962. *Income and welfare in the United States*. New York: McGraw-Hill.

Morgan, James N., Richard F. Dye, and Judith H. Hybels. 1977. Results from two national surveys of philanthropic activity. In U.S. Department of the Treasury, *Research papers* 1:157–323. Washington, D.C.: GPO.

Morgan, James N., Ismail A. Sirageldin, and Nancy Baerwaldt. 1966. *Productive Americans*. Ann Arbor, Mich.: Institute for Social Research.

Owen, David E. 1967. *English philanthropy, 1660–1960*. Cambridge, Mass.: Harvard University Press.

Phelps, Edmond, ed. 1975. *Altruism, morality and economic theory*. New York: Russell Sage.

Pleck, Joseph H., and Michael Rustad. 1980. Husbands' and wives' time in family work and paid work in the 1976–76 study of time use. Wellesley, Mass.: Wellesley College Center for Research on Women. Mimeo.

Pollak, Robert A., and Michael L. Wachter. 1975. The relevance of the household production function and its implications for the allocation of time. *Journal of Political Economy* 83:255–77.

Roistacher, Elizabeth A., and James N. Morgan. 1974. *Charitable giving property taxes, and itemization on federal tax returns, a final report from a national survey.* Ann Arbor, Mich.: Institute for Social Research.

Roistacher, Elizabeth A., James N. Morgan and F. Thomas Juster. 1974. Preliminary report to the commission on private philanthropy and public needs. Ann Arbor, Mich.: Institute for Social Research.

Rosenthal, Joel T. 1972. *The purchase of paradise, gift giving and the aristocracy, 1307–1485.* London: Rutledge and Kegan Paul.

Sills, David. 1957. *The volunteers.* Glencoe, Ill.: The Free Press.

Smith, Constance, and Anne Freedman. 1972. *Voluntary associations.* Cambridge, Mass.: Harvard University Press.

Smith, David Horton. 1973. *Voluntary action research, 1973.* Lexington, Mass.: D.C. Health, Inc.

Thiessen, Victor. 1968. Who gives a damn? Ph.D. diss., University of Wisconsin.

Titmuss, Richard. 1972. *The gift relationships: From human blood to social policy.* New York: Random House.

U.S. Bureau of Labor Statistics. 1965. *Consumer expenditures and income, total U.S., urban and rural, 1960–71 survey of consumer expenditures.* BLS Report no. 237–97.

U.S. Department of Labor, Manpower Administration. 1969. *Americans volunteer.* Manpower/Automation Research Monograph no. 10. Washington, D.C.: GPO.

Weisbrod, Burton A. 1977. *The voluntary nonprofit sector.* Lexington, Mass.: Lexington Books.

Wolozin, Harold. 1975. The economic role and value of volunteer work in the United States: An exploratory study. *Journal of Voluntary Action Research* 4:23–42.

Comment   Daniel S. Hamermesh

In this study Professor Morgan has epitomized what the Survey Research Center has become most noted for: the production of interesting numbers

Daniel S. Hamermesh is a professor of economics at Michigan State University, East Lansing, Michigan, and a research associate of the National Bureau of Economic Research.

based on survey results. This particular set of numbers on the magnitudes and directions of inter- and intrafamily transfers is important to anyone interested in problems of labor supply, taxation, discrimination, or the measurement of well-being. The figures will provide substantial grist for the mills of economists seeking to test theories of household behavior.

The paper stresses intrafamily transfers especially. It claims, based on the valuation of their size, that the death of private support for dependent family members has been announced a bit prematurely, that reliance on publicly provided income maintenance is much less extensive than we thought. This claim rests on the valuation of time spent in household production, which Morgan rates at $6 per hour. If this is too high, as I believe it is, we should not abandon our preconceptions about the relative importance of public and private transfers as rapidly as this paper would have us do.

One way to get an upper bound on the value of time spent in home production is to ask: What would it cost to purchase the services in the market? The average woman age 30–34 (see table 6.A.1) does 1338 hours of housework. This is undoubtedly an underestimate of the amount performed by a nonworking mother with two small children, since Morgan's average includes unmarried women and married women with no small children. Therefore, assume 2000 hours is a fair guess of the hours spent in household production by a full-time housewife with children. Based on Gauger and Walker (1980), I estimate that in 1979 dollars the cost of purchasing the services provided by a housewife with one child under age 5 and the other under age 12 is $11,000. We thus find that $5.50/hour is all the market values her services.

.   The $5.50 is clearly an upper bound, even for prime-age women. It ignores the fact that higher wages must be paid in the market to induce people to leave the home, to compensate for commuting costs and work in an unpleasant environment, and so forth. Also, because one can mix leisure and work much more readily at home than in the market, the supply price of an hour of household production is likely to be far less than the cost of purchasing the same hour in the market. Third, even if an hour purchased in the market did cost $6, an hour of the nonspecialist's time at home is not worth $6: I am quite sure no one would buy my services as a plumber, glazier, or carpenter for $6. This last consideration means that the value of housework performed by men in the sample (who do not specialize in housework) is especially overstated. Finally, the $6 per hour figure is far too high even as a price of time in the market for many persons in the sample: I doubt the average 4-year-old girl could have commanded $6/hour for the thirty hours of housework Morgan lists for her, and similarly for the roughly five hundred hours per annum performed by men 65 + and the thousand hours performed by women 65 + . One should note that these points have little to do with the selection biases that Morgan refers to; those are statistical problems, these are economic ones.

What is an appropriate figure if $6 is not? I am not sure, but I would bet it is much closer to the one-third of the market wage that has been estimated as the value of time spent commuting than it is to the full market wage. That being so, and noting that $6 was around the average wage rate in 1979, valuing the average person's housework at $2/hour seems reasonable. In that case the aggregate value of housework is $273 billion rather than the $818 billion implied by the average of 606 hours of housework per annum per person in the Panel Study of Income Dynamics sample. This recalculation alone reduces the total amount of intrafamily transfers by $171 billion, from $695 billion to $524 billion.

Intrafamily transfers seem even smaller compared to interfamily and socially provided transfers when the latter are adjusted for underreporting. Morgan's aggregates of $5.0, $2.6, and $71.5 billion for unemployment insurance, workers' compensation, and Social Security compare to official total benefits received in 1979 of $8.6, $8.4, and $90.6 for these programs. Here too, another bias is introduced that leads to an overstatement of the case for the importance of intrafamily transfers.

The only calculation that might cause a downward bias in the size of intrafamily transfers is the attribution of contributory transfer income evenly to husbands and wives. Since the primary beneficiaries of Social Security, as well as unemployment insurance and workers' compensation, are disproportionately males, this clearly overstates (understates) the income received by females (males). Insofar as the calculations already show a slightly greater net lifetime transfer from males to females than vice versa, they are biased down. The bias, though, is likely to be tiny given the small size of contributory transfers relative to other sources of income.

Morgan constructs seemingly arbitrary equivalence scales among family members, counting persons aged 14 + as one, 6–13 as .86, 3–5 as .57, and those below age 3 as .29. This equivalence is used to reflect "needs" and thus allocate the family income among family members. I am not sure what "needs" means, indeed; as an economist I find the term somewhat repugnant. Certainly if one values a housewife's time at the market wage, the amount of the family's full income transferred to a newborn child must exceed the amount implied by a "need" equaling .29 of an adult's. More important, do men and women consume equal amounts of the household's full income, or, as many feminists claim, do men receive a disproportionate share based on claims stemming from their market work? If so, net transfers by men aged 25 + are overstated while those of women are understated.

The last section of the paper is quite separate from the rest; it represents an attempt to point out the importance of distinguishing leisure time from time spent in household and market production in comparing well-being across families. Though I am not bothered by comparisons of income across families, nor by attempts to compare full incomes by valuing carefully time spent in home production, an interfamily comparison of utility, even though it is called "well-being" and is specified ex ante as a Cobb-Douglas function with coefficient $\alpha = .5$, is hard to swallow. It should suffice to note that leisure is important in measuring GNP, though Nordhaus and Tobin (1972) and others have already noted this.

Morgan has greatly overstated the size of intrafamily transfers by overvaluing time in home production and underestimating the correlation of gross contributions and "needs," and he has overestimated interfamily transfers by overvaluing time. Nonetheless, the raw data he presents are provocative; they pose some interesting mysteries and should lead to some fruitful extensions. Two of these caught my attention, and there are undoubtedly others. First, in table 6.2 there is a consistent inverse-U shaped relation between age and gifts of money and time, and the receipt of gifts of *time* bears a U-shaped relation to age. However, the incidence of receipt of *monetary* gifts is monotonically decreasing with age. This may result from differential underreporting of gifts by age, but why should the differential exist for time but not for money? Conversely, it may reflect the observation that people 65 and over decumulate wealth very slowly, if at all, and reduce their spending on goods as they age (Hamermesh 1984); that being so, emergency gifts of money are not needed, though emergency gifts of time may be required to complement goods as inputs in household production, especially among the oldest people. This is consistent with the sharp jump in the reported incidence of receipt of gifts of time in the 75+ age category.

Morgan's data can and should be used to examine differences in intrafamily transfers by husbands and wives across education groups and by race. Do these correlations correspond to what theories of marital sorting would predict? How do households compensate for the presence of discrimination in the market by reallocating effort in household production? Finally, on a corrected version of the data underlying figure 6.4, are the actuarial present values of net transfers by men and women equal, and, if not, how do these reflect adjustments to market discrimination? Clearly, Morgan's major contribution here is the provision of data that can enable social scientists to answer questions about the nature of exchange within households and its response to market forces.

References

Gauger, William H., and Kathryn E. Walker. 1980. *The dollar value of household work*. Ithaca, N.Y.: Cornell University, College of Human Ecology.

Hamermesh, Daniel S. 1984. Consumption during retirement: The missing link in life-cycle theory. *Review of Economics and Statistics* 66:1–7.
Nordhaus, William, and James Tobin. 1972. Is growth obsolete? *NBER Fiftieth Anniversary Colloquim*. New York: Columbia University Press.

7 Income Transfers and the Economic Status of the Elderly

Sheldon Danziger, Jacques van der Gaag,
Eugene Smolensky, and Michael K. Taussig

7.1 Introduction

The massive growth of income transfers over the last thirty years, particularly those to the elderly, is a central feature of our recent economic history. In 1950, the Social Security Old Age and Survivors Insurance (OASI) trust fund paid 3.48 million retired workers and survivors, 2.3 percent of the population, a total of $1.02 billion in benefits, or just 0.45 percent of U.S. Personal Income. In contrast, in 1979 retirement and survivors' benefits under OASI amounted to $93.13 billion, or 4.79 percent of Personal Income, and the number of recipients numbered 30.35 million, or 13.8 percent of the population.[1] Furthermore, the advent of Medicare and Medicaid in 1965 and of the Supplemental Security Income program (SSI) for the elderly in 1974 (to replace the state-administered old age assistance programs), and the rapid growth of federal and state and local government worker retirement programs, accounted for billions of dollars of additional transfers going totally or disproportionately to the elderly. The elderly are the largest group of

Sheldon Danziger is director of the Institute for Research on Poverty and professor of social work at the University of Wisconsin, Madison; Jacques van der Gaag is an economist in the Development Economics Research Department of the World Bank in Washington, D.C.; Eugene Smolensky is professor of economics at the University of Wisconsin, Madison; and Michael K. Taussig is professor of economics at Rutgers University.

This research was supported in part by a grant from the U.S. Department of Health and Human Services (HHS-5IA-7901) and by funds granted to the Institute for Research on Poverty and to the Brookings Institution by the Office of the Assistant Secretary for Planning and Evaluation of the Department of Health and Human Services. Daniel Feaster and Lyle Nelson provided computational assistance. William Birdsall, Robert Lampman, David Lindeman, Marilyn Moon, James Morgan, Joseph Quinn, and Barbara Torrey offered helpful comments on an earlier draft. The opinions and conclusions expressed are those of the authors, not of any agency or institution that has provided funds.

239

recipients of government income transfer payments in this country, as well as in other economically developed countries. The expected future growth of these benefits has become a matter of major concern for economists and the general public. These facts justify careful examination of certain key aspects of income transfer programs for the elderly.

The implicit transfer policy question obviously is: Would increments at the margin to elderly rather than nonelderly households be equitable? This paper does not explicitly address this normative question. Rather, it addresses a prior factual question: How well-off are the elderly relative to the nonelderly? To that end it examines in some detail how the measured effect of transfers on the economic status of the elderly depends on the underlying income and recipient unit concepts.

How economically well-off are the elderly? The simplest method of assessing the economic status of a group like the elderly is to compare their average money income to the average of the rest of the population or of other groups. Our point of departure in undertaking this study is the familiar one that the validity of such comparisons often depends critically on the income and recipient unit concepts that are used to generate the underlying size distributions of economic status both before and after transfers.[2] We will present several alternative measures of the relative economic status of the elderly based on a number of different treatments of the income and recipient unit concepts. We begin with comparisons that include transfers and taxes. We then deduct taxes and examine the effects. Finally, we also deduct transfers and evaluate the consequences.

The paper proceeds as follows. Section 7.2 discusses a new data set created by the authors for dealing with some well-known, but unresolved, problems in the measurement of economic status. Section 7.3 then uses these new data to generate estimates of the economic status of consumer units headed by elderly and nonelderly persons, including transfers. In this section, income and consumption measures of economic well-being receive about equal attention. Section 7.4 reports the differential effects of income transfers on the economic status of the elderly and the nonelderly. Because we know of no reasonable way to estimate what consumption would be in the absence of transfers, this section concentrates on income measures of economic well-being. Section 7.5 summarizes the main findings of the paper and offers some implications for public transfer policies.

7.2 The Data

Economists have often expressed dissatisfaction with the quality of the data available for measuring economic well-being. How is it possible to compare the effect of income transfers on the relative economic status of any group in the population when the income concept in existing data sets is known to be severely deficient in some crucial respects? This circumstance is particularly troublesome, of course, when the deficiencies of the data are known to be nonrandom between two or more groups and therefore cannot be assumed to cancel each other out when making intergroup comparisons. This general problem is especially pertinent when comparing the economic status of the elderly with that of the rest of the population. We have therefore resorted to two corrective procedures. First, we compare measures of economic well-being based on consumption as well as on income. Second, we create a new data set that corrects for one of the more important deficiencies in existing consumption and income data. To be specific, we have combined data from the 1972–73 Consumer Expenditure Survey (CEX) with data from the Inventory of Consumer Durables (CD) of the same survey to make consumption and income measures from the CEX correspond more closely to the concepts used in standard economic theory.

The CEX data have been described in detail in, among other sources, U.S. Department of Labor, Bureau of Labor Statistics (1977) and in King (1978). We therefore discuss here only those aspects of the data directly relevant to this study. First, we have restricted our analysis to consumer units interviewed in 1973, thereby eliminating problems associated with relative price changes between 1972 and 1973. In addition, we eliminated consumer units that were not full-year participants and also those for which income records were incomplete. We were left with a sample of 9494 consumer units.[3] The elderly are defined to be all consumer units headed by a person aged 65 or over; the nonelderly, as all units headed by a person aged 64 or younger. (We note in passing that the 5.5 percent of persons in institutions and group quarters were not covered in the CEX; consequently, elderly persons living in nursing homes were not included in this study.)[4]

The quality of the income data is difficult to assess. Underreporting of income is a serious problem in any household survey. Factor payments reported by consumer units in the CEX are only 91 percent of the amount in the National Income Accounts. The shortfall differs by income source. Ninety-two percent of wages and salaries are reported, but only 78 percent of federal public assistance transfers and 54 percent of state and local transfers (Dalrymple 1980). The biases for comparisons of the income of the elderly and the nonelderly are offsetting to some extent. The elderly are more likely to receive transfers and less likely to receive wage and salary income than the nonelderly. But the elderly receive a much larger share of federal transfers as compared to state and local transfers than do the nonelderly. Furthermore, Radner (1981) has reported that the elderly underreported their money income considerably more than did the nonelderly in the 1973 Current Population Survey. The same bias is likely to hold in the CEX. Finally, the CEX does not include most types of government-provided in-kind income (the only exception is food stamps), most of which are received by the elderly, or employer-provided fringe benefits, most of which are received by the nonelderly. Thus, neither the direction nor the magnitude of the bias by age is known.

Consumption expenditures as measured in the CEX are defined as out-of-pocket expenditures.[5] This definition differs from that in the National Income Accounts, especially with regard to durable purchases. If, for instance, a household buys a new car and pays in cash, the total expenditure appears in consumption. However, if the household makes a down payment and borrows the rest, only the down payment plus the monthly finance charges are counted as consumption. If the "down payment" consists of an old car, only the finance charges are counted. Since it is likely that elderly households own a more extensive stock of durables than younger households, ignoring the contribution of durables (including owner-occupied houses) to both income and consumption would bias comparisons across age groups.

To deal with this problem, we combined data from the CD with the CEX to obtain consumption and income measures that are more closely related to the consumption and income flow concepts of economic theory. The CD public use tape provides information on the presence of major durables, minor durables, vehicles and furnishings in all households in the 1972–73 CEX. We matched the information on the CD tape with the expenditure data on the CEX tape to obtain a measure of household consumption that excludes expenditures on durables made during the year of the survey, but includes the value of consumption flows (service flows) from all durables present in the household (for a complete description, see van der Gaag et al. 1981 and appendix A). We included service flows from major durables and vehicles only. The value of most minor durables (toaster, mixer, hair dryer, etc.) is small enough to warrant treating them as nondurables. The CD tape does not contain information on the value of house furnishings, which prevents us from calculating service flows from furniture. The services derived from owner-occupied housing are included as a substitute for expenditures on home purchases in the consumption measure and as an addition to the income measure.

The reported measures of income and consumption are quite different from the adjusted, theoretically more appropriate, ones. The results vary both by age of the household head and by income class. One surprising outcome of these adjustments is that "consumer expenditures" from the CEX is a pretty good proxy for total "consumption" by nonelderly households. The corrections for service flows from, and expenditures on, owner-occupied homes, durables, and vehicles tend to cancel so that, on average, the ratio of reported to adjusted consumer expenditures is 1.00 ($9813/$9807 in table 7.1). For elderly households, however, adjusted

Table 7.1 Quintile Shares, Gini Coefficients, and Means for Consumption and Income after Taxes, 1973: CEX Consumption and Income Measures Reported and Adjusted for Durable Flows

	Quintile Shares					Gini Coefficient	Mean Economic Status
	1	2	3	4	5		
I. All consumer units							
1. Reported CEX consumption	6.26	11.91	17.11	23.58	41.14	.351	$ 8,855
2. Adjusted consumption	6.90	12.64	17.45	23.56	39.44	.327	9,014
3. Reported CEX income after taxes	4.75	11.16	17.21	24.32	42.56	.382	11,115
4. Adjusted income after taxes	4.96	11.14	17.19	24.50	42.21	.377	12,989
II. Consumer units, head age < 65							
1. Reported CEX consumption	7.39	12.78	17.40	22.90	39.52	.321	9,813
2. Adjusted consumption	7.80	13.25	17.74	23.10	38.10	.303	9,807
3. Reported CEX income after taxes	5.81	12.39	17.69	23.65	40.48	.348	12,260
4. Adjusted income after taxes	5.78	12.17	17.73	23.95	40.37	.348	14,217
III. Consumer units, head age > 64							
1. Reported CEX consumption	6.34	11.43	16.64	22.62	42.96	.361	4,963
2. Adjusted consumption	6.51	12.07	16.99	22.79	41.65	.348	5,794
3. Reported CEX income after taxes	5.14	9.23	14.54	21.87	49.22	.436	6,455
4. Adjusted income after taxes	5.20	9.72	15.14	22.39	47.54	.421	7,997

consumer expenditures exceed reported consumption, on average, by 17 percent ($5794/$4963 in table 7.1).

In contrast to the effects on consumption, income after direct state and federal taxes changes considerably, *both* for elderly and for all other consumer units, after we add to the CEX income measure the estimated rental value of durables, vehicles, and owner-occupied houses. For example, for elderly households in the first quintile of the size distribution of income for the whole sample, the change is as large as 40 percent; for the nonelderly in the same quintile, it is 24 percent. On average, our adjusted income measure is 16 percent higher than the reported measure from the CEX for consumer units under age 65 ($14,217/$12,260) and 24 percent higher ($7997/$6455) for the elderly.

Table 7.1 provides further details on the effects of our adjustments of the CEX measures of consumption and income after taxes, for all consumer units and then separately for units headed by the elderly (age 65 and over) and the nonelderly. The size distributions—before and after our adjustments—are each summarized by their quintile shares, Gini coefficients, and means. Adjusting income and consumption to incorporate flows from durable goods generally results in higher mean economic welfare and lower inequality for all groups than is shown by the reported CEX data. These results cast doubts on the empirical findings of other studies that have used the reported CEX data (or Current Population Survey data or other data sets that do not account for service flows from durable goods), especially those studies that have made comparisons across age groups.

7.3 Measures of Economic Status

We turn now to the relative economic status of the elderly under different treatments of the income and recipient unit concepts. The vast literature on empirical measures of inequality has examined the issues involved in defining these concepts in depth, and we will not repeat here all the familiar points.[6] Instead we present a number of such measures with a brief discussion of why each is included. We then proceed to compare and contrast their empirical implications. All the estimates reported are based on the adjusted consumption and income data discussed in section 7.2.

One measure of economic status we emphasize is income before taxes, but including cash transfers and the bonus value of food stamps (YBT). We do so, even though transfers are properly the subject of the next section, because YBT is the closest approximation in the CEX to the Current Population Survey's (CPS) widely used money income measure. Because the elderly receive favorable tax treatment in the federal personal income tax and in many state and local taxes, any before-tax measure understates their relative economic status. Hence, a second measure employed is income after direct taxes (YAT). Taxes are considered as negative transfers and are discussed in the next section of this paper. However, because YAT is our best proxy for command over resources, it is our favored income measure in this section.

Our third measure of economic status is consumption (C). If the life-cycle hypothesis about lifetime saving patterns is valid, then a consumption measure would result in less-biased comparisons of the economic status of the elderly and the nonelderly than an income measure. The reasoning underlying this assertion is stated in a recent study of the issues concerning the measurement of poverty:

> Measuring money spent on consumption rather than money income has frequently been offered as an alternative definition of well-being because it eliminates much of the transitory phenomenon of unexpected gains and losses manifest in current income figures. In other words, consumption stands as a proxy for long-run income. Available data indicate that replacing income with consumption as a poverty measure may have significant effects on the poverty count. Since at very low incomes, expenditures for consumption more often than not exceed income, a current income measure produces higher poverty counts than a consumption measure. In particular, a consumption measure would reduce the number of young poor, who are frequently suffering only temporary poverty, and the number of aged poor who can maintain consumption by drawing upon savings.[7]

Although our own recent paper finds strong evidence contradicting the predictions of the life-cycle hypothesis about the consumption behavior of the aged (Danziger et al. 1982), we nevertheless present consumption as an alternative to our income measures.

Having settled on these three "income" concepts, we turn to the recipient unit. The average consumer unit headed by a person between the ages of 35 and 54 includes twice as many persons as the average unit headed by persons over 65. This suggests that some adjustment for unit size is needed, but the appropriate adjustment is not obvious. One extreme approach is to make no adjustments at all, that is, YBT, YAT, and C are defined on a consumer-unit basis. The arguments in support of this conventional approach stress the voluntary nature of household formation and the presumed utility gained by persons who choose to share their incomes with spouses, children, or any other members of the unit (Lebergott 1976; Pollak and Wales 1979). If person A with a substantial income marries person B with no income, whose utility decreases? Indeed, the new consumer unit of two persons presumably has higher utility than the maximum utility level of the previous two single-person units.

The opposite extreme is to adjust for differences in unit size by redefining consumption and income on a per capita basis, (C/N) and (YAT/N), where N is the number of persons in the unit. The per capita transformation of consumer unit consumption or income is easy to understand and mathematically convenient, but has little else to recommend it.[8] A per capita income measure of economic status implies, for example, that when person A with a given income marries person B with no income, her or his utility is halved; and further, that when the couple have two (planned) children, it is halved again. Per capita income or consumption measures ignore all economies of scale and specialization and—relative to alternative equivalence scales—maximize the distortion in any money income measure of economic status that ignores the value of leisure time and nonmarket production. With this caveat, we will proceed to use the C/N and YAT/N measures to highlight the extreme effects of adjusting consumer unit consumption and income for differences in family size and composition.

Finally, we define four additional measures of economic status: the welfare ratios C/N^*, YAT/N^*, C/N^{**}, and YAT/N^{**}, where N^* and N^{**} proxy the number of equivalent adults in a consumer unit derived from two different equivalence scales. The constant-utility equivalence scale denoted by N^* is based on the theoretical framework of the Extended Linear Expenditure System (see van der Gaag and Smolensky 1982). The scale denoted by N^{**} is that implicit in the official U.S. poverty lines (the Orshansky poverty lines). The two equivalence scales are quite different (see appendix B for a more complete discussion), although they lead to quite similar empirical results in this study. The constant-utility equivalence scale is less sensitive to family size because all commodities are considered in the Extended Linear Expenditure System on which it is based, while the Orshansky scale is based solely on varying food requirements with family size, for which economies of scale are less than for total consumption.

We have then three income concepts—income before taxes (YBT), income after taxes (YAT), and consumption (C). We also have four recipient unit concepts—the household, the two equivalence scales, and the per capita adjustment (see table 7.2). Rather than report on all twelve cells, however, we report on only nine: income before taxes (YBT), income after taxes (YAT), and consumption (C) on a per consumer unit basis; per capita income after taxes (YAT/N), and per capita consumption (C/N); the welfare ratios based on our constant-utility equivalence scale for income (YAT/N^*) and for consumption (C/N^*); and the welfare ratios based on the equivalence scale implicit in the Orshansky poverty lines for income (YAT/N^{**}) and consumption (C/N^{**}). Income after taxes is our preferred income concept, since it is our best indicator of a unit's command over resources, and N^* is our preferred equivalence scale because it is derived from demand theory.

Table 7.2   **Alternative Measures of Economic Status: Income and Recipient Unit Concepts**

		Recipient Unit Concepts		
Income Concepts	Per Consumer Unit	Constant-Utility Equivalence Scale	Orshansky Equivalence Scale	Per Capita
YBT	YBT			
YAT	YAT	YAT/N^*	YAT/N^{**}	YAT/N
C	C	C/N^*	C/N^{**}	C/N

Table 7.3 reports our estimates of quintile shares, Gini coefficients, and means for our nine measures of economic status for all consumer units. There are considerable differences in the mean level of economic status and of inequality among these distributions. As expected, the level of income after taxes is lower than that of income before taxes, and the level of consumption is even lower. The size distribution of income, whether measured by the quintile shares or the Gini coefficients, becomes more equal as one moves from YBT to YAT to C. Our welfare ratio adjustments are normalized independently. As a result, their means cannot be compared. However, these adjustments to both income and consumption show lower inequality than do the unadjusted counterparts. According to the Gini coefficients, per capita income and per capita consumption are distributed more unequally than their unadjusted counterparts, but the ranking is ambiguous because the Lorenz curves of the respective distributions intersect: the per capita distributions have larger shares of total income or consumption in the bottom quintiles even though they are more unequal as ranked by comparisons of Gini coefficients. Therefore we cannot give unambiguous social welfare rankings unless we specify a social inequality aversion parameter (Atkinson 1970). Note finally that the use of either welfare ratio as the measure of economic status results in unambiguously less measured inequality than the distribution based on per capita income or per capita consumption.

Table 7.4 gives the age-disaggregated counterparts of the data in table 7.3. The two age groups are the nonelderly (household head is less than 65) and the elderly (head is 65 and over). Consider first the data for YBT. Mean YBT for the elderly is only about half that for the nonelderly, and the distribution for the elderly is considerably more unequal. Deducting taxes from income, or looking at consumption, moves the elderly closer in terms of both means and Ginis, but large gaps remain. This simple relationship does not hold, however, once we turn to the distribution of per capita income after taxes and per capita consumption expenditures. According to both of these results, units headed by the elderly are almost

Table 7.3   Quintile Shares, Gini Coefficients, and Means by Alternative Measures of Economic Status, All Consumer Units, 1973

	Quintile Shares					Gini Coefficient	Mean Economic Status
	1	2	3	4	5		
1. Income before taxes (YBT)	4.59	10.68	16.92	24.76	43.04	.391	$14,918
2. Income after taxes (YAT)	4.96	11.14	17.19	24.50	42.21	.377	12,989
3. Consumption (C)	6.90	12.64	17.45	23.56	39.44	.327	9,014
4. Constant utility welfare ratio—income (YAT/N*)	6.58	12.83	17.63	22.94	40.02	.333	1.86[a]
5. Constant utility welfare ratio—consumption (C/N*)	8.70	13.84	17.64	22.33	37.49	.286	1.32[a]
6. Poverty line welfare ratio—income (YAT/N**)	5.99	12.21	17.11	23.10	41.59	.353	3.60[a]
7. Poverty line welfare ratio—consumption (C/N**)	8.08	13.29	17.32	22.25	39.06	.307	2.54[a]
8. Per capita income (YAT/N)	5.78	11.08	15.99	22.65	44.50	.385	5,204
9. Per capita consumption (C/N)	7.13	11.75	15.87	21.79	43.46	.360	3,756

Each consumer unit's income is entered once in the computation of the summary measures of economic status.

[a]These measures have been normalized with a family of four as the reference group.

as well-off on average as are units headed by the nonelderly—$4852 vs. $5291 for YAT/$N$ and $3625 vs. $3788 for C/N. The Gini coefficient of YAT/N is also quite similar for the two groups, .382 and .385, while the Gini of C/N is substantially lower for the elderly, .328 vs. .368. The distributions based on our welfare ratio measures are between those of the unadjusted and the per capita measures. We conclude from these results that comparisons of the relative economic status of the elderly and nonelderly are more sensitive to the treatment of the recipient unit (per consumer unit, per capita, per equivalent adult) than they are to the treatment of the income concept (YBT, YAT, C).

Table 7.5 is identical to table 7.4 except for the method of weighting the recipient units. In table 7.4 we follow the standard practice of constructing size distributions by taking each consumer unit's economic status as *one* entry in the size distribution, whatever the number of persons in the unit. As Danziger and Taussig (1979) have argued, this conventional approach is inconsistent with individualistic social welfare functions in which each person's welfare is valued equally. In table 7.5 we use an alternative weighting procedure that counts the income of a unit of n persons one time for *each* of the n persons in the unit. This equal-person-weighting procedure is more appropriate than the standard equal-unit-weighting procedure if we are to interpret the inequality parameter estimates as measures of inequality among individuals.[9] Because the incomes of consumer units are positively correlated with the number of persons in the unit, we expect to find less inequality in the equal-person-weighting results.

A comparison of the corresponding entries in tables 7.4 and 7.5 shows that this expectation is fulfilled for units headed by the nonelderly. For all nine measures of economic status, inequality is unambiguously smaller when computed with equal-person weighting. For the three income measures that do not adjust for unit size, the means are higher, while for five of the six measures that are adjusted for unit size, they are lower. For units headed by the elderly, except for the per capita measures, inequality is lower and the means are higher. However, the effects of person weighting are less equalizing for the elderly than for the nonelderly. The contrast between the magnitudes of the changes resulting from person weighting for the two groups reflects differences between them in the relation between size of income (or consumption) and the size of the consumer unit, and the fact that the elderly live in smaller units on average with much less variation in size.[10]

Table 7.6 briefly summarizes our findings (all based on the equal person weights, as in table 7.5). The economic status of units headed by the elderly is about 60 percent of that of units headed by the nonelderly where either income after direct taxes or consumption per unit is the measure of economic status. By per capita income or consumption mea-

Table 7.4   **Quintile Shares, Gini Coefficients, and Means by Alternative Measures of Economic Status, 1973, Consumer Unit Weights, by Age**

	Quintile Shares					Gini Coefficient	Mean Economic Status
	1	2	3	4	5		
I. Consumer units, head age < 65							
1. Income before taxes (YBT)	5.50	11.88	17.68	24.21	40.73	.356	$16,471
2. Income after taxes (YAT)	5.78	12.17	17.73	23.95	40.37	.348	14,217
3. Consumption (C)	7.80	13.25	17.74	23.10	38.10	.303	9,807
4. Constant utility welfare ratio—income (YAT/N^*)	6.85	13.23	18.08	22.96	38.87	.318	1.91
5. Constant utility welfare ratio—consumption (C/N^*)	9.02	14.24	17.66	22.06	37.03	.278	1.34
6. Poverty line welfare ratio—income (YAT/N^{**})	6.34	12.67	17.37	23.04	40.57	.340	3.74
7. Poverty line welfare ratio—consumption (C/N^{**})	8.36	13.49	17.25	22.14	38.76	.301	2.62
8. Per capita income after taxes (YAT/N)	5.65	11.22	15.96	22.79	44.37	.385	5,291
9. Per capita consumption(C/N)	7.05	11.57	15.67	21.54	44.17	.368	3,788

II. Consumer units, head age > 64

1. Income before taxes (YBT)	4.93	9.14	14.40	21.73	49.80	.444	8,604
2. Income after taxes (YAT)	5.20	9.72	15.14	22.39	47.54	.421	7,997
3. Consumption (C)	6.51	12.07	16.99	22.79	41.65	.348	5,794
4. Constant utility welfare ratio—income (YAT/N*)	6.44	10.96	15.63	22.12	44.84	.380	1.63
5. Constant utility welfare ratio—consumption (C/N*)	7.79	12.83	17.16	22.64	39.58	.318	1.21
6. Poverty line welfare ratio—income (YAT/N**)	5.85	10.44	15.75	22.28	45.68	.395	3.04
7. Poverty line welfare ratio—consumption (C/N**)	7.30	12.58	17.37	22.83	39.91	.325	2.22
8. Per capita income after taxes (YAT/N)	6.36	10.96	15.63	22.26	44.8	.382	4,852
9. Per capita consumption (C/N)	7.51	12.50	16.72	22.86	40.41	.328	3,625

Each consumer unit's income is entered once in the computations of the summary measures of economic status.

Table 7.5   Quintile Shares, Gini Coefficients, and Means by Alternative Measures of Economic Status, 1973, Person Weights, by Age

	Quintile Shares					Gini Coefficient	Mean Economic Status
	1	2	3	4	5		
I. Consumer units, head age < 65							
1. Income before taxes (YBT)	6.30	12.65	18.05	23.55	39.46	.331	$18,064
2. Income after taxes (YAT)	6.63	12.98	18.29	23.66	38.44	.321	15,702
3. Consumption (C)	8.64	13.91	18.13	23.06	36.27	.276	10,667
4. Constant utility welfare ratio—income (YAT/N*)	7.44	13.62	18.25	22.89	37.79	.302	1.91
5. Constant utility welfare ratio—consumption (C/N*)	9.55	14.70	18.13	22.45	35.14	.255	1.31
6. Poverty line welfare ratio—income (YAT/N**)	6.62	12.86	17.50	23.06	39.96	.331	3.50
7. Poverty line welfare ratio—consumption (C/N**)	8.68	13.74	17.73	22.43	37.42	.286	2.39
8. Per capita income after taxes (YAT/N)	5.69	11.52	16.45	22.68	43.67	.376	4,313
9. Per capita consumption expenditures (C/N)	7.15	12.50	16.50	21.82	42.02	.343	2,975

II. Consumer units, head age > 64

1. Income before taxes (YBT)	4.93	9.74	14.77	21.96	48.60	.431	9,892
2. Income after taxes (YAT)	5.24	10.38	15.54	22.49	46.35	.407	9,155
3. Consumption (C)	6.91	12.54	17.09	22.66	40.79	.335	6,498
4. Constant utility welfare ratio—income (YAT/N*)	6.40	11.29	15.72	22.13	44.46	.375	1.68
5. Constant utility welfare ratio—consumption (C/N*)	8.16	12.95	17.33	22.57	38.98	.308	1.21
6. Poverty line welfare ratio—income (YAT/N**)	5.72	10.70	15.82	22.45	45.32	.392	3.17
7. Poverty line welfare ratio—consumption (C/N**)	7.32	12.67	17.48	22.89	39.64	.321	2.26
8. Per capita income after taxes (YAT/N)	5.78	10.89	15.87	22.50	44.96	.389	4,609
9. Per capita consumption (C/N)	7.16	12.43	17.18	22.79	40.44	.331	3,339

NOTE: Each consumer unit's income is entered as many times as there are persons in the unit in the computations of the summary measures of economic status.

Table 7.6   The Economic Status of Elderly Units Relative to Nonelderly Units: A Summary[a]

	Measure of Economic Status								
	(1) YBT	(2) YAT	(3) C	(4) YAT/N*	(5) C/N*	(6) YAT/N**	(7) C/N**	(8) YAT/N	(9) C/N
1. Mean economic status of elderly									
Mean economic status of nonelderly	.55	.58	.61	.88	.92	.91	.95	1.07	1.12
2. Gini coefficient for elderly									
Gini coefficient for nonelderly	1.30	1.27	1.21	1.24	1.21	1.18	1.12	1.03	.97
3. Percent of elderly in bottom quintile									
Percent of nonelderly in bottom quintile	3.46	3.10	3.36	1.86	1.73	1.69	1.44	.97	.79
4. Percent of bottom quintile who are elderly[b]	30.9	28.7	30.3	19.4	18.3	17.9	15.7	11.2	9.3

[a]All results are based on equal person weights, as in table 7.5.
[b]Persons in consumer units with elderly heads are 11.5 percent of all persons.

sures, however, the elderly are somewhat better-off than younger consumer units. The welfare ratio measures lie in between.[11] They show the elderly to be 88–95 percent as well-off as the nonelderly. Row 2 summarizes the data on relative inequality. The per capita measures show similar degrees of inequality for the two groups. On the other measures, the Gini coefficient is from 12 to 30 percent greater among units headed by the elderly. The data in row 3 show that elderly units are more than three times more likely to be in the lowest quintile of the size distribution of economic status than nonelderly units if we rank consumer units on the basis of income before or after taxes or consumption, but about 3 percent *less* likely on a per capita income, and about 20 percent less likely on a per capita consumption, basis. The welfare ratio measures show the elderly to be 44–86 percent more likely to be in the lowest quintile. Finally, the last row shows that about 30 percent of the units in the bottom quintile are elderly when the measures of economic status are not adjusted by any equivalence scale, about 10 percent based on the per capita measures, and 16–20 percent for the welfare ratio measures.

We can now summarize the numerous numbers in this section:

- Units headed by the elderly are clearly worse-off economically than those headed by the nonelderly on the basis of income before or after taxes or consumption, if no adjustments for family size and composition are made.
- They are about as well-off as the nonelderly on a per capita basis, whether judged by income after taxes or by consumption.
- The results on the basis of the constant utility welfare ratio measures and the welfare ratio measures based on the implicit Orshansky poverty line equivalence scales are intermediate between these two extremes.
- These estimates strongly suggest that the consumer unit issue is more important than the income concept (consumption vs. income) issue in resolving the question of the relative economic status of the elderly.

7.4   The Net Effects of Transfers on Economic Status

We now turn to the role of the net effects of transfers and taxes on the economic status of elderly units relative to nonelderly units, and on the degree of inequality within each age group. Some tax effects are apparent in the comparisons already made between YBT and YAT. However, both of these measures include transfer income, which we now isolate for special attention.

The CEX attempted to obtain a rather full accounting of transfers—private as well as public. Data were collected, and hence included in YAT, on all the public cash transfers (Social Security, railroad retirement, federal retirement, state and local retirement, unemployment insurance, public assistance, workers' compensation, and "all other money receipts"). In addition, the CEX collected data on the bonus value of food stamps, which are also included in YAT. Questions were not asked about other in-kind public transfers.

As with most surveys, underreporting of transfers is a problem. Taking the National Income Accounts as the benchmark, Social Security benefits are underreported by 3 percent. Other transfer payments average 78.3 percent of their benchmark, with different underreporting rates for each program. Dalrymple (1980) attempted several corrections for underreporting and found they do not have a large impact on a variety of inequality measures.

Table 7.7 presents five pretransfer income measures of economic status for both the elderly and the nonelderly. For each consumer unit, the pretransfer measure is defined as the value of income net of all transfers received. After netting out transfers, we order all consumer units by size of pretransfer income and weight each person's economic status equally. Thus the pretransfer distributions in table 7.7 are comparable to the corresponding post-transfer distributions from table 7.5. The assumed counterfactuals in the pretransfer measures of economic status are naive. In the absence of transfers, pretransfer incomes (and the size and composition of consumer units) would undoubtedly be different from the measured values. Because we do not have sufficient estimates of all the behavioral responses to the availability of transfers, however, we adopt the conventional assumption of no behavioral responses. The counterfactual for what consumption would have been in the absence of transfers is more difficult to conceptualize. As a result, we focus only on the effects of transfers on income.

Transfers raise the mean economic status of the nonelderly by almost 5 percent and lower inequality among them by about 7 percent. The effects for the elderly are much larger—the mean economic status of the elderly is raised over 50 percent and inequality among them is reduced by about 30 percent.

Table 7.7 also tells us something about the role of taxes. Comparing YBT and YAT shows that taxes of the nonelderly average 13 percent of before-tax income, while the elderly pay 7.5 percent. Taxes also slightly reduce within-group inequality—2 percent for the nonelderly and 3 percent for the elderly. For each group, transfers have a larger effect than taxes on both average levels of economic status and the degree of within-group inequality.[12]

Table 7.8 summarizes the data from table 7.7 and provides additional information on consumer units in the bottom quintile. A comparison of tables 7.6 and 7.8 shows that, based on the income measures of economic status, transfers greatly increase the relative economic status of the

Table 7.7   Gini Coefficients and Means, Alternative Measures of Economic Status, Including Transfers and Less Transfers, 1973, Person Weights, by Age

	Total Income		Total Income Less Transfers		Percentage Change[a]	
	Gini Coefficient	Mean Economic Status	Gini Coefficient	Mean Economic Status	Gini Coefficient	Mean Economic Status
I. Consumer units, head age < 65						
1. Income before taxes (YBT)	.331	$18,064	.356	$17,342	−7.0%	+4.2%
2. Income after taxes (YAT)	.321	15,702	.348	14,981	−7.8	+4.8
3. Constant utility welfare ratio (YAT/N*)	.302	1.91	.331	1.82	−8.9	+4.9
4. Poverty line welfare ratio (YAT/N**)	.331	3.50	.357	3.34	−7.3	+4.8
5. Per capita income after taxes (YAT/N)	.376	4,313	.399	4,111	−5.8	+4.9
II. Consumer units, head age > 64						
1. Income before taxes (YBT)	.431	9,892	.593	6,649	−27.3	+48.8
2. Income after taxes (YAT)	.407	9,155	.575	5,912	−29.2	+54.9
3. Constant utility welfare ratio (YAT/N*)	.375	1.68	.577	1.06	−32.7	+58.5
4. Poverty line welfare ratio (YAT/N**)	.392	3.17	.569	2.02	−31.1	+56.9
5. Per capita income after taxes (YAT/N)	.389	4,609	.567	2,889	−31.4	+59.5

[a]Defined as $100 \cdot$ [Economic Status − (Economic Status Less Transfers$_i$)]/Economic Status Less Transfers$_i$, where i = Gini coefficient or mean.

Table 7.8   The Pretransfer Economic Status of Elderly Consumer Units Relative to Nonelderly Units: A Summary[a]

	(1) $\widehat{Y}$BT	(2) $\widehat{Y}$AT	(3) $\widehat{Y}$AT/N*	(4) $\widehat{Y}$AT/N**	(5) $\widehat{Y}$AT/N
1. Mean economic status of elderly					
Mean economic status of nonelderly	.38	.40	.58	.61	.70
2. Gini coefficient for elderly					
Gini coefficient for nonelderly	1.67	1.65	1.68	1.59	1.42
3. Percent of elderly in bottom quintile					
Percent of nonelderly in bottom quintile	4.78	4.65	3.72	3.40	2.67
4. Percent of bottom quintile who are elderly[b]	38.22	37.60	32.54	30.59	25.70

$\widehat{Y}$BT = YBT less transfers (which is roughly equal to factor income).
$\widehat{Y}$AT = YBT less transfers and less taxes (which is roughly equal to after-tax factor income).
[a]All results are based on equal person weights, as in tables 7.5, 7.6, and 7.7.
[b]Persons in consumer units headed by the elderly are 11.5 percent of all persons.

elderly. Their relative mean economic status increases by about 50 percent after transfers. The other row comparisons confirm this finding. We conclude that the effect of transfers on the relative economic status of the elderly is large and does *not* depend on the choice of any particular measure of economic status. The pretransfer measures of economic status are as sensitive to the treatment of the recipient unit as are the post-transfer measures.

We gain further insights into the effects of transfers by disaggregating our CEX sample according to various demographic characteristics. Table 7.9 presents data, for eight mutually exclusive age-race-sex groups, on income before taxes and transfers (roughly, factor income, $\widehat{YBT}$); transfers, R; taxes, T; the net transfer ratio, $(R - T)/\widehat{YBT}$; and income after taxes and transfers, YAT. All of the elderly groups have higher net transfer ratios than their nonelderly counterparts. Simple, two-way comparisons of elderly and nonelderly groups, with roughly similar incomes before taxes and transfers, also show substantial differences in the net transfer ratios. For example, on average, white female-headed consumer units under age 65 and white male-headed units age 65 and over have roughly comparable factor incomes, but the latter group enjoys a much higher transfer income. Elderly males also pay less in taxes than the women and thus have higher income after taxes and transfers (YAT). The net transfer ratio for the men is positive; for the women it is negative.

Table 7.9   **Taxes, Transfers, and Net Transfer Ratios by Demographic Group, 1973**

Age-Race-Sex of Consumer Unit Head	$\widehat{YBT}$ [a]	Taxes T	Transfers R	Net Transfer Ratio $(R - T)/$ $\widehat{YBT}$	YAT[b]
White male					
< 65	$18,187	$2,649	$ 457	−.118	$16,040
> 64	7,240	794	3,463	+.369	9,910
Nonwhite male					
< 65	12,960	1,531	824	−.055	12,253
> 64	2,728	140	2,606	+.904	5,195
White female					
< 65	8,518	1,126	1,054	−.008	8,445
> 64	3,867	412	2,423	+.379	5,878
Nonwhite female					
< 65	4,231	437	1,943	+.356	5,737
> 64	2,127	271	1,835	+.736	3,691
All consumer units	13,964	1,930	1,123	−.058	12,997

[a]$\widehat{YBT}$ = YBT − Transfers = income before taxes and before transfers.
[b]YAT = $\widehat{YBT}$ − Taxes + Transfers = income after taxes and after transfers.

A similar comparison can be made between the consumer units headed by a nonwhite female under age 65 and those headed by a white female over age 65. In both cases, the elderly group receives higher net transfers, and experiences a higher net transfer ratio. Again, although we do not show the data, these findings are insensitive to the measure of economic status.

A similar analysis for consumer units classified by more detailed categories of the head's age (data not shown), shows that the net transfer ratios for heads less than 62, 62–64, 65–71 and over 72 are −.105, −.003, +.282, and +.621, respectively. Thus the net transfer ratio rises monotonically with the age of the head.

Table 7.10 gives further estimates of net transfer ratios for the same eight age-race-sex groups. To hold income approximately constant, net transfer ratios are calculated within each quintile of $\widetilde{YBT}$ for the whole sample. The results strongly confirm the positive relationship between age and net transfers. Within any quintile, the elderly enjoy a higher net transfer ratio than their race-sex counterparts and their quintile as a whole. For example, in the third quintile, the net transfer ratio for consumer units headed by white males under age 65 is −.089, while that for units headed by white males age 65 and over is .188.

We add further detail to our findings with a descriptive regression of

Table 7.10   **Net Transfer Ratios by Demographic Group, by Income Quintile**

Age-Race-Sex of Consumer Unit Head	Quintile of Income Before Taxes and Transfers (YBT)					
	1	2	3	4	5	Total
White male						
< 65	1.00	.009	−.089	−.118	−.149	−.118
> 64	2.06	.593	.188	.021	−.109	.369
Nonwhite male						
< 65	2.28	.003	−.078	−.121	−.096	−.055
> 64	2.41	.443	*	*	*	.904
White female						
< 65	1.40	−.015	−.079	−.089	−.131	−.008
> 64	1.88	.408	.016	*	*	.520
Nonwhite female						
< 65	2.55	.125	−.055	*	*	.356
> 64	2.28	*	*	*	*	.736
All consumer units	1.77	.127	−.067	−.110	−.145	−.058

A negative number means that the group's taxes exceed its transfers; a positive number, that transfers exceed taxes. A number that exceeds 1.00 means that net transfers are more than half of total income. The upper limits of the first four income quintiles are: $3,694; $9,043; $14,480; and $21,140.

*Cell has less than twenty consumer units.

the determinants of the amount of net transfer per consumer unit (table 7.11). The results in the first column are for the whole sample; those in column 2 are for units headed by nonelderly, and those in column 3 are for units headed by the elderly. The largest difference in the columns is the mean net transfer, which is negative ($-\$1627$) for the nonelderly and positive (\$2372) for the elderly.

Net transfers, holding income before taxes and transfers constant, increase monotonically with age. For the elderly, net transfers are lower for nonwhites and females, reflecting the fact that Social Security payments, which are the largest component of net transfers, are positively related to past earnings. For the same reason, net transfers are substantially higher for those with liquid assets in excess of \$1500. For the elderly, net transfers are, surprisingly, more income-tested than for the nonelderly—a one dollar increase in $\widetilde{YBT}$ reduces net transfers by 28 cents for the elderly and by 17 cents for the nonelderly.

More detailed regressions that decompose the net transfer into nonwelfare transfers, welfare transfers, and taxes (not shown) indicate that, holding $\widetilde{YBT}$ constant, the probability of transfer receipt rises and the probability of tax payment falls with the age of the consumer unit head. Given receipt, and holding $\widetilde{YBT}$ constant, nonwelfare transfers rise with age and welfare transfers fall with age; given that taxes are paid and holding $\widetilde{YBT}$ constant, taxes paid fall with age.

We made one further attempt to refine our measure of the proelderly bias in the tax-transfer system. Burkhauser and Warlick (1981) show that current-period analysis overstates the "true" redistributive impact of Social Security because a portion of current Social Security transfers are best viewed as a return to prior contributions. They estimate the annuity value of each individual's total (employer plus employee shares) Social Security tax contributions and denote the difference between current benefits and the estimated annuity value as the "transfer component." They estimate that the transfer component was, on average, 73 percent of the current transfer in 1972.

Burkhauser and Warlick (1981) generously gave us access to their data. We constructed a matrix of the ratios of the transfer component to the total benefit. All Social Security recipients were classified by five age categories, their race, sex, and by marital status, and by seven Social Security benefit classes. The current Social Security benefit of each recipient in the CEX was multiplied by the appropriate ratio and the transfer component was derived. The earned annuity component was treated in the same manner as private pension income, that is, as a part of $\widetilde{YBT}$, income before taxes and transfers.

Table 7.12 presents the same data as table 7.9, except that the net transfer ratios are now computed with the annuity component excluded from the numerator and included in the denominator. The pattern is the

Table 7.11   Regression Results: The Determinants of Net Transfers[a]

	All Households	Head < 65	Head > 64
Constant	81.32	159.92	1836.27
Family size	254.03	220.96	585.02
	(18.84)	(18.73)	(83.55)
Age of head:			
< 35	−156.17	−249.92	—
	(79.35)	(77.43)	—
55–61	291.10	201.73	—
	(102.32)	(98.78)	—
62–64	671.27	569.18	—
	(148.87)	(144.29)	—
65–71	2219.80	—	—
	(117.93)	—	—
72+	2513.97	—	127.71
	(111.83)	—	(138.69)
Nonwhite	311.36	491.78	−878.59
	(100.37)	(106.81)	(260.74)
Female	233.37	792.73	−927.95
	(75.93)	(87.32)	(54.32)
Before tax, before transfer income (YBT)	−0.19	−0.17	−0.28
	(0.003)	(0.003)	(0.008)
Northeast	−57.40	−100.69	25.92
	(83.58)	(90.92)	(191.22)
Northcentral	−177.36	−234.60	−161.80
	(77.12)	(83.31)	(181.70)
West	7.64	−63.34	123.40
	(84.6)	(90.69)	(206.38)
Urban	202.36	72.47	605.51
	(65.61)	(71.77)	(148.30)
Home owner	258.59	224.30	742.69
	(69.47)	(71.77)	(151.98)
Assets > $1500	121.08	−132.73	1094.69
	(65.72)	(71.95)	(146.50)
R^2	.504	.437	.427
Number of observations	9,494	7,661	1,833
Mean of dependent variable	−855.20	−1627.3	2371.9

Standard errors appear below regression coefficients. The constants for the regressions in columns 1 and 2 are estimates of the net transfer of a unit headed by a white male between the ages of 35 and 54 who lives outside an urban area in the southern region and has assets worth less than $1,500.
[a]Net transfers are defined as cash transfers less direct taxes.

Table 7.12   **Taxes, Transfers, and Net Transfer Ratios with the Annuity Component of Social Security Treated as Pretransfer Income by Demographic Group, 1973**

Age-Race-Sex of Consumer Unit Head	$\widehat{YBT}$ [a]	Taxes T	Trans- fers R	Net Trans- fer Ratio $(R - T)/\widehat{YBT}$	YAT[b]
White male					
< 65	$18,232	$2,649	$ 457	−.120	$16,040
> 64	8,027	794	2,677	+.235	9,910
Nonwhite male					
< 65	13,022	1,531	762	−.059	12,253
> 64	3,247	140	2,087	+.600	5,195
White female					
< 65	8,579	1,126	993	−.016	8,445
> 64	4,264	412	2,026	+.379	5,878
Nonwhite female					
< 65	4,281	437	1,893	+.340	5,737
> 64	2,384	271	1,581	+.549	3,691
All consumer units	13,964	1,930	963	−.069	12,997

[a]$\widehat{YBT}$ = YBT − Transfers = income before taxes and before transfers.
[b]YAT = $\widehat{YBT}$ − Taxes + Transfers = income after taxes and after transfers.

same as table 7.9, although the differences between the elderly and nonelderly are less pronounced. The adjusted net transfer ratios for the elderly in table 7.12 are about 60–70 percent of the corresponding entries in table 7.9. The tax-transfer system clearly treats the elderly more favorably than their nonelderly counterparts, even after the annuity component of Social Security has been removed from measured transfers.

7.5   Summary and Conclusions

In the United States the concern with the economic status of the elderly has expressed itself politically in the last three and a half decades in the massive growth of Social Security retirement and other transfers. The ongoing policy issue is whether current benefit levels in these transfer programs are now sufficient to accomplish their purpose of maintaining the consumption standards of elderly retirees relative to those of the predominantly nonelderly workers who are taxed to finance these programs. The logical first step in resolving this issue is to measure accurately the economic status of the elderly relative to the nonelderly, and the second is to evaluate the quantitative role of net transfers in determining the total resources available to the elderly.

This paper has addressed these two tasks. We began by creating a new microdata set matching the 1972–73 Consumer Expenditure Survey with the Inventory of Consumer Durables. The match enabled us to estimate consumption flow and income flow measures of economic status for consumer units. This procedure increased the measured consumption and income of the elderly considerably and the income of the nonelderly, but barely affected the measured consumption of the nonelderly. We then used the adjusted consumption and income measures together with various adjustments for differences in family size and composition to produce estimates of economic status.

We concluded that the relative economic status of units headed by the elderly is very sensitive to how, if at all, the unit's income is adjusted for differences in size and composition, but is much less sensitive to the choice of consumption or income as the measure of economic status. We then presented evidence on the effects of transfers on the economic status of the elderly. The effect is large, as expected, and the results are not sensitive to our choice of a measure of economic status, nor to our adjustments for differences in the size and composition of consumer units.

Although many elderly individuals are poor, when we take into account taxes, transfers, and household size, the elderly enjoy higher economic status than some other groups (e.g., households headed by women). Current policy, however, is to take from the nonelderly poor (through cuts in Aid to Families with Dependent Children and Food Stamps) while holding the elderly harmless. There is talk of deindexing OASI and SSI benefits, which would reduce benefits for the elderly poor as well as all other elderly. Ruled out is the possibility of making Social Security benefits subject to the income tax, which would not adversely affect the elderly poor. We do not know whether these policy proposals flow from normative judgments, political swaps, or incorrect perceptions of the economic status of the elderly. If perceptions of the relative economic status of the nonelderly underlie these policy decisions, our paper suggests reconsideration to be in order. Whether measured by current income or by consumption, where adjusted for consumer unit size and composition, the economic status of the elderly was on average quite similar to that of the nonelderly in 1973. If this study could be replicated using current data, we would expect to find that the elderly are even better-off now relative to the nonelderly.[13]

Appendix A *Description of Methodology and Results of Estimating Service Flows from Durables and Owner-Occupied Houses*

For the present study[14] we treat consumer units whose members own certain types of durables and units living in their own homes as if they rent these assets to themselves. Rental values are added to income and consumption, while expenditures on durables are subtracted from consumption. Thus we correct for the distortions that occur when expenditures on a new durable good are included in the reported CEX consumption measure, but the value of services from durables already owned is excluded. This, of course, is especially relevant when comparing home owners and renters. For renters, rent payments are included in consumption, but a similar category of consumption expenditures is not included for home owners.

The CEX tape contains an estimated rental value of owner-occupied houses. This value is added to both the consumption and income measures for home owners. Mortgage interest payments, property taxes, and property insurance payments were subtracted from consumption expenditures. About 10 percent of the home owners failed to report a rental value. This missing data problem was dealt with in a straightforward way, with the aid of a hedonic rental value equation.

To obtain rental values for durable goods other than housing, we matched data from the CEX tape with data from the Inventory of Consumer Durables. The latter data set reports information on the presence, purchase price, and date of acquisition of major and minor durables, furnishings, and vehicles for each unit on the CEX tape. This information is used to compute yearly service flows from durables and vehicles in the way described below.[15]

Major durables on the CD tape include cooking stoves, refrigerators, dishwashers, washing machines, television sets, and so forth.[16] If a durable is present in a unit, and we have the additional information that the durable was purchased, received as a gift, or acquired with the purchase of a house, the unit is referred to as an *owner*. All other units are referred to as *nonowners*.

Thus nonowners include units that rent their durables. The rent paid will show up as an expenditure on the CEX tape, which is appropriate. Nonowners also include units for which the use of a durable is included in the shelter rent of a house or apartment. This will result in an underestimate of the amount of services consumed from that durable. While shelter is slightly overestimated, total consumption will be measured correctly.

The service flow in year t from a durable good is defined as

$$S_t = r_t p_t + (p_t - p_{t+1}),$$

where r_t is the interest rate in year t, and pt is the price of the durable at the beginning of year t.

Thus, S_t equals the sum of the market rate of return on the amount invested in the durable as valued at the beginning of the year, plus the change in the price of the durable during the year. Since, for each durable that has been acquired s years ago,

$$p_t = (1 - \sigma)^s p_0,$$

with p_0 the value of the durable at the time of acquisition, and σ the economic depreciation rate, we have:

$$\begin{aligned} S_t &= r_t p_t + (1 - \delta)^s p_0 \\ &= (r_t + \delta)(1 - \delta)^s p_0. \end{aligned}$$

We arbitrarily set the interest rate, r_t, equal to .07.[17] The depreciation rate for δ was constructed using information on the life expectancy of durables and durable specific prices indices.

To be able to calculate S_t for each durable in the unit, we had to deal with a serious missing data problem. The value of the durable at the time of acquisition, p_0, was reported only when the durable was acquired in 1972 or later.

We employed the following model to impute the value of a durable for owners who do not report p_0:

	y is unknown	if $d = 0$,
(A1)	$y = \alpha' X_1 + \epsilon_1$	if $d = 1$,
(A2)	$d = \beta' X_2 + \epsilon_2,$	

where y is the logarithm of the value of the durable; d is a dummy variable: if $d = 1$, the value is reported; if $d = 0$, the value is not reported; X_1 and X_2 are vectors of exogenous variables, to be discussed below; α and β are coefficients to be estimated; and ϵ_1 and ϵ_2 are disturbance terms. We further assume

$$\begin{bmatrix} \epsilon_1 \\ \epsilon_2 \end{bmatrix} \sim N \left(\begin{bmatrix} 0 \\ 0 \end{bmatrix}; \begin{bmatrix} \sigma_1^2 & \sigma_{12}^2 \\ \sigma_{21}^2 & \sigma_2^2 \end{bmatrix} \right) \text{ and } \sigma_2^2 = 1.0.$$

The vector X_1 includes after-tax income and family size to represent the unit's economic means and needs. The age and marital status of the head are also included in the equation, as are variables representing region, city size information (living within an SMSA or not), and an urban-rural dummy variable.[18]

The vector X_2 contains those variables that are assumed to influence the probability and frequency of buying a certain durable. They include after-tax income, family size, home ownership, and the age and marital status of the unit's head.

The estimation procedure is as follows:

First the β's of equation (A2) are estimated using a Probit specification. The sample consists of all owners.

Second we obtain consistent estimates of the α's in equation (A1) by means of an ordinary least-squares (OLS) regression of the following equation:

(A3) $y = \alpha' X_1 + \alpha_1 \lambda_1 + v,$

where λ_1 is the inverse of the Mills's ratio obtained from the Probit equation, and v is a disturbance term. The sample consists of all owners reporting the value of the durable at the time of acquisition. Table 7.A.1 is an example of the results.

The first column can be interpreted as the probability that the owner of an electric stove acquired this stove within the past two years. This

Table 7.A.1   Estimation Results of the Model Predicting the Value of an Electric Stove (*t*-values in parentheses)

Independent Variables	Probit Equation Yes/No Reported Value (equation A2)		Equation A3 (with λ_1)	Equation A3 (without λ_1)
Constant	−.290	(2.80)	−1.475 (3.39)	2.141 (5.12)
Income	.005	(1.99)	— —	— —
Log income	—	—	.305 (6.86)	.317 (7.06)
Family size	.003	(.21)	−.012 (.67)	−.007 (.41)
Home owner	−.744	(12.31)	— —	— —
Age < 25	1.346	(8.56)	.370 (2.30)	−.191 (1.68)
25–35	.500	(7.95)	.103 (1.16)	−.154 (2.12)
> 50	−.221	(1.35)	−.025 (.29)	.131 (1.59)
Male	.177	(2.33)	— —	— —
Married			.252 (2.87)	.227 (2.56)
Northcentral			−.190 (2.18)	−.202 (2.29)
South			−.112 (1.36)	−.138 (1.66)
West			−.042 (.46)	−.064 (.71)
SMSA			.014 (.18)	.001 (.01)
Rural			.053 (.58)	.050 (.54)
λ_1			.618 (4.88)	—
R^2			.108 —	.087 —

Number of observations: 3730.
Number of reporters: 1040.

probability decreases significantly with the age of the head (age 36–50 is the omitted class). It is also significantly lower for home owners than for non–home owners. After-tax income has a slight positive effect on this probability. These results are in accordance with what common sense would predict.

The second column records the results of estimating equation (A3). The value of an electric stove at the time of acquisition increases with income, as expected. Very young units buy more expensive stoves than do older ones. Units with a married head buy more expensive items than do those with unmarried heads.[19] Furthermore, there are some regional differences. Owners in the Northcentral region spend less on an electric stove than owners in the rest of the nation. Finally, note that λ_1 has a very significant effect, .618, with a t-value of 4.88; the null hypothesis of no systematic selection in the sample is therefore rejected.

Comparing columns 2 and 3 shows that the estimates for the coefficients of the age of the head are seriously biased, unless we correct for the systematic selection of reporters and nonreporters. The predicted value of equation (A1) was deflated to correct for price changes during the year of acquisition and 1972–73. This deflated value was used to create a service flow for each durable in each unit. Since part of our study addresses distributional aspects of income and consumption, a random term was added, drawn from a normal distribution with variance $\hat{\sigma}_{NR}$, the estimated variance of the subsample of owners who were nonreporters.

Vehicles were treated in the same way as other major durables. Table 7.A.2 displays income and consumption data before and after adding service flows from owner-occupied houses and durables. A sensitivity analysis revealed that our results are stable for a large range of plausible values for the depreciation rate, δ, and the interest rate, r. This result should not come as a surprise, since a large part of our adjustments consists of the rental value of owner-occupied houses. This rental value is not affected by our assumptions concerning δ and r.

The first comparison of table 7.A.2 presents the mean values of observed after-tax income. The familiar result is that average income for the elderly is far below the average income of nonelderly. The same holds for total consumption expenditures, as reported by BLS. Not surprisingly, older units are more likely to own their homes than younger ones, but the average rental value of owner-occupied housing is slightly higher for the nonelderly: $1414 vs. $1261. The sum of interest payments on mortgages and home insurance payments is almost twice as high for nonelderly as for elderly units.[20] If we measure the consumption of durable goods and vehicles by their service flows, younger units consume, on average, $543 a year, while older ones consume only $278. Measured by expenditures on durables, however, the numbers read $1280 and $395.

Table 7.A.2   **Consumption and Income before and after Adjusting for the Rental Value of Owner-Occupied Housing, and Service Flows from Durables and Vehicles (CEX-1973, after-tax income quintiles)**

	Quintiles					
	1	2	3	4	5	Mean
Reported after-tax income						
< 65 years	2,706	6,281	9,565	13,454	23,645	$12,282
65+	2,616	5,949	9,396	13,272	25,611	6,471
Reported consumption expenditures						
< 65	4,607	6,708	8,673	10,514	15,536	9,824
65+	3,064	5,138	6,623	8,484	11,803	4,963
Percentage home owners						
< 65	.276	.346	.534	.709	.799	.569
65+	.572	.726	.790	.802	.879	.675
Rental value home						
< 65	437	591	1,077	1,714	2,615	1,414
65+	904	1,213	1,666	1,985	2,671	1,261
Housing cost (mortgage, interest payments, etc.)						
< 65	131	229	493	858	1,351	684
65+	160	330	388	616	936	313
Rental value durables & vehicles						
< 65	201	341	484	673	814	543
65+	139	274	389	479	940	278
Expenditures on durables & vehicles						
< 65	424	791	1,137	1,377	2,173	1,280
65+	186	398	667	800	1,037	395
Consumption (adjusted)						
< 65	4,690	6,619	8,604	10,668	15,441	9,817
65+	3,760	5,896	7,624	9,532	13,441	5,794
After-tax income (adjusted)						
< 65	3,344	7,213	11,126	15,842	27,074	14,239
65+	3,659	7,436	11,451	15,737	29,222	8,011
Ratio adjusted consumption to reported consumption						
< 65	1.02	.99	.99	1.02	.99	1.00
65+	1.23	1.15	1.15	1.12	1.14	1.17
Ratio adjusted income to reported income						
< 65	1.24	1.15	1.16	1.18	1.15	1.16
65+	1.40	1.25	1.22	1.19	1.14	1.24

Thus, consumption of durables is seriously overestimated by expenditures on durables, especially for the nonelderly.

It turns out that "consumer expenditures" is a pretty good proxy for the "consumption" of the nonelderly. The corrections for owner-occupied housing, durables, and vehicles tend to cancel. On average the ratio of corrected consumption to consumer expenditures is 1.00. For elderly households, however, the results are quite different. "Consumer expenditures" seriously underestimate total consumption. On average, the corrections increase consumption by the elderly by 17 percent.

Income changes considerably both for the elderly and the nonelderly. For elderly units in the first quintile, the change is as large as 40 percent. For the nonelderly it is 24 percent. On average, income increases 16 percent for the nonelderly and 24 percent for the elderly.

Consumption and income measures usually do not include service flows from durables and owner-occupied housing. As our results show, this deficiency seriously compromises these measures as welfare indicators. This problem seems particularly important when welfare comparisons are made among consumer units at various stages in the life cycle.

Appendix B *Derivation and Estimation of Constant Utility Equivalence Scale*

As Muellbauer (1979), building on the work of Barten (1964), has shown, true—that is, constant utility—equivalence scales can be constructed for consumer units of various sizes and composition, once a system of demand equations derived from a utility framework has been estimated. However, because of a well-known identification problem inherent in this approach, additional information is generally needed to calculate a complete equivalence scale. Van der Gaag and Smolensky (1982) and Kakwani (1980) demonstrate that this identification problem—central in the literature on household equivalence scales—can be circumvented if Barten's approach of incorporating household characteristics in a demand system is applied to Lluch's (1973) Extended Linear Expenditure System.

The estimation of true household equivalence scales then proceeds as follows:

First, a set of linear Engel curves, household characteristics included, is estimated.

From these estimates the parameters of the underlying utility function (Stone-Geary) are calculated.

Finally, using the expenditure function dual to the Stone-Geary utility function, the following ratio is calculated:

$$E = \frac{e(u_0 \mid h_1)}{e(u_0 \mid h_0)},$$

where $E(\cdot)$ is the expenditure function, giving the minimum amount of money needed for a household with characteristics h to reach utility level u.

Though the resulting equivalence scale is generally a function of the chosen utility level u_0 (and, hence, of income), the estimated scale turned out to be very stable over a large range of incomes. We therefore applied a constant scale here, one that does not vary with incomes. This scale is presented in table 7.A.3. The equivalence scale obtained is generally reasonable, though it differs quite a bit from scales commonly employed.[21] The age and sex of the household head are important vari-

Table 7.A.3   **Constant Utility Equivalence Scale[a]**

Consumer Unit Composition	Age of Head of Consumer Unit			
	35	35–54	55–64	65+
One person				
Male	60	63	56	47
Female	50	53	46	37
Two persons				
Husband and wife	77	80	73	64
Female head, child 6–11	56	60	53	—
Three persons				
Couple, child < 6	76	80	73	64
6–11	88	91	84	75
12–17	90	93	86	77
18+	94	98	90	82
Four persons				
Couple, 2 children < 6	83	87	80	71
6–11, < 6	85	89	82	73
6–11	95	98	91	82
12–17, 6–11	97	100	93	84
12–17	97	100	93	84
18+, 6–17	110	113	106	98
18+	101	105	97	89
Five persons[b]				
Couple, 3 children 6–11	91	94	87	—
12–17, 6–11	102	105	98	—
18+, 6–17	115	119	112	—

[a]A consumer unit consisting of a husband and wife with two children, age 12–17 and 6–11, is 100.

[b]Adding more children to the household adds 4 or 5 percentage points to the scale up to a family size of eight persons. After that only 2 to 3 percentage points should be added.

ables. From their consumption behavior at given income levels, it can be concluded that elderly and female-headed households seem to "need" fewer consumption goods to reach a given utility level than do younger households, especially those headed by men.[22] The scale is also very sensitive to the age of children, much more so than with respect to family size. This is in sharp contrast with, for instance, the equivalence scale implicit in the official U.S. poverty lines, in which the age of children plays no role, but family size is very important.

Table 7.A.4 displays the ratio of the poverty line to the constant utility scales for selected households. For elderly male singles and couples, respectively, the Orshansky scale is 17 and 6 percent higher than our scale. The Orshansky scale is also higher for units with more than five persons. The poverty (Orshansky) line equivalence scale is obtained by specifying food "needs" for households of different composition. One would expect an equivalence scale that is based solely on food requirements to be more sensitive to family size than one that is based on expenditures on all commodities. Economies of scale in, for instance, housing and transportation, are much larger than for food.

Our scale in table 7.A.3 does have two oddities. First, the difference between single men and single women seems quite large. Second, it is unlikely that the addition of one young child to a childless couple would leave their economic "needs" unaffected. However, these results are direct "translations" of the regression results, as are the results with respect to the age of the consumer unit head. We therefore use it as our

Table 7.A.4   **Ratio of Poverty Line Equivalence Scale to Constant Utility Scale of Table 7.A.3**

| | Age of Head of Consumer Unit | |
Consumer Unit Composition	35–54	65+
1: male	.92	1.17
2: husband, wife	.91	1.06
3: husband, wife 1 child[a]	1.00	n.a.
4: husband, wife 2 children[b]	1.00	n.a.
5: husband, wife 3 children[c]	1.00	n.a.
6: husband, wife 4 children	1.12	n.a.

n.a = not applicable, because few consumer units with an elderly head have more than two persons.
[a]Child is 6–11 years old for the constant utility equivalence scale.
[b]One child is 6–11 years, the other is 12–17 years for the constant utility equivalence scale.
[c]Two children are 6–17, the other is over 18 for the constant utility equivalence scale.

preferred method for adjusting incomes for differences in the size and composition of consumer units.

Notes

1. The OASI benefit and beneficiary data are from Robertson (1981), tables 4.1 and 4.2, pp. 42–43. The U.S. Personal Income and population data are from U.S. President (1982), table B-20, p. 255 and table B-28, p. 265.
2. See Moon (1977) and Moon and Smolensky (1977) for discussions of the issues.
3. We did not, however, adjust the weights used to expand the sample to represent the entire U.S. population
4. About 10 percent of all elderly persons (2.0 million) live in consumer units where the head is under 65, while about 3 percent of all nonelderly persons (5.4 million) live in units where the head is over 65. As will be discussed in note 11, our results are not sensitive to our choice to classify all persons by the age of the head of the unit rather than by their own age.
5. See U.S. Department of Labor, Bureau of Labor Statistics (1977) for a complete description of the excluded items. Consumption data are from the interview survey only. Expenditure items collected only in the diary were excluded and, as a result, we underestimate total consumer expenditures by about 12–15 percent. Our measures of income and consumption do not include the value of leisure and thus understate the "full income" of the elderly relative to the nonelderly.
6. Danziger and Taussig (1977) provide a comprehensive review.
7. U.S. Department of Health, Education, and Welfare (1976), p. 30. Many of the same points were repeated more recently in U.S. Department of Health, Education, and Welfare (1979). See, for example, pp. 30–31.
8. Nonetheless, per capita income is widely used to make comparisons of economic welfare across countries or over time in one country.
9. Watts and Peck (1975), Atkinson and Harrison (1978), and Kuznets (1976) also advocate the use of equal-person weights in estimating summary measures of inequality.
10. The mean consumer unit size in our sample is 3.00 persons per unit. Unit size generally declines with age of head, and is less than 2.00 for units where the head is over 64 years. Our choice of person weighting is designed to account for these differences.
11. As mentioned above, all persons in a consumer unit are classified as elderly if the head is over 65 years of age, and as nonelderly if the head is less than 65. Classifying as elderly those nonelderly persons who live in units headed by the elderly and as nonelderly those elderly in nonelderly units could bias our conclusions concerning the relative economic status of the two groups. We attempted to gauge the extent of the bias by reclassifying all persons according to their own age. Thus persons under 65 living with the elderly were counted as nonelderly, and those over 65 living with the nonelderly were classified as elderly. As a result, 3.7 percent of persons shifted categories. This, or any alternative classification, requires an assumption about how much of a unit's income accrues to each person. In this paper, to be consistent, we follow the standard procedure and assume that all persons in a unit share equally, whatever the age of the head. This assumption leads to relatively small changes in our results. For example, the ratio of the per capita income of the elderly to that of the nonelderly rises to 1.12 from 1.07. The results would undoubtedly differ if we assumed (as did Moon 1977) that elderly persons in nonelderly units with incomes above the poverty line received less than an equal share of the nonelderly unit's income. Of course, once the assumption of unequal sharing is introduced, it has implications for men versus women, and adults versus children in all units. Because we have no reliable evidence about the actual degree of income sharing, we are unable to pursue this issue.

12. Of course, not all taxes are included in our tax variable. On the other hand, not all transfers in our sample are reported in full.

13. According to published Current Population Survey data (U.S. Bureau of the Census 1981), the ratio of the mean income of elderly families to the mean income of all families increased from .66 to .71 between 1973 and 1980. While these data are not directly comparable to ours, an upward trend in the relative economic status of the elderly would probably be found if we had a Consumer Expenditure Survey for a recent year.

14. This appendix draws heavily on van der Gaag et al. (1981), which contains more detailed information on the estimation and imputation discussed below.

15. In what follows we restrict ourselves to all households interviewed for the CEX in 1973. Furthermore, we restrict ourselves to service flows from major durables and vehicles. The value of most minor durables (toaster, mixer, hair dryer, etc.) is small enough to warrant treatment as nondurables. Unfortunately, the CD tape does not contain information on the value of house furnishings.

16. For a complete listing, see section D of the code book for the BLS Inventory of Consumer Durables public-use tape.

17. In June 1973 interest rates ranged from 6.3 percent on taxable U.S. bonds, to 7.2 percent on three-month treasury bills, to 8 percent on prime commercial paper. In general these were considerably higher rates than had prevailed in the preceding few years. See U.S. President (1982).

18. This list of independent variables is not derived from any theory of the acquisition of durables. Our only goal is to get an unbiased estimate of y. Alternative specifications were tried but none improved the coefficient of determination of the equation.

19. We emphasize here that all these results should be interpreted for owners only, that is, very young units buy more expensive stoves than older ones, *if* they buy. We are not interested in the unconditional expected value of y, since we impute y only for those units that are reported to be owners.

20. Edward Budd has called our attention to the fact that our imputation for the rental value of owner-occupied homes is about 18 percent larger than the amount reported in the National Income and Product Accounts. This might lead to an overestimate on the relative economic status of the elderly because they are more likely to be home owners. However, our general conclusions on relative economic status are confirmed even when we do not make our adjustments for home ownership.

21. Our equivalence scale is a direct transformation of the estimation results of the demand system. Hence it depends directly on the way we incorporated characteristics of the unit in the demand equation. For instance, no attempt was made to interact the sex of the unit's head with the age of the head. In fact, both variables were simply included as additive dummy variables. Consequently, the "difference" between male- and female-headed consumer units is the same for all age groups. In subsequent work, it might be worthwhile to experiment with various alternatives for incorporating characteristics of the unit in the system of demand equations.

22. The same results were obtained from estimating the Extended Linear Expenditure System (ELES) using regional price variation to identify all parameters (see van der Gaag, Smolensky, and Lee 1984). Thus the conclusion that elderly consumer units "more efficiently" produce utility is not attributable to the savings assumptions implicit in ELES, nor to the fact in these data that the elderly are substantial savers. For more on the savings behavior of the elderly, see Danziger et al. (1982).

References

Atkinson, A. B. 1970. On the measurement of inequality. *Journal of Economic Theory* 2:244–63.
Atkinson, A. B., and A. J. Harrison. 1978. *The distribution of personal wealth in Britain.* London: Cambridge University Press.
Barten, A. P. 1964. Family composition, prices and expenditure patterns. In *Econometric analysis for national economic planning*, ed. R. P. E. Hart, G. Mills, and J. K. Whitaker. London: Butterworth.
Burkhauser, R., and J. Warlick. 1981. Disentangling the annuity from the redistributive aspects of Social Security. *Review of Income and Wealth* 27, no. 4:401–21.
Dalrymple, R. 1980. The sensitivity of measured comprehensive inequality to aggregation, reranking and underreporting. Ph.D. diss., Department of Economics, University of Wisconsin-Madison.
Danziger, S., J. van der Gaag, E. Smolensky, and M. K. Taussig. 1982. The life-cycle hypothesis and the consumption behavior of the elderly. Discussion Paper no. 697–82, Institute for Research on Poverty, University of Wisconsin-Madison.
Danziger, S., and M. K. Taussig. 1977. *Conference on the trend in economic inequality in the U.S.* Special Report no. 11. Institute for Research on Poverty, University of Wisconsin-Madison.
———. 1979. The income unit and the anatomy of income distribution. *Review of Income and Wealth* 25, no. 4:365–75.
Gaag, J. van der, S. Danziger, E. Smolensky, and M. Taussig. 1981. From consumer expenditures to consumption. Manuscript. Institute for Research on Poverty, University of Wisconsin-Madison.
Gaag, J. van der, and E. Smolensky. 1982. Consumer expenditures and the evaluation of levels of living. *Review of Income and Wealth* 28, no. 1:17–27.
Gaag, J. van der, E. Smolensky, and M. Lee. 1984. Consumer demand and the distribution of welfare in the U.S. Manuscript in process. Institute for Research on Poverty, University of Wisconsin-Madison.
Kakwani, N. C. 1980. *Income inequality and poverty.* New York: Oxford University Press.
King, J. 1978. *The 1972–73 Consumer Expenditure Survey. The measure of poverty.* Technical paper 8. U.S. Department of Health, Education, and Welfare. Washington, D.C.: GPO.
Kuznets, S. 1976. Demographic aspects of the size distribution of income: An exploratory essay. *Economic Development and Cultural Change* 25:1–94.
Lebergott, S. 1976. *The American economy, income, wealth, and want.* Princeton, N.J.: Princeton University Press.

Lluch, C. 1973. The extended linear expenditure system. *European Economic Review* 4, no. 1:21–32.

Moon, M. 1977. *The measurement of economic welfare.* New York: Academic Press.

Moon, M., and E. Smolensky, eds. 1977. *Improving measures of economic well-being.* New York: Academic Press.

Muellbauer, J. 1979. McClements on equivalence scales for children. *Journal of Public Economics* 12, no. 2:221–31.

Pollak, R., and T. Wales. 1979. Welfare comparisons and equivalence scales. *American Economic Review* 69, no. 2:216–21.

Radner, D. 1981. Adjusted estimates of the size distribution of family money income for 1972. Social Security Administration, Office of Policy, Working Paper no. 24. Washington, D.C.: U.S. Department of Health and Human Services.

Robertson, A. H. 1981. *The coming revolution in Social Security.* McLean, Va.: Security Press.

U.S. Bureau of the Census. 1981. *Money income and poverty status of families and persons in the United States: 1980,* Series P-60, no. 127. Washington, D.C.: GPO.

U.S. Department of Health, Education, and Welfare. 1976. *The measure of poverty.* Washington, D.C.: GPO.

————. 1979. *Work, income, and retirement,* ed. T. A. Gustafson. Technical Analysis Paper no. 18, Office of Income Security Policy, Office of the Assistant Secretary for Planning and Evaluation. Washington, D.C.: GPO.

U.S. Department of Labor. Bureau of Labor Statistics. 1977. *Consumer Expenditure Survey series: Interview survey 1972–73.* Report no. 455-4. Washington, D.C.: GPO.

U.S. President. 1982. *Economic report of the President.* Washington, D.C.: GPO.

Watts, H., and J. Peck. 1975. On the comparison of income redistribution plans. In *The personal distribution of income and wealth,* ed. J. D. Smith. New York: National Bureau of Economic Research.

Comment   Barbara Boyle Torrey

Introduction

This paper addresses two basic questions that are raised by the enormous growth of transfer programs since 1940: (1) How well-off are the aged today relative to the nonaged? (2) How much of the present eco-

Barbara Boyle Torrey is a fiscal economist with the Office of Management and Budget, Washington, D.C.

nomic status of the aged is provided by transfers? The comparison of economic status between the aged and nonaged is complicated because the groups have different sources of income, forms of consumption, and life-styles. The biological relationship between these two groups is linear, but the economic relationships are more complex. In recognition of these complexities the authors used the 1972 Consumer Expenditure Survey (CEX) and the related Inventory of Consumer Durables to develop a data base that is more appropriate to the economic comparisons between age groups than the data bases generally used.

Although some of the methods in this analysis are not commonly used, the most important and controversial part of this study is likely to be its conclusions, because they contradict strongly held public opinion. Therefore these comments will focus on the conclusions and suggest how the results could be modified by the biases in the study and potential future trends. Then some of the public policy implications will be discussed.

How the Measurement of Economic Status
Affected the Conclusions

The first and most prominent conclusion, of course, is that the economic status of the aged is approximately 90 percent of the economic status of the nonaged when equivalence scales are used. If a value can be ascribed to leisure, then the aged would almost certainly be as well-off as the nonaged if not considerably better-off.

However, as noted by the authors, this conclusion is very sensitive to the measurement of the economic unit. The sensitivity of the unit concept suggests that this is where we should be concentrating future research. Some would argue that no adjustment is necessary to make different size households equivalent because people have voluntarily chosen their family size to maximize their utility. While this may be true to some extent for the nonaged, it is hard to argue that it is as true for the aged who no longer have the option of having more children or, in many cases, of marrying. Therefore, when comparing the aged and nonaged, an equivalence adjustment for different kinds of households is useful.

The constant utility equivalence scale used in this paper is based on consumption patterns of different kinds of households for food, housing, clothing, transportation, etc. The authors' estimates suggest that contrary to life-cycle theory, the aged continue to save rather than dissave. This result was also found in the Survey of Changes in Consumer Finance and in the 1960–61 CEX. In fact, the aged continue to save at least the same percentage of their income even though their income after taxes decreases as they get older. One explanation of this behavior may be that saving becomes more important to people as they get older and have fewer opportunities to increase their income. And, in fact, saving may become so important that the aged are willing to forego some consumption to achieve a target level. If this were true, it would not be surprising to see different consumption patterns in men and women. Aged women should have more need to save since they will live longer and therefore are more threatened by declining income than men. But it also suggests that utility measures that look only at consumption may assume too quickly that utility remains constant as the consumption of the aged drops.

An evaluation of the general economic status of the aged and nonaged requires not only a measurement of the mean economic status but also the distribution around the mean. Therefore the second conclusion—that the Gini coefficient for the aged using equal person weights and equivalence scales was 18–24 percent higher than for the nonaged—is important.

However, when the Gini coefficient is measured using equal unit weights, which is more common, the difference in inequality is reduced to 16 percent and 19 percent for the two measures that used equivalence scales; and on a per capita basis, income inequality actually becomes less for the aged than for the nonaged. Using either unit weights or person weights creates some problems of interpretation. It is easier to interpret the results if unit weights are used for economic measures unadjusted for unit size and if person weights are used for the economic measures adjusted for unit size. This would also tend to reduce the variance in the ratios of the Gini coefficients for the different measurement concepts.

The aged income distribution would be relatively more unequal if it were not for transfer payments. And this leads to the third conclusion that public transfers raise the mean economic status of the aged about 56 percent and reduce inequality among them by about 30 percent. But the admitted naive assumption that there are no behavioral effects from the enormous public tax and transfer system means that the estimated effects of transfers on economic status of the aged are upper bounds. One of the authors, in fact, has recently surveyed the literature on how income transfer programs have affected work and concluded that up to one-half of the decline in the older male labor force (and therefore the decline in their wage income) since 1950 is because of the Social Security program's work disincentives.

The final conclusion that the authors leave for the reader to make is that an adequate retirement income for the aged population had, in general, been achieved by 1973 in the United States. Other studies, such as the one recently done by Michael Hurd and John Shoven, support this conclusion, but none of the studies is as comprehensive in providing alternative ways to verify the results. Although some aged do not have adequate means, the majority appear now to have achieved economic independence, largely because of the public transfer programs. This accomplishment is not only unheralded, but is also denied by public opinion, as a recent Harris poll suggests. Part of the reason for the misperception may be that the relative economic status of the aged has fluctuated quite significantly in the past. Although we do not have comparable historical data for the better measurement concepts used in this paper, there is historical information for the ratio of the median total money income of aged families with all families. Between 1950 and 1967 this ratio decreased 16 percent, but between 1967 and 1980 it increased 24 percent. (The ratio of median total money income for unrelated individuals 65 and over to all unrelated individuals did not change from 1950 to 1980.) Apparently public perception has lagged behind the major improvements that took place in the relative economic status of the aged in the 1970s.

The Potential Effect of Research Biases and Future Trends
on Relative Economic Status

How well the conclusions of this paper can be applied to the future depends in part on the biases in the research and how future trends may affect the populations described. The CEX data base, while better than most data bases, is still imperfect. Three specific qualities of the CEX suggest that the relative economic status of the aged could be underestimated in this study and therefore improve relative to the nonaged in the future.

The major omission in the CEX for the purposes of this study is the information on Medicare services for the aged and the employer health insurance for the nonaged. Of course, a number of conceptual problems are introduced when including medical costs in a measurement of economic status. But because the medical utilization rate significantly differs between the aged and nonaged and because consumption of medical services is to some extent voluntary, it should not be completely ignored. Because Medicare and employer health insurance are not of equal value, their omission produces a bias in the results. The total compensation comparability study by the Office of Personnel Management estimated that in 1979 the value of the employer health insurance benefits to employees in industry was $1045. This compensation did not go to all employees, but of those it did go to it usually provided family health benefits. The insurance value of Medicare net of institutional care expenditures was $1011 *per enrollee* in 1979. Therefore, if both of these values were added to the income of the aged and nonaged, the economic status measured by income of the aged would be increased relative to the nonaged. In addition, if these insurance values of health benefits are actuarial estimates of consumption, then consumption measures of economic status for the aged would likewise increase relative to the nonaged. And a utility scale developed on consumption data omitting these measures of health consumption would undervalue the aged's equivalence scale and therefore reduce to some extent the difference between the aged and nonaged.

There are two other reasons why the CEX data base may underestimate the economic status for the aged: Over 50 percent of the CEX respondents in 1973 who were 65 and over had a ninth grade education or less. Also, only 65 percent of the people 65 and over owned their own home. We already know that the future aged will be significantly better educated than the present aged both absolutely and relative to the nonaged. And the 1975 Retirement History Study suggested that subsequent aged cohorts will have higher rates of home ownership. This means that both earnings histories, which are directly related to education, and assets, which are directly related to home ownership for the aged, are likely to increase in the future and improve the economic status of the aged.

However, at least two future demographic trends could reduce the economic status of the aged relative to the nonaged. In another paper, the authors estimated that the mean income after taxes of couples over 71 was 81 percent of the income of couples 65–71 years old (84 percent for single females and 101 percent for single men). This difference in income will tend to reduce the economic status of the aged as more of the aged become 71 and older (35 percent in 1970; 39 percent in 1990; and 44 percent by 2000).

In addition, both the Census and the Social Security actuaries project that the difference in life expectancies for men and women will continue to increase over time. Since women's retirement income is lower than men's the trend of increasing the ratio of aged women to men in the future would tend to lower the future economic status of the aged as a whole. However, this also could be offset to some extent by the improving work histories of the future cohorts of retired women.

The net effect of all these factors cannot be predicted, but they will tend to offset each other to some extent. Public policy, of course, will not wait to be made until we know what the net effects will be.

Public Policy Implications

The authors discuss one major public policy implication of their conclusions, which is that the aged should not be disproportionately favored relative to specific needy groups in the society, such as poor, female-headed families. Therefore such options as taxing Social Security benefits should be considered as a deficit reduction measure before further cuts in transfers to less-privileged groups are taken. Although taxing Social Security benefits would reduce the rate of return on Social Security contributions to upper-income recipients, this should not be a binding constraint on the allocation of resources.

The aged today look almost as heterogeneous in terms of income distribution as the nonaged. And therefore, like the nonaged, their poverty problems can no longer be solved by broad, general programs without enormous costs. Although much of the credit for the past reduction in both poverty and the Gini coefficient for the aged can be attributed to Social Security, it will be a particularly inefficient vehicle to solve the remaining income problems of the poor, when most of the aged are no longer poor.

The authors' recommendations to tax Social Security benefits could be generalized to a reevaluation of all the tax expenditures for the aged. Total tax expenditures for the aged are worth an estimated $16.4 billion in 1983, which make them together the third largest federal "program" for the aged, not counting the retirement programs for federal employees. Federal revenues would be increased 2.5 percent if these exemptions were eliminated. Of course, elimination would lower the mean economic status of the aged slightly, but it would also lower their Gini coefficient.

The other major non-needs-tested federal program for the general aged is the provision of free and complete medical care to all veterans 65 and over. This costs over $1 billion today and will double by 1990 as the size of this population doubles.

But other questions should also be addressed. The present aged have inherited a substantial windfall from Social Security and Medicare. That windfall is partly responsible for their present economic status and their ability to accumulate and protect private assets. The next generation will inherit the private assets of their parents, which are considerable, given the saving and consumption pattern of this cohort of aged. And they will inherit it without an estate tax. Providing a windfall to the poor or to the aged has generally been acceptable public policy. But to have the side effects of the windfall to the aged passed on to the nonpoor, nonaged children tax-free should raise questions about the future distribution of income.

Of course, longer-term issues are raised by the conclusions in this paper. Should the economic parity of the aged with the nonaged that is demonstrated in this paper be maintained, and if so how and by whom? If the present economic parity of the aged is to be maintained, then that amount of total personal income that is required to finance the federal transfers to the aged will have to increase from approximately 7 percent in 1980 to 8 percent by 1990 and 15 percent at the peak of the baby-boom retirement. Alternatively, other public goals would have to be sharply curtailed. If the nonaged increased their taxes to maintain the relative economic status of the aged through 2010, but then did not raise their tax rates further, the economic status of the aged who retire later would deteriorate 25 percent relative to the nonaged. Under those conditions, if the aged wanted to maintain their present relative economic status, they would have to increase their own assets or retirement age.

And this raises the question of whose responsibility it is to maintain some economic parity between the aged and nonaged. In 1975 the federal government was paying 78 percent of all retirement payments to the aged and 54 percent of their health care. The private sector was paying 15 percent and 37 percent, respectively, with the state and local governments paying the rest. Is this present division of responsibility what we want to assume for the future? Or should we suggest that both the private sector and individuals take more responsibility in the future for maintaining the approximate economic parity that this paper has described in 1973.

The issues of whether economic parity should be maintained between the aged and nonaged, and if so how and by whom, are the obvious long-term policy shadows cast by the results of this paper.

8 The Role of Income Transfers in Reducing Inequality between and within Regions

David Betson and Robert Haveman

8.1 Introduction

Convergence of per capita or per household income among states or regions in the postwar period is well known (see U.S. Department of Commerce 1978, 1981; Hanna 1957). Income growth rates in the South and the Southwest—the Sun Belt—have exceeded those in the older and richer northern and New England states—the Snow Belt. Traditionally northern industries such as textiles and furniture have migrated to the southern states while new technology industries have concentrated their growth in the South and the Southwest.

This narrowing of regional inequality has occurred simultaneously with two other postwar phenomena—an exceptionally rapid increase in public income transfers and the essential stability of the degree of inequality in the overall distribution of post-transfer income (see Danziger, Haveman, and Plotnick 1981). In this paper, we will explore the anatomy of the regional convergence of incomes and relate this convergence to the high and stubborn level of overall income inequality. In addition, we will explore the pattern of within-region inequality among the regions. The primary questions we will ask and attempt to answer are:

1. What role have income transfers played in the observed reduction of income inequality among regions of the country?

2. Which regions display the greatest income inequality, and for which regions has the inequality within the region changed the most over time?

David Betson is a professor of economics at the University of Notre Dame; and Robert Haveman is professor of economics at the University of Wisconsin, Madison.

This research was supported in part by funds granted to the Institute for Research on Poverty by the U.S. Department of Health and Human Services under the provisions of the Economic Opportunity Act of 1964. The authors wish to thank Lyle Nelson for his research assistance, and Luise Cunliffe for the preparation of the various data tapes.

283

3. To what extent have income transfers offset the high and growing inequality in the distribution of market income within regions?

4. In which regions have income transfers been used most effectively in reducing market income inequality?

5. What factors determine the impact of transfers in reducing inequality within states and regions?

The focus of this paper is on individual regions and differences among them. This focus deserves comment. What is there about regional groupings of people that makes them a relevant unit of analysis? While analyses of differences in average incomes or income inequality among racial groups or age groups are common fare and require little defense, studies of regional differences in average income or inequality are often viewed as suspect and artificial. What makes such studies worthwhile?[1]

To be sure, individual members of racial or age groupings are inexorably identified with their group; membership in these clubs is not voluntary. Such is not the case with regions. Those not pleased with the opportunities implied by the average incomes or the income inequality in their current location are, in principle at least, free to choose another. While migration costs do exist and provide some rationale for focusing on regional groupings, immobility cannot be relied on as the sole basis for regional analysis; nor can the proposition that individuals view others in their region as a more accurate comparison group than members of their race or age cohort.

Our defense for analyzing income and inequality differences among regions, and the impact of income transfers on these differences, is a straightforward one. For whatever reason, people are interested in differences in regional performance; in whether the South is poorer or growing more rapidly than the North. Perhaps this reflects a view that a viable federalism requires that the variance in economic performance among regions be minimized. Perhaps it only reflects interest in the outcome of the competitive process that exists among states or regions in a federal system.

While this interest in regional performance exists generally among the population, it is apparently magnified among national policymakers. Legislative measures are typically designed with regional equity as an explicit objective, and congressional requests for analysis of regional impact are common. Indeed, in many legislative measures, considerations of regional performance form the primary bases for the allocation of funds. Revenue sharing is an important example. And in those measures the indicators of regional performance used are precisely those of this study: differences in average income among regions, differences in regional income growth, and differences in inequality among regions (as indicated by regional unemployment rates or regional rates of poverty incidence). Our regionally based measurements and estimates are designed to meet this interest.

8.2   Income Transfers and Their Growth, 1965–81

Public spending on income transfers is large and has grown rapidly in recent years as new programs have been enacted, benefit levels in existing programs have been increased, and eligibility requirements have been loosened. In 1981 expenditures on these programs are estimated to reach almost $300 billion, an amount that is about 10 percent of the Gross National Product.

Table 8.1 lists the major income transfer programs and shows their expenditures for 1965 and 1979 and estimates for 1981. These programs are divided into two types: social insurance and public assistance. Within

Table 8.1   Expenditures on Major Income Transfer Programs

		Public Expenditures (billions of current dollars)		
	Date Enacted	1965	1979	1981 (estimate)
Social insurance				
Cash benefits:				
Social Security (OASDI)	1935	$16.5	$102.6	$137.0
Unemployment insurance	1935	2.5	11.2	18.7
Workers' compensation	1908	1.8	9.9	14.8
Veterans' disability compensation	1917	2.2	6.8	7.5
Railroad retirement	1937	1.1	4.3	5.2
Black lung	1969	NE	0.6	0.9
In-kind benefits:				
Medicare	1965	NE	29.1	38.4
Public assistance (welfare)				
Cash benefits:				
Aid to Families with Dependent Children (AFDC)	1935	1.7	10.8	12.8
Supplemental Security Income (SSI)[a]	1972	2.7	6.8	8.5
Veterans' pensions	1933	1.9	3.6	4.1
General assistance	NA	0.4	1.2	1.5
In-kind benefits:				
Medicaid[b]	1965	0.5	21.8	27.6
Food Stamps	1964	0.04	6.8	9.7
Housing assistance	1937	0.3	4.4	6.6
Total expenditures		$31.6	$219.9	$293.3
Total expenditures as a percentage of GNP		4.6	9.1	10.0

Sources: *The Budget of the United States Government, Fiscal Year, 1981*, and its appendix for 1979 and 1981 estimates. Plotnick and Skidmore (1975) for 1965 data. Social insurance programs condition benefits on contributions based on previous employment; public assistance programs condition benefits on current income and assets (means-tested).

NA = not applicable, varies by states.
NE = nonexistent.
[a] Aid to the Blind, Aid to the Permanently and Totally Disabled, and Old Age Assistance in 1965.
[b] Medical Aid to the Aged in 1965.

each category are programs providing cash income and others providing in-kind benefits.

The programs have two basic objectives—replacing income losses from events that are largely outside an individual's control, and assuring a minimum level of economic support to those who have little other income. The first objective is largely served by social insurance programs for which eligibility and benefit levels depend on past contributions and some identifiable problem, such as old age, death of spouse, illness, disability, or unemployment. One does not have to prove financial need to claim benefits. Social insurance accounts for nearly three-quarters of the expenditures.

The second objective is served by the public assistance (welfare) programs for which inadequate economic means is the chief eligibility criterion. Receipt of welfare benefits is not conditioned on past contributions. Benefits are asset- and income-tested—they vary inversely with income from private sources and social insurance.

These income transfer programs have grown rapidly in recent years with expenditures increasing from 4.6 percent of GNP in 1965 to 10.0 percent in 1981. Table 8.2 shows the increase in both the number of beneficiaries of the cash transfer programs and the size of the average benefit and compares this growth with that of census money income. In 1965, 37 percent of all households received a cash transfer; by 1978, 42 percent were recipients. The last column shows that the average transfer for recipient households increased by 55.3 percent, while census money income increased by only 20 percent.

Given the targeting of income transfers on those experiencing income losses and those without adequate economic means, the growth in these expenditures would be expected to have narrowed income differences in a wide variety of dimensions. In this paper we will focus on two—income differences *within* regions (states) and income differences *among* regions (states).

8.3 Cash Transfers and Inter- and Intrastate Income Differentials—A Static View

Although the convergence of average state incomes has been well documented, substantial differences in average household incomes still exist among states. Table 8.3 presents the mean household income by four different income concepts in 1975 for the fifty states and the District of Columbia. The four income concepts are:

Y_1 = Cash income from wages, salaries, rents, dividends, interests, and miscellaneous sources (i.e., "market income").

$Y_2 = Y_1$ plus social insurance income.

$Y_3 = Y_2$ plus welfare income (i.e., "post-transfer income").

$Y_4 = Y_3$ minus taxes paid (i.e., "post-tax, post-transfer income").[2]

Table 8.2 Cash Income Transfers and Census Money Income of Households[a] in Constant 1978 Dollars, 1965 and 1978

	1965		1978		1965–78
	Mean for Recipient Households	Percent of Households Receiving	Mean for Recipient Households	Percent of Households Receiving	Real Growth of Mean
Social Security and railroad retirement	$ 2407	22%	$ 3747	26%	55.7%
Public assistance[b]	2006	5	2079	8	3.6
Other cash government transfers[c]	1801	18	2973	17	65.1
One or more cash transfers[d]	2532	37	3931	42	55.3
Total census money income	13767	—	16518	—	20.0
Cash transfers as a percentage of money income	6.8%	—	10.0%	—	—

SOURCE: Computations by authors from 1966 Survey of Economic Opportunity and March 1979 Current Population Survey.

[a]Households include families and unrelated individuals. The programs represented here differ from those in table 8.1. The Census does not gather data on in-kind transfers, nor does it disaggregate cash transfers by program to the extent shown in table 8.1.

[b]Includes Aid to Families with Dependent Children, Supplemental Security Income (Old Age Assistance, Aid to the Blind, and Aid to the Permanently and Totally Disabled in 1965), and General Assistance.

[c]Includes unemployment compensation, workers' compensation, government employee pensions, and veterans' pensions and compensation.

[d]The mean value in this row exceeds the mean for any individual category, and the percentage receiving one or more transfer is lower than the sum of rows 1–3, because some households receive more than one transfer.

Table 8.3   **Mean State Household Income—1975**

	Number of Households (in 1000)	Mean Income of State			
		Y_1	Y_2	Y_3	Y_4
Northeast	17458	13716	14994	15318	11997
1 ME	384.	10949.	12096.	12343.	10115.
2 NH	295.	12850.	14033.	14218.	11672.
3 VT	170.	11276.	12332.	12658.	10081.
4 MA	2083.	13736.	14966.	15246.	11864.
5 RI	329.	12497.	13844.	14110.	11288.
6 CT	1092.	15519.	16770.	16988.	13496.
7 NY	6699.	13564.	14787.	15175.	11535.
8 NJ	2438.	15487.	16777.	17067.	13690.
9 PA	4058.	12932.	14350.	14660.	11746.
Northcentral	19798	13854	14998	15245	12008
10 OH	3620.	13702.	14866.	15092.	12129.
11 IN	1827.	13688.	14790.	14962.	11917.
12 IL	3837.	14875.	15988.	16287.	12674.
13 MI	3085.	14157.	15447.	15769.	12419.
14 WI	1554.	14103.	15282.	15519.	11879.
15 MN	1340.	13788.	14891.	15113.	11548.
16 IA	1005.	13570.	14688.	14876.	11695.
17 MO	1730.	12111.	13216.	13476.	10792.
18 ND	209.	13822.	14783.	14945.	11763.
19 SD	226.	11951.	12900.	13128.	10902.
20 NB	549.	13426.	14384.	14576.	11553.
21 KS	816.	13457.	14549.	14695.	11643.
South	23847	12252	13269	13568	10890
22 DE	194.	15050.	16124.	16330.	12334.
23 MD	1385.	16874.	17771.	17981.	13516.
24 DC	287.	14609.	15335.	15725.	11361.
25 VA	1709.	14533.	15415.	15622.	12107.
26 WV	643.	10641.	12417.	12725.	10482.
27 NC	1862.	11554.	12463.	12795.	10103.
28 SC	896.	11541.	12500.	12830.	10338.
29 GA	1675.	11792.	12590.	13098.	10536.
30 FL	3241.	11881.	13309.	13561.	11223.
31 KY	1157.	10860.	12080.	12418.	10081.
32 TN	1460.	11174.	12196.	12489.	10281.
33 AL	1242.	10928.	11968.	12295.	9978.
34 MS	762.	9848.	10749.	11279.	9327.
35 AR	757.	9990.	11094.	11414.	9419.
36 LA	1225.	12018.	12900.	13313.	10803.
37 OK	996.	12105.	13103.	13368.	10563.
38 TX	4356.	12765.	13564.	13807.	11191.

Table 8.3 (continued)

	Number of Households (in 1000)	Mean Income of State			
		Y_1	Y_2	Y_3	Y_4
West	13851	14303	15342	15641	12054
39 MT	258.	13026.	14103.	14319.	11184.
40 ID	281.	12828.	13874.	14097.	11075.
41 WY	131.	14593.	15467.	15629.	12585.
42 CO	928.	14527.	15295.	15475.	11896.
43 NM	384.	12424.	13341.	13696.	11078.
44 AZ	803.	13096.	14252.	14483.	11400.
45 UT	382.	13779.	14684.	14910.	11816.
46 NV	224.	14756.	15651.	15847.	12602.
47 WA	1286.	14028.	15174.	15382.	12402.
48 OR	863.	12926.	14123.	14320.	11031.
49 CA	7943.	14556.	15608.	15961.	12160.
50 AK	111.	23407.	23916.	24234.	17055.
51 HA	257.	17444.	18404.	18833.	13905.
Total	75044.	13395.	14511.	14002.	11659.

The data in table 8.3 contain a number of patterns. First, for market income (Y_1), the gap between the highest and lowest state is substantial— $9848 (Mississippi) to $23,407 (Alaska). The ratio of the highest to the lowest is 2.4. For census income (Y_3), the gap is smaller—$11,279 (Mississippi) to $24,234 (Alaska)—and the ratio of the highest to the lowest falls to 2.1. Because of income transfers, the ratio is reduced by about 15 percent. When taxes are accounted for as well, the gap again narrows— from $9327 (Mississippi) to $17,065 (Alaska)—and the ratio of the highest to the lowest falls to 1.8. At a point in time, the tax-transfer system makes an important contribution to narrowing the regional disparity in average household incomes.

The above numbers document the substantial regional disparities in average incomes that still exist. Related questions concern the extent to which these disparities contribute to total inequality in the nation, and the role of the tax-transfer system in reducing these regional differentials. One measure of inequality that can be decomposed into a measure of inequality among states and inequality within the states is the Theil measure of income inequality (see appendix B for a description of the Theil index and its decomposition). Indeed, the Theil index of total inequality among households in the nation (T_T) has two components— the level of Theil inequality in per household income among regions (T_A) and the average level of Theil inequality in per household income within regions (T_W). Thus,

(1) $$T_T = T_A + T_W.$$

Table 8.4   Theil Indices of Inequality for the Four Income Concepts, 1975

	Y_1	Y_2	Y_3	Y_4
T_W	.974	.531	.291	.220
T_A	.006	.005	.004	.003
T_T	.979	.536	.296	.223

For 1975 the total level of household income inequality (T_T) and its two components (T_A and T_W) are shown in table 8.4 for the four income concepts. Several patterns are clear in this table:

1. The major component of total inequality among households (T_T) for all of the income concepts is inequality among households within states (T_W) rather than inequality in mean household income among the states (T_A). For Y_1, T_A accounts for only about .7 percent of T_T; for Y_4, T_A accounts for about 1.3 percent of T_T. If all differences in average incomes among states were eliminated while the level of inequality among households within states was left untouched, total inequality among households in the nation would decrease by less than 2 percent.

2. At a point in time, 1975, transfers cause a decrease in T_A inequality—from .006 to .004, a decrease of 23 percent. Transfers have a substantially larger effect on T_W—a decrease from .97 to .29, or 70 percent. For T_T, total income inequality, transfers effected a reduction of 69 percent. The tax-transfer system accounted for a reduction of 77 percent in T_W, 48 percent in T_A, and 77 percent in T_T.

Analogous to the question of inequality in the average income per household among the states is the question of the extent to which the states are similar to each other in terms of the level of income inequality within each state. Table 8.5 presents the pattern of inequality within states for all of the states. The four income concepts used in measuring this gap between the rich and poor within states are the Y_1, Y_2, Y_3, and Y_4 concepts, and the Theil index within states is the indicator of inequality.

As with mean household income differences, states also differ substantially in terms of within state inequality. States in the South generally have the most substantial inequality, with the Northcentral region displaying the smallest gap between rich and poor. For market incomes (Y_1), the ratio of the most unequal distribution of income (Mississippi) to the least unequal (Wisconsin) is 2.2. For post-transfer income (Y_3), the disparity among states in terms of within-state inequality falls substantially, and the ratio of the most unequal to the least unequal decreases to 1.3. When taxes are accounted for, all states have even less within-state inequality. However, the ratio of the most unequal to the least unequal rises slightly to 1.4. Overall one can conclude that the tax-transfer system not only dramatically reduces the overall level of inequality within states, but also reduces the dispersion in within-state inequality. That is, the

Table 8.5   **Theil Indices of Income Inequality Within States—1975**

	Y_1	Y_2	Y_3	Y_4
Northeast	1.072	.608	.296	.223
1 ME	.970	.468	.286	.221
2 NH	.772	.408	.266	.214
3 VT	.947	.509	.292	.220
4 MA	.949	.549	.284	.216
5 RI	1.143	.546	.297	.227
6 CT	.844	.512	.307	.239
7 NY	1.225	.705	.307	.221
8 NJ	.919	.544	.282	.220
9 PA	1.058	.571	.281	.217
Northcentral	.888	.486	.278	.209
10 OH	.873	.458	.258	.198
11 IN	.775	.381	.263	.200
12 IL	1.021	.620	.296	.223
13 MI	.915	.540	.267	.204
14 WI	.697	.401	.260	.186
15 MN	.781	.421	.271	.196
16 IA	.789	.407	.284	.214
17 MO	1.102	.508	.303	.230
18 ND	.758	.404	.304	.230
19 SD	.815	.394	.287	.230
20 NB	.811	.418	.295	.224
21 KS	.750	.385	.276	.207
South	1.042	.531	.306	.235
22 DE	.822	.463	.280	.204
23 MD	.760	.482	.292	.222
24 DC	1.066	.690	.368	.256
25 VA	.763	.419	.285	.216
26 WV	1.301	.562	.277	.213
27 NC	.908	.477	.280	.206
28 SC	.999	.487	.261	.199
29 GA	1.221	.626	.288	.218
30 FL	.983	.498	.311	.247
31 KY	1.142	.569	.320	.250
32 TN	1.093	.518	.291	.228
33 AL	1.336	.613	.318	.247
34 MS	1.516	.655	.317	.246
35 AR	1.252	.503	.294	.227
36 LA	1.232	.669	.334	.262
37 OK	1.176	.553	.341	.249
38 TX	.878	.475	.295	.230

Table 8.5 (continued)

	Y_1	Y_2	Y_2	Y_4
West	.876	.575	.297	.216
39 MT	.799	.400	.283	.209
40 ID	.730	.388	.264	.195
41 WY	.690	.380	.279	.220
42 CO	.702	.429	.284	.216
43 NM	1.072	.589	.305	.233
44 AZ	.858	.465	.296	.227
45 UT	.730	.405	.270	.207
46 NV	.738	.419	.294	.229
47 WA	.796	.460	.284	.221
48 OR	.817	.430	.284	.208
49 CA	.933	.560	.301	.213
50 AK	.534	.430	.310	.226
51 HA	.784	.549	.294	.215

SOURCE: Calculations by authors from 1976 Survey of Income and Education.

tax-transfer system not only reduces the Theil index within all states, but it also tends to make states more similar in their levels of inequality.[3]

We have discussed how the tax-transfer system has affected the differences among states in two separate dimensions: average state income and the degree of within-state inequality. To bring together these two dimensions of regional inequality at a point in time, we have defined an indicator of the differences among states, which is the sum of the relative variation in these two dimensions. This indicator is based on the relative variance among states in each of the two dimensions. This summary index of income and inequality differences across states, RV_T, can be used to describe the overall role of transfers in the convergence of states—the convergence in average incomes among states ($RV_{\bar{Y}}$) and the convergence of within-state inequality (RV_{IN}).[4] In table 8.6, we present RV_T along with its components for the four income concepts as computed from the 1975 Survey of Income and Education (SIE).

Table 8.6   **Measures of Differences Among States, 1975**

Income Concept	$RV_{\bar{Y}}$	RV_{IN}	RV_T
Y_1	.012	.031	.042
Y_2	.010	.027	.037
Y_3	.009	.004	.013
Y_4	.007	.005	.011

SOURCE: Computed by authors from the Survey of Income and Education, 1975.

Several interesting patterns emerge from the measures of the differences among states shown in table 8.6. First, when market income (Y_1) is used as the basis of comparison, the relative dissimilarity among states is caused primarily by differences in within-state inequality. But when transfers are accounted for (Y_3), the index of overall differences among states falls by 68 percent, primarily because of a dramatic fall in the component of the index attributable to inequality within states (RV_{IN}). Further, when Y_3 is the income concept used as the basis of comparison, relative dissimilarity in within-state inequality (RV_{IN}) is reduced to one-half the magnitude of $RV_{\bar{Y}}$. When income before transfers (Y_1) is the income concept used, RV_{IN} is three times $RV_{\bar{Y}}$. Second, after adding in the effect of taxes (Y_4), we see that states become even more similar, but the effect is not as dramatic as the effect of transfers. In summary, the measures of differences among states presented in table 8.6 suggest that the tax-transfer system does have a dramatic effect in reducing differences among states. This effect is primarily the result of the reduction of the dissimilarity among states in within-state income inequality.

These statistics, then, suggest a major role of income transfers and taxes in decreasing observed income inequality at a point in time. For 1975, the tax-transfer system reduced inequality in all the dimensions on which we are focusing: (1) among households in the nation (T_T), (2) among households within states (T_W), and (3) among states (T_A). Income transfers have decreased income inequality within states relatively more than they have decreased the inequality in average household income among the states. RV_{IN} falls from .031 to .004 in moving from Y_1 to Y_3—a decrease of 87 percent. $RV_{\bar{Y}}$, however, drops from .012 to .009, a decrease of 19 percent. Transfers have caused states to be more alike in terms of the rich-poor disparity within states (RV_{IN}) than in terms of mean income differences among them. This suggests that the often noted convergence in regional incomes is caused in part by the growth in transfers, but that other factors have also played an important role. To answer this question more completely, changes in T_T inequality over time need to be decomposed.

8.4 Income Transfers and Intra- and Interstate Income Differences—A View across Time

Growing income transfers can affect inequality over time in a variety of ways. In this section we will try to identify the impact of the transfer system on a number of inequality measures over time. In particular, to what extent have transfers contributed to changes in:

1. inequality in household incomes within states (T_W) over time?
2. inequality in mean household income among states (T_A) over time?
3. inequality in household incomes within the nation (T_T) over time?
4. inequality in the rich-poor gap among states (RV_{IN}) over time?

Table 8.7   Theil Indices of Inequality within Regions (T_W), Inequality among Regions, (T_A), and Total Inequality (T_T) for Y_1 and Y_3, 1967–79

	Y_1			Y_3		
Year	T_W	T_A	T_T	T_W	T_A	T_T
1967	.959	.008	.967	.348	.007	.355
1968	.916	.007	.924	.333	.006	.339
1969	.910	.007	.917	.336	.006	.342
1970	.996	.006	1.002	.350	.006	.356
1971	1.034	.006	1.040	.348	.005	.353
1972	1.052	.006	1.058	.349	.005	.354
1973	1.063	.005	1.069	.338	.004	.342
1974	1.100	.005	1.105	.337	.004	.341
1975	1.099	.005	1.104	.333	.004	.337
1976	1.099	.006	1.105	.332	.005	.336
1977	1.099	.005	1.104	.332	.004	.336
1978	1.049	.004	1.053	.335	.003	.339
1979	1.017	.004	1.022	.341	.003	.344

SOURCE: Calculations by authors from 1968–80 Current Population Surveys.

Table 8.7 presents Theil indexes for the years 1967–79 based on microdata from the Current Population Surveys for 1968–80, with states aggregated to twenty regions. The indices for Y_1 and Y_3 are shown. Several patterns are of interest:

1. Total inequality in market income (T_T for Y_1) *increased* from 1967 to 1979 from .967 to 1.022. Its pattern was somewhat irregular—declining during the 1960s, increasing steadily until the mid-1970s, and falling in 1978 and 1979.

2. Total inequality in census money income (T_T for Y_3) was nearly constant at about .35, although a smaller negative trend can be observed, at least until 1977. Hence, the increasing inequality in market income is not observed for post-transfer income. Transfers contributed to this difference.

3. Inequality in market income among households within regions (T_W for Y_1) increased markedly from .959 to 1.017 from 1967 to 1979. The distribution of census money income within regions (T_W for Y_3) stayed approximately constant at about .34, again implying a strong offsetting role for income transfers.

4. Inequality in average household income among regions (T_A) decreased substantially from 1967 to 1979, irrespective of the income concept chosen. For market income (Y_1), a measure largely unaffected by transfers, the decrease was from .0080 to .0044, a decrease of 46 percent. For post-transfer income (Y_3), the decrease was from .0070 to .0035—a 50 percent reduction. Transfers have contributed little if anything to the convergence among states over time in average incomes.

The role of transfers in decreasing aggregate income inequality among households at a point in time (T_T) has increased over time. This is shown in table 8.8 in both absolute (column 1) and relative (column 2) terms. In absolute terms, income transfers reduced the aggregate Theil index among households in the nation (T_T) by about .6 points in the late 1960s. By the late 1970s, this impact had grown to about .7 points. In percentage terms, transfers reduced pretransfer inequality by about 63 percent in the late 1960s; by the late 1970s, this had increased to about 68 percent. The reason for this increased impact of transfers is shown in columns 3 and 4 of table 8.8. The percent of households receiving transfers increased from 34 to 43 percent from 1967 to 1979. During the same period, transfers as a percent of total census income rose from 6.2 to 8 percent.

The contribution of transfers to the reduction in overall regional differences is shown in table 8.9. The impact indicators shown are for (1) the absolute and percentage impact of transfers on the relative variance of average household income among regions ($RV_{\bar{y}}$), (2) the absolute and percentage impact on the relative variance of within-region inequality among regions (RV_{IN}), and (3) the summary indicator of income and inequality differences among regions (RV_T). In column 4, transfers are seen to have reduced the relative variance of mean incomes among states by between 9 and 20 percent. This effect has been growing over time. In column 5, the impact of transfers on the reduction of the relative variance

Table 8.8   **Impact of Transfers on Total Inequality and the Growth of Transfers, 1967–79**

Year	Absolute Impact of Transfers on Total Inequality ($T_{TY_1} - T_{TY_3}$)	Percentage Impact of Transfers on Total Inequality [$(T_{TY_1} - T_{TY_3})/T_{TY_1}$]	Percent of Households Receiving Transfers	Percent of Y_1 Which is Transfer Income
1967	.613	63.4	34.1	6.2
1968	.584	63.3	35.2	6.5
1969	.575	62.7	36.2	6.3
1970	.646	64.5	39.4	7.2
1971	.687	66.0	40.4	8.0
1972	.704	66.6	30.6	8.2
1973	.727	68.0	40.2	8.5
1974	.764	69.1	43.1	9.5
1975	.767	69.5	45.7	9.2
1976	.769	69.6	44.1	8.9
1977	.768	69.6	42.5	8.5
1978	.714	67.8	42.1	8.2
1979	.678	66.3	43.0	8.0

SOURCE: Calculations by authors from the 1968–80 Current Population Surveys.

Table 8.9   Overall Differences among States and the Percentage Impact of
                   Transfers on These Differences, 1967–79

	Differences among States in Y_1			Percentage Reduction in Differences Attributable to Transfers		
Year	$RV_{\bar{Y}}$	RV_{IN}	RV_T	$RV_{\bar{Y}}$	RV_{IN}	RV_T
1967	.015	.021	.036	11.3	48.3	32.8
1968	.014	.021	.035	11.4	62.2	42.3
1969	.013	.025	.038	11.4	41.1	30.9
1970	.012	.019	.031	9.1	34.2	24.7
1971	.011	.015	.026	11.6	49.5	33.4
1972	.011	.020	.031	14.1	50.8	37.8
1973	.010	.027	.037	17.7	70.3	56.0
1974	.010	.026	.035	18.1	61.9	49.8
1975	.009	.016	.025	14.6	54.1	39.8
1976	.011	.021	.032	18.9	59.7	45.9
1977	.009	.027	.035	17.0	78.3	62.9
1978	.008	.022	.030	17.7	72.1	58.3
1979	.008	.025	.033	20.2	74.1	60.8

SOURCE: Calculations by authors from the 1968 and 1980 Current Population Surveys.

of within-state inequality ranges from 48 to 78 percent and has been growing rapidly since 1967. The last column of table 8.9 shows the effect of transfers on overall convergence among states. The effect of transfers on this indicator is also growing over time, rising from 33 percent in 1967 to 61 percent in 1979.

From these comparisons, the following propositions would seem to hold. First, the convergence in average household market income among regions from 1967 to 1979 (indicated in table 8.7 by the decrease in T_{A,Y_1} or by the change in $RV_{\bar{Y}}$ in table 8.9) dampened the impact of the marked increase in within-region market income inequality during this period (indicated in table 8.7 by the increase in T_{W,Y_1}) on the level of overall inequality. Second, the substantial decrease in observed inequality in average income among regions from 1967 to 1979 (as indicated by the decrease in T_{A,Y_1} in table 8.7) is primarily the result of a decrease in market income inequality. This is indicated by the change in T_{A,Y_1} from .008 to .004 over the 1967–79 period—with little if any increase in the absolute impact of transfers on inequality among regions. While transfers decreased inequality in average household income among regions by .001 in 1967 (a 13 percent reduction), they accounted for a .0009 decrease in inequality between regions in 1979 (a 20 percent reduction). Third, the role of transfers in the overall convergence of states (as measured by decreases in RV_T over time) has been primarily through reducing the disparity among states in the level of within-state inequality (i.e., in reducing RV_{IN}).

8.5 Patterns of Intraregional Inequality and the Impact of Transfers

In this section, we look more carefully at the patterns of intraregional inequality at a point in time, and changes in this pattern across time. In particular, we attempt to assess the impact of the level, growth, and distribution of transfers on intraregional inequality, both at a point in time and over time.

8.5.1 Regional Growth in Market Incomes and Transfers, 1967–79

The first three columns of table 8.10 show the pattern of regional growth in market income (Y_1) and income transfers over the period of 1967 to 1979. In the first column of table 8.10, the growth in real average household income (Y_1) is shown for the various regions. For the nation as a whole, average real market income grew 9.1 percent over the thirteen-year period. This overall average conceals substantial differences in regional growth rates. These extend from a negative 2.7 percent growth (New York) to growth of 20.8 percent in Alabama and Mississippi.

The second column in table 8.10 shows the real growth in transfer income per household from 1967 to 1979, by region and for the nation as a whole. While the percentage increase for the nation is 43 percent, it varies by region from − 32 percent (Washington, D.C.) to 71 percent (Pennsylvania). The highest rates of increase occurred in the Northeastern states (58.7 percent); the Western states have had the lowest transfer growth rates (38.1 percent). The third column in table 8.10 shows the percentage change in the ratio of income transfers to market income (Y_1) for each of the regions from 1967 to 1979. For the United States, transfers as a percent of pretransfer income increased from 6.7 percent to 8.7 percent, a 31 percent increase. For individual regions (excluding Washington, D.C.), the change in the ratio of transfer income to Y_1 ranges from 7 percent to 67 percent.

Inspection of the table shows that the increase in transfers as a percent of income was greater over the period for states in the higher-income Northeast region than it was for the other regions, especially the South and West. This pattern reflects the more rapid growth in the market income denominator of the southern and western states than in the Northeast, as well as the somewhat slower growth of income transfers in the South. In short, the rapid increase in market incomes in the southern and western states (which account for over 90 percent of total income)

Table 8.10   Regional Growth in Incomes, Transfers, and Their Impact on Inequality: 1967–79

	Percentage Change in:					Transfer Impact Index[a]
	Y_1	Transfers	Transfer/Y_1	T_{wY_1}	T_{wY_3}	
Northeast	4.1	58.7	52.5	16.1	.7	4.7
1 ME VT NH MA CT RI	10.2	38.5	25.7	.4	.8	-.1
2 NY	-2.7	62.8	67.4	24.8	.7	7.0
3 NJ	4.4	64.8	57.9	13.1	-7.1	7.6
4 PA	7.9	71.5	59.0	21.2	7.3	3.9
Northcentral	9.6	50.2	37.0	2.4	-1.9	1.5
5 OH	5.8	61.5	52.7	10.9	-5.2	5.7
6 IN	4.5	45.9	39.5	8.1	6.7	.4
7 IL	8.5	48.9	37.2	5.2	-1.4	2.3
8 MI WI	9.2	62.2	48.5	17.6	1.8	5.2
9 IA MN ND SD NB KS MO	16.3	36.1	17.0	-15.1	-3.9	-4.4

South	15.8	38.1	19.3	3.3	−7.5	3.8
10 DC	4.6	−32.0	−35.0	9.0	.3	3.1
11 DE MD VA WV	13.3	26.5	11.7	−2.4	−14.1	4.9
12 NC SC GA	16.1	50.0	29.2	16.9	−9.7	9.4
13 FL	11.5	19.5	7.2	−18.2	−6.6	−4.2
14 KY TN	13.6	67.3	47.3	17.8	−7.9	7.9
15 AL MS	20.8	42.1	17.7	6.8	−11.7	5.9
16 LA AR OK	20.3	34.8	12.1	−2.2	−1.5	−.2
17 TX	18.8	47.7	24.3	7.5	1.0	2.4
West	7.1	24.4	16.3	1.1	.7	.1
18 AZ NV MT ID WY CO NM UT	17.5	25.6	6.9	−7.9	8.0	−6.0
19 WA OR HA AK	12.8	34.3	19.0	−11.4	−11.1	−.2
20 CA	2.5	22.0	19.1	9.7	3.9	2.0
Total	9.1	43.2	31.3	6.0	−1.9	2.7

SOURCE: Calculations by authors from 1968 and 1980 Current Population Surveys.

aSee text section 8.5.3 for description of this index.

from 1967 to 1979 overwhelms the impact of transfer income which grew somewhat more rapidly in the North than in other regions.

8.5.2   The Patterns of Change in Intraregional Inequality, 1967–79

In the fourth and fifth columns of table 8.10, we show an index of the change in within-region inequality in both Y_1 and Y_3 from 1967 to 1979 for each of the twenty regions and for the United States. The index shown is the percentage change in T_W from 1967 to 1979 for both Y_1 and Y_3.

Several patterns are evident. Consider first the change in the pattern of within-region inequality in market income (Y_1). In fourteen of the twenty regions, market incomes became more unequal (as measured by T_{W,Y_1}) from 1967 to 1979. The percentage increase in inequality was the greatest for New York (+25 percent) and Pennsylvania (+21 percent). Florida and Iowa et al. displayed the greatest reduction in pretransfer inequality, with percentage changes of −18 and −15, respectively. Among census regions, the increase in Y_1 inequality within regions was the greatest for the Northeast (increasing 16.1 percent); the West recorded the smallest increase (1.1 percent).

For post-transfer income (Y_3), the pattern is quite different—eleven of the regions showed a reduction in inequality from 1967 to 1979. The greatest percentage reductions in post-transfer income inequality were experienced by Delaware et al. (−14 percent) and Alabama-Mississippi (−12 percent); the greatest percentage increases in post-transfer income inequality were recorded for Arizona et al. (+8 percent) and Pennsylvania (+7 percent). All of the southern regions recorded decreases in post-transfer inequality, except the District of Columbia and Texas. While the South showed a reduction in post-transfer inequality within the region of 7.5 percent, both the West and the Northeast had only slight reductions in post-transfer inequality.

8.5.3   The Contribution of Transfers to the
Reduction of Within-Region Inequality Over Time

The patterns in table 8.10 suggest that in nearly all regions transfer income has worked to offset generally increasing inequality in the distribution of market income (Y_1). In some regions (e.g., Ohio, Illinois, North Carolina et al.), inequality in post-transfer income (T_{W,Y_3}) decreased from 1967 to 1979 in spite of an increase in pretransfer income inequality (T_{W,Y_1}); in other regions, census income inequality has increased from 1967 to 1979 in spite of increased transfers. And, in a few regions, post-transfer inequality increased from 1967 to 1979 by more than pretransfer inequality, suggesting that the growth in transfers did not contribute to a decrease in inequality.

The last column in table 8.10 is an attempt to indicate the role of transfers in decreasing the inequality in census income within states

(T_{W,Y_3}) over time. The index of the role of transfers used in the table is the difference between the percentage impact on inequality of transfers in 1967 and that recorded for 1979, that is,

$$\frac{T_{W,Y_1}^{1979} - T_{W,Y_3}^{1979}}{T_{W,Y_1}^{1979}} \times 100 - \frac{T_{W,Y_1}^{1967} - T_{W,Y_3}^{1967}}{T_{W,Y_1}^{1967}} \times 100.$$

For example, if for some region transfers reduced inequality between Y_1 and Y_3 by 40 percent in 1979, but only reduced it by 29 percent in 1967, a score of 11 would be recorded for this index.

Again, several patterns can be observed. First, in six of the twenty regions the index has a negative sign, indicating that transfers played a less strong equalizing role in these regions in 1979 than in 1967. Three options are possible here: (1) inequality in Y_3 increased by more than Y_1 inequality from 1967 to 1979, (2) inequality in Y_3 fell by less than Y_1 inequality from 1967 to 1979, and (3) inequality in Y_3 increased while Y_1 inequality decreased. All three options are represented in the six regions with negative indices. However, for fourteen of the twenty regions transfers played a more equalizing role in 1979 than in 1967.

Second, the reduction in inequality of post-transfer income beyond what would be expected if post-transfer inequality changed at the same pace as pretransfer inequality is greatest in New York, New Jersey, North Carolina et al., and Kentucky-Tennessee. Third, for the United States as a whole, transfers played a stronger role in decreasing within region inequality in 1979 than in 1967. The weighted average reduction in within-region inequality in post-transfer income from 1967 to 1979 is 8 percentage points greater than the weighted average change in within-region pretransfer inequality. Finally, transfers played a substantially greater role in reducing within-region inequality over time in the Northeast and the South than in the West and Northcentral regions.

These results document the increases in inequality in market income within regions from 1967 to 1979, and indicate the major role income transfers have played in mitigating that increase. A related question is: Have regions become more or less alike over time in the extent of the rich-poor gap within the region? Is there convergence or divergence among the regions in within-region inequality over time?

8.5.4 The Convergence in Intraregional Inequality, 1967–79, and the Role of Transfers

In table 8.11, the within-region inequality of each of the twenty regions is shown for each of the income concepts (Y_1, Y_2, Y_3), for 1967 and 1979. The Theil index (T_W) is the measure of the rich-poor gap within each region, and each regional Theil index is stated as a fraction of the weighted average within-region Theil for the United States. For 1967, the highest Theil within ratio for Y_1 is 1.45 (Louisiana et al.); the lowest is .84

Table 8.11   Ratio of within-Region Inequality to the Nation's Average, 1967 and 1979

	1967			1979		
	Y_1	Y_2	Y_3	Y_1	Y_2	Y_3
Northeast	.974	.973	.952	1.069	1.115	.982
1 ME VT NH MA CT RI	.969	.858	.882	.917	.917	.906
2 NY	1.041	1.140	1.036	1.225	1.386	1.064
3 NJ	.871	.940	1.020	.929	1.001	.967
4 PA	.947	.869	.877	1.082	.993	.960
Northcentral	.930	.874	.930	.899	.921	.934
5 OH	.926	.903	1.007	.969	.980	.974
6 IN	.903	.686	.796	.921	.729	.866
7 IL	.897	.876	.918	.890	1.083	.923
8 MI WI	.843	.818	.899	.935	.990	.934
9 IA MN ND SD NB KS MO	1.037	.965	.964	.830	.792	.944

South	1.333	1.154	1.127	1.106	1.003	1.068
10 DC	1.119	1.438	1.191	1.150	1.579	1.218
11 DE MD VA WV	.978	1.084	1.089	.900	.892	.954
12 NC SC GA	.949	1.037	1.083	1.047	.951	.997
13 FL	1.283	.972	1.051	.989	.914	1.001
14 KY TN	1.097	1.118	1.095	1.218	.999	1.028
15 AL MS	1.420	1.398	1.327	1.431	1.201	1.195
16 LA AR OK	1.453	1.483	1.144	1.340	1.160	1.149
17 TX	1.024	1.080	1.117	1.038	.965	1.151
West	.923	.980	.967	.881	.971	.997
18 AZ NV MT ID WY CO NM UT	.906	.875	.864	.786	.781	.951
19 WA OR HA AK	.889	.921	1.011	.743	.874	.917
20 CA	.942	1.040	.995	.975	1.094	1.054

SOURCE: Calculations by authors from 1968 and 1980 Current Population Surveys.

(Michigan-Wisconsin). The difference is .61. For Y_3, the highest 1967 ratio is 1.32 (Alabama-Mississippi); the lowest is .79 (Indiana). This is a difference of .53, substantially smaller than the high-low difference for Y_1. The reduction in the range from .61 to .53 is attributable to income transfers.

The same pattern is observed for 1979. The highest ratio for Y_1 in 1979 is 1.43 (Alabama-Mississippi); the lowest is .74 (Washington et al.), for a difference of .69. This increase in the difference among regions in within-region inequality in Y_1 from 1967 to 1979 is consistent with earlier data indicating the increasing inequality in market incomes generally. The highest ratio for Y_3 in 1979 is 1.22 (D.C.); the lowest is .91 (Maine et al.), for a difference of .31. This decrease in the range from .69 to .31 is attributable to income transfers in 1979.

From these crude comparisons, it appears that:

1. There has been divergence in within-region inequality in pretransfer income from 1967 to 1979. The range in the within inequality ratio increased from .61 to .69 from 1967 to 1979.

2. There has been substantial convergence in the rich-poor gap in post-transfer income among regions from 1967 to 1979. The range in the within inequality ratio decreased from .53 to .31 from 1967 to 1979.

3. The switch from divergence to convergence in within-region inequality is attributable to the growth of transfers from 1967 to 1979.

4. In 1967 transfers reduced the range of within-region inequality among regions from .61 (Y_1) to .53 (Y_3), a 13 percent decrease. In 1979 transfers reduced the range of inequality among regions from .69 (Y_1) to .31 (Y_3), a 55 percent decrease.

The extent of convergence in the regional rich-poor gap (as measured by the Theil inequality index) among the regions, and the role of transfers in this convergence, is also shown in table 8.12. Comparing Y_1 and Y_3, the same patterns are observed as described above for the range. Namely:

1. The regions *diverged* over time in terms of inequality in pretransfer income. The measure of variation among the regions increased from .021 to .025, an increase of 22 percent.

2. The regions *converged* over time in terms of inequality in post-transfer income. The measure of variation among the regions decreased from .011 to .007, a decrease of 39 percent.

Table 8.12   Index of the Relative Variance in the Extent of Within-Region Inequality (RV_{IN}), 1967 and 1979

	Y_1	Y_2	Y_3
1967	.021	.026	.011
1979	.025	.026	.007

3. The swing from a 22 percent *increase* in disparity among the states in within-region inequality (for Y_1) to a 39 percent *decrease* in disparity among the regions in within-region inequality (for Y_3) is attributable to the growth in income transfers and their improved targeting on low-income households.

4. In 1967, transfers accounted for the reduction from .021 to .011 in disparity among the regions in the rich-poor gap from Y_1 to Y_3. This is a reduction of 48 percent. In 1979, transfers reduced the among-region disparity from .025 (Y_1) to .007 (Y_3), a reduction of 74 percent. The impact of transfers in reducing the disparity among the regions in the variation in the regional rich-poor gap in 1979 is more than 150 percent of the 1967 impact of transfers.

An important and puzzling pattern is observed in table 8.12. Within each of the years, the disparity in within-region inequality recorded for Y_2 is about the same as that for Y_1. Social insurance transfers, it appears, do not serve to *reduce* the disparity among states in the extent of within-region inequality. This pattern can also be observed in table 8.11 where, in 1967, fifteen of the twenty regions are shifted away from a ratio of unity in moving from Y_1 to Y_2; for 1979, eleven of the twenty regions are so shifted. This pattern remains unexplained.

8.6   The Determinants of the Impact of Transfers in Reducing Within-Region Inequality—A Preliminary Examination

This evidence, then, suggests that transfers have resulted in a decrease in the dispersion of incomes within states, and that this contribution to reduced within-state income differences has increased over time. For nearly all states at any point in time, the distribution of pretransfer income (Y_1) is more unequal than the distribution of post-transfer income (Y_3). The contribution of transfers to this reduction in inequality—measured as $(T_{W,Y_1} - T_{W,Y_3})$—varies substantially across states, however. For example, in 1975, this indicator ranged from .22 to 1.20. The question is: What determines the impact of transfers in reducing the inequality of income within states at a point of time?

Here we adopt two approaches in describing the role of transfers in decreasing within-state inequality. As appendix B shows, decomposing the change in Theil inequality from Y_1 to Y_3 suggests that the impact of transfers on within-state inequality depends largely on η (the percentage of the households within a state that are transfer recipients) and θ (the proportion of the total income of recipients accounted for by transfers). Our first approach focuses on this decomposition and measures the effect of both η and θ on the reduction of within-state inequality ($T_{W,Y_1} - T_{W,Y_3}$), which we will designate as I. In this formulation, then,

(2) $$I = \delta_0 + \delta_1 \eta + \delta_2 \theta + \epsilon_1.$$

However, neither η nor θ are, themselves, exogenous variables. For example, the percentage of households that are recipients (η) depends on the demographic characteristics of the state. Ceteris paribus, states with more older or retired households, for example, would expect to have a larger proportion of households receiving transfers—a larger η. Similarly, states with larger family sizes would, ceteris paribus, have a larger ratio of transfer to total income for those receiving transfers—a larger θ. A more appropriate statement of the determinants of the impact of transfers on within-state inequality would then be:

(3) $\eta = \alpha'Z + \epsilon_2,$

(4) $\theta = \beta'Z + \epsilon_3,$

(2) $I = \delta_0 + \delta_1\eta + \delta_2\theta + \epsilon_1,$

where Z is a vector of exogenous determinants of η and θ, chosen to reflect the characteristics of states likely to influence the number of transfer recipients in the state (η) and the benefits they on average receive (θ).

In this formulation, the true determinants of I are viewed as having their impact through η and θ, two instruments which can be thought of as the extensive margin of transfer recipiency and the intensive margin, respectively. If η and θ are assumed to be the outcome of an implicit market for transfers, the Z vector must include state characteristics reflecting both the demand for transfers (e.g., the incidence in the population of groups likely to be eligible for transfers) and the supply of transfers (e.g., tastes of the population for poverty reduction).

If, in fact, the impact of transfers on inequality in the state is the outcome of this market process, the determinants of I could be understood by simply regressing I on Z.

(5) $I = \Pi'Z + \epsilon_4.$

In what follows, results from both models are shown. In the first, the exogenous Z variables are viewed as having their impact on I through η and θ; in the second, these factors are viewed as direct determinants of I. The estimates shown are for 1975 and rely on state data taken from the Survey of Income and Education. The vector of Z variables is:

  1. the state unemployment rate (UR),
  2. the percent of the state's household heads that is female (FEHD),
  3. the percent of the state's population that is over 65 (AGED),
  4. the average family size of the state's households (FSIZ).

Because transfer programs are targeted on the aged and families headed by a female, FEHD and AGED are demand-side variables. The family-size-conditioned nature of many transfers causes FSIZ to reflect the demand for transfers as well. UR captures both the demand for transfers by those who are unemployed and covered by unemployment insurance and, insofar as it reflects the performance of a state's economy, the ability of the state to supply transfers.[5]

Consider first the framework in which the exogenous determinants of I are viewed as working through η and θ. The first three columns of table 8.13 present the regression results for this model. All of the exogenous variables have the expected sign in explaining the variance in both η—the extent of transfer recipiency—and θ—the "depth" of transfer support. And all of them are significant. The AGED variable has the largest impact on both η and θ. A one percentage point increase in AGED increases both the percent of the population who are recipients and the percent of the income of recipients accounted for by transfers by more than one percentage point. While the unemployment rate (UR) has an important impact on the percent of the population receiving transfers (η), its effect on the relative level of transfers received by recipients (θ) is significant but small. The small effect on θ presumably reflects the role of UR in capturing both demand- and supply-side effects.

The third column shows that both η and θ are very significant determinants of I—the impact of transfers on inequality. Their relative magnitudes suggest that the role of transfers in reducing inequality works more strongly through the level of transfers received by recipients (θ) than through the number of households receiving transfers (η). This is as we would expect. Given the pro-poor character of transfers, a larger impact on inequality is expected from targeting an increment of transfers on existing recipients than from extending the number of recipients. In terms

Table 8.13   The Determinants of η, θ, and I, 1975 (*t*-values in parentheses)

Independent Variables	Dependent Variables				
	η	θ	$I^{*a,b}$	I^{*a}	$\bar{Z}$
CONSTANT	$-.29$ (2.4)	$-.14$ (1.3)	.07 (2.0)	$-.41$ (2.6)	—
UR	1.35 (5.8)	.41 (2.0)	—	1.10 (3.5)	.072
FEHD	.31 (2.1)	.39 (4.3)	—	.62 (4.5)	.16
AGED	1.23 (9.2)	1.03 (8.7)	—	1.48 (8.2)	.19
FSIZE	.15 (4.4)	.09 (3.1)	—	.22 (4.9)	2.82
$\bar{\eta}$	—	—	.58 (3.6)	—	.50
$\bar{\theta}$	—	—	.79 (3.8)	—	.40
R^2	.72	.66	.90	.66	—
N	51	51	51	51	—

[a]The impact variable (I^*) is expressed as the percentage change in the index of inequality $[(T_{W,Y_1} - T_{W,Y_3})/Y_{W,Y_1}]$. The mean of I^* is .67, indicating that, on average, transfers reduced within-state inequality as measured by the Theil index by 67 percent. Among the states, I^* ranged from .42 to .79.

[b]This equation was estimated by two-stage least squares.

of inequality reduction, the intensive margin is more important than is the extensive margin.

The direct effect of the exogenous variables on the impact of transfers on inequality (I) is shown in the fourth column of table 8.13. All of the variables have the expected sign, and all are significant. As expected, the proportion of the population older than 65 (AGED) is the most significant variable in explaining the impact of transfers on inequality. The arc elasticities for the independent variables are:

$$UR \quad +.08$$

$$FEHD \ +.10$$

$$AGED +.29$$

$$FSIZ \quad +.07$$

Hence, a 1 percent increase in the share of the aged population increases the impact of transfers on inequality by .3 percent; relative increases in the other variables have a substantially smaller effect on the inequality reducing impact of transfers. While transfers, then, reduce inequality within all regions and states, their impact is greater the higher the unemployment rate of the region, the larger the average family size in the region, the higher the proportion of female-headed families in the region,   · and, especially, the larger the aged proportion of the region's population.

8.7   Summary and Conclusions

As is well known, income transfers are targeted on the low-income population and, hence, are equalizing. Moreover, the larger the transfers relative to nontransfer income are, ceteris paribus, the greater is the reduction in inequality for which they are responsible. Numerous studies have documented the impact of transfers in reducing poverty, reducing inequality in the size distribution of income, reducing inequality between groups (e.g., blacks and whites, elderly and nonelderly, intact and female-headed families), and reducing the inequality *within* particular groups, such as the elderly, blacks, and the disabled.

This study is in that tradition. We have focused on groups of individuals identified by their region of residence, sometimes by states and sometimes by regional groupings of states. A number of questions have been posed regarding the level and the dispersion of the incomes of these regional groupings of individuals—both across the groups and within the groups; both at a point in time and across time.

The questions posed and the results obtained are as follows:

1. How different are the states in terms of per household income?

• In 1975 the gap between the states was substantial—in terms of pretransfer, pretax income (Y_1) the ratio of the highest to the lowest state is 2.4. The ratio falls to 1.8 when post-transfer, post-tax income (Y_4) is used.

2. Does the inequality in average income among the states contribute very much to the aggregate level of inequality in the nation?

• Using the Theil index, the differences in average income among the states accounts for only about 2 percent of the total level of national income inequality. Inequality among people within states accounts for the rest.

3. How different are the states in the extent of inequality among their citizens?

• In terms of Y_1, the ratio of the Theil index of the most unequal to the least unequal state is 2.2. The ratio falls to 1.4 when Y_4 is used. In sum, substantial disparity exists among states in the extent of within-state inequality, but the disparity is far less for post-transfer income than for pretransfer income.

4. Which states are the most unequal in the distribution of income among their citizens; which are the least unequal?

• The distribution of income is most unequal within the southern states; the northcentral and northeastern states have the least inequality. This is true irrespective of the income concept used.

5. At a point in time, have transfers contributed substantially to a reduction in average income differences among states?

• In 1975 the dispersion of average post-transfer income (Y_3) among states (as measured by the Theil index) was 23 percent less than the dispersion of average pre-transfer income (Y_1). Transfer income accounts for this reduction.

6. At a point in time, have transfers contributed substantially to a reduction in inequality within states?

• Again using the Theil index, transfers caused a very substantial decline of 70 percent in average inequality within the states in 1975.

7. To what extent have transfers caused states to converge over time in both income levels and income inequality?

• Consider the period from 1967 to 1979. Using an index of state differences which combine both average income differences and inequality differences, transfers caused an overall reduction in the index from .042 to .013, a reduction of 68 percent. Of this .029 reduction, about 90 percent was from a reduction of differences among states in inequality; about 10 percent was from a reduction in state average income differences.

8. To what extent has income inequality within regions changed over time?

• Using market income (Y_1), average inequality within states increased from 1967 to 1979. The Theil index of within-region inequality increased from .96 to 1.02. For fourteen of twenty regions, the Theil index for Y_1 increased from 1967 to 1979. For post-transfer income, within-region inequality stayed at about .34. Eleven of the twenty regions showed a decrease.

9. Has the inequality in average incomes across regions declined over time?

- The Theil measure for Y_1 shows a decline of 46 percent from 1967 to 1979; that for Y_3 shows about a 50 percent reduction. Differences in average incomes among states have declined enormously from 1967 to 1979, irrespective of the income concept.

10. What role have transfers played in decreasing overall inequality over time?

- From 1967 to 1979 Theil inequality among all households increased from .97 to 1.02, using Y_1. For Y_3, the Theil index stayed constant at about .35. The effect of transfers has been to offset the growing inequality in market incomes over time. In the late 1960s, transfers reduced inequality by about 63 percent; this increased to about 68 percent in the late 1970s.

11. Regions have converged over time in both average incomes and inequality. What role has the transfer system played in this convergence?

- Using our index of state differences, transfers increased their impact in reducing the index of *overall* state differences (RV_T) from 33 percent in 1967 to 61 percent in 1979. The contribution of transfers in reducing income inequalities within states (RV_{IN}) increased from 48 to 74 percent over the same period. The impact of transfers in reducing state income differences ($RV_{\bar{Y}}$) was small, but increased from 11 to 20 percent. In sum, transfers contributed substantially and increasingly to decreases in overall income inequality and inequality within regions. The contribution of transfers to observed convergence in average incomes among regions was small over the entire period, but increased slightly. The bulk of the convergence in average incomes among states was the result of more rapid growth in Y_1 in the poorer southern regions over this period.

12. For which regions did transfers increase their impact in reducing inequality over time?

- The South and the Northeast experienced a growing impact of transfers in reducing inequality, relative to the remaining regions.

13. Has the impact of transfers in decreasing the differences among regions in within-region income inequality increased or decreased?

- From 1967 to 1979 states became more divergent in the inequality in the distribution of market income (Y_1), but converged in the inequality of post-transfer income (Y_3). The impact of transfers in reversing the divergence in market income inequality can be described in several ways:

—In 1967 transfers reduced the *range* among regions in within-region inequality by 13 percent; in 1979, by 54 percent.

—In 1967 transfers reduced the *relative variance* among regions in within-region inequality by 48 percent; in 1979, by 74 percent.

14. At any point in time, transfers contribute to a reduction in inequality within all states and regions. What characteristics cause the impact of transfers on inequality to be greater in some states than in others?

• At the margin, the impact of transfers on inequality is greater if the increment is used to increase the benefits of existing recipients, rather than enlarging the number of recipients. The marginal impact of transfers on inequality reduction is larger in states with higher unemployment rates, larger average family sizes, a higher proportion of female-headed families, and especially, a higher proportion of aged persons.

The equalizing role of transfers in the economy can be clearly seen in this region-based analysis, both at a point in time and over time. At a point in time (1975), transfers (1) reduce average income differences among states by about *13 percent*, (2) reduce inequality within states by about *32 percent*, and (3) reduce differences in within-state inequality among states by about *60 percent*. Over time, the transfer system has grown rapidly, both as a share of total income and in terms of the number of households who are recipients. As a result, from 1967 to 1979 transfers (1) reversed the trend toward overall inequality in market incomes, (2) increased their contribution to the reduction in overall inequality from 64 percent to 68 percent, (3) increased their contribution to reducing inequalities within states from 48 to 74 percent, (4) increased from 11 to 18 percent their contribution to the reduction in average income differences among states, (5) increased from 42 to 75 percent their contribution to the convergence in within-state income inequalities among regions, and (6) increased their contribution to reducing the overall index of state income differences from 33 to 61 percent.

A more vivid and broadbrush picture of the regional impact of transfers can be seen by focusing only on the income and inequality differences between the South and the North over time. The pattern of differences between these two regions and changes in these differences reflect the general national pattern, and clearly portrays the role of income transfers.

Across the entire period from 1965 to 1979, the South had both a lower average income and greater inequality in the distribution of income than did the North. Over that period, however, the South-North disparity in both average income and inequality was reduced. The convergence in average incomes was primarily caused by a more rapid increase in market incomes in the South than in the North over this period. The source of the convergence was economic growth; income transfers had little to do with it. Indeed, while ratio of income transfers to market income was greater in the South than in the North over the entire period, the increase in this ratio in the northeast and northcentral states exceeded that in the South and the West over the period.

At the beginning of the period, market incomes in the South were distributed substantially more unequally than in the North. While market income inequality increased in both regions over the period, the trend toward more inequality was greater in the North than in the South. However, in both regions the distribution of census money income became slightly more equal from 1965 to 1979 and, indeed, the regions became more alike in their final income distributions. Both the reduction in census money income inequality and the convergence of the regions over the period are attributable primarily to the growth in and allocation of income transfers.

These transfer income patterns, while complex, do have policy implications. Here we will mention only the most prominent of them and do so in the form of questions:

1. If a continued downward trend in the degree of inequality among regions, or continued reductions in inequality within regions, is valued by society, what is the likely impact of reduced transfers on these indicators of economic performance? Will cuts in transfers promote increased inequality within regions and increase disparity in inequality among regions, or will the policy changes maintain the reductions in inequality in both dimensions that have already been achieved?

2. The growth in transfers over the past fifteen years has been dominated by the federal transfer system. What will be the effect of transferring discretion over the level and composition of transfers from the federal to state governments? Will the loss of federally mandated programs and benefit minima seriously erode the contribution of transfers to reducing within-region and total inequality, and to reducing the disparity among regions in within-region inequality.

3. To what extent will the renewed emphasis on economic growth continue to yield reductions in the inequality of average incomes among regions? Or will future economic growth reverse the pattern of impacts experienced over the last fifteen years?

4. Are policies other than income transfers available to mitigate or reverse the trend toward increased market income inequality within regions (and within the nation)? Is the future sectoral composition of growth, with its emphasis on high-technology, skill-intensive activities, likely to exacerbate this problem of growing market income inequality? And, if so, does this not call for continued emphasis on income transfers if the overall small reductions in final income inequality are to be maintained?

Finally, we would emphasize the tentative nature of our results. They clearly raise as many research questions as they answer. Our effort has largely been one of measurement and documentation; the causes of the changes we have uncovered here have only been briefly explored. While we have made a first effort to determine which regional characteristics have accounted for the within-region reductions in inequality attributable to transfers, the analysis neglected a number of higher moments of the Theil measure which could have played a role. Moreover, the determinants that we did identify are primarily permanent regional characteristics which have little to do with transfer policy measures that could be used to influence the inequality reduction potential of transfers.

A few extensions of this research are immediately obvious. First, our determinants analysis is based on cross-section state data for a single year, 1975. This analysis could be extended by enlarging the data base to the twelve years of available Current Population Survey tapes, though at the cost of regional detail in any year from 50 to 20. The variation introduced by the time series data could enable more precise identification of both the regional characteristics and policy variables affecting the distributional effects of transfers. Second, we have considered only a subset of the full range of transfers affecting regional incomes and the inequality of their distributions; in-kind transfers, additional cash transfers, and fringe benefits could be merged onto the data tapes, and the impacts of this more full-blown definition of transfers on regional incomes and inequalities could be analyzed. Finally, our analysis has looked only at first-round regional and distributional impacts of transfers and taxes. These policies generate both consumption reallocations and labor supply effects which, in a general equilibrium context, work their way through the economy, changing prices, outputs, and wages differentially by regions. Analytic models exist for exploring the regional and distributional implications of these second-, third-, and fourth-round effects of transfers (see Golladay and Haveman 1977). For simulated transfer policy changes less extensive than the transfers analyzed here, the full pattern of regional and distributional impacts have been found to vary substantially from the first-round effects.

Appendix A *Data Bases Used in Study: CPS and SIE*

Two separate data bases have been employed in this study. The major data source is the Survey of Income and Education (SIE) conducted in 1976. It contains demographic and economic information for roughly 150,000 households across the United States in calendar year 1975. This data base was chosen as the primary data base for the sole reason that it is the most recent public-use data source that is statistically large enough to allow analysis to be performed on the state level.[6] While the SIE does allow state-by-state analysis, it unfortunately provides but one point in time to view the regional dispersions in incomes. Thus, to see if the patterns observed in the SIE data for 1975 persist over time, we also employed a series of Current Population Surveys (CPS) from 1968 to 1980. This series of microdata bases allows us to track the regional dispersion of incomes for twenty regions (clusters of states) for the calendar years 1967 through 1979.

In this study we employed four different income concepts: market income (Y_1), market income plus social insurance benefits (Y_2), post-transfer income (Y_3), and post-tax and post-transfer income (Y_4). A more precise definition of each of these concepts is given in table 8.A.1. One should note that some difference does exist between the SIE and CPS

Table 8.A.1   Definitions of Income Concepts Used in Study

	SIE	CPS
Market Income (Y_1) =		
Wages and salaries +	X	X
Self-employment income +	X	X
Interest, dividends, and rental income +	X	X
Private employment retirement benefits +	X	X
Public employee retirement benefits +	X	
Alimony, child support and other	X	X
Market Income Plus Social Insurance (Y_2) =		
Y_1 +	X	X
Social Security and railroad retirement +	X	X
Worker's compensation +	X	X
Veterans' benefits +	X	X
Unemployment compensation +	X	X
Public employee retirement benefits		X
Post-Transfer Income (Y_3)		
Y_2 +	X	X
Aid to Families with Dependent Children +	X	X
Supplemental Security Income (OAA) +	X	X
General assistance +	X	X
Food Stamps +	X	
Earned income tax credit	X	
Post-Tax, Post-Transfer Income (Y_4) =		
Y_3 −		
Federal income tax −	X	
FICA payroll tax −	X	
State income tax	X	

"X" indicates that the income source was included in the income concept and data base.

Table 8.A.2   Control Totals for Y_1 (billions of dollars)

Year	Control Total	Value on CPS Tape	% Captured on Tape
1967	$576	$453.3	78.7
68	627	503.6	80.3
69	683	561.0	82.1
70	717	596.1	83.1
71	763	635.6	83.3
72	831	704.2	84.7
73	926	774.8	83.7
74	1006	826.9	82.2
75	1063	907.2	85.4
76	1167	1002.0	85.9
77	1293	1111.5	86.0
78	1457	1244.1	84.0
79	1630	1406.7	86.3
	Control total[a]	SIE tape[a]	
1975	1080	1004.9	93.0

SOURCES FOR Y_1 TOTALS: For 1970, 1972–79: *Statistical Abstract 1980*, p. 445, table 738. Y_1 control total = personal income − transfer payments + personal contributions for social insurance − other labor income. For 1968, 1969, 1971: *Statistical Abstract 1973*, p. 324, table 526. For 1967: *Statistical Abstract 1970*, p. 316, table 480.
[a]Public employee retirement included.

definitions, primarily with respect to public employee retirement benefits. In the SIE, we treated public employee benefits as private retirement benefits and included them in market income. However, the CPS data base did not allow us to separate public employee retirement benefits from other insurance programs; hence, they were included in the Y_2 measure of income on the CPS data base.

Tables 8.A.2 through 8.A.4 present control totals from other published sources and the amounts that we "capture" on the individual data bases for the three major sources of income. Table 8.A.2 provides this information on market income (Y_1), while tables 8.A.3 and 8.A.4 provide the same information for the two additions to Y_1 that comprise post-transfer income: namely, social insurance and cash welfare benefits. As one can see from the tables, the SIE provides the best "capture rate" on all three sources of income, which also suggests its use as a primary data source.

Table 8.A.3   Control Total for Social Insurance (billions of dollars)

Year	Control Total	Value on CPS Tape	% Captured on Tape
1967	37.710	26.512	70.3
68	42.482	30.589	72.0
69	46.131	33.130	71.8
70	55.609	40.486	72.8
71	65.687	47.976	73.0
72	72.781	55.412	76.1
73	84.821	64.191	75.7
74	98.556	77.218	78.3
75	123.431	80.432	65.2
76	135.289	85.174	63.0
77	145.452	90.231	62.0
78	155.391	97.877	63.0
79	n.a.	108.595	—
	Control total[a]	SIE tape[a]	
1975	106.286	83.741	78.8

SOURCES FOR SOCIAL INSURANCE TOTALS: For 1970, 1975, 1977–78: *Statistical Abstract 1980*, p. 336, table 539. For 1976: *Statistical Abstract 1979*, p. 332, table 530. For 1974: *Statistical Abstract 1977*, p. 324, table 507. For 1971–73: *Statistical Abstract 1975*, p. 285, table 453. For 1968–69: *Statistical Abstract 1971*, p. 275, table 435. For 1967: *Statistical Abstract 1970*, p. 280, table 420.

[a]Public employee retirement included.

Table 8.A.4   Control Totals for Cash Welfare (billions of dollars)

Year	Control Total	Value on CPS Tape	% Captured on Tape
1967	5.449	3.641	66.8
68	6.306	4.388	69.6
69	7.560	4.841	64.0
70	9.221	6.115	66.3
71	11.797	6.996	59.3
72	14.144	7.643	54.0
73	14.840	8.033	54.1
74	16.287	10.097	62.0
75	19.867	11.365	57.2
76	21.412	12.454	58.2
77	23.353	13.303	57.0
78	24.082	13.530	56.2
79	n.a.	14.237	—
	Control total[a]	SIE tape[a]	
1975	24.561	21.824	88.9

SOURCES FOR CASH WELFARE TOTALS: For 1970, 1973–78: *Statistical Abstract 1980*, pp. 332–33, table 534. Control totals calculated by subtracting Medicaid, Food Stamps (except SIE), and other from public aid total. For 1972: *Statistical Abstract 1975*, p. 281, table 447. For 1971: *Statistical Abstract 1973*, p. 287, table 461. For 1967–69: *Statistical Abstract 1970*, p. 277, table 416.

[a]Includes Food Stamps.

Appendix B *The Theil Index of Income Inequality*

Decomposition of the Theil Index by States

H. Theil (1967) proposed a measure of inequality containing a number of desirable properties and based on information theory. One of these properties was that the overall index could be easily decomposed into a measure of the extent of inequality between and within some specified groupings of the observations. The groupings used in this study were the states or regions in which households resided.

The Theil index of total income inequality in a population can be written as:

$$T = \sum_i \frac{1}{N} \ell n \, (\bar{Y}/Y_i),$$

where N = the number of households, Y_i = the ith household income, and $\bar{Y}$ = the mean income in the population.

Assume now that the population has been allocated according to the location of their residence, that is, their state (or region). Theil has shown that the aggregate index T_T can be decomposed as:

(A1) $T_T = T_A + T_W,$

where

$$T_A = \sum_{j=1}^{M} \frac{1}{M} \ell n \, (\bar{Y}/\bar{Y}_j),$$

$$T_W = \sum_{j=1}^{M} \eta_j \sum_{i \in S_j} \frac{1}{N_j} \ell n (\bar{Y}_j/Y_i),$$

and M = the number of states, N_j = the number of households in the jth state, $\eta_j = N_j/N$, S_j = the set of individuals who reside in the jth state, and Y_j = mean household in jth state.

Upon examination, T_A is the Theil inequality index of the states' mean level of incomes while T_W is the weighted average of within levels of income inequality for the M states. Thus the overall Theil index (T_T) can be decomposed into two separate components: the inequality between states (measured by their mean incomes), and the weighted average across the states of the individual inequality within states.

A Decomposition of the Impact of Transfers
on the Theil Index of Inequality

In this paper, we measured the impact of transfers as the difference between census money income (Y_3) and market income (Y_1). Thus to describe the role of transfers in reducing overall inequality and inequality between and within states, we only have to consider the effect of changing the income concept on equation (A1). We can decompose the effect of transfers in reducing overall inequality into two effects: the change in inequality in average income among states (change in T_A), and the change in the weighted average across states of the within-state level of inequality (change in T_W). That is:

$$T_{T1} - T_{T3} = (T_{A1} - T_{A3}) + (T_{W1} - T_{W3}),$$
$$= \Delta T_A \quad + \quad \Delta T_W$$

where the second subscript refers to the income concept employed. The first term in this decomposition measures the extent to which overall inequality is reduced because of the reduced variation in state mean income attributable to transfers; the second term measures the extent to which the weighted average across states of within-state inequality is reduced by transfers. The second term can be rewritten as:

$$\Delta T_W = \sum_j \eta_j (T_{1j} - T_{3j}),$$

where

T_{kj} = the Theil inequality index for jth state defined for the kth income concept.

$$= \sum_{i \in S_j} \frac{1}{N} \ell n(\bar{Y}_k/Y_{ki}).$$

Thus ΔT_W is the weighted average of the change in each state's own index of inequality using the state's share of the population as weights.

The decomposition of the impact of transfers on any individual state's inequality index requires some explanation. In order not to further complicate the notation, we will drop the subscript referring to the state, although it should be understood that the impact of transfers on inequality within a state is being decomposed.

To decompose the impact of transfers within a state, first divide the state's population into two groups: those households that receive transfers ($i \in S_R$) and those which do not ($i \notin S_R$). Using the decomposition procedure described above, but employing recipiency of transfers as the grouping classification, the Theil index for income concepts Y_1 and Y_3 can be decomposed as follows:

$$T_k = [\ln(\bar{Y}_k/\bar{Y}_{kNR}) + \ln(\bar{Y}_k/\bar{Y}_{kR})] + [\eta_R \sum_{i \in S_R} \ln(\bar{Y}_{kR}/Y_{ki})$$
$$+ (1 - \eta_R) \sum_{i \notin S_R} \ln(\bar{Y}_{kNR}/Y_{ki})]$$

for k = 1 and 3 where $\bar{Y}_k$ = mean state income for k income concept, $\bar{Y}_{kR}$ = mean recipient income for k income concept, $\bar{Y}_{kNR}$ = mean nonrecipient income for k income concept, R = number of households receiving transfers, and $\eta_R = R/N$ = the percent of the population receiving transfers.

Using this decomposition, we can interpret the first bracketed expression as an index of the difference in average income between the nonrecipient and recipient populations using the kth income concept (denoted as T_{kG}). The second bracketed expression is the weighted average of the inequality within the two groups (denoted as T_{kD}). Hence, the reduction in inequality resulting from transfers (I) can be written as

$$I = T_1 - T_3 = (T_{1G} - T_{3G}) + (T_{1D} - T_{3D}) = \Delta T_G + \Delta T_D.$$

Now note that since Y_1 equals Y_3 when $i \notin S_R$, ΔT_D can be written as

$$\Delta T_D = \eta_R \sum_{i \in S_R} \frac{1}{R} [\ell n(\bar{Y}_{1R}/Y_{1i}) - \ell n(\bar{Y}_{3R}/Y_{3i})]$$

$$= \eta_R [\ell n\left(\frac{\bar{Y}_{1R}/\bar{Y}_{3R}}{1 - \bar{\theta}}\right) + T_\theta],$$

where θ_i = the share of the household's income which comes from transfers equal to

$$\frac{Y_{3i} - Y_{1i}}{Y_{3i}} = \frac{TR_i}{Y_{3i}},$$

TR_i = the household's transfers, $\bar{\theta}$ = the mean θ in the recipient population, and

$$T_\theta = \sum_{i \in S_R} \frac{1}{R} \ell n\left(\frac{1 - \bar{\theta}}{1 - \theta_i}\right),$$

which is the Theil index of inequality of the relative share of market income in the recipient population.

Thus the total impact of transfers on within-state inequality can be decomposed as

$$I = \Delta T_G + \eta_R D_\theta,$$

where
$$D_\theta = \ell n\left(\frac{\bar{Y}_{1R}/\bar{Y}_{3R}}{1 - \bar{\theta}}\right) + T_\theta,$$

which is an index of the dispersion of θ in the recipient population.

This decomposition can be given the following interpretation. The term ΔT_G can be interpreted as a measure of the degree to which the gap in incomes between the recipients and nonrecipients is reduced, on average. Thus, if transfers raise the incomes of recipients relative to nonrecipients, ΔT_G must be positive.

The second term, D_θ, requires some explanation. Consider the situation where every recipient receives a transfer such that $\theta_i = \bar{\theta}$, or equal to

$$TR_i = Y_{1i}\bar{\theta}/(1 - \bar{\theta}),$$

In this case, it can easily be demonstrated that D_θ is equal to zero. Hence, D_θ can be interpreted as the impact on total inequality of the divergence of actual transfers from the zero variance standard. The sign of D_θ is difficult to assign. The second term T_θ, since it is a Theil index, will always be positive. However, using Jensen's inequality, the first term of D_θ is seen to be positive only if, within the recipient population, transfers are not strongly positively correlated with pretransfer income.

One final decomposition of the impact of transfers can be noted:

$$\ell n(1 - X) = - \sum_{j=1}^{\infty} \left(\frac{X^j}{j} \right) \text{ where } 0 \le X \le 1.$$

Since θ_i will by definition always be between zero and one j

$$T_\theta = \sum_{i \in S_R} \frac{1}{R} \sum_{j=1}^{\infty} \frac{\theta_i^j - \bar{\theta}^j}{j}.$$

The fourth-order approximation of T_θ hence can be written as

$$T_\theta = \frac{\sigma_\theta^2}{2} + \frac{s(\theta)}{3} + \frac{k(\theta)}{4} + \frac{\sigma_\theta^2 \bar{\theta}}{2} (2 + \beta\bar{\theta}) + \bar{\theta}s(\theta),$$

where $\sigma_\theta^2 = $ variance of θ, $s(\theta) = $ skewness of θ, and $k(\theta) = $ kurtosis of θ. (Note: A fourth-order approximation will be needed if $\bar{\theta}$ lies between .3 and .6 and higher-order terms will be needed if θ lies above .6).

Hence T_θ can be interpreted as the index of the distribution of the relative importance of transfers in the recipient population. From empirical experience, $\bar{\theta}$ is the dominant moment in this decomposition, hence, given that $s(\theta)$ is sufficiently nonnegative, T_θ will be positively related to the average "dependency" of the recipient population on transfers ($\bar{\theta}$).

Notes

1. Our brief attention to this question here is a result of the helpful conference comments of Peter Gottschalk.

2. See appendix A for a detailed description of the definitions of the four income concepts and the data bases from which these numbers were computed.

3. Throughout this paper we have assumed that comparisons made between Y_1 and Y_3 are the appropriate comparisons to be made to assess the impact of transfers. However, we should note that the existence of transfer affects, through labor supply savings and consumption behavior, not only the level but also the distribution of market incomes. Thus the approximate basis of comparison would be the distribution of market incomes that exist in the absence of transfers. Work by Betson, Greenberg, and Kasten (1980) and Golladay and Haveman (1977) suggest that the use of Y_1 as a basis of comparison might tend to overstate the redistributive impact of transfers.

4. To derive this measure of overall convergence, let us first "standardize" the two dimensions of comparison as

$$\text{Rel}_{\text{Rich}} = \frac{\bar{Y}_S - \bar{Y}_T}{\bar{Y}_T}$$

= relative richness of the Sth state;

$$\text{Rel}_{\text{In}} = \frac{T_S - T_W}{T_W}$$

= relative inequality of the Sth state,

where $\bar{Y}_S$ = mean income of the Sth state; T_S = within-state Theil inequality index of the Sth state; $\bar{Y}_T = \Sigma \eta_S \bar{Y}_S$ = average state mean income; $T_W = \Sigma \eta_S T_S$; and η_S = population share of the Sth state.

The summary measure of overall convergence can then be defined as:

$$RV_T = \Sigma \eta_S \left[\left(\frac{\bar{Y}_S - \bar{Y}_T}{\bar{Y}_T} \right)^2 + \left(\frac{T_S - T_T}{T_T} \right)^2 \right]$$

$$= RV_{\bar{Y}} + RV_{\text{IN}},$$

where

$$RV_{\bar{Y}} = \frac{\Sigma \eta_S (Y_S - Y_T)^2}{\bar{Y}_T^2}$$

= the relative variance of the state's mean income;

$$RV_{\text{IN}} = \Sigma \frac{\eta_S (T_S - T_W)^2}{T_W^2}$$

= relative variance of within-state inequality.

One should note that $RV_{\bar{Y}}$ and T_A are both measures of the relative dispersion in mean state incomes. However, RV_{IN} and T_W are measuring quite different concepts. While RV_{IN} is a measure of the relative variance of within-state inequality (T_S), T_W measures the average within-state level of inequality.

5. A variety of other variables exists with some claim to reflecting supply- or demand-side influences on the volume of income transfers within a state, including race, health status, education, and relative income. Strong intercorrelations among these and between them and the included variables led to their exclusion from the final regression. The variables included reflect population characteristics that directly determine transfer eligibility and benefit awards.

6. The 1980 public-use census tapes which would be statistically large enough to perform state-by-state analysis are not yet available.

References

Betson, D., D. Greenberg, and R. Kasten. 1980. A microsimulation model for analyzing alternative welfare proposals: An application to the program for better jobs and income. In *Microsimulation models for public policy analysis*, ed. R. Haveman and K. Hollenbeck. New York: Academic Press.

Danziger, S., R. Haveman, and R. Plotnick. 1981. How income transfers affect work, savings, and the income distribution: A critical review. *Journal of Economic Literature*, September. Vol. 19, pp. 975–1028.

Golladay, F., and R. Haveman. 1977. *The economic impacts of tax-transfer policy: Regional and distributional effects.* New York: Academic Press.

Hanna, F. 1957. Analysis of interstate income differentials: Theory and practice. In *Regional income: Studies in income and wealth.* Report of the National Bureau of Economic Research. Princeton, N.J.: Princeton University Press.

Plotnick, R., and F. Skidmore. 1975. *Progress against poverty: A review of the 1964–1974 decade.* New York: Academic Press.

Theil, H. 1967. *Economics and information theory.* Chicago: Rand McNally.

U.S. Department of Commerce, Bureau of Economic Analysis. 1978. Regional differences in personal income growth, 1929–1977. In *Survey of current business*, October. GPO.

————. 1981. Regional and state projections of income, employment, and population to the year 2000. In *Survey of Current Business*, November. GPO.

U.S. Department of Commerce, Bureau of the Census. *Statistical abstract of the United States.* Washington, D.C.: GPO.

Comment   Peter Gottschalk

The authors start from two well-known observations. First, there has been a convergence of mean incomes between states over the last decade. Second, transfer payments have increased substantially over the same period. This rise in transfers has served to offset the increasing inequality of market incomes leading to a fairly stable degree of inequality of post-transfer income. The authors ask whether the increased transfers explains not only the stability in the personal income distribution but also the convergence of average incomes across states.

Since the authors summarize their conclusions clearly, I will not repeat all their conclusions here. However, in case the massive amount of documentation hides what I consider to be the most interesting conclusion, let me stress it. Less than 2 percent of the overall inequality in market-generated income (or in any of their post-tax or post-transfer income concepts) is caused by inequality *among* states. This implies that

Peter Gottschalk is a professor of economics at Bowdoin College, Brunswick, Maine, and is affiliated with the Institute for Research on Poverty.

even if we were to institute a fully effective regional policy, which would totally equalize average incomes among states, this would have a negligible impact on overall inequality unless it also decreased within-state inequality. This is a striking conclusion of crucial importance in the debate about whether regional policy should be designed to achieve distributional goals.

My comments are divided into two parts. First, I review some of the specific measures used by the authors and suggest some changes. Second, I ask why one would be interested in decomposing changes in inequality into changes attributable to within-state differences and changes attributable to among-state differences.

Methodological Issues

I would like to raise two issues about the methodology used by the authors. The first focuses on the use of relative variances to describe convergence among states. The second focuses on the regressions used to determine the effectiveness of transfers in reducing inequality.

Index of regional inequality. In describing the convergence among states, the authors define an index which is equal to the sum of the variance of the states' relative incomes plus the variance of their relative Theil indexes. I consider each in turn.

The variance of relative mean income is simply an alternative to the among-state Theil index used in the rest of the paper. Since these conceptually measure very much the same thing, all conclusions are basically the same using either index of inequality.

The variance of the relative Theil indexes, however, does add a new dimension. The inclusion of transfers may make the distribution of post-transfer income more similar across states, not only by bringing mean incomes closer together but also by making the spread of these distributions more alike. The latter element is captured by the variance of the relative Theil indexes. Inasmuch as policymakers value having the same degree of inequality in all states, this attribute will enter their social welfare function.

To summarize the two elements of convergence (similar means and inequality), the authors compute the sum of these two relative variances. This part of the paper would have benefited from an explicit discussion of the normative basis for this particular summary measure. By taking the sum of two indexes, the authors implicitly assume that both dimensions have equal weight in the social welfare function. My guess is that the actions of policymakers would reveal a much higher value placed on equalizing incomes among states than on equalizing inequality. This implies that a composite index would place a higher weight on reducing the relative variance of means.

Determinants of regional inequality. The second methodological issue I would like to explore is the authors' explanation of factors that cause transfers to be more or less effective in reducing pretransfer inequality. The decomposition of the difference between the pre- and post-transfer Theil indexes in the appendix is a useful contribution. The authors show that when inequality is measured by the Theil index, the impact of transfers in reducing inequality depends on three factors: (1) the portion of the population receiving transfers; (2) the reduction in the income gap between recipients and nonrecipients, and (3) the dispersion of the distribution of the percentage of income that comes from transfers.

It is interesting to compare this decomposition with the decomposition of income sources, using the variance of log income as the measure of inequality. Using the authors' notation, and letting R be the ratio of post-transfer to pretransfer income, it can be shown easily that the impact of transfers in reducing the log variance is equal to

$$\text{var}(y_3) - \text{var}(y_1) = \text{var}(r) - 2\,\text{cov}(ry_1),$$

where lower-case letters represent logarithms. The reduction in inequality from including transfers, therefore, depends on the amount of variation in the size of the transfers (as represented in the variance of r) and whether transfers are correlated with pretransfer income (as captured by the covariance). While I prefer the simplicity of the log variance measure, the authors have provided a useful service by showing us the counterpart using the Theil measure.

Their empirical work, however, is not closely linked to their theoretical appendix. The authors posit a linear approximation to the relationship between the reduction in inequality caused by transfers and two factors: the proportion of the population receiving transfers (η) and the *average* ratio of transfers to total income for recipients in the state (θ). Their appendix, however, shows that the reduction in inequality depends not only on the state means but also on higher-level moments.

This makes intuitive sense. Suppose a state had a larger proportion of people receiving transfers or that the average ratio of transfers to income was higher in the state. How much would this decrease inequality? The answer depends on the extent to which transfers go to people in the lower tail of the distribution. Using log variance to decompose makes this obvious, since there is a covariance term in the expression.

The paper would have been improved by calculating these upper-level moments. The authors could then have regressed all these components of I (the impact of transfers) on state characteristics. The total impact of the state characteristics could then have been calculated using the accounting framework developed in the appendix.

The regression results could also have been made more useful if the authors had included some instruments to reflect the endogenous, policy-relevant variables which affect the effectiveness of transfers in reducing inequality. These would show what legislative changes could be made to improve the effectiveness of transfers. While states can do relatively little to change the age composition of their population, they can change benefit levels or expand AFDC to include families with an unemployed parent. Without such policy handles, the equations remain merely descriptive devices that do not suggest ways states can change their own destinies.

Normative Issues

The authors' are right in claiming that since policymakers are interested in regional distribution issues, for whatever reason, this is sufficient ground for being interested in the authors' study. However, it may be useful to further explore the underlying rationale to identify possible conflicts between the goal of regional equality and other goals. I will devote the rest of my comments to this issue.

As the authors point out, there is a long tradition of subdividing the population into groups and looking at the within- and between-group inequality. Notably, people have looked at the inequality between the races, among experience groups, and between sexes. The question is why one is interested in any specific grouping of the population. It is only a mechanical matter to calculate these between-group inequality measures. The question I am raising is whether grouping the population according to the state they live in has a clear normative basis.

We need to determine some normative reason for focusing on place of residence as a grouping variable. Any decomposition into between and among inequality implies that we care not only about the total inequality but also about the relative importance of the between and within inequality. To focus attention on this element, I propose that we think in terms of changes in the economy that would keep total inequality constant but change the mix of between and within inequality. Does the relative size of these two components of total inequality have any normative implication?

First, we may inherently be concerned about some types of between-group inequality. This is clearly the case when we think of black-white inequality. Equal average incomes across races might be a legitimate goal in itself. If we are forced to hold inequality constant, we would prefer to see a larger percentage of the inequality attributed to within-race inequality rather than between-race inequality. In this case we may be intrinsically interested in the size of the between-group inequality. Does this hold for states?

Do we feel better knowing that states are totally equal and that all inequality comes from differences in incomes within states? My answer to this question depends crucially on the amount of interstate mobility. If people are born into a state and can never leave that state, then any increase in among-state inequality decreases the expected income of some people who are tied to a particular locale. In this sense it is equivalent to being black. It may, therefore, be of interest in its own right. On the other hand, if people are mobile, there may be little intrinsic reason to care whether inequality comes from differences among states or within states. Another way of stating this is that we may not be willing to accept greater total inequality in order to change the relative importance of among-state inequality.

A second reason we might be interested in this question focuses on within-state inequality. Suppose deprivation is relative. If persons living in poor states view their condition in relationship to other people in the same state, then we should applaud any decrease in the relative importance of within-state inequality. An *increase* in among-state inequality matched by offsetting reductions in within-state inequality may increase social welfare. Again, we are interested in the decomposition of inequality, but in this case we would like to see the relative size of the within inequality diminished.

While certain circumstances may arise where the relative size of these two components of inequality may enter the social welfare function, many popular arguments seem to view regional equalization only as a means to achieving the goal of reducing poverty or total inequality. In this light the authors' paper is extremely useful, for it shows that if regional development increases the mean income of poor states, but does nothing to the within-state inequality, it will have little impact on total equality. Only programs targeted at decreasing within-state inequality are likely to have a large impact. The question one would then want to raise is why these should be regional programs? Why should programs not be targeted at the poor directly if a reduction in their numbers is the goal?

Summary

The authors have presented a massive body of evidence which takes a good deal of time to digest. For anyone seriously interested in within- and among-state inequality, the authors have provided a gold mine. It seems difficult to imagine many additional numbers that anyone would still want to be calculated. The strength of the paper lies in its processing a huge amount of information and clearly presenting the results. What remains to be done by those in this field is to develop the normative foundations and the theoretical links between policy instruments and increases in this dimension of social welfare.

9   Trends in Social Security Wealth by Cohort

Robert Moffitt

This paper has a simple and straightforward purpose: to calculate the present value of Social Security payroll taxes and benefits received for a series of cohorts who have reached retirement age since the system began in 1937. Such a calculation is of interest for at least two reasons. First, despite the great ink spillage on Social Security in the 1970s, one will search in vain for a simple historical calculation of the type presented here. While a number of calculations have been made of the internal rates of return to Social Security taxes and of related present values (e.g., Aaron 1977; Brittain 1972; Burkhauser and Warlick 1979; Feldstein and Pellechio 1977; Freiden, Leimer, and Hoffman 1976; Pechman, Aaron, and Taussig 1968; and others), none have systematically examined trends in Social Security wealth for the entire period since 1937, nor have any presented a systematic analysis of the causes of the trends in Social Security wealth. This is not to say, however, that there is not already widely perceived conventional wisdom on what the postwar trends have been. This conventional wisdom (as several fellow economists at the University of Maryland and the Brookings Institution have confirmed) is that (a) cohorts retiring to date have received more in present-value terms than they have paid in; (b) that the magnitude of the net present value of benefits minus taxes, representing the across-cohort or intergenerational transfer provided by the system, was greatest for the earliest cohorts and has steadily fallen over time (at least in some relative sense); and (c) that (a) and (b) are simple reflections of a pay-as-you-go system, for in such a system the benefits of each group of retirees are

Robert Moffitt is a professor of economics at Rutgers University.

The author would like to thank Olivia Mitchell, Marilyn Moon, and Joseph Quinn for comments.

financed by the taxes of the contemporaneous group of workers, implying that the first few retiring cohorts will have paid in very little and therefore will do very well relative to their contributions. The calculations in this paper confirm these prior concepts in their broad outlines, but the exact senses in which they are true are clarified considerably. In addition, in at least one particular (whether the transfer has increased or decreased over time) the calculations show that in a sense the conventional wisdom is quite misleading, if not incorrect.

A second motivation for this exercise—which provided the stimulus for my original interest in these calculations—relates to the behavioral question of whether the Social Security system has historically had any effects on savings and hence the capital stock (Feldstein 1974) or on labor supply or retirement (Burkhauser and Turner 1978). Most of the time-series studies of these questions (see Danziger, Haveman, and Plotnick 1981 for a review) have relied on a calculation of the total value of Social Security wealth, which is very unlike that calculated here. The wealth series calculated by Feldstein (1974) and Munnell (1974), and updated more recently by Leimer and Lesnoy (1980)—I shall call it the FMLL series—calculates for each group of individuals of a certain age the present value of future benefits minus only the present value of future taxes to be paid; past taxes are not included. The exclusion of past taxes is suggested by analogy with the Ando-Modigliani-Brumberg model of life-cycle consumption, in which consumption is assumed to be a function of the present value of two variables: that of the future income stream, plus that of assets as of the current time, rather than as of the beginning of the life cycle. In a fully funded Social Security system, one in which past taxes are accumulated in a reserve fund for future retirees, the economy-wide value of contemporaneous assets would include the value of this reserve fund and hence the present value of past taxes. But in a pay-as-you-go system, one in which taxes are quickly paid out as benefits, no reserve fund is present and hence the model in no way represents past taxes. This would seem to call for some modification of the Ando-Modigliani-Brumberg model for an examination of Social Security, for it is rather difficult to see how the life-cycle effects of Social Security can be estimated when the value of past taxes paid in is assumed to have no effect on behavior. This paper in no way directly addresses this modeling issue, but clearly an alternative approach to examining the time-series evidence on Social Security would be to start with a more strictly cohort-defined Social Security wealth variable of the type developed here.[1]

9.1 Preliminaries

The Social Security Act of 1935 established the basis for the Old Age, Survivors, and Disability Insurance program in the United States. However, the 1935 Act merely provided the basis for the present program; it has changed enormously since then. For example, the 1935 Act provided only for retirement benefits—benefits for survivors of covered workers and for dependents were enacted at later dates. Also, under the initial Act benefits were much lower than now, payroll tax rates were considerably less, and coverage of the working population was below what it is today. In a series of amendments to the Act since 1935, benefits have been increased and liberalized, tax rates have been raised, and coverage has been broadened.

Nevertheless, the structure of the program for present purposes has always been roughly the same. Covered workers are required to pay a legislated percent of their earnings up to a legislated amount, termed the taxable maximum earnings level. Employers are required to pay an equal percentage of their employees' earnings up to the same maximum. At the age of 65, or somewhat earlier since early retirement has been permitted, individuals who have accumulated sufficient quarters of coverage are entitled to benefits of various types. Four types of benefits represent the bulk of the system's expenditures. One represents payments to retired men who are entitled to benefits under their earnings records; another is the equivalent payment to women entitled under their earnings records; a third is the payment to wives who choose to take the amount to which they are entitled under their husbands' earnings records; and the fourth is the payment to aged widows who are entitled to survivor benefits under their late spouses' earnings records. In all cases the single most important characteristic of the system is that benefits are not directly based on taxes paid in. Rather, they are based on a weighted average of lifetime earnings, the weights being determined by a fairly complicated formula which has changed over time. Hence the relationship between contributions and benefits is indirect and often very loose.

The conceptual basis for the calculations of the net present value of benefits minus taxes is simple. Taxes began to be paid in 1937; benefits began to be paid in 1940. For each birth cohort that has reached retirement age since 1940, the calculation desired requires a stream of tax payments and benefit payments at each age in that cohort's lifetime. Summed and discounted, the requisite net present value is obtained. However, the available published data are not in perfect form for this calculation. Benefits of various types are generally available by age and sex in each year, as are the number of benefit recipients of each type. In the upper age ranges the data are often grouped into broad age intervals, requiring some interpolation to obtain amounts for smaller age intervals. Unfortunately, tax payments by age and sex are not available. Consequently, data on annual earnings by age and sex are used in conjunction with the relevant payroll tax rate to estimate tax payments.[2] Since payments are made only up to a certain maximum, and since only median earnings are available, some assumption regarding the distribution of earnings must be made to determine how many individuals are and are not at the maximum.

For the purposes of this paper, life-cycle streams of taxes and benefits are calculated for eight cohorts spaced at five-year intervals. The tax and benefit payments are in turn grouped into five-year age intervals beginning at age 15 and running up to age 74. The final 75+ category is open-ended. All data sources and algorithms are reported in appendix A.

This is perhaps the appropriate point to note several caveats to the analysis. First, since aggregate data are used in the calculations, inferences regarding individuals within cohorts are difficult and, at times, hazardous. Whether the present value of benefits equals that of taxes for any individual or group of individuals within a cohort cannot be ascertained. A fortiori, only intergenerational transfers created by Social Security are presented here; intragenerational transfers are not examined. Second, it should be pointed out that welfare inferences based on these calculations are also hazardous. Since individuals can adjust their saving behavior, their dates of retirement, their earnings amounts over their lifetime, and their family types (they can sometimes alter the type of benefit they receive), the ultimate value of the net transfer is to a certain extent endogenous. This problem is common to virtually all studies of the distributional impact of transfers. Third, no wealth values are calculated for cohorts who have not yet reached retirement age. Since their future taxes and benefits are subject to legislative changes, their wealth values are inherently a matter of speculation.[3]

9.2   Results

9.2.1   Benefit and Tax Trends

Table 9.1 shows the mean real monthly benefit paid to each of the eight cohorts when they reach the 65–69 age category. Each cohort is denoted by the year in which the cohort reached the median age in this category (67). All dollar amounts in this paper are in real 1967 dollars. As the table indicates, benefits have always been greatest for retired male workers, as should be expected on the basis of their high earnings profiles. However, neither benefits for men nor for the three categories of women have risen smoothly over time. Nominal benefits were unchanged between the Social Security Amendments of 1939 and 1950, causing real benefits to fall over this period. Hence the 1947 cohort began at a lower level than the 1942 cohort. However, the 1950 Amendments greatly increased benefit levels, the percentage increase ranging from 47 to 63 percent depending on the benefit type. These benefit increases applied across the board and increased the benefits of all retirees at all ages, not just new

Table 9.1   Benefit Amounts and Replacement Rates by Cohort[a]

Cohort[c]	Monthly Benefit at Age 65–69				Benefit Replacement Rate at Age 65–69[b]			
	Retired Males	Retired Females	Wives	Widows	Retired Males	Retired Females	Wives	Widows
1942	47	41	27	41	.23	.36	.13	.20
1947	44	32	22	32	.20	.36	.10	.15
1952	67	47	35	52	.23	.34	.12	.18
1957	91	67	44	63	.29	.45	.14	.20
1962	101	72	46	77	.29	.45	.13	.22
1967	96	74	43	82	.25	.38	.11	.21
1972	149	117	69	116	.25	.49	.15	.25
1977	155	119	71	126	.32	.46	.14	.25

[a]All dollar amounts are in real 1967 dollars.

[b]Benefit as percent of earnings at age 62. Male earnings used for all but retired females.

[c]Year in which cohort is age 67.

retirees. Real benefit growth was substantially lower in the subsequent years, and even fell again in real terms in the early 1960s, another period of a faster price growth than nominal benefit growth. A second explosion of benefits occurred in the late 1960s and early 1970s, generating real benefit increases comparable in percentage terms to those of the early 1950s.

The table also shows the replacement rates of those in the 65–69 age category for each cohort, representing the ratio of benefits to the earnings of the same cohort five years earlier. Although replacement rates have wavered quite a bit, they have very slowly increased for some benefit types. On the whole, however, there have been no major changes in their values.

Figure 9.1 shows the benefit profiles of male retirees of each cohort as it aged from the 65–69 category. Benefits change over time for a cohort for several reasons: new members of the cohort retire, perhaps at different (presumably larger) benefit levels; other members of the cohort die, probably with lower benefit levels; women change from dependent to

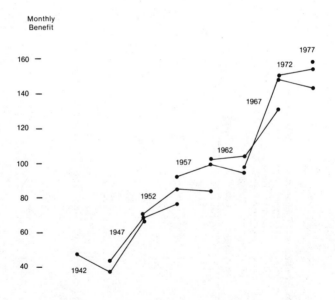

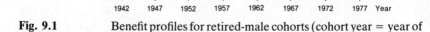

Fig. 9.1   Benefit profiles for retired-male cohorts (cohort year = year of age 67): ages 65–69, 70–74, 75+

survivor status, probably with an increase in the benefit level; and legislation or lack of it allows the real value of benefits for the same individual to change. The figure indicates the last of these effects completely dominates the life-cycle growth of benefits during retirement. Sharp increases in benefits occurred in the early 1950s and late 1960s, regardless of the age of the recipient. In addition, the shape of the profile varies greatly from cohort to cohort; it is sometimes convex, sometimes concave, sometimes relatively flat (as during the late 1950s and early 1960s). This extreme unevenness would seem to pose some problems for the standard life-cycle model with complete certainty, for it is difficult to see how these benefit profiles could have been correctly anticipated.

Table 9.2 shows the number of recipients per capita of each type at the base age range 65–69. Although more than 80 percent of men and women in the 1977 cohort received benefits, only 8 percent of men and 5 percent of women in the 1942 cohort did. These extremely low recipiency rates should cast some doubt on the extent to which early cohorts did well under the system, for while those actually receiving benefits may have done famously, very few actually received them (presumably because they had not accumulated sufficient quarters of covered earnings). Unlike the standard model of a pay-as-you-go system in which all the elderly are immediately blanketed into the system at its start, in the U.S. system eligibility was highly restricted in the beginning.

Figure 9.2 shows the recipiency rate profiles for male retirees in each cohort. Unlike the benefit profiles, here the shapes are consistently concave over time. Recipiency rates rose more rapidly for the early cohorts as they aged, probably because a disproportionately large number became eligible (i.e., attained insured status) at later ages. In addition, as recipiency rates approach 100 percent, there must by necessity be a leveling-off of the profiles.

Table 9.3 shows some of the relevant trends affecting tax payments

Table 9.2   **Recipients Per Capita at Age 65–69**

Cohort	Retired Males	Total	Females Retired Females	Wives	Widows
1942	.08	.05	.01	.03	.01
1947	.12	.11	.02	.06	.03
1952	.30	.29	.11	.12	.06
1957	.52	.58	.26	.22	.10
1962	.66	.74	.35	.25	.14
1967	.70	.78	.41	.22	.15
1972	.78	.83	.47	.20	.16
1977	.84	.87	.52	.19	.16

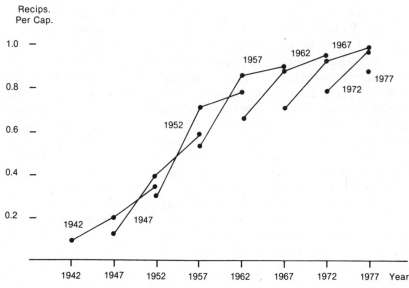

Fig. 9.2   Cohort profiles of male recipients per capita: ages 65–69, 70–74, 75+

over the period since 1937. Notably, tax rates stayed quite low until the early 1960s, when they began to rise steadily. As a consequence, the cohorts considered here paid very little tax into the system. Even the latest cohort considered in this paper, that aged 67 in 1977, was already 50 years old in 1960 when the tax rates began to rise. Hence, the peak of the earnings profile had passed or was near to passing. The table also shows that the real value of the taxable maximum has gone through uneven

Table 9.3   **Trends in Tax Payments and Coverage**

Year	Tax Rate[a]	Annual Taxable Earnings Maximum	Fraction of Covered Workers at Maximum	Covered Male Workers Age 40–44 Per Capita
1937	.010	9,646	.03	.54
1942	.010	8,174	.08	.69
1947	.010	5,682	.21	.67
1952	.015	5,816	.27	.82
1957	.020	6,213	.29	.92
1962	.029[b]	6,522	.30	.91
1967	.036[b]	8,118	.25	.91
1972	.041[b]	9,000	.24	.89
1977	.044[b]	11,752	.14	.89

[a]OASI only. Employers and employees each.
[b]Rounded off from a number with more significant digits.

changes over the period, also presumably difficult to forecast. The real maximum declined from 1937 to 1947 and rose thereafter. But apparently it did not rise as fast as earnings, for the percent of covered workers paying the maximum tax rose steadily until 1962, after which it declined as the real maximum accelerated. The increases in the percentage of workers hitting the taxable maximum reinforces the effect of low marginal taxes and lowers further the percentage of earnings actually paid in the form of taxes for these cohorts.

9.2.2   Social Security Wealth

The value of Social Security wealth, S, is calculated as the difference between the present value of benefits, SB, and taxes, ST. The term "Social Security wealth" as used in this paper will always refer to *net* wealth (net of taxes, that is). It will be zero in an actuarially fair system. The benefit value is calculated as:

$$(1) \qquad SB = \frac{1}{N_{17}} \sum_{k=1}^{4} \sum_{a=62}^{75+} \frac{R_a^k \; B_a^k}{(1+r)^{a-17}},$$

where R_a^k denotes the number of recipients of benefit type k at age a, B_a^k is the mean real benefit of type k at age a, N_{17} is the population size at age 17, and r is the real rate of interest. In most of the calculations, r is assumed to equal .03, as assumed by FMLL, although S is also calculated for other interest rates. The trends in wealth across cohorts are not significantly affected by this choice, although obviously the absolute amount of calculated wealth will be. It should be noted too that a few projections of benefits are required for the calculation of SB, namely (1) the benefits of those aged 75+ for the 1972 cohort and (2) the benefits of those aged 70–74 and 75+ for the 1977 cohort. For these projections, benefits are assumed to grow over these age ranges at the same rate as they did for the previous cohort. As an approximation this should be sufficiently close to probable actual experience.

It should also be noted that SB is divided by the number of individuals alive at age 17, putting the wealth measure on a per capita basis. Thus SB represents the aggregate value of all benefits received by all members of a cohort, but on a per capita basis. This definition will become important below, for it is not the same as the wealth value of recipients only—it includes all those who die before reaching retirement age and those who reach retirement age but do not receive benefits. As a result, the measure SB can grow as a result of increased life expectancy and increased coverage and recipiency rates, as well as from increased benefit levels for those who receive benefits. Although the growth of benefits for recipients alone is of some interest by itself, the measure here is the more comprehensive one necessary to compare each cohort as a whole to each other cohort as a whole.

The present value of tax payments is the following:

(2)
$$\text{ST} = \frac{1}{N_{17}} \sum_{a=17}^{75+} \frac{C_a \, T_a}{(1+r)^{a-17}},$$

where C_a is the number of covered workers at age a, and T_a is the mean tax payment at age a per covered worker. Both are equal to zero if the cohort is at an age prior to 1937. The tax payment is calculated as:

(3)
$$T_a = p_a \left[u_a \, Y_a + (1 - u_a) \, YM_a \right]$$
$$+ p_a \left[u_a \, Y_a + (1 - u_a) \, YM_a \right] (1 - s_a),$$

where u_a is the estimated fraction of the cohort at age a whose earnings are below the taxable maximum, p_a is the payroll tax rate at age a, Y_a is the value of earnings conditional on being below the maximum, YM_a is the value of the taxable maximum earnings at age a, and s_a is the non–Social Security personal tax rate on earnings. The tax payment is composed of an employee component and an employer component, with the latter deflated by $(1 - s_a)$ because it is not subject to tax. Note that the usual assumption of complete shifting of the employer portion onto the employee is followed here. Finally, the value of Social Security wealth is $S = \text{SB} - \text{ST}$.

Before presenting the results of the wealth calculation, the basic principles of a developing pay-as-you-go system should be briefly mentioned (Samuelson 1958; Diamond 1965; Aaron 1966). In a simple economy in which real wages grow at the rate g and the labor force grows at the rate n, a pay-as-you-go system in which all tax receipts are immediately paid out as benefits can attain a long-run equilibrium under which each individual obtains a rate of return $(n + g)$ on his payroll contributions. Both productivity growth and labor-force growth allow each cohort to "borrow" against future generations at this rate in Ponzi fashion. If the interest rate r is equal to $(n + g)$, the cohort could have done equally well with private savings and hence the program is actuarially fair. If r is greater (less) than $(n + g)$, the program is less (more) than actuarially fair and each cohort receives a negative (positive) lifetime net wealth increment. However, in the beginning such a system must give the first generation of retirees a net rate of return greater than $(n + g - r)$, for these cohorts did not pay a full lifetime of taxes but receive the full amount of receipts from current workers. Therefore in the immature phase of the system the value of the intergenerational transfer should fall, at least relative to wage growth, and should approach some equilibrium level.

Main Results

The results of the net wealth calculation for the eight cohorts are shown in table 9.4. As the table indicates, each member of the cohort born in 1892 who was alive at age 17 (i.e., in 1909) received a net present value of

Table 9.4   **Trends in Social Security Wealth By Cohort (1967 dollars)**

Cohort	S	Absolute Change	Five-Year Growth Rate (%)
1942	$ 24	$ 39	163
1947	63	82	130
1952	145	95	66
1957	240	116	48
1962	356	88	25
1967	444	100	23
1972	544	53	10
1977	597	—	—

$24. The absolute size of this number is small because (1) it is discounted back to age 17 since that is the beginning of the life cycle (multiply by about four to get age-65 values); (2) it is in 1967 dollars; and (3) it includes many nonrecipients, almost 70–90 percent of the members of the first cohort (see figure 9.2). More important is the *relative* size of the wealth values across cohorts. For the 1977 cohort, S was $597, about 25 times greater—implying an average annual growth rate (in real terms) of about 14 percent. The results immediately answer some of the basic questions regarding trends in Social Security wealth. First, it has risen in absolute value for all cohorts reaching retirement age up to 1977. This is not incompatible with an immature, or developing, pay-as-you-go Social Security system, but it is also not necessary; in the usual model of such a system the absolute value of wealth falls over time. To the extent that the caveat about welfare implications mentioned above is ignored, it appears that the absolute size of the intergenerational transfer received by more recent cohorts is larger that that received by early cohorts. Second, however, the growth rate of the wealth value has indeed slowed over time, consistent with expectations. The absolute value of the difference from one cohort to the next rose until the 1960s and appears to have begun falling by 1977. The growth rate of wealth, exceedingly large at first, has fallen with every succeeding cohort.

Components of Growth

Equally important is the determination of what has caused this particular growth pattern. Table 9.5 breaks down the net wealth values into their benefit and tax components (SB and ST) and subcomponents. The table shows that growth in benefits has dominated the growth in net wealth, for changes in net wealth were almost entirely determined as a result of significant benefit growth combined with tiny tax growth (SB grew from $27 to $815 while ST only from $4 to $218). ST remained small and grew very little in absolute terms until the 1970s. The subcomponents of SB

Table 9.5   **Components of Growth in Social Security Wealth ($S = SB - ST$)**

Cohort	Total	SB[a]				ST[a]		
		Retired Males	Retired Females	Wives	Widows	Total	Males	Females
1942	$ 27	$ 19	$ 3	$ 3	$ 3	$ 4	$ 3	$ 0[b]
1947	71	46	10	7	9	8	7	1
1952	161	97	30	15	20	17	14	2
1957	270	149	62	25	34	30	25	5
1962	408	202	108	33	65	52	41	11
1967	533	246	158	37	92	89	68	21
1972	693	321	224	43	105	148	110	38
1977	815	365	262	43	144	218	156	61

[a]Components may not add up exactly because of rounding error.
[b]0.3.

show that over most of the period the benefits of male retirees contributed the most in absolute terms to its growth. However, since the 1960s, benefits claimed by women on the basis of their own earnings records (retired females) have grown in approximately the same amounts as those of men. Correspondingly, the growth of benefits claimed by dependent wives has virtually halted. This is an interesting result, presumably caused by the increase in the number of working wives with significant lifetime wage profiles. As wives' earnings increase, the benefits for which they are eligible alone also increase. Since the law automatically grants wives the larger of either the benefit for which they are eligible alone or that for which they are eligible under their husbands' records (usually about 50 percent of his benefit), wives' earnings growth should result in a gradual switching from the wives category to the retired females category.

Table 9.6 shows the results of further decomposing the change in S from cohort to cohort into several parts. The formula for SB can be rewritten as:

$$(4) \qquad SB = \frac{N_{17}^m}{N_{17}} \sum_{a=62}^{75+} \frac{N_a^m}{N_{17}^m} \frac{R_a^1}{N_a^m} \frac{B_a^1}{(1+r)^{a-17}}$$

$$+ \frac{N_{17}^f}{N_{17}} \sum_{a=62}^{75+} \sum_{k=2}^{4} \frac{N_a^f}{N_{17}^f} \frac{R_a^k}{N_a^f} \frac{B_a^k}{(1+r)^{a-17}},$$

where N_a^m is the size of the male population at age a, and N_a^f is the size of the corresponding female population, and where $k = 1$ denotes male retired-worker benefits, and $k = 2, 3,$ and 4 denote the three female benefit types. The change in SB from cohort to cohort may thus be decomposed into changes in (a) the fraction of the cohort that is male at age 17; (b) the sex-specific life probabilities (fraction of population

Table 9.6 Decomposition of Growth of Social Security Wealth[a] (percentages × 100)

Cohorts	Benefits per Recipient				Recipients per Capita			Taxes per Capita					
	Total	Replacement Rate[b]	Benefit Growth	Earnings[c]	Total	Basic[b]	Growth	Total	Taxes per Covered Worker	Coverage Rate[d]	Level of Employment	Life Probabilities	Age in 1937
1942–1947	16	−9	28	1	65	55	11	−4	0	−4	1	6	−7
1947–1952	19	12	−19	33	58	148	−30	−4	0	−3	0	7	−6
1952–1957	29	41	−21	13	61	143	−43	−7	−3	−1	−2	7	−7
1957–1962	57	0	28	26	34	69	−27	−11	−7	−2	−2	6	−8
1962–1967	65	−63	72	67	36	38	−1	−27	−16	−7	−2	19	−14
1967–1972	101	155	−120	102	18	53	−33	−40	−27	−6	−3	26	−15
1972–1977	87	−62	35	117	86	85	5	−99	−84	−13	4	44	−35

[a]Numbers for each cohort pair calculated as $(S_{t+1}^i - S_t)/(S_{t+1} - S_t)$, where S_t is the actual net wealth value for cohort t (see table 9.4), and S_{t+1}^i is the value of wealth which cohort t+1 would have had if variable i had changed but all other variables had remained at cohort t values. Since the decomposition is only a first-order Taylor series approximation, horizontal sums do not sum to 100.
[b]At age 65–69.
[c]At age 60–64.
[d]Number of covered workers divided by level of employment.

surviving to each age); (c) the benefit recipiency rate per capita; and (d) the size of the benefit.

The formula for ST can be rewritten as the following:

$$
(5) \qquad \text{ST} = \frac{N_{17}^m}{N_{17}} \sum_{a=17}^{75+} \frac{N_a^m}{N_{17}^m} \frac{C_a^m T_a^m}{N_a^m} \frac{1}{(1+r)^{a-17}}
$$

$$
+ \frac{N_{17}^f}{N_{17}} \sum_{a=17}^{75+} \frac{N_a^f}{N_{17}^f} \frac{C_a^f T_a^m}{N_a^f} \frac{1}{(1+r)^{a-17}}.
$$

Thus the growth in ST can be decomposed into changes in the fraction of the population that is male at age 17; changes in life probabilities; and changes in per capita taxes paid.

Table 9.6 shows the results of computing the fractions of the change in S from cohort to cohort that result from each of these factors alone. To interpret the table, compare the relative magnitudes and signs of the percentages horizontally, across the rows. (The percentages need not add to 100—see the table.) For example, 65 percent of the change in S from the 1942 cohort to the 1947 cohort was a result of a change in the recipiency rate; only 16 percent was a result of changes in the benefit. Increased taxes account for only a small -4 percent of the change; growth in life expectancy for only a $+6$ percent; and the fact that the later cohort started paying taxes at an earlier age and hence paid more taxes accounted for a relatively small -7 percent. The table also shows a decomposition of benefit growth into growth in the basic 65–69 benefit replacement rate, changes in benefits over the retirement period, and changes in earnings; a decomposition of the change in the recipiency rate into changes in the basic recipiency rate at age 65–69 and the growth of recipiency over the retirement period; and a decomposition of changes in per capita taxes into portions resulting from changes in taxes paid per covered worker, coverage as a percent of employment, and the employment rate (employment per capita). See appendix A for an exact statement of the decomposition. The results show that the growth in benefits between the 1942 and 1947 cohorts was mostly a result of what is called benefit growth—that is, growth of benefits *during* retirement (i.e., after age 69). This can be seen back in figure 9.1 as well. On the other hand, the growth in the recipiency rate appears to be mostly a result of growth in the basic (i.e., age 67) recipiency rate, rather than in the growth rate of recipiency during retirement. Finally, the wealth-depressing effect of tax growth appears to be almost entirely a result of growth in coverage for the 1942–1947 change rather than from changes in tax rates or employment growth.

Moving down the table, the magnitudes often grow in absolute value. This is just a result of the fact that, as taxes grow, benefits must also grow to produce an equivalent net wealth increase. The more important point is that the relations between the magnitudes within horizontal rows of the table change over time.[4] In the early years of the program most of the growth was a result of increases in the recipiency rate, rather than changes in the benefit, as just mentioned for the 1942–1947 change. However, the importance of the latter has gradually increased and that of the former has fallen, with the result that benefit growth has been more important quantitatively since the 1950s. This should be expected on the basis of the leveling-off of recipiency growth discussed previously. Also, it appears that the determinants of the change in the benefit itself have fluctuated dramatically, sometimes more a result of a higher age 65–69 benefit (the replacement rate column) and sometimes more a result of a higher growth rate of benefits at later ages (the benefit growth column). Again, figure 9.1 demonstrates why this instability is to be expected. Simple growth in earnings has also apparently accounted for an increasing share of the growth in benefits: with a fixed replacement rate, benefits will naturally rise at the same rate as earnings. There is no particular rationale for this pattern, for it has resulted from the different ways the Social Security formula has been changed over time. The table also shows the determinants of the recipiency rate, where it seems that increases in the basic rate (i.e., age 67) has been more important than the growth of recipiency during retirement in raising net wealth from cohort to cohort.

The depressing effect of taxes paid in has been relatively slight over most of the period presented here, at least until the 1970s. Also, although in the early years what growth did occur in taxes was mainly a result of coverage growth (0 vs. −4 and 0 vs. −3), tax growth since then has resulted more from the basic change in tax payments per covered worker. The growing importance of taxes paid in is also reflected by the growing negative percentage accounted for by age at entry in 1937, for this implies more years of tax payments in the lifetime.

Finally, the results indicate that changes in life expectancy have a net positive effect on the growth of S, although increases in life expectancy increase both benefits and taxes. Although its importance was slight during the early years of the program, it has grown to such an extent that the impact of increased life expectancy amounts in magnitude to almost 50 percent of the net change in S from the 1972 to the 1977 cohorts.

Life-Cycle Patterns of Wealth

Figure 9.3 shows the life-cycle path of cumulative net Social Security wealth for the most recent cohort. The paths of the other cohorts are similar in shape, although each cohort of an older age began paying taxes at a later date. S is negative until the cohort reaches retirement age because only taxes have been paid in. For the cohort in the figure, as well as all the other cohorts, (1) S is always still negative in the 60–64 age range, despite the increased frequency of early retirement, and (2) S is

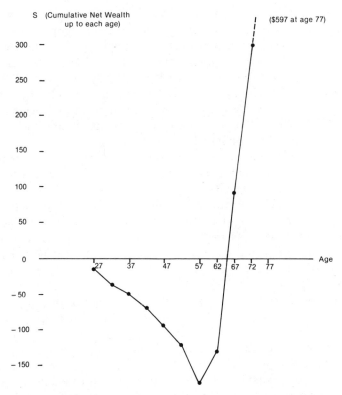

Fig. 9.3   Life-cycle net Social Security wealth profile for 1977 cohort

always positive in the subsequent, 65–69 age range. Thus from the perspective of the cohort as a whole—although not necessarily from that of a particular individual—the system has paid off already by age 69. It is also interesting to note that there is an enormous growth of S in the last age category of $75+$. That this holds for all cohorts, not just that in the figure, is demonstrated in table 9.7, which shows the value of S during retirement age for each cohort. The growth rate at the final point, often more than 100 percent, implies an extremely large payoff at older ages. Put differently, if all members of the cohort were to die at age 75, net wealth would often be only one-half of what it actually turns out to be. Thus the receipt of benefits by those aged $75+$ constitutes a large fraction, if not the largest, of net wealth.

Alternative Wealth Measures

Table 9.8 provides additional evidence on the growth of S. The first columns show the values of S calculated for different values of r. While the magnitude of S changes in the expected direction, the trends in

Table 9.7   **Life-Cycle Growth of Social Security Wealth (S)**

	Age			
Cohort	60–64	65–69	70–74	75 +
1942	−2	2	7	24
1947	−5	1	21	63
1952	−12	15	72	145
1957	−24	47	136	240
1962	−29	72	171	356
1967	−46	61	217	443
1972	−97	100	284	544
1977	−137	90	290	597

Table 9.8   **Additional Wealth Measures: Internal Rates of Return, Benefit-Cost, and Earned-Wealth Indicators**

	S			Internal Rate of Return	SB/ST	Relationship to Earned Wealth	
Cohort	r = .02	r = .03	r = .04			V	S/V
1942	42	24	13	.195	6.8	4,600	.005
1947	112	63	36	.196	8.9	4,565	.014
1952	254	145	83	.197	9.5	4,375	.033
1957	420	240	137	.165	9.0	4,376	.055
1962	627	356	203	.141	7.8	4,839	.074
1967	789	444	249	.116	6.0	5,398	.082
1972	975	544	301	.099	4.7	6,566	.083
1977	1,089	597	321	.085	3.7	7,767	.077

absolute amounts and in growth rates obtained previously are not affected. The table also shows the internal rates of return for each cohort. After remaining more or less constant at around 20 percent (in real terms, recall) for the early cohorts, the rate of return has fallen steadily to about 8 percent for the most recent cohort. That these real rates are considerably higher than .03 or any other possible real rate of return to private savings over this period is just another indication of the large net intergenerational transfer that has been provided to cohorts retiring to date. The decline of these rates of return is again to be expected in a developing system as described above. The table also shows the ratio of SB to ST, the benefit-cost ratio frequently employed as a measure of the generosity of the system. This particular ratio rose for the first three cohorts but, like the rate of return, has fallen since then.

The final columns in the table show the results of an attempt to gauge the importance of Social Security wealth relative to private, earned wealth. Suppose that the present value of lifetime earnings is V and that total wealth is thus $W = S + V = V(1 + S/V)$.[5] There is also presumably some cohort utility function $U(W)$. In a growing economy we should expect V and hence W to grow, but in an immature pay-as-you-go Social Security system we should also expect S/V to gradually fall (to zero if the equilibrium is at an actuarially fair level). A case could be made on this basis that it is the change in S/V—rather than the change in the internal rate of return, benefit-cost or cost-benefit ratios, or absolute sizes or growth rates of S—that should determine the relative well-offness of successive cohorts.

Estimates of V are not possible to obtain directly because earnings data by age, which are needed to construct cohort-specific earnings profiles, are not available before 1937. However, these pre-1937 age-earnings profiles can be estimated by extrapolating backward from the post-1937 age-earnings profiles, with due allowance for the general level of economic activity and hence for the Depression. To do this the post-1937 age-earnings data were pooled into a single regression, and an age-earnings profile was estimated (with dummies for World War II and including an index of the general level of earnings) and then used to generate an age-earnings profile for each cohort from which a value for after-tax lifetime earned wealth, V, was obtained (see appendix B).

The results of this exercise are shown in table 9.8. As the table indicates, the ratio S/V appears to have risen all the way up to the 1972 cohort, contrary to expectations. Thus, it appears that S has risen at a sufficiently high rate so that successive cohorts through the early 1970s appear to actually have been made better-off by the system than previous cohorts! This arises simply because S, though growing at steadily lower rates, has nevertheless continued to grow at a faster rate than earnings.

This result does not appear to be a consequence of an underestimate of the growth rate of V. To be sure, the results of the regression exercise produce a V that actually fell for the first three cohorts in the table. The explanation for this trend arises from the fact that the Depression occurred at a more crucial stage in the lifetime working careers of the 1947–1957 cohorts than the 1942 or later cohorts. Whereas, for example, the 1942 cohort was already 54 years old in 1929—the working career almost over and the earnings profile already dipping—the three successive cohorts were anywhere from 39 to 49 years old in 1929, at the peak of their earnings profiles. The depressing effect on lifetime earnings was consequently disproportionately large for the latter groups. Nevertheless, to check the accuracy of the S/V calculation, ratios of S to cohort earnings at various 1937 wages were also calculated, ratios requiring no estimation procedures at all. The results, shown in appendix B, show precisely the same pattern as that of S/V in table 9.8.

For the eight cohorts examined here this also means that a conventional inequality calculation will show that the Social Security system has increased inequality. For example, the coefficient of variation of V over the eight cohorts is 16, whereas that of $(S + V)$ is 18. Across these particular eight cohorts, that is, the better-off have been made still better-off. Of course, this is to a great extent a misleading analogy with conventional distributional criteria, for there has been no redistribution from earlier cohorts to more recent cohorts except in the negative sense that there was a failure to redistribute more, intergenerationally speaking, toward the early cohorts. The point is, however, that all the net wealth increments are intergenerational transfers from future cohorts to current cohorts, and the fact that S/V has been rising implies only that the more recent cohorts have been redistributing more, proportionately speaking, from future cohorts than previous generations did. Moreover, since an increase in S/V cannot continue indefinitely in a pay-as-you-go system—indeed, it has already begun to fall—it is to be presumed that an extension of this analysis to future cohorts would be capable, at some point, of generating a reduction in the coefficient of variation measured across all cohorts.

One puzzle remains: How could S/V rise at all for so long in a pay-as-you-go system? The answer, it turns out, is that the system was not in fact pay-as-you-go until the mid-1960s. When benefits began to be paid in 1940, benefit levels were far below what they could have been if all tax receipts (or even most of them) had been disbursed. In 1940, in fact, the trust fund was 40 times the size of benefit payments. The fund gradually fell over the following two decades until the mid-1960s, where it has stabilized at a level deemed appropriate for contingencies only (i.e., sudden shortfalls in revenues). Thus the intergenerational transfer was intentionally kept low for the early cohorts.

9.2.3   Remarks on Interpretation and on Future Trends

It may be helpful in interpreting these results to put them into context by comparing them with other Social Security wealth measures. The wealth measure presented here is simple in concept: it measures the amount each cohort put in and the amount each got out. Aside from having to project a few benefit amounts for the most recent cohorts, all the numbers used in these calculations are actual magnitudes of taxes and benefits historically paid and received. This is a much simpler and more straightforward task than is the calculation of other wealth measures in the literature, most of which require assumptions regarding the expectations of individuals. For example, estimating the wealth of cohorts not yet retired requires not only estimating what benefits and taxes will be in the future, but also how cohorts at each age will perceive those benefits and taxes. Even in the wealth measure considered by FMLL, which is intended to be a historical measure, it is assumed that each cohort at each age forms a perception of its own wealth only loosely based on actual past experience or actual future experience. Thus, for example, much of the discussion of the FMLL wealth measure has revolved around the appropriateness of different expectational assumptions. In the wealth measure constructed in this paper, on the other hand, no such issues arise because no decisions of this type are necessary in its construction. The study here is closely analogous to studies of the distribution of transfer benefits, inasmuch as both are examinations, to the greatest extent possible, of actual benefits received. In addition, although different wealth measures are appropriate for different purposes, a measure showing simply how well different cohorts have actually done historically seems quite important to examine. In fact, as mentioned at the beginning of the paper, it is surprising that it has not been examined before.

The wealth measure here is also similar to those used in transfer-benefit studies in the respect that both generally ignore behavioral effects. For example, to the extent that individuals have retired early to obtain higher wealth increments, the present values presented here are an exaggeration of true welfare measures. It is for this reason that the FMLL measure estimates wealth assuming an age 65 retirement for all, but such a restriction is not appropriate when one is simply measuring actual benefits received.[6] As mentioned at the beginning of the paper, the welfare implications of the measures presented here are consequently clouded by this possibility, and by the questions of the extent to which private saving is displaced and the extent to which a stream of unexpected changes in wealth yields lower utility than the same stream had it been expected.

Although future trends in Social Security wealth have not been considered here, the results may have some implications for such trends. There are again two different questions: What will actually happen? What do current cohorts perceive will happen? What will actually happen is, of course, up to the U.S. Congress and can only be a matter of political speculation. What is more interesting is the nature of the constraints within which Congress will have to operate. Clearly the net wealth increment for future cohorts must be smaller than it has been for those considered in this paper, as a result of the maturation of a pay-as-you-go system. But unless productivity growth and labor-force growth are extremely low over the next 30–40 years, a positive net wealth increment will be possible on average. However, since the lump in the age distribution will pass through the high-earnings range in the next decade or two, maintaining a more-or-less constant net wealth increment will require building up a transitional trust fund for the financing of later benefits. To have a pay-as-you-go system on average, the surplus and deficit years must cancel out in the long run only.

Regarding how current cohorts perceive their future wealth, and therefore how their current behavior is affected, the calculations here raise the question of the relative importance individuals attach to past historical trends rather than to the future possibilities just mentioned. If individuals only examine past historical trends, the results presented here should generate the expectation of a much more generous system in the future than now, for the absolute value of the net wealth increment has risen continuously for all cohorts retired to date. Although the growth rate of that increment has fallen, it is still positive and large. Any type of adaptive expectations model would presumably generate this kind of result. Yet the more unfavorable possibilities for the future appear to have gained widespread recognition. Consequently, where the average citizen's opinion of the future lies—between the extremes of a more generous system and a possibly bankrupt one—is a question I leave to more intrepid analysts.

9.3   Summary

Net Social Security wealth, equal to the present value of benefits minus taxes, has risen in absolute value for all cohorts having reached retirement age since the inception of the Social Security system. However, the absolute change in wealth and its rate of growth have fallen. The growth of wealth thus far has been predominantly a result of benefit growth; taxes have affected net wealth very little, though this will change for future cohorts. Beyond this, the exact determinants of the growth in wealth have fluctuated a great deal over time, being a result at differing times of changes in recipiency rates, benefit-replacement rates, growth rates of benefits over the retirement period, and life probabilities. The one unexpected finding was that net Social Security wealth grew faster than earnings all the way into the 1970s, implying that cohorts retiring later have been made better-off in proportionate terms than cohorts retiring earlier.

Appendix A   *Wealth Algorithms and Data Sources*

The value of net Social Security wealth, S, is calculated for each cohort as the difference between the present value of benefits, SB, and the present value of taxes, ST. The formula for SB is:

$$SB = F_{17}^m Y_{62}^m RR_{67}^1 BR_{67}^1 \sum_{a=62}^{75+} \frac{P_a^m G_a^1 H_a^1}{(1+r)^{a-17}}$$

$$+ F_{17}^f Y_{62}^f RR_{67}^2 \sum_{a=65}^{75+} \frac{P_a^f G_a^2 H_a^2}{(1+r)^{a-17}}$$

$$+ F_{17}^f Y_{62}^m \sum_{k=3}^{4} RR_{67}^k BR_{67}^k \sum_{a=65}^{75+} \frac{P_a^f G_a^k H_a^k}{(1+r)^{a-17}},$$

where

$$F^i_{17} = N^i_{17}/N_{17} \text{ (see text), sex } i;$$

$$Y^i_{62} = \text{annual earnings of workers of age 60-64, sex } i;$$

$$RR^k_{67} = \text{recipiency rate of benefit type } k, \text{ equaling } R^k_{65-69}/N^i_{65-69}, \text{ where } i = m \text{ for } k = 1, \text{ and } i = f \text{ for } k = 2, 3, 4;$$

$$BR^k_{67} = B^k_{65-69}/Y^i_{62}, \text{ where } i = m \text{ for } k = 1; \text{ and } i = f \text{ for } k = 2; \text{ and } i = m \text{ for } k = 3, 4;$$

$$P^i_a = N^i_a/N^i_{17}, \text{ sex } i;$$

$$G^k_a = B^k_a/B^k_{67};$$

$$H^k_a = RR^k_a/RR^k_{67}.$$

Here $k = 1$ if a male retired worker; $k = 2$ if a female retired worker; $k = 3$ if a wife; and $k = 4$ if a widow. This formula was used in the decomposition reported in table 9.6, with BR representing the replacement rate; G representing the growth rate of benefits during retirement; Y^i_{62} representing earnings in that table; RR^k_{67} representing the basic recipiency rate; and H representing the growth rate of recipiency during retirement.

The formula for ST is:

$$ST = F^m_{17} \sum_{a=17}^{75+} P^m_a E^m_a W^m_a T^m_a \frac{1}{(1+r)^{a-17}}$$

$$+ F^f_{17} \sum_{a=17}^{75+} P^f_a E^f_a W^f_a T^f_a \frac{1}{(1+r)^{a-17}},$$

where

$$E^i_a = \text{employment of sex } i \text{ at age } a, \text{ divided by } N^i_a;$$

$$W^i_a = \text{number of covered workers of sex } i \text{ at age } a, \text{ divided by } E^i_a;$$

$$T^i_a = \text{estimated tax payments of covered workers of sex } i \text{ at age } a$$
$$= p_a(2 - s_a) [u^i_a YB^i_a + (1 - u^i_a) YM_a];$$

$$p_a = \text{payroll tax rate at age } a;$$

$$s_a = \text{non-Social-Security tax rate at age } a;$$

$$u^i_a = \text{fraction of workers of sex } i \text{ at age } a \text{ below the taxable maximum};$$

$$YB^i_a = \text{mean earnings of sex } i \text{ at age } a \text{ if below } YM_a;$$

$$YM_a = \text{taxable maximum earnings level at age } a.$$

The estimate of u^i_a assumes that earnings among covered workers is distributed exponentially, as appears to be the case (see the *Annual Statistical Supplement of the Social Security Bulletin, 1977–1979*, p. 93). Under the exponential assumption it can be shown that

$$u_a^i = 1 - \exp[-\text{YM}_a/(1.44\ Y_a^i)],$$

where the factor of 1.44 is introduced to convert median earnings to mean earnings. The formula for the truncated mean of an exponential distribution can also be used to generate a value for earnings below the maximum:

$$\text{YB}_a^i = 1.44\ Y_a^i\ u_a^i - \text{YM}_a\ (1 - u_a^i).$$

The above formulation of ST was used in the decomposition reported in table 9.6, with taxes per covered worker represented by T_a^i, coverage represented by W_a^i, and employment by E_a^i.

The data sources are as follows:

(1) Population by age and sex, post-1937: Leimer and Lesnoy 1980 (LL), appendix G; pre-1937: interpolated from decennial census figures from 1900–1940 Censuses.

(2) Number of recipients of each benefit type by age: LL, appendix G.

(3) Number of covered workers by sex and age: LL, appendix G.

(4) Payroll tax rate from 1937: *Annual Statistical Supplement (ASS) of the Social Security Bulletin, 1977–1979.*

(5) Taxable maximum earnings levels: *1977–1979 ASS.*

(6) Median earnings by age and sex since 1937: *1977–1979 ASS*, p. 90; *1972 ASS*, p. 63; and *1968 ASS*, p. 55.

(7) Non-Social-Security tax rate by year: ratio of tax payments to personal income from National Income and Product Accounts.

(8) Employment by sex and age: *1980 Handbook of Labor Statistics*, table 18, for post-1947; interpolated from employment and age-specific, labor-force data for 1937–1946 reported in *Historical Statistics of the United States*, U.S. Bureau of the Census.

(9) Benefits by type by age: *annual ASS* and *Social Security Yearbooks* from 1940 to date.

(10) Current Price Index used to deflate all nominal values: *Historical Statistics*, p. 210.

Appendix B *Estimation of After-Tax Earned Wealth*

The formula for V, the after-tax value of cohort earnings discounted to age 17, is:

$$V = F_{17}^m \sum_{a=17}^{75+} P_a^m E_a^m \frac{(Y_a^m + \text{TE}_a^m)(1 - s_a)}{(1 + r)^{a-17}}$$

$$+ F_{17}^f \sum_{a=17}^{75+} P_a^f E_a^f \frac{(Y_a^f + \text{TE}_a^f)(1 - s_a)}{(1 + r)^{a-17}}$$

where TE_a^i is the employer portion of the payroll tax, and all other variables are as defined in appendix A. Note that the employer portion of the tax is added to observed earnings to be consistent with the shifting

Table 9.A.1   Post-1937 Earnings Regressions[a]

	Male	Female
Age (A)	.36*	.33*
Age Splines:[b]		
22+	−.20*	−.33*
27+	−.11*	−.02
32+	−.02	.06
37+	−.03	−.02
42+	.00[d]	.00[d]
47+	−.02	−.04
52+	.00[d]	.00
57+	−.03	−.06*
62+	−.17*	−.09*
67+	.08*	−.06*
72+	−.01	.02
Log W^c	1.28*	2.10*
Max (log W − 4.5, 0)	−.93*	−.43*
World War II dummy: = 1 if year is 1942, 1943, 1944, or 1945	.06	−.19*
Constant	−6.29*	−10.00*
R^2	.94	.93

*Significant at the 10 percent level.
[a]Dependent variable: logarithm of $E_a^i(Y_a^i + \text{TE}_a^i)$.
[b]Of the form: Max $(A − A_i, 0)$, where A_i is the denoted age.
[c]W = real average weekly earnings of production workers in manufacturing by year (source: *Historical Statistics*, p. 169, and 1980 *Handbook of Labor Statistics*, p. 188).
[d]Less than .005 in absolute value.

Table 9.A.2   **Wealth-Earnings Ratios by Cohort**

Cohort	S/Y^m_{60-64}	S/Y^m_{55-59}	S/Y^m_{50-54}
1942	.010	a	a
1947	.024	.024	a
1952	.042	.047	.051
1957	.064	.063	.070
1962	.085	.085	.089
1967	.095	.094	.099
1972	.098	.103	.107
1977	.099	.096	.105

[a]Earnings data not available.

assumption employed in the calculation of ST. Note too that Y represents conditional earnings (i.e., of workers only); it must be deflated by the employment rate to obtain per person earnings in the entire cohort.

The terms in V involving ages after 1937 can be obtained from the data reported in appendix A, but portions of each cohort's profile prior to 1937 cannot. Nor are employment data by sex and age available prior to 1937. Instead, all the cohort age data post-1937 were pooled into a single regression and the earnings equations shown in table 9.A.1 were estimated. The results were used to impute a value for expected earnings pre-1937 (or, more precisely, a value for the employment rate times the sum of full earnings—see the footnotes to the table). Implicitly it is assumed that the shape of the age profile remained unchanged prior to 1937; only the intercept, changing as a result of the average manufacturing wage, was altered. Because this imputation is obviously subject to some error, ratios of V to available post-1937 annual male earnings were also calculated. The results are shown in table 9.A.2. As the table indicates, the trends are the same as those in S/V reported in the text.

Notes

1. There is also the question of the extent to which the net transfer eventually received by any cohort was actually perceived at younger ages, and there is the need for determining how cohorts not yet retired perceive their Social Security wealth. Still, it would seem preferable to assume that wealth perceptions are based on the actual experience of existing retirees rather than on the latest projections of the Social Security Administration. For one attempt to model perceptions in this fashion, see Moffitt (1981).

2. Another major difference between the wealth value calculated here and that calculated in the FMLL algorithm is that the latter assumes that all individuals at each point in time have the same income, regardless of age. This undoubtedly distorts the shape of true cohort earnings profiles and hence the calculation of tax payments.

3. However, a few projections are made in the calculations below, although only for the remainder of the lifetimes of those who have already retired by 1977.

4. The sex ratio is not shown in table 9.6 because it has stayed virtually constant over the period and hence accounts for none of the change in S.

5. Assume no inheritance or other forms of non-life-cycle unearned income.

6. In any case, it would be difficult to do in the context of this paper. Although the benefits of those retiring at age 65 in each year can be obtained separately in the data, the benefit streams of this subset of individuals as they age and their particular lifetime earnings streams cannot be broken out from aggregate data.

References

Aaron, H. 1966. The Social insurance paradox. *Canadian Journal of Economics* 32 (August):371–74.

———. 1977. Demographic effects on the equity of Social Security benefits. In *Economics of public services*, ed. Martin Feldstein and Robert Inman. New York: Macmillan.

Brittain, J. 1972. *The payroll tax for Social Security*. Washington, D.C.: The Brookings Institution.

Burkhauser, R., and J. Turner. 1978. A time-series analysis on Social Security and its effect on the market work of men at younger ages. *Journal of Political Economy* 86 (August):701–15.

Burkhauser, R., and J. Warlick. 1979. Disentangling the annuity from the redistributive aspects of Social Security. Discussion paper 562-79. Institute for Research on Poverty, University of Wisconsin-Madison.

Danziger, S., R. Haveman, and R. Plotnick. 1981. How income transfers affect work, savings and the income distribution. *Journal of Economic Literature* 3 (September):975–1028.

Diamond, P. 1965. National debt in a neoclassical growth model. *American Economic Review* 55 (December):1126–50.

Feldstein, M. 1974. Social Security, induced retirement, and aggregate capital accumulation. *Journal of Political Economy* 82 (September/October):905–26.

Feldstein, M., and A. Pellechio. 1977. Social Security wealth: The impact of alternative inflation adjustments. Working paper 212. Cambridge, Mass.: National Bureau of Economic Research.

Freiden, A., D. Leimer, and R. Hoffman. 1976. Internal rates of return to retired worker-only beneficiaries under Social Security, 1967–1970. Paper no. 5. Washington, D.C.: Office of Research and Statistics, Social Security Administration.

Leimer, D., and S. Lesnoy. 1980. Social Security and private saving: A reexamination of the time series evidence using alternative Social Security wealth variables. Working Paper no. 19. Washington, D.C.: Office of Research and Statistics, Social Security Administration.

Moffitt, R. 1981. Interrupted life-cycle models and the dynamic effect of Social Security on saving. Mimeo. Rutgers University.

Munnell, A. 1974. *The effect of Social Security on private saving.* Cambridge, Mass.: Ballinger.

Pechman, J., H. Aaron, and M. Taussig. 1968. *Social Security: Perspectives for reform.* Washington, D.C.: The Brookings Institution.

Samuelson, P. 1958. An exact consumption-loan model of interest with or without the social contrivance of money. *Journal of Political Economy* 66 (December):467–82.

Comment   Joseph F. Quinn

The paper by Robert Moffitt has two goals, to provide a systematic examination of the trends in Social Security wealth since the beginning of the system in 1937 and to analyze the causes of these trends. The paper begins with a discussion of the conventional wisdom on Social Security wealth; that

(1) the cohorts that have retired up to now have received far more than an actuarial return on their contributions;

(2) the size of the bonus (the intergenerational transfer) has fallen over time; and

(3) this pattern is exactly what you would expect in a pay-as-you-go system.

Early generations had little time to contribute, and they were able to profit from the growth in productivity and population over the subsequent decades—the chain-letter effect. This paper basically confirms the conventional wisdom, with an exception noted below.

The paper begins with a short description of OASI—the retirement and survivors' components of Social Security. It emphasizes the important point that the relationship between contributions and benefits is very loose. This is certainly true for individuals. Some die early or work forever and therefore never receive benefits; others retire early and live and collect for decades. There are individual winners and losers. But this is also true for cohorts, in which these individual differences wash out. The analogies between Social Security and welfare programs are stronger, I believe, than those between Social Security and pension or insurance plans. This is important because it is the main reason for a study such as this—cohorts as a whole can gain or lose.

The paper follows the actual flows of Social Security contributions

Joseph F. Quinn is a professor of economics at Boston College.

(from employees and employers) and benefits for eight cohorts of Americans, and asks whether each cohort gained or lost, how much, and why. The cohorts are defined by five-year intervals—the first includes those aged 65–69 in 1942, and the last those aged 65–69 in 1977. No calculations are done on those who have not reached the traditional retirement age of 65, since the books are not yet closed on them. Actually, the books are not yet closed on anyone still alive. Despite the emphasis on actual benefits paid, therefore, some future projections have to be made for the last two cohorts. Moffitt assumes that benefits will grow in the future at the same rate that they did for the previous cohort during the same age intervals (70–74 and 75 +). This probably exaggerates the growth, since it projects the dramatic increases of the early 1970s into the late 1970s and early 1980s. But this is unlikely to alter the basic flavor of the results. All the data, by the way, are aggregate.

Table 9.1 and figure 9.1 show that real benefits have been rising over time, but by no means smoothly. In fact, there were several periods of real decline, and two periods of dramatic increase—the early 1950s and the early 1970s. (This was back in the days when Congress would bring home the bacon periodically [after each 6–8 points of accumulated inflation, it appears] with well-publicized and universally applauded benefit increases. Unfortunately for current representatives, one Congress decided to capture the present discounted value of all future applause and indexed the benefits once and [perhaps] for all.) Since earnings were rising over time along with benefits, the replacement rates in table 9.1 have risen less dramatically than benefit levels alone.

Table 9.2 and figure 9.2 document the dramatic increase in recipiency rates—from under 10 percent of the total cohort aged 65–69 in 1942 to near 90 percent by 1977. Part of this is explained by individuals reaching eligibility by obtaining the necessary quarters of coverage, but most is from the extensions of coverage to new categories of individuals over the years.

Moffitt then turns to the debit side of the ledger—taxes. This side is more difficult, since the aggregate tax data are not available by age and sex. The contributions are therefore estimated on the basis of earnings data (which are available by age and sex) and tax rates. Since only median earnings are available, Moffitt has to assume a functional form for the earnings distribution to determine how many people are over the maximum taxable amount. It is interesting to note how low the maximum contributions were until the 1960s. The youngest group in this sample (those 65–69 in 1977) was already 50 when Social Security taxes really began to rise. This is why they all made out so well, and why we will not.

The heart of this paper brings the two sides together and calculates Social Security *wealth* for each cohort—defined as the difference between the present discount values of benefits and taxes. This is a confusing name, given how wealth is usually defined in the literature. Moffitt is calculating net or windfall wealth, the *increment* in wealth which the system has provided or the excess over what the cohort "deserved." If the cohorts' taxes equaled their benefits, Moffitt's calculated wealth would be 0.

The basic results are given in table 9.4 and are described in somewhat unusual terms. Both the benefit and tax streams are discounted down, with a 3 percent interest rate, to the year in which the cohort was aged 17. The difference (the cohort windfall) is then divided by the entire population of the cohort at age 17. This makes for small numbers. For example, the oldest cohort, aged 15–19 in 1909, received an average increment of $24 each, in 1967 dollars. This is not the annual flow. This is the per capita stock equivalent of all the windfall ahead. Admittedly, $24 long enough ago can be a lot of money. I've read that the $24 the Indians received for the Island of Manhattan, if wisely invested, would be worth more than the entire island is worth today. Oh, for an IRA in 1626.

The age to which one discounts obviously makes no difference to relative magnitudes, which is the central focus of the paper. But dividing by the population rather than by the number of people in the system or the number of eventual recipients does. In the early years, Moffitt is averaging together a much larger average subsidy to those people in the system with the zeros of those who were not. Whether this is appropriate depends on what the purpose of these numbers is—a topic to which I'll return.

With this definition, Moffitt finds that the net Social Security transfer to each succeeding cohort has grown over time, to nearly $600 per person (at age 17 in 1967 dollars) for the last group. This is nearly a tenfold increase in the thirty years since 1947. The increase would be less dramatic if restricted to those in the Social Security system. The rate of growth of the wealth increment has fallen steadily, down to about 2 percent per year by 1977.

Moffitt then decomposes these basic trends in a number of ways. He shows that the increase in the wealth bonus has been dominated by the benefit side—huge benefit increases partially offset by much more modest tax increases. In table 9.6 both the benefit and tax components are further decomposed into such elements as the coverage of the system, benefit and tax rates per person covered, and life expectancy. It is difficult to know what to carry away from this table. Some of the components change so drastically from period to period that generalization seems impossible. For example, the initial replacement rate component of benefits per recipient in table 9.6 changes from -63% to $+155\%$ to -62% over the last three cohorts, while benefit growth changes from $+72\%$ to -120% to $+35\%$. What do we learn from such erratic movements?

Table 9.8 includes some miscellaneous wealth indicators. It shows that the patterns of wealth bonuses over time are similar under various discount rates (2, 3, and 4 percent). The main point of the paper is restated in terms of internal rates of return. They are always positive, obviously, and far in excess of any realistic real rate of return. They have dropped, however, from nearly 20 percent (in real terms) for the first three cohorts to just under 10 percent for the last two. The chain letter, it appears, is coming to a halt.

In a final interesting set of calculations, Moffitt estimates the proportion of total lifetime earnings that the Social Security bonus represents. In an actuarially fair system, it would be 0. He finds, surprisingly, that the ratio actually rose through 1972 (when it reached 8.3 percent), and has only fallen since then. Although this wealth bonus has been growing at slower and slower rates, it has nonetheless, until just recently, been growing faster than earnings.

This paper describes and discusses a new series on Social Security wealth. It is basically an accounting paper—appropriate for this conference—and an interesting one. It does not focus on either explaining or predicting behavior. My comments have less to do with what is in the paper than with what is not. I would like to suggest how this work might be incorporated into a larger piece which I think would be a very significant contribution to this growing literature.

A lot of concepts of Social Security wealth are in circulation. At the aggregate macro level, there are series by Feldstein (1974), Munnell (1974), Barro (1978), Leimer and Lesnoy (1980), and others. With individual microdata, wealth definitions have been developed by Blinder, Gordon and Wise (1983), David and Menchik (1981), Hurd and Shoven (1981), and Burkhauser and myself (1983). They are proliferating, and it is beginning to become confusing.

Is one of these definitions of Social Security wealth right and the others misguided? No. It is not an issue of right and wrong, but rather of appropriate and inappropriate—to a specific policy question. As I see it, there are two main reasons for a series on Social Security wealth. The first concerns income and wealth distributions. The Social Security system is picking and filling a great number of pockets, and the sums involved are large. One is tempted to ask how it all comes out. How do the rich fare? The poor? Men and women? Single and married persons? Early and later generations? These are interesting questions which require a certain definition of Social Security wealth.

The second major focus is the explanation and prediction of behavior. The Social Security Administration transfers huge sums of money, and it is inconceivable that this transfer does not have behavioral impacts. The major areas studied thus far have been savings behavior, labor supply and retirement decisions and, more recently, bequests. These research problems also require definitions and calculations of Social Security wealth.

What is conspicuously absent from the literature is an exposition of how these various concepts of Social Security wealth differ and which is appropriate for which policy issue.

In the estimation of any of these series, a number of decisions have to be made. These decisions affect the final numbers. Let me mention three.

How should benefits be measured, by what was actually dispersed or by what was expected at some previous time? As an example, there were huge real increases in benefits in the early 1970s, as Moffitt documents. These were huge windfall gains to recipients which, I suspect, were not anticipated. How should they be treated? It depends, obviously, on the question being asked. If the distributional impact of Social Security is being studied, the windfalls should be included in the calculation, as Moffitt does. On the other hand, if one is analyzing the actual retirement decisions of individuals in 1969, these unanticipated real gains are irrelevant. It would be better to base wealth calculations on expected future benefits, regardless of whether these expectations proved accurate or not.

Should benefits be measured as actual or potential? By working beyond 65, an individual reduces his Social Security wealth below what it would have been if he had chosen earlier retirement. Social Security wealth is endogenous because it depends on labor supply decisions. The distributional impact depends on the Social Security benefits actually claimed by an individual or a cohort. Yet it would be a grave error to use this concept in a behavioral study, where an exogenous concept is needed. To use the actual amount would be to reverse causation. Those who continue to work, even if totally unaffected by their retirement income options, will obviously end up with lower Social Security wealth than those who do not. But to deduce that the low wealth (thus misdefined) forced or induced the additional work would be wrong.

A final issue is the treatment of past taxes. Most Social Security wealth series ignore them completely and define current wealth as the discounted stream of future benefits minus any future taxes to be paid. Moffitt's series is different, because all taxes and benefits are counted. Which approach is correct? As always with economic questions, it depends.

It is not clear from this paper what the purpose of these calculations is. Moffitt mentions two motivations: First, this series had never been calculated. Second, the author has an interest in the impact of Social Security on aggregate savings and capital stock. Yet most of the paper seems to deal with intergenerational income redistribution rather than savings behavior.

I will summarize this point, specifically and in general. This paper is weak on why this particular series is of interest. How and why does it differ from other series? What policy question is it designed to answer? In general, wealth series are proliferating. In the absence of an effective freeze movement to counter this proliferation, a paper elucidating the differences between and uses of these series would be a welcome addition.

My last suggestion for additional research is much easier said than done. This is one prerogative of being a discussant—to suggest to others what you know you would not do yourself. The once nearly unanimous support for Social Security is eroding. Much of the current political upheaval on this topic stems from precisely the issue that Moffitt has addressed here. Due to long-run changes in demographic structure and productivity growth, the chain letter is coming to a halt. Many members of the current generation of contributors feel that Social Security will leave them net losers. Do we learn anything from this analysis about whether this conventional wisdom is true or when it will become true? This would obviously require projections of future benefits—an undertaking that Moffitt has wisely avoided. But it might well explain, in very simple terms, an extremely important current additudinal shift.

References

Barro, Robert J. 1978. *The impact of Social Security on private saving.* Washington, D.C.: American Enterprise Institute.

Blinder, Alan, Roger Gordon and Donald Wise. 1983. Social Security, bequests and the life-cycle theory of saving: Cross-sectional tests. In *The Determinants of National Saving and Wealth*, ed. Franco Modigliani and Richard Hemming, 89–122. New York: Macmillan.

Burkhauser, Richard V., and Joseph F. Quinn. 1983. The effect of pension plans on the pattern of life cycle compensation. In *The measurement of labor cost*, ed. Jack Triplett, 395–415. Studies in Income and Wealth, vol. 48. Chicago: University of Chicago Press.

David, Martin, and Paul Menchik. 1981. The effect of Social Security on lifetime wealth accumulation and bequests. Discussion paper 671. Madison, Wis.: Institute for Research on Poverty, University of Wisconsin.

Feldstein, Martin. 1974. Social Security, induced retirement, and aggregate capital accumulation. *Journal of Political Economy* 82 (September/October):905–26.

Hurd, Michael, and John Shoven. 1983. The economic status of the elderly: 1969–1979. NBER Income and Wealth Conference, Baltimore, Maryland.

Leimer, Dean, and Selig Lesnoy. 1980. Social Security and private saving: a reexamination of the time series evidence using alternative Social Security wealth variables. Working paper 19. Washington, D.C.: Office of Research and Statistics, Social Security Administration.

Munnell, Alicia. 1974. *The effect of Social Security on private saving.* Cambridge, Mass.: Ballinger.

10   Raising the Normal Retirement Age under Social Security: A Life-Cycle Analysis

Jennifer L. Warlick and Richard V. Burkhauser

10.1   Introduction

Concern for the current and future financial soundness of Social Security has led to numerous proposals which would decrease the system's total obligations. Perhaps the best known proposal would raise the "normal" retirement age, that is, the age at which full Social Security benefits are paid, to 68. Its proponents argue that the proposal is reasonable since Americans are living longer and projected labor market demand for older workers will rise in the future. Best of all, by itself the proposal would go a long way toward restoring the financial soundness of the system. The National Commission on Social Security (1981) estimates that the version of the proposal which it recommends (described in greater detail below) would eliminate two-thirds of the long-run deficit which is equivalent to 1.52 percent of taxable payroll over the period 1980–2054, projected by the 1980 Trustee's Report. This decrease is twice as large as that associated with any of the additional four recommendations designed to reduce Social Security outlays made by the Commission.

Some reductions in benefits is a necessary solution for those who believe the financial integrity of the Social Security system is in danger and that future increases in taxes are inappropriate. Consequently, rather than discuss the relative merits of tax increases versus benefit reductions,

Jennifer L. Warlick is a professor of economics at the University of Notre Dame; and Richard V. Burkhauser is a professor of economics at Vanderbilt University and affiliated with the Institute for Public Policy Studies at Vanderbilt.

Support for this research was provided in part by funds granted to the Institute for Research on Poverty by the U.S. Department of Health and Human Services under the provisions of the Economic Opportunity Act of 1964. Simonette Samuels provided valuable computer assistance and Karen Holden, John R. Wolfe, and Robert Moffitt provided helpful comments on a previous draft.

this paper takes a careful look at the effect that a change in normal retirement age to 68 would have on Social Security liabilities. In addition, we show how different types of beneficiaries would be affected by this form of benefit reduction.

Our major point is that the savings attributable to the proposal will not accrue from changes in retirement age as long as the adjustments made to benefits for early and delayed retirement are approximately actuarially fair. Rather, under a system of fair actuarial adjustments, savings will be because of a lifetime reduction in benefits which is independent of the age of retirement. Postponement of retirement will result in additional savings only if workers are induced to retire so late as to be subject to less than fair actuarial bonuses such as those existing under the current system. If workers cannot be induced to postpone retirement but follow present retirement patterns, total savings attributable to the proposal, as well as the reduction in total lifetime benefits experienced by most individuals, will be equivalent to those generated by an across-the-board reduction in benefits. These two methods of achieving the same savings are distinguished however by their impact on persons who currently elect early retirement at ages less than 65. These workers would not be permitted to receive benefits under the proposal to raise the initial retirement age to 65. To the degree that they value early payments at a rate above the plan's actuarial rate, they suffer additional losses. In the extreme case of workers who die before reaching age 65, they receive no benefits at all although other family members would be eligible for survivor's benefits. In contrast, an across-the-board decrease in benefits (e.g., a 20 percent reduction in all benefits) maintaining the current provisions for early retirement at age 62 is neutral with respect to mortality experience. Workers who elect early retirement would simply receive 20 percent less than under the current system. This difference has important distributional implications to the extent that mortality experience is correlated with race and income status.

A group that would be substantially affected by the proposal is low-wage workers who retire early under the current system. The Supplemental Security Income (SSI) program offsets to a large degree the reduction in OASI benefits for these low-wage workers thereby substantially increasing their life-cycle Social Security wealth relative to its level at age 65 (Burkhauser and Smeeding 1981). If these workers are no longer permitted to retire nor enroll in SSI prior to age 65, they will experience a substantial reduction in Social Security wealth. However, SSI will still play an important role in protecting these workers from additional losses and in almost totally mitigating the losses of low-income workers who retire at age 65 under the current rules. This is the case because, then as now, SSI will offset the actuarial reductions for workers retiring at age 65–68. To the extent that low-wage workers are eligible for and choose to enroll in SSI, the program shifts the burden of the proposal to medium- and high-wage workers.

The remainder of this paper develops these points as follows. In section 10.2 we summarize our methodology, which employs a life-cycle analytic framework, and outline the calculation of the measures used in the comparison of the costs of current and proposed legislation. In section 10.3 we describe the National Commission proposals and simulate their effect on the costs and income distribution of Social Security. Qualifications, implications, and possible extensions of this paper are discussed in the concluding section.

10.2   Methodology

In this paper we evaluate the effects of a change in benefit rules using the lifetime of individual workers as the relevant period of analysis. Our measure of the savings attributable to the proposal is the change in worker's Social Security wealth (W_R), that is, the present value of future benefits at the time of retirement. We do not attempt to compute total savings across the retired population to the system, but rather concentrate on the effect of the proposal on representative workers.

This multiperiod measure is preferred to a single-period measure because the latter may be positive in the initial years of an individual's retirement (between age 62 and 65, for instance, when no benefits are paid out under the proposal) only to become negative for the balance and majority of his retirement. The outcome of a single-period analysis which aggregates across individuals at different stages of retirement in a particular year is dependent on the distribution of the retired population by time elapsing since retirement. In years when the proposal delays the retirement of large numbers of workers age 62–65 relative to those retired, the savings attributable to the proposal would appear quite large. In contrast, if the cohort of workers forced to postpone retirement is small relative to those retired, a single-period measure could show increased costs. Having shown how the proposal affects the Social Security wealth of workers with different wage histories, we separate this wealth into two parts— wealth based on total lifetime Social Security contribution by the worker and his employer and wealth based on welfare transfers—and see how this mix of annuity and redistribution in the system is affected. Finally we look at how this mix is affected when SSI is considered.

The specific measures used in our analysis are Social Security wealth (W) at retirement age (R), the present value of all contributions to the system at retirement age (C_R), and the welfare transfer component of Social Security wealth (T_R). Each of these measures $(W_R, C_R, \text{and } T_R)$ is computed for three hypothetical workers who can retire at various ages: 62, 65, 68, and 71 years. The hypothetical workers represent three workers earning in each year of their work life the minimum wage, the median wage for all covered male workers, and the maximum wage as defined by the maximum taxable earnings base. In our examples we assume all workers were age 62 in 1982, and all present values are evaluated from 1982.

Social Security wealth at the point of retirement (W_R) is equal to the sum of expected OASI benefits (b_R) over the worker's remaining life discounted by the probability of survival (p_k) in each period (k) and the interest rate (d):

$$(1) \qquad W_R = \sum_{k=1}^{99-R} b_R p_k (1 + d)^{-(k-1)}.$$

Expected OASI benefits (b_R) are calculated, as described in the appendix, from hypothetical wage histories beginning with 1951 and continuing through to the year of retirement. Possible years of retirement are 1982, 1985, 1988, and 1991. For years before 1978, annual wages for the minimum wage earner equal the statutory minimum wage times 2000 hours. Annual earnings for the median wage earner in years prior to 1978 are equal to the median wage of the cohort of male earners age 30–34 in 1951 in covered employment. Annual earnings for the high-wage worker in years prior to 1983 are equal to the maximum taxable earnings base in each year respectively. Annual wages must be projected for years after 1982 for the maximum-wage earner and for years after 1977 for the minimum- and median-wage earners. For the time interval ending in 1982, wages are projected forward by the rate of growth in wages for the period 1951 through the last year of reported wages. We assume real annual wage growth of 2 percent for years after 1982. The Primary Insurance Amounts (PIA), derived from Average Indexed Monthly Earnings (AIME) based on these wage histories, are adjusted by a series of actuarial factors representing a variety of early and delayed retirement options. A full discussion of these derivations is provided in the appendix. Eight scenarios are simulated for each type of worker (see table 10.1). The life expectancies employed are for males and are taken from Bureau of Vital Statistics figures for 1972. The discount rate (d) assumed three values alternately: 2, 5, and 10 percent. The tables shown in the next section assume a rate of 2 percent.

The value of the individual's total contributions at the point of retirement (C_R) is equal to the sum of annual OASI taxes paid both by the individual $(t_{ak} w_k)$ and by the individual's employer $(t_{bk} w_k)$ compounded by a rate of interest (r_j).[1] Thus,

$$(2) \qquad C_R = \sum_{k=1}^{Y-1938} w_k (t_{ak} + t_{bk}) \prod_{j=k+1}^{Y-1938} (1 + r_j),$$

where Y is equal to the year of retirement. The wages employed are those in the hypothetical wage histories. The tax rates are equal to the legally specified contribution rates for OASI in each year. The rate of interest (r_j) is equal to the interest rate on U.S. Government Bonds prevailing in each year. Interest rates were projected for years after 1977 following the same procedure used to project wages. This is only one of several possible rates that could have been used. The rate of return resulting from use of bond rates is lower than that resulting from other alternatives such as the annual yield plus the rate of increase in average stock prices.

The welfare transfer component of Social Security (T_R) is equal to the difference between the Social Security wealth (W_R) and lifetime contributions (C_R).

The ultimate savings of the proposal to the system will depend on the labor force response of older workers. We do not attempt to predict that response in our simulations. Rather we calculate the value of the variables defined above for a range of retirement ages which include the most important possibilities. Thus our simulations yield estimates of the potential savings associated with a wide range of responses. Not only do we identify the savings that will accrue if workers choose to retire at the same age under the proposal as under current law, but we also show how savings vary when workers opt for different retirement ages.

10.3   Results

Several proposals to raise the normal retirement age have been aired at public forums. Among these, we have chosen to focus on that recommended by the National Commission on Social Security, primarily because it is more fully specified than most and because it has been the subject of careful analysis. The specifics of the proposal are as follows:

1. The earliest age of eligibility for full retirement benefits should be raised from 65 to 68.

2. The age at which reduced benefits are available should be raised from 62 to 65.[2]

3. The age at which the earnings test no longer applies should be raised from 72 to 75.

4. The asymmetry between the reduction for early retirement and credit for delayed retirement should be eliminated either by raising the credit to its actuarial equivalent, or by raising the credit by a smaller factor and by increasing the reduction.

The Commission recommends a gradual phase-in of its proposal beginning in January 2001 with full implementation in 2012. Our simulations reports its effect assuming full implementation in 1982.

Table 10.1 presents eight different scenarios simulated for low-, median-, and high-wage workers. In the first three rows the age of first

Table 10.1   Simulation Results for Eight Retirement Scenarios

	(1)	(2)	(3)	(4)	(5)	(6)	(7)	(8)
		Full				W_R		Transfer
	Age of	Benefits	Actuarial	Annual				Component[a]
	Retirement	Available	Adjustment	Benefit				
Scenario	(R)	at Age:	Factor	(b_R)	2%	5%	10%	T_R
				(a) Low-Wage Worker				
1	62	65	.80	$2,801	$35,341	$28,200	$20,978	$21,038
2	65	65	1.00	3,550	33,941	25,188	16,483	19,638
3	68	65	1.09	3,934	27,366	18,782	10,672	13,063
4	62	68	.64	2,241	28,273	22,560	16,782	13,970
5	65	68	.81	2,876	27,360	20,273	13,228	13,057
6	68	68	1.00	3,610	24,990	17,123	9,693	10,687
7	71	68	1.09	4,016	19,036	11,900	5,629	4,733
8	71	68	1.28	4,715	22,738	14,316	6,896	8,435

				(b) Median-Wage Worker			
1	62	65	.80	$5,108	$64,450	$51,248	$38,258	$29,920
2	65	65	1.00	6,453	61,268	45,368	29,563	26,738
3	68	65	1.09	7,121	48,230	32,803	18,273	13,700
4	62	68	.64	4,086	51,561	41,142	30,606	17,031
5	65	68	.81	5,227	49,305	36,434	23,646	14,775
6	68	68	1.00	6,533	43,930	29,800	16,503	9,400
7	71	68	1.09	7,223	32,147	19,567	3,614	−2,383
8	71	68	1.28	8,481	38,806	23,912	10,893	4,276
				(c) High-Wage Worker			
1	62	65	.80	$5,338	$67,356	$53,746	$39,982	$25,692
2	65	65	1.00	7,005	66,646	49,383	32,222	24,982
3	68	65	1.09	8,026	54,740	37,329	20,922	13,076
4	62	68	.64	4,270	53,885	42,997	31,997	12,221
5	65	68	.81	5,674	53,661	39,687	25,800	11,997
6	68	68	1.00	7,364	49,892	33,944	18,927	8,228
7	71	68	1.09	8,451	38,025	23,295	10,461	−3,639
8	71	68	1.28	9,924	45,815	28,379	13,128	4,151

[a]The difference between total contributions into the system and the present value of future benefits discounted at 2 percent at age 62. Contributions equal $14,303, $14,530, and $14,664 for the low-, median-, and high-wage worker, respectively.

eligibility for full Social Security benefits is 65, and we observe a worker's Social Security benefits when he retires at ages 62, 65, and 68 alternately. In all cases we assume that the worker is a male without a dependent spouse.[3]

In the next three rows we assume normal retirement is at age 68 and again look at the Social Security benefits of a worker who retires at ages 62, 65, and 68 evaluated at age 62. In the final two rows we again assume age 68 is normal, but now the worker retires at age 71. In column 3 we show the actuarial reduction factor used to adjust the benefits for different ages of acceptance. For example, row 1 refers to a worker who retires at age 62 and receives yearly benefits which are only 80 percent of his current PIA.[4] If he retires at age 65 he receives the full PIA, and at age 68 he receives 1.09 of his PIA.

Column 4 shows the annual benefit in 1982 dollars associated with the wage histories of the three workers. Notice that annual benefits increase when a worker delays retirement. This occurs both because higher earning years are substituted for earlier years of lower earnings in calculating a worker's AIME and because the actuarial adjustment factors in column 3 are applied to the full PIA. The next three columns show Social Security wealth (W_R) evaluated at age 62 with discount rates of 2, 5, and 10 percent. The final column shows the welfare component of OASI (T_R) which is defined as the difference between C_R (not shown) and W_R evaluated at 2 percent (column 5).

Notice that under current law W_R is approximately equal at a 2 percent rate whether benefits are accepted at age 62 or age 65 for each of our workers (scenarios 1 and 2). Hence between age 62 and 65 the system provides only a slight penalty for those who postpone benefit acceptance. If benefits are postponed to age 68, W_R falls dramatically. The system clearly penalizes those who postpone acceptance past age 65. At discount rates of 5 and 10 percent, the system penalizes postponement past age 62, thereby effectively reducing net earnings at later ages and inducing retirement.[5]

10.3.1 Reductions in Social Security Wealth, Holding Retirement Age Constant

The effects of the change in normal retirement age from 65 to 68, holding the actual age of retirement constant at 62, can be seen by comparing rows 1 and 4 of table 10.1. In the case of the median-wage worker (panel b), the annual benefit falls from $5,108 to $4,086, a decline of 20 percent. This must be the case since the actuarial reduction factor falls from .80 to .64. Notice also that Social Security wealth evaluated at 2 percent falls from $64,450 to $51,561 or 20 percent. W_R also falls by 20 percent in columns 6 and 7. This result does not vary with the age of retirement, so long as the age of retirement is unaffected by adoption of the proposal. For example, comparing rows 2 and 5 of column 5 shows that W_R for the median-wage worker who retires at age 65 under both the current system and the proposal falls from \$61,268 to \$49,305 or by 20 percent. The same result is obtained from rows 3 and 6 for the worker retiring at 68. It follows that if the proposal does not induce a worker to alter his retirement plans, the change in normal retirement age has the same effect as a constant reduction in benefits across all periods.

10.3.2   Changing Retirement Ages: The Actuarially Fair Case

The National Commission proposal sets age 65 as the age of first eligibility for reduced benefits, thus forcing workers who would currently retire at age 62 to postpone retirement for three years. As can be seen by comparing row 5 of column 5 with rows 1 and 4, this forced postponement has little additional impact on Social Security wealth. W_R now falls from \$64,450 to \$49,305 or by 23 percent, with incremental savings equaling only 3 percent. Although this result is at first surprising, it is simply explained by the fact that the adjustment factors for early retirement are actuarially fair for most workers. That is, W_R is approximately equal at all ages of retirement 62 through 65. Thus the major effect of the proposal results from the switch to a new set of actuarial adjustment factors (the drop from .80 to .64 at age 62). So long as the factors are actuarially fair, little savings are to be gained by postponing retirement. Postponement of retirement to age 68 (row 6) caused W_R to fall by an additional 9 percent or a total of 32 percent, from \$64,450 to \$43,930. Thus the total decline attributable to postponement of retirement from age 62 to 68 is 12 percent.[6] While this decline is certainly nontrivial and indicates that the proposed factors are not actuarially fair at a discount rate of 2 percent, it is less than what might be expected of a postponement of retirement of six years. Review of the relevant values of W_R for the low- and high-wage worker reveals smaller reductions from postponing retirement (9 and 6 percent, respectively).

10.3.3   Changing Retirement Ages: The Actuarially Unfair Case

When the system is actuarially fair, postponing benefit acceptance does not affect Social Security wealth. But when the system is designed to be less than actuarially fair, postponing benefit acceptance reduces W_R. Consider the case of the median-wage worker who currently retires at 65 (row 2). If he retires at age 65 under the proposal (row 5), his Social Security wealth falls by 20 percent from \$61,268 to \$49,305 (column 5). If he postpones benefit acceptance until age 68 (row 6), his W_R falls another 8 percent to \$43,930. Assuming that the proposal incorporates the same credits for delayed retirement as the current system (3 percent annually), postponement of benefit acceptance another three years to age 71 causes W_R to fall an additional 20 percent, bringing the total reduction to 48 percent. When the delayed retirement credit is raised to its actuarial equivalent, as proposed by the National Commission, the loss in wealth resulting from postponing benefits is substantially reduced. This is best seen by comparing rows 6, 7, and 8 of column 5. The actuarial adjustment level is a critical policy parameter whose effect is not well understood.

Table 10.2 summarizes the effect of moving normal retirement age to 68 for age combinations shown in table 10.1. It shows the percentage change in Social Security wealth that would result from adoption of the proposal as measured in the life-cycle framework. Panels (a), (b), and (c) refer to low-, median-, and high-wage workers, respectively. The results are generally quite similar across these different workers. The columns of table 10.2 refer to the age of retirement under current law while the rows refer to age of retirement under the proposal. The numbers in parentheses are the actuarial reduction factors (column 3 in table 10.1). Entries are defined as the difference between the Social Security wealth evaluated at 2 percent paid under the respective scenario's (column 5 in table 10.1) divided by wealth paid under the current law. For example, for the median-wage worker who retires at age 62 under current and proposed

Table 10.2   **Percentage Change in Social Security Wealth Resulting from Raising the Normal Retirement Age to 68**

	Current Law		
Proposal	62 (.80)	65 (1.00)	68 (1.09)
(a) Low-Wage Earner			
62 (.64)	20%	*	*
65 (.81)	23	20	*
68 (1.00)	29	26	9
71 (1.09)	46	44	30
71 (1.28)	36	33	17
(b) Median-Wage Earner			
62 (.64)	20%	*	*
65 (.81)	23	20	*
68 (1.00)	32	28	9
71 (1.09)	50	48	33
71 (1.28)	40	37	20
(c) High-Wage Earner			
62 (.64)	20%	*	*
65 (.81)	20	20	*
68 (1.00)	26	25	9
71 (1.09)	44	43	31
71 (1.28)	32	31	16

*We assume that workers do not choose to retire earlier under the proposal than under current law.

law, the reduction in wealth is equal to 20 percent or ($64,450 − $51,561)/$64,450 (table 10.1, panel b, column 5, rows 1 and 4).

It is evident from table 10.2 that the greatest savings to the system accrue from a life-cycle perspective when workers retire at later ages than they do under current law and actuarial adjustments remain unfair. This will be partly accomplished because the National Commission proposal would prohibit retirement at age 62. However, if workers retired at 65 this would have little additional affect on life-cycle savings for the system. Total lifetime liabilities would fall only if such workers continue to work beyond age 65.

10.3.4   Changes in Net Social Security Wealth: The Welfare Transfer Component of OASI

Implementation of the proposal would reduce Social Security wealth net of contributions over the life cycle, which we have called the welfare component of OASI (T_R) and others would call true Social Security wealth (see Moffitt in this volume). If the Social Security system resembled private sector insurance, T_R would be zero. The fact that benefits are only loosely related to contributions and that the system has paid benefits to workers as though they contributed to the system throughout their work lives means that most workers have received a positive T_R.

Raising the normal retirement age to 68 will reduce T_R. This is seen in table 10.3. The table entries are derived from column 8 of table 10.1 and are equal to the difference in the values of T_R for the paired scenarios divided by T_R for the current retirement year. For example, the reduction experienced by our median-wage worker who retires at age 62 under both current law and the proposal is equal to ($29,920 − $17,031)/$29,920 or 43 percent. Entries in excess of 100 percent indicate that a positive welfare component under current law is replaced by a negative transfer component under the proposal; that is, under the proposal actual Social Security wealth is less than the value of lifetime contributions into the system.

A review of table 10.3 indicates that the welfare component of Social Security wealth is significantly reduced under the proposal. The reduction increases dramatically as retirement is postponed past 65. Our median-wage worker currently retiring at 62 would see T_R cut in half if he retired at 65 under the proposal. Postponement of retirement to 71 completely eliminates T_R (a reduction of 108 percent) and leaves him with Social Security wealth ($32,147) which equals only 93 percent of contributions ($34,530). Table 10.3 suggests that the proposal to raise the normal retirement age to 68 would have the effect of bringing Social Security benefits much closer to what might now be obtained in a private insurance system and for some workers might actually result in benefits below those obtainable in the private sector.

Table 10.3   **Percentage Reduction in the Portion of a Worker's Social Security Wealth Representing a Welfare Transfer**

	Current Law		
	62 (.80) (1)	65 (1.00) (2)	68 (1.09) (3)
	(a) Low-Wage Earner		
62 (.64)	34%	*	*
65 (.81)	38	34	*
68 (1.00)	49	46	18
71 (1.09)	78	76	64
71 (1.28)	60	57	35
	(b) Median-Wage Earner		
62 (.64)	43%	*	*
65 (.81)	51	45	*
68 (1.00)	69	65	31
71 (1.09)	108	109	117
71 (1.28)	86	84	69
	(c) High-Wage Earner		
62 (.64)	52%	*	*
65 (.81)	53	52	*
68 (1.00)	68	79	37
71 (1.09)	114	115	128
71 (1.28)	84	83	68

*See note at table 10.2.

10.3.5   How Changes in Interest Rates Affect Workers' Wealth

Up to this point we have assumed that all workers have a discount rate of 2 percent. While it is true that a 2 percent real rate may be the appropriate market value of future benefits, or in the case of the government, the appropriate opportunity cost of current liability, it is not clear that it is appropriate as a measure of all workers' discount rates.[7] In the case where low-wage workers have a higher discount rate than high-wage workers and are unable to borrow against their Social Security wealth, the picture changes dramatically. Now rather than being virtually indifferent between taking benefits between age 62 and 65, as was the case at 2 percent, low-wage workers who wait until age 65 to retire experience significant reductions in their Social Security wealth. Under current law, W_R at age 65 is 11 and 21 percent less than at age 62 for discount rates of 5 and 10 percent, respectively (table 10.1, columns 6 and 7, rows 1 and 2). At a 5 percent discount rate, a worker who currently retires at 62 but is forced to retire at 65 under the proposal faces a 28 percent reduction in W_R ([\$28,200 − \$20,273]/\$28,200) compared to a 23 percent reduction at a discount rate of 2 percent. This reduction of 28 percent is 40 percent more than his high-wage counterpart's reduction (table 10.2, row 2, column 1). At 10 percent he loses 37 percent of W_R or 85 percent more than his high-wage counterparts. The losses for postponement past age 65 are even greater. A similar result would occur if low-wage earners had systematically higher mortality rates than their higher wage counterparts. In either of these cases, workers with higher discount rates would prefer across-the-board benefit cuts to increases in normal retirement age.

10.3.6   The Interaction of OASI and SSI

This effect is mitigated to some degree when the Supplemental Security Income program (SSI) is brought into the analysis. SSI is a federally funded guaranteed income program for the low-income aged (65 and over), blind, and disabled. Although eligibility for SSI is conditioned on both income and assets, persons 65 years and older may continue to work and still be eligible for SSI benefits. The first $65 of earnings per month are totally disregarded and each additional dollar of earnings in excess of $65 reduces the guarantee by fifty cents. Thus in 1982, an aged worker with no other income could earn up to $7488 and still be eligible for SSI. After an initial disregard of $20 per month, Social Security benefits reduce the SSI guarantee dollar for dollar. Whether working or retired, the hypothetical low-wage worker in our simulations is eligible for SSI benefits under each of the eight scenarios except number 2.[8] Although it is true that almost half of those aged persons eligible for SSI choose not to participate (Warlick 1982), the picture created by panel (a) of table 10.1 is inappropriate for the low-income worker who is eligible for and accepts SSI. Consequently, in table 10.4 we simulate the case of such a low-wage worker. SSI benefits have been added to OASI benefits in the calculation of the total annual benefit (column 4) and the combined value of SSI and OASI wealth (W_R') (columns 5, 6, 7).

The interaction of SSI and OASI has two important effects on our low-wage worker. First, the addition of SSI substantially increases combined OASI and SSI wealth. For instance in the case of early retirement (scenario 1) W_R evaluated at 2 percent increases from $35,341 in table 10.1 to $41,969 in table 10.4 when SSI is included.

Second, it substantially alters the relative values of W_R' across scenarios. This change in W_R' is confirmed by comparing table 10.2 with table 10.5. The entries in table 10.5 are constructed in the same manner as those in table 10.2, with each entry defined as the difference in W_R' for the relevant pairs of scenarios divided by W_R' for the current age of retirement. Under current law, a low-wage worker retiring at age 62 receives $2801 in OASI benefits at ages 62–64 (table 10.1, scenario 1). At age 65 and over, his annual OASI benefit is supplemented by $679 of SSI. Total Social Security wealth (W_R') evaluated at 2 percent is equal to $41,969 rather than the $35,341 shown in table 10.1. If this worker postpones

Table 10.4   **Simulation Results Including SSI for a Low-Wage Worker**

Scenario	(1) Age of Retire- ment (R)	(2) Full Benefits Available at Age:	(3) Actuarial Adjust- ment Factor	(4) Annual Benefit (b_R)	(5)	(6) W_R	(7)	(8) Transfer Component (T_R)
					2%	5%	10%	
1	62	65	.80	$3,480*	$41,969	$33,149	$24,256	$27,666
2	65	65	1.00	3,550	33,941	25,187	16,483	19,638
3	68	65	1.09	3,934	29,217	20,479	12,147	14,914
4	62	68	.64	3,480**	40,366	31,590	22,763	26,063
5	65	68	.81	3,480	33,258	24,677	16,145	18,955
6	68	68	1.00	3,610	26,841	18,820	11,169	12,538
7	71	68	1.09	4,016	20,887	13,599	7,104	6,584
8	71	68	1.28	4,715	24,589	16,013	8,372	10,286

*Benefit at ages 62–64 consists only of OASI benefits and equals $2,801.
**Benefit at ages 62–64 equals $2,241.

Table 10.5   **Percentage Change in Total System Benefits to a Low-Wage Worker Resulting from Raising the Normal Retirement Age to 68**

Proposal	Current Law		
	62 (.80)	65 (1.00)	68 (1.09)
62 (.64)	4%	*	*
65 (.81)	21	2	*
68 (1.00)	36	21	8
71 (1.09)	50	38	29
71 (1.28)	41	28	16

*See note at table 10.2.

retirement to age 65 (scenario 2) he receives annual OASI benefits of $3550, an amount too large for him to be eligible for SSI. W_R' in this case is $33,941. Thus postponement of retirement in the presence of SSI reduces W_R' by 21 percent compared to the world without SSI in which wealth is approximately equal at 2 percent whether benefits are accepted at age 62 or age 65.

Thus the age of first eligibility critically affects low-wage workers. If these workers are no longer permitted to retire prior to age 65, they will experience a 21 percent reduction in Social Security wealth (W_R') regardless of SSI (see table 10.5, row 2, column 1). In contrast, if they are permitted to retire at age 62, SSI will continue to offset the actuarial reduction and they will experience only a small decline in wealth (4 percent). Even if low-wage workers are not permitted to retire prior to age 65, SSI will play an important part in protecting those workers from additional losses and in almost totally mitigating the losses of low-wage workers who retire at age 65 under the current rules. Notice in table 10.5 that a worker who retires at age 65 under the proposal is only 2 percent worse-off than he is under current law. This is the case because SSI offsets the actuarial adjustment between ages 65 and 68 in the same manner that it does for workers who take benefits early under the current law. Comparing scenarios 2 and 5 of table 10.4 shows that W_R' evaluated at 2 percent falls by a mere 2 percent from $33,941 to $33,258. Thus, although a proposal disallowing acceptance at age 62 would significantly disadvantage low-wage workers who would currently opt for early retirement, low-wage workers who would retire at 65 under both systems could protect themselves from the substantial reductions experienced by their high-wage counterparts by enrolling in SSI.

Because SSI benefits are financed by general revenues and OASI by the payroll tax, the increased use of SSI by those receiving low OASI benefits will shift the revenue burden of supporting such workers toward general revenues. Therefore the effect on OASI savings in table 10.2 greatly overestimates the savings on total revenues. In addition, to the degree that low-wage workers currently take OASI benefits at age 62, table 10.5 shows that virtually no savings will occur unless the option to receive benefits at age 62 is removed from OASI.

10.4   Conclusion, Qualifications, and Policy Implications

In this paper we have estimated a life-cycle measure of the savings that would accrue from implementation of the proposal of the National Commission on Social Security to raise the normal retirement age to 68. Our estimates reveal that the greatest savings accrue when workers elect to retire at later ages under the proposal than under current law and when delayed retirement credits are less than actuarially fair. It remains to be seen how workers will adjust their retirement decisions in response to a higher retirement age. Clearly an unexpected change in Social Security wealth will lower the wealth of individuals and lead them to work more than they anticipated over the life cycle. The closer they are to their planned retirement age when this occurs, the more likely they are to postpone retirement rather than work more hours per year. But this increase in years of work would be offset to some degree by actuarially unfair Social Security adjustments. For instance, workers with discount rates greater than 2 percent are likely to accept Social Security benefits before age 68. The same is true for low-wage workers eligible for SSI.

Postponing normal retirement is in many ways the equivalent of an across-the-board reduction in benefits, and both types of cuts would substantially reduce the welfare component of Social Security causing the system to yield benefits much closer to those provided by private insurance. But if low-wage workers have higher discount rates or lower life expectancies than their higher-wage counterparts, postponing the age of Social Security acceptance as a means of reducing benefits puts a disproportionate burden on low-wage workers and is clearly worse than across-the-board cuts in benefits from their perspective. This burden is mitigated by SSI for those low-wage workers who choose to participate in this program, especially if OASI acceptance at age 62 is still allowed. But obstacles such as the lack of information, the stigma of welfare receipt, and the complexity of the enrollment process currently discourage almost one-half of all eligible aged persons from participating in SSI.

These conclusions require qualifications on several grounds. First, they are based on simulations for hypothetical workers with low-, median-, and high-wage histories which may not reflect the actual experience of current or future beneficiaries. Interpretation of the results for the median-wage earner requires special caution because the median earnings used in the calculations are a mixture of the earnings for part-time and full-time workers, rather than the earnings of a worker in the approximate middle of the earnings distribution (Schulz 1981). Second, the simulation results are sensitive to the assumptions regarding the interest rate at which contributions are compounded, the method used to project earnings records into the future, and life expectancies used in the calculation of Social Security wealth. The percentage changes in Social Security benefits (table 10.2) show only slight sensitivity to the choice of discount rate, however. Third, the simulations refer to the cohort of workers attaining age 62 in 1982. It is likely that future cohorts will do slightly worse and thus more workers will have negative T_R.

In light of these qualifications an obvious extension of this paper is to repeat the simulations with the earnings histories of actual workers from the entire distribution of earnings. So doing would allow examination of the redistributive effects of the proposal across workers occupying different positions in the income distribution and of different marital and entitlement status.

Three policy implications flow from these conclusions. First, our analysis indicates that the largest savings accrue only when workers postpone retirement past age 68. While the fall in Social Security wealth will increase work effort, it is still the case that, given the option, workers will tend to preserve their diminished Social Security wealth by taking it at the earliest age possible. Hence few workers are likely to wait until age 68 or beyond to retire. Workers would be more likely to retire past 68 if the National Commission's proposal to increase actuarial adjustments past this age were achieved, but to do this would reduce system savings.

Second, up to this point in the history of the system virtually all workers have received a positive T_R. As Moffitt shows (this volume) and as we showed in Burkhauser and Warlick (1981), T_R is falling. Raising the normal retirement age to 68 will substantially reduce T_R for all workers within OASI. For low-income workers, however, the welfare transfer aspect of OASI will to a larger degree be picked up by SSI, if they apply for benefits and if OASI benefits are still available at age 62. For those who favor a disentangling of the annuity and redistributive goals of OASI this is a plus, but for others it is another example of a two-track system in which the poor are singled out for stigma-inducing treatment. For those concerned with overall budget reductions, we show that OASI savings will be offset to some degree by increases in SSI.

Finally, the argument has been made that portions of Social Security benefits in excess of payroll tax contributions should be subject to income taxation (Levy 1980). Because high-wage as well as low-wage earners receive substantial transfers under the current system, taxing this component of Social Security benefits would redistribute benefits toward those with the greatest need. The general decline of the transfer component under the most likely of the proposal scenarios and its total elimination for some median- and high-wage earners mitigates this argument.

Appendix

Under current law, monthly retirement benefits are derived from a figure referred to as the Primary Insurance Amount (PIA).[9] The PIA is based on an individual's earnings averaged over the work life (AIME). Earnings for years 1951 up to and including the year the individual becomes eligible for benefits (currently age 60) are indexed to compensate older workers for general increases in real wages and in the taxable wage base under Social Security which would otherwise advantage younger (disabled) workers. The index in each year is equal to the ratio of median earnings of the covered population in the year the worker reaches age 60 to median wages in that year. Earnings for the year in which the worker becomes 60 and all years thereafter up to the year of retirement are not indexed. Not all years are included in the calculation of AIME. The number of years averaged (the "computation years") is equal to the number of years which elapsed between 1951 or the individual's twenty-first birthday, whichever is later, and the year in which the individual reaches age 62, minus five. Thus the number of computation years for the individuals reaching age 62 in 1982 in our examples is 26 ($1982 - 1951 = 31 - 5 = 26$); for an individual reaching 62 in 1985, 28 years are used, and so on up to a maximum of 35 for cohorts reaching 62 in 1991 and later. Years with the highest earnings are selected for the computation years. Any years up to the year of retirement may be included. AIME is equal to the total earnings (some of which will be indexed) in the "computation years" divided by the number of months in those years. AIME may be recomputed in years following retirement to take account of high earnings in those years if doing so increases AIME. AIME cannot be lowered by low-earning years subsequent to retirement.

For individuals who become eligible for retirement in 1979 or later, the PIA is determined by application of a mathematical formula to AIME. The formula is progressive, that is, the percentage of AIME replaced by benefits declines as average earnings rise. For individuals reaching age 62 in 1979 the formula is 90 percent of the first $180 of AIME, plus 32 percent of AIME over $180 and through $1085, plus 15 percent of AIME in excess of $1085. The dollar amounts in this formula, denoted the "bend points," are automatically adjusted on an annual basis for increases in average wages.

The normal age of retirement, that is, that age at which an individual may draw a benefit equal to 100 percent of PIA, is currently 65.[10] Workers may elect to receive benefits as early as age 62, but benefits are reduced by 5/9 of 1 percent for each month of entitlement before age 65 (6.67 percent annually), reflecting the fact that they will be paid over a longer period of time. The reduction approaches actuarial fairness for most workers; that is, the present value of future benefits paid over the remaining lifetime of the beneficiary is approximately the same at any age of first receipt age 62 through 65.

An individual who wishes to work past the normal age of retirement can choose to delay receipt of benefits. This is desirable because benefits are reduced for earnings in excess of a specified limit (the "exempt amount") for workers less than age 72.[11] In the event that an individual delays retirement, benefits are increased by 1/12 of 1 percent of PIA for each month (3 percent annually) that benefits are not drawn between ages 65 and 72. This credit is less than actuarially fair: Individuals delaying retirement cannot hope to recoup foregone benefits over their remaining lifetimes.

Notes

1. This assumes that the full incidence of the Social Security payroll tax is shifted to the employer following Brittain (1971). In contrast, Hamermesh (1979) and Vroman (1971) suggest that the tax is only partially shifted onto labor.

2. Under the proposal, earnings would continue to be indexed up to and including the second year of first eligibility, but the age defined by this rule would rise from 60 to 63. The period for computing the AIME would be measured at age 62 so that the maximum number of years to be averaged would remain 35 (National Commission on Social Security 1981).

3. As seen in Moffitt (this volume), the number of couples earning Social Security benefits in their own right makes this the dominant case. The increasing work effort of women will continue the trend away from dependent spouse benefits. Another action that will further this trend is the move toward earnings sharing which would end spouse benefits and replace them with equally shared earnings records of a married couple.

4. Reduction factors of .64, .81, and 1.28 are used in rows 4, 5, and 8 following the National Commission, which asserts that when using a 2 percent real discount rate these are the actuarially fair rates. The adjustment factor of 1.09 in rows 3 and 7 is not actuarially fair but is used currently by Social Security to adjust PIA for retirement past age 65.

5. There is a growing literature on the effects of Social Security on labor supply. See Danziger, Haveman, and Plotnick (1981) for an excellent review of this literature.

6. In an actuarially fair system, W_R would be equal at all ages of retirement. Although we have employed the schedule of adjustment factors designated as actuarially fair by the National Commission, the results of our simulations show that they are only approximately fair for our hypothetical workers at discount rates of 2, 5, and 10 percent. This result underscores the importance of the worker's discount rate in his evaluation of the relative value of W_R at different ages of retirement.

7. As Blinder, Gordon, and Wise (1980 and 1981) and Burkhauser and Turner (1981) show, evaluating Social Security wealth and its effect on work depends critically on the interest rate employed.

8. In the simulations, the size of the SSI benefit varies with annual earnings until the time of retirement, at which point it is fixed in real terms. SSI benefit levels for future years are projected from 1982 at a rate equal to the historic rate of growth of low-income wages less 1 percent. We assume that wages are the sole source of income until the time of retirement. We assume Social Security benefits are the sole source of non-SSI income during retirement.

9. The description of current law is taken from U.S. Department of Health, Education, and Welfare (1978).

10. Benefits drawn at age 65 may be less than 100 percent of PIA if the individual has earnings in excess of the exempt amount under the earnings test. If the individual is married to someone who is not entitled to benefits in his or her own right, total benefits to the couple will equal 150 percent of PIA.

11. Beneficiaries between ages 65 and 72 can earn $5,500 in 1982 without affecting the amount of their benefits. The amount of exempt earnings for persons under 65 is $3960. Benefits are reduced by $0.50 for each $1.00 of earnings above the exempt amount.

References

Blinder, Alan, Roger Gordon, and Donald Wise. 1980. Reconsidering the work disincentive effects of Social Security. *National Tax Journal* 33 (December):431–42.

———. 1981. Rhetoric and reality in Social Security analysis—A rejoinder. *National Tax Journal* 34 (December):473–78.

Brittain, John. 1971. *The payroll tax for Social Security*. Washington, D.C.: The Brookings Institution.

Burkhauser, Richard V., and Timothy M. Smeeding. 1981. The net impact of the Social Security system on the poor. *Public Policy* 29, no. 2 (Spring):159–78.

Burkhauser, Richard V., and John Turner. 1981. Can twenty-five million Americans be wrong? A response to Blinder, Gordon, and Wise. *National Tax Journal* 34 (December):467–72.

Burkhauser, Richard V., and Jennifer L. Warlick. 1981. Disentangling the annuity from the redistributive aspects of Social Security. *Review of Income and Wealth* 27 (December):401–21.

Danziger, Sheldon, Robert Haveman, and Robert Plotnick. 1981. How income transfer programs affect work, savings, and the income distribution: A critical review. *Journal of Economic Literature* 19 (September):975–1028.

Hamermesh, Daniel S. 1979. New estimates of the incidence of the payroll tax. *Southern Economics Journal* (April):1208–19.

Levy, Mickey D. 1980. *The tax treatment of Social Security: Should the exclusion of benefits be eliminated?* Washington, D.C.: American Enterprise Institute for Public Policy Research.

National Commission on Social Security. 1981. *Social Security in America's future*. Washington, D.C.: GPO.

Schulz, James H. 1981. Pension policy at a crossroads: What should be the pension mix? *The Gerontologist* 21, no. 1 (February):46–53.

U.S. Department of Health, Education, and Welfare. 1978. *Social Security handbook*. Washington, D.C.: GPO.

Vroman, Wayne. 1971. *The payroll tax for Social Security*. Washington, D.C.: The Brookings Institution.

Warlick, Jennifer L. 1982. Participation of the aged in SSI. *Journal of Human Resources* 17, no. 2 (Summer):236–60.

Contributors

David Betson
Department of Economics
University of Notre Dame
South Bend, Indiana 46556

Edward C. Budd
Department of Economics
Pennsylvania State University
University Park, Pennsylvania 16802

Richard V. Burkhauser
Department of Economics
Vanderbilt University
Nashville, Tennessee 37235

Sheldon Danziger
Institute for Research on Poverty
University of Wisconsin
Madison, Wisconsin 53706

Robert Eisner
Department of Economics
Northwestern University
Evanston, Illinois 60201

Harvey Galper
The Brookings Institution
1775 Massachusetts Avenue, N.W.
Washington, D.C. 20036

Peter Gottschalk
Department of Economics
Bowdoin College
Brunswick, Maine 04011

Daniel S. Hamermesh
Department of Economics
Michigan State University
East Lansing, Michigan 48824

Robert Haveman
Department of Economics
University of Wisconsin
Madison, Wisconsin 53706

Robert Hutchens
New York School of
   Industrial Relations
Cornell University
P.O. Box 1000
Ithaca, New York 14853

Robert Lampman
Department of Economics
University of Wisconsin
Madison, Wisconsin 53706

Robert Moffitt
Department of Economics
Rutgers University
New Brunswick, New Jersey 08903

Marilyn Moon
The Urban Institute
2100 M St. N.W.
Washington, D.C. 20037

James N. Morgan
Survey Research Center
Institute for Social Research
The University of Michigan
P.O. Box 1248
Ann Arbor, Michigan 48106

Benjamin A. Okner
Office of the Secretary
U.S. Treasury Department
15th & Pennsylvania Avenue, N.W.
Washington, D.C. 20220

Edgar O. Olsen
Department of Economics
University of Virginia
Charlottesville, Virginia 22901

Janice Peskin
Congressional Budget Office
House Annex #2
2nd & D Streets, S.W.
Washington, D.C. 20515

Joseph F. Quinn
Department of Economics
Boston College
Chestnut Hill, Massachusetts 02167

Daniel B. Radner
Office of Research and Statistics
Social Security Administration
1875 Connecticut Avenue, N.W.
Washington, D.C. 20009

Timothy M. Smeeding
Department of Economics
University of Utah
Salt Lake City, Utah 84112

Eugene Smolensky
Department of Economics
University of Wisconsin
Madison, Wisconsin 53706

Michael K. Taussig
Department of Economics
Rutgers University
New Brunswick, New Jersey 08903

Eric Toder
Office of Tax Analysis
U.S. Treasury Department
15th & Pennsylvania
    Avenue, N.W.
Washington, D.C. 20220

Barbara Boyle Torrey
Office of Management and Budget
Executive Office of the President
726 Jackson Place, N.W.
    Room 6026
Washington, D.C. 20503

Jacques van der Gaag
World Bank
Room I-8135
1818 H Street, N.W.
Washington, D.C. 20433

Jennifer L. Warlick
Department of Economics
University of Notre Dame
South Bend, Indiana 46556

T. Cameron Whiteman
Apartment 1
2203 42nd Street, N.W.
Washington, D.C. 20007

Kathy A. York
Department of Economics
University of Virginia
Charlottesville, Virginia 22901

Author Index

Subject Index

Age-related transfers, 47–48, 51–52, 55–60; data quality on, 241–42; distributional effects of, 52–53; elderly people, income and consumption measures of well-being for, 240–70; elderly people, economic well-being by socioeconomic group, 259–63; elderly people, Orshansky scale for, 244–48; elderly people, tax effects for, 256–59; in-kind versus money, 241–42; Lorenz curves and Gini coefficients, 53; underreporting of, 255–56

Altruism, 3–4

Business transfers, 13, 21

Capital gains and losses, transfer income as source of, 25–26, 40–41

Differentially taxed assets: allocational and distributional effects, 93–121; implicit and explicit taxation, 115–19; implicit transfers, 87–89

Distribution of income, 4, 37. *See also* Gini coefficients; Lorenz curves

Dividend payments, transfer measures, 13

Full effective tax rates, 87–88, 117–19; distributional effects of, 91–93; versus traditional approach, 89–93

Gini coefficients: age-related transfers to elderly, effects of, 53, 248–55; household sector transfers, effects of, 55–60

Government transfers, 15, 19–21

Hicks-Haig income, 25
Hicksian equivalent variation, 178–79, 181–90; in-kind transfers, 3, 177–78; preference schedules, 190–92; public housing, benefit measures for, 187–92
Households: sectoral transfer payments, 37–38, 40–42; transfers, types of, 16, 20–21

Income transfers, public assistance versus social insurance, 285–86
In-kind transfers, 1, 3; budgetary effects, 140; collective consumption, treatment as, 43; direct versus indirect subsidies, 140, 152–55; distributional impact, 140–47; economic efficiency, valuation approaches related to, 141–47; equity benefits, 147; government cost approach, 141, 143–44; household sector, 39–40; market value approach, 3, 141–43; Marshallian versus Hicksian measures, 177–79; means versus non-means tested values, 139; measurement and valuation approaches, 3–4, 43–44, 140–47; Medicare, 147–60; NIPA measurement of, 10–12, 22–23; nonrecipient benefits, 146–47, 152–60; public housing programs, 3, 148, 150–55, 160–64; public versus private, 3–4; recipient value approach, 141, 145–46; social benefit value approach, 141, 144–45
Insurance funds, 16, 20, 44–45

386